OCCASIONS OF GRACE

An historical and theological study of the Pastoral Offices and Episcopal Services in the Book of Common Prayer

Byron David Stuhlman

The Church Hymnal Corporation
445 Fifth Avenue
New York, NY 10016

5 4 3 2 1

TABLE OF CONTENTS

AUTHOR'S PREFACE

This present work brings to a conclusion the study which I began in *Redeeming the Time* of the liturgy of the church as an architecture of time. *Redeeming the Time* focussed its attention on the three temporal cycles of the "regular services" of the church — that is, those services which follow the three cycles of time regulated by the calendar: the liturgical day, the liturgical week, and the liturgical year. Those services are related to the rhythms of the corporate life of the church. I identified in that book another cycle of liturgical rites as well — those occasional offices known a Pastoral Offices in the Book of Common Prayer 1979, which follow not the rhythms of the calendar and of the corporate dimension of the Christian life, but the rhythms of the personal life of the Christian. In the present book I turn my attention to these rites, and to those occasional offices known as Episcopal Services in the Book of Common Prayer 1979. Episcopal Services are sometimes assimilated to the pastoral offices as rites which relate to the role of Christians in the church's ministry, but the logic of these services makes it theologically preferable, I believe, to relate them not to occasions in the lives of individual Christians, but rather to occasions in the life of the parish and the diocese. The church understands rites for both kinds of events as "occasions of grace" — ways in which the turning points in the lives of Christians and Christian communities are transformed by being brought into relation with the crucified and risen Christ. It is that conviction which underlies the title for this work.

The forms of worship for these occasions found in the Book of Common Prayer have historically been one of the strengths of Anglicanism. Anglicans ritualize these occasions in a convincing and appealing way, and many other denominations in the English-speaking world have drawn on those forms of worship in devising their own rites. But Episcopalians have often not understood the reason for this strength sufficiently. The reason is not that we are good at "ceremonial" matters. The real strength of these services lies in the way in which they give concrete expression to the way the crucified and risen Christ touches our lives to transform them on such occasions. One purpose of this book is to explore the theological connections between these services and the faith which they articulate at a deeper level, so that we may make them more effective tools for shaping our lives according to the gospel.

To do that, I have set the study of these services in the context of an analysis of the course of their development in the liturgical tradition, in order to measure the 1979 rites according to the standards of scripture and tradition. This, however, is a more difficult task for the occasional offices than it is for the regular services, for Scripture often gives little attention to these rites, and the church has often adapted local cultural forms with too little attention to the issue of whether these forms are consistent with the norms of the gospel. To assist the reader in this project, I have provided fairly detailed analyses of the structure of the rites at various stages in their development and a selection of key texts. I hope that this will provide readers with materials to understand the evaluation which I make of these rites and to form their own judgments of the current rites. In presenting this material I have tried to sketch out a theology of these rites as means for the sanctification of the personal life of the Christian and for the life of the local Christian community.

I owe the insights developed in both *Redeeming the Time* and this present book to Alexander Schmemann and to Howard Galley, both of whom contributed to my understanding of the church's liturgy as an "architecture of time." Like *Redeeming the Time*, this book draws on the research which I did under the supervision of Geoffrey Wainwright for my doctoral dissertation at Duke University, "An Architecture of Time: A Critical Study of Alexander Schmemann's Liturgical Theology." Several persons took time to read the manuscript of this work and to offer suggestions. I am particularly indebted to Robert Prichard of Virginia Seminary for his suggestions, many of which have been incorporated into the final revision of the manuscript.

Byron David Stuhlman

EDITORIAL PRACTICES

Citations from the Book of Common Prayer

Citations from the Book of Common Prayer use the abbreviation BCP followed by the date of the edition. In most cases I have left the 1549 and 1552 texts as printed, rather than modernizing the spelling and punctuation. All American editions are printed in parallel columns in the work by Paul Marshall cited below. Citations are taken from the following sources unless otherwise noted:

BCP 1549   1549 English edition:
            E. C. S. Gibson, ed., *The First and Second Prayer Books of Edward VI* (New York: E. P. Dutton, 1910).

BCP 1552   1552 English edition:
            E. C. S. Gibson, ed., *The First and Second Prayer Books of Edward VI* (New York: E. P. Dutton, 1910).

BCP 1662   1662 English edition (Oxford: University Press);
            also in Paul V. Marshall, *Prayer Book Parallels: The public services of the Church arranged for comparative study* (New York: Church Hymnal, 1989).

BCP 1789   1789 American edition:
            in Paul V. Marshall, *Prayer Book Parallels: The public services of the Church arranged for comparative study* (New York: Church Hymnal, 1989).

BCP 1892   1892 American edition:
            in Paul V. Marshall, *Prayer Book Parallels: The public services of the Church arranged for comparative study* (New York: Church Hymnal, 1989).

| BCP 1928 | 1928 American edition (New York: Church Hymnal); also in Paul V. Marshall, *Prayer Book Parallels: The public services of the Church arranged for comparative study* (New York: Church Hymnal, 1989). |
| BCP 1979 | 1976 American edition (New York: Church Hymnal); also in Paul V. Marshall, *Prayer Book Parallels: The public services of the Church arranged for comparative study* (New York: Church Hymnal, 1989). |

Translation of foreign texts

I have preferred to follow the older custom of retaining the second person singular in translation of Latin and Greek texts because this requires less alteration of the original syntax for graceful English and so allows a translation closer to the original. Some translations are my own. In other cases, I have adapted the translations of others and noted the alteration.

INTRODUCTION: OCCASIONS OF GRACE

The Regular Services of the Church and the Pastoral Offices

The Christian church roots its life in the crucified and risen Christ, who is the mystery of our salvation. The regular services of the church are those rites which ground the life of the Christian community in the paschal mystery of Christ — his death and resurrection — as that mystery finds concrete expression in the temporal rhythms of the day, the week, and the year. Their purpose has been described as the sanctification of time. They constitute an architecture of time by which the church is transformed by passing over with Christ into the life of the world to come. At sunrise and sunset each day the church celebrates the crucified and risen Christ as the sun of righteousness that knows no setting and the light that darkness has never quenched. On the Lord's Day each week at the eucharist the church grounds its existence in the crucified and risen Christ as the word of truth and the bread of life. In the baptismal eucharist of the Easter vigil each year the church renews its participation in Christ's passover from death to life.

But individual Christians and local Christian communities also have rhythms to their own lives — personal and communal rhythms which find their meaning, as the rhythm of the corporate life of the whole church finds its meaning, in Christ's death and resurrection. If we lose sight of the occasions which punctuate the rhythms of these personal and communal dimensions of Christian existence, we fail to relate the mystery of salvation to persons and local communities whose lives are to be transformed by that mystery. The rites proper to these rhythms are "occasional offices" which constitute the final two cycles of the church's liturgy — the cycle of the Christian's life and the life of local Christian communities as they are graced at their critical moments, their turning points, by the crucified and risen Christ so that these turning points become "occasions of grace." It is these occasional offices that are the focus of this book.

"Pastoral Offices" is the name which the Book of Common Prayer 1979 gives to those "occasional offices" which are related to important turning points in the lives of individual Christians. The principal pastoral offices included in the Book of Common Prayer 1979 and the *Book of Occasional Services* are the two series of rites in preparation for baptism (one associated with the baptism of adults and one associated with the baptism of children), the series of rites in preparation for reaffirmation of the baptismal covenant, the form for Commitment to Christian Services, the rites for marriage and for religious profession, the Reconciliation of a Penitent, rites associated with the church's ministry to the sick and suffering, and rites associated with the burial of the dead.

"Episcopal Services" is the name which the Prayer Book gives to those "occasional offices" which are related to important turning points in the life of the local Christian community — the diocese or the parish. They are called "Episcopal Services" because the bishop ordinarily presides at their celebration, though in some cases the bishop may delegate to someone else the right to preside.[1] The principal episcopal services included in the Book of Common Prayer 1979 are the Ordination of Bishops, Priests, and Deacons, the Celebration of a New Ministry, and the Consecration of a Church.

This analysis yields the following framework for understanding the church's services:

1. **Regular Services:** The Daily Office, the Holy Eucharist, and Holy Baptism as the distinctive rites of the church's corporate worship in the daily, weekly, and annual cycles of the calendar;

2. **Pastoral Offices:** occasional offices concerned with turning points in the personal lives of individual Christians;

3. **Episcopal Services:** occasional offices at which a bishop presides and which structure the life of the local Christian communities — the diocese and the parish.

The regular services are concerned with the sanctification of time. The pastoral offices are occasional offices concerned with the sanctification of the life of the Christian. Episcopal services are occasional offices concerned with the sanctification of the life of the local Christian community.[2]

In the distinctive services of each of the cycles of time — the regular services appointed for the day, the week, and the year — the Christian Church celebrates and enters into the paschal mystery of the death and resurrection of Christ. In the occasional offices Christ's cross and resurrection, which have been inscribed on our personal lives and the lives of our local communities through our participation in the regular services of the church, further shape the contours of those lives. That is the function of the pastoral offices and episcopal services. As the regular services of the church take the simple realities of our lives — sunrise and sunset, a story, a meal, a bath — and transform their meaning by relating them to Christ's death and resurrection, so the pastoral offices seek to stamp the cross on the common turning points of our personal lives. Likewise the episcopal services seek to conform the communal life of the church in the local community to the crucified and risen Christ as that church exercises his royal priesthood.

The Liturgical Provisions for Occasional Offices

The Euchologies and Sacramentaries: The ancient euchologies of Eastern Christians and sacramentaries of Latin-speaking Christians[3] included rites for these occasions of grace as an integral part of their contents. The euchology or sacramentary was the celebrant's book: it included the texts needed by the celebrant (whether bishop or presbyter) for any service at which he presided. Provision was made for both regular services and occasional services. Similar books were provided for other orders: the gospel book for deacons, the lectionaries for readers, and the psalters and collections of antiphons and responsorial verses for cantors and choirs. The congregation had no book of its own, for the congregational parts of a service were either easily memorized texts used repeatedly (like the congregational texts of the ordinary of the eucharist), or texts given out at a particular service by the cantor and repeated by the congregation (like the refrain to the gradual psalm at the eucharist).

The Pontifical and the Ritual: In the middle ages, the liturgical books of Latin-speaking Christians were reorganized, and books with complete texts (including rubrics and parts for celebrants, readers, deacons, singers, and congregation) for each rite or group of rites were issued. From this reorganization came the missal for the eucharist and the breviary for the daily office. Other services eventually were collected in two books: what was variously known as the *rituale*, the *manuale*, or the *agenda* contained those occasional offices at which a presbyter presided, and what eventually came to be called the *pontificale*[4] contained those occasional offices at which a bishop presided.[5] In the course of this development, the rites in each of these last two collections came to be thought of as primarily the concern of the presbyter or the bishop; the fact that such rites properly involved the ministry of the whole church was often lost sight of; and the corporate worship of the church ceased to be understood as the appropriate context for many of these ministrations.

The Book of Common Prayer: At the Reformation, the Church of England issued a single, simplified book which contained the complete texts for what had been included in the missal, the breviary, the ritual, and the pontifical. By including the occasional offices of the ritual and the pontifical in the Book of Common Prayer, the Anglican tradition recovered (at least in theory) the corporate context of these ministrations, gave expression to the balance between the corporate and the personal dimensions of the Christian life, and emphasized the church's pastoral concern for its members. The pastoral offices and the episcopal services particularize the paschal mystery which is the basis of the church's common life and release the transforming power of that mystery in the personal life of Christians and in the lives of local Christian communities.

The Relation of Pastoral Offices and Episcopal Services to the Eucharist

Although the pastoral offices and episcopal services are related to occasions in the lives of individual Christians and local Christian communities which cannot be scheduled according to the calendar, the majority of them are intended to be celebrated in the context of one of the regular services which follow the rhythm of the day, the week, and the year. The table in Appendix 1 spells out in detail the relationship of Pastoral Offices and Episcopal Services in the book of Common Prayer and the Book of Occasional Services to the temporal rhythms of the regular services. In the Book of Common Prayer 1979 most of these occasional services are set in the context of a eucharist, so that the occasion is sealed with the reception of communion.[6] This integration of the rites with the eucharist was the intentional design of the Standing Liturgical Commission, which set out the rationale in this way:

> In all the Pastoral Offices [and also in the Episcopal Services], the Commission has had in mind that the Holy Communion should be the climactic action, or the context within which the service is placed.[7]

The format is usually as follows, although not every service is structured in exactly the same way or has all of the following components:

Gathering or Entrance	Special forms to introduce the office or service
Ministry of the Word	Special propers except on Sundays and feasts
Rite Proper to the Office	Special forms of commitment
	Special forms of the prayers of the people
	Ritual action and prayer of blessing proper to the rite
	(Subsidiary formulas and actions)
Holy Communion	Proper preface if appointed
	Proper postcommunion prayer if appointed.

Note that this format ordinarily brings together the commitment, the ritual action, and the prayer of blessing (consecration) proper to the particular office. In addition, it allows the context for the ritual action and prayer of blessing to be set by the special provisions for the gathering and the liturgy of the word and the whole action to be sealed by communion. The key to understanding the theology of each rite is the central ritual action and the prayer of blessing which usually accompanies it: these give each rite its particular "shape" in Gregory Dix's terms. In the Byzantine tradition this prayer of blessing often took the form of a "prayer with bowed heads" (*kephaloklisia*). In the West the prayer could take this form (a prayer over the people or *super populum* like those found in early sacramentaries for the blessing at the end of the eucharist),[8] but in important rites it often took a more solemn form similar to that of the eucharistic prayer — sometimes beginning with an introductory dialogue and often sung to the preface tone (like the thanksgiving over the water at baptism in the Book of Common Prayer 1979[9]).

Interpreting the Occasional Offices and the Occasions that They Mark

This book is ultimately a study in liturgical theology — an attempt to understand the life of Christians on the basis of the liturgical rites for important occasions in their personal lives and their life in the community of faith (that is, on the basis of the pastoral offices and episcopal services). Its method is that which came to be known as "comparative liturgy"[10] in the first part of this century and has more recently been described as "the structural analysis of liturgical units."[11] This method involves analyzing rites in the context of their historical development and of their place in the liturgy of the church as a whole. Since the time of Dom Gregory Dix, it has been recognized that the *shape of the ritual action* is as important as the *words of the liturgical text* in this enterprise.

In Anglicanism, continuity has been an important criterion of all liturgical rites: they are judged by their conformity to scripture and tradition, in the conviction that scripture and tradition bear true testimony to the proper way of relating these rites to Christ. Theological interpretation therefore begins with historical analysis of the way in which rites have developed. Again and again in the Book of Common Prayer 1549, Archbishop Cranmer refers to scripture and the "ancient fathers," the "ancient writers," "the primitive church," or "ancient authors."[12] For that reason, subsequent revisions of the Book of Common Prayer have usually been made with intentional reference to liturgical tradition.

In both *Redeeming the Time* and this present work, I have therefore set each rite in the context of its historical development, usually looking at the literature of the New Testament, the first several centuries, the middle ages, the Reformation, and the present revision. I have paid particular attention to developments in the Byzantine East as well as the Latin West for the first millennium and a half, for Anglicanism has considered itself the heir of the Greek East as well the Latin West. Not all the pastoral offices and episcopal services follow exactly the same line of development. A major shift in one office might occur at a quite different era from a major shift in another office. I have therefore organized the narrative in each chapter to follow the major stages of the development of each rite, rather than trying to impose a completely uniform shape on each chapter.

Four factors stand out as particularly important in analyzing the rite prescribed for a particular pastoral office or episcopal service in a liturgical formulary:

1. Its place in the overall structure of the church's liturgy — in this case its function as a pastoral office or an episcopal service;
2. The particular ritual action which is the characteristic feature of the service and the principal prayer of blessing associated with that ritual action;
3. The biblical texts (often assigned as eucharistic propers), formulas for administering the rite, and other prayers associated with the rite, all of which serve to establish the context for the interpretation of the rite, but in later rites sometimes undercut the meaning of the principal prayer of blessing or blur its focus;
4. Other ritual actions and texts associated with the rite, which properly reenforce (but sometimes distort) the meaning of the principal ritual action.

I shall pay particular attention to these factors in analyzing each of the rites in its various stages of development and in the conclusion draw the strands together to fashion a theology of the pastoral offices and the episcopal services. Since this present work is intended as a theological as well as an historical analysis of the occasional services, it includes an evaluation of the historical developments. The remainder of this introduction is devoted to the perspective from which the task of evaluation is pursued in this present work.

The Liturgical Inculturation of the Gospel

The gospel finds concrete expression in every culture in which the church takes root. It addresses us where we are and, when we respond faithfully, transforms the culture of which we are a part. The gospel takes concrete form in the church's liturgy and through the liturgy shapes and forms us. In this way the liturgy serves not only to glorify God but also to sanctify us, and liturgical formation — the way ritual action forms and shapes us as Christians — is one of the concrete expressions of the Spirit's work of sanctification. Because the world remains fallen until God's kingdom comes, however, the church — when it is true to its calling — remains to some extent a counterculture in every culture in which it is planted. It is always the *ekklesia* — the people of God "called out" of the world. As such it can never simply accept cultural forms as it finds them, but must transform them so that they are reshaped by the cross and resurrection of Christ and the transforming power of the Holy Spirit.

The regular services of the church — the daily office, the Holy Eucharist, and the baptismal liturgy — are securely anchored in Scripture and tradition and contemporary forms of these rites can be tested according to these criteria. But this is far less true of the occasional offices. Scripture often gives little or no direction for such services, and the church therefore borrowed ritual forms native to local cultures far more freely for them. Here we see much greater variation from place to place and age to age, and tradition is a far less reliable criterion in the evaluation of the rites. In many cases reference to Christ was simply superimposed on local cultural forms without really transforming those forms. Cultural institutions are very deeply rooted and encode particular understandings of the institutions of human society (such as family and marriage, the distribution of power in the order of the common life, communal responses to deviations from conventional social norms, and understandings of sickness and death). As we interpret the pastoral offices and episcopal services, we shall need to be particularly vigilant about how adequately the rites of the church in any particular age or culture articulate the ways in which all things are made new by Christ's death and resurrection and the gift of the Spirit. We also need to be aware that because of the particularity of cultural forms some traditions articulate a more adequate Christian understanding of particular institutions (such as marriage or the authority conferred by ordination) than other traditions do. When the occasional services function properly, they shape and transform such institutions according to the norms of the gospel. But it is very easy, in rites where the church "borrows" ritual forms from other cultures, for the process to work in reverse, so that the ritual forms do not transform the culture from which they are adapted but distort the gospel. In evaluating the occasional offices in the course of this study, I shall be particularly concerned with trying to discern whether the cultural norms of a particular age and culture have distorted the evangelical vision which should find expression in these rites. This somewhat countercultural perspective is different from the more usual Anglican perspective on these rites, which arose in an established church that worked from a less critical perspective on the fusion of the gospel with local cultural forms.

Studies of the eucharist and the rites of initiation have made the ritual structures and texts for these services readily accessible to students of the Book of Common Prayer. That is less true of the other services contained in the Prayer Book, and I have therefore included in this study a fairly detailed analysis of ritual structures and have provided translations of key texts for these rites. It is my hope that these materials (when tested against the norms of the gospel) will help the reader discern the ways in which important moments in the personal lives of individual Christians and in the corporate life of congregations can indeed be occasions of grace, in which the crucified and risen Christ transforms every aspect of human life through the power of the Holy Spirit.

ENDNOTES

[1]The ordination of a bishop is reserved to the presiding bishop or another bishop by delegation from the presiding bishop; the ordination of diocesan deacons and presbyters may be delegated by the diocesan bishop to another bishop; the celebration of a new ministry may be delegated by the diocesan bishop to another minister.

[2]For a fuller discussion of this way of classifying the services of the Book of Common Prayer, see the concluding chapter of this book.

[3]Sacramentaries began to appear in the West about the end of the sixth century, as formularies used for particular services by the bishops of major sees were collected and organized. The earliest surviving manuscript of a sacramentary dates from the eighth century. Western sacramentaries are usually organized as sets of prayers for use at the eucharist in calendric sequence, with the ordinary of the eucharist and texts for other rites either inserted into this sequence or appended to it. Euchologies of the Byzantine rite usually begin with the ordinary of the office and the eucharistic liturgies, followed by various prayers and orders for other rites. Because the celebrant has no "proper" texts for the eucharist (texts which vary according to feast or season) the calendar plays very little role in organizing the contents of the euchologies. The earliest surviving manuscript of a Byzantine euchology dates from the eighth century.

[4]Originally, this title was given to the chronicle of the actions of the popes. Anglicans have sometimes called such a book the "ordinal" because it contained the rites for ordination.

[5]These are the most important of the books. Other books include collections of *ordines* (rubrics for various services, sometimes with texts — the predecessor of the *rituale* and the *pontificale*), customaries (setting out the practices for particular churches or religious orders), the martyrology (with

daily notices of commemorations), and the *processionale* (for processions in the course of the year).

[6]The primary exceptions are some rites which are part of a process leading up to some form of the baptismal commitment or its renewal (rites of the catechumenate and related processes), the rite for the reconciliation of a penitent, and preliminary services before the burial eucharist.

[7]Standing Liturgical Commission, *Pastoral Offices*, Prayer Book Studies 24 (New York: Church Hymnal, 1970), page 7. Although this study was not concerned with Episcopal Services, the same holds true for them.

[8]At the eucharist these are the prayers "over the people" (*super populum*) found in some sacramentaries for every proper but later restricted (as in the *Book of Occasional Services*) to Lenten propers.

[9]The ordination prayers are also solemn prayers of this sort in the Roman tradition and in the Book of Common Prayer 1979, although the use of the preliminary dialogue with these prayers is later than the text of these prayers themselves. The ordination rites in the Book of Common Prayer 1979 do not use such a dialogue for their ordination prayers, and the dialogue has also been dropped in the reformed Roman rites.

[10]The term comes from Anton Baumstark, who set out the method is the book *Comparative Liturgy*, revised by Bernard Botte and translated by F. K. Cross, (Westminster, MD: Newman Press, 1958).

[11]It is Juan Mateos who developed the discipline in this way. For a discussion of the method as developed by Mateos and his disciples, see Robert Taft, *Beyond East and West: Problems in Liturgical Understanding* (Washington, DC: Pastoral Press, 1984), chapters 10 and 11.

[12]BCP 1549, Preface, Holy Baptism, The First Day of Lent, Preface to the Ordinal (pages 3, 236, 281, and 292).

PART I

THE PASTORAL
OFFICES

CHAPTER 1

JOURNEYS ON THE WAY OF THE CROSS

RITES IN PREPARATION FOR BAPTISM AND RITES RELATED TO THE AFFIRMATION OF THE BAPTISMAL COVENANT

Until 1979 both baptism and confirmation were grouped in the Book of Common Prayer among the pastoral offices. The 1979 Book of Common Prayer, however, removed baptism from the pastoral offices. The recommended times for baptism in this book are the ancient baptismal feasts of Easter, Pentecost, and the Feast of the Baptism of Christ (the Sunday after Epiphany), a new baptismal feast (All Saints' Day or Sunday), and the occasion of the bishop's visitation. In other words, baptism is treated as a regular service of the church, the proper liturgy of the baptismal feasts. This is the way in which it was celebrated in the classic liturgies of the fourth and fifth centuries.

Baptism undeniably has pastoral dimensions, however, even if it is not classified as a pastoral office. In the Book of Common Prayer 1979 and its authorized supplement, *The Book of Occasional Services*, this pastoral dimension finds expression in various related rites which are classified as pastoral offices (in the terminology of the Book of Common Prayer) and pastoral services (in the *Book of Occasional Services*). In the Prayer Book itself we find grouped with the pastoral offices Confirmation (understood not as an initiatory service, but as a rite for the Affirmation of the Baptismal Covenant) and a similar service, A Form of Commitment to Christian Service. *The Book of Occasional Services* includes as Pastoral Services three series of rites related to baptism. Two of these series of rites are designed as processes of preparation for baptism itself — Preparation of Adults for Holy Baptism and Preparation of Parents and Godparents for the Baptism of Infants and Young Children. The third series of rites is a parallel process which culminates in Confirmation — Preparation of Baptized Persons for the Reaffirmation of the Baptismal Covenant.

The very complex story behind these present rites unfolds in this chapter in the following stages:

1. The Baptismal Journey for Adults in the Classic Rites;
2. The Baptismal Journey for Children in the Classic Rites;
3. The Breakdown of the Original Initiatory Pattern in the West;
4. Baptism and Confirmation in the Book of Common Prayer up to 1979;
5. The Initiatory Pattern of the Book of Common Prayer 1979.

The 1979 provisions restore the initiatory pattern of stage 1 and to a lesser extent that of stage 2. The breakdown of stage 3 issued in a separate service of confirmation, consisting of the concluding portion of the baptismal rite which in the West was eventually reserved as a distinct rite to be administered by the bishop. This rite raises a host of historical and theological problems which the 1979 revision sought to resolve by treating it not as an initiatory rite, but as a rite of "intensification" — an Affirmation of the Baptismal Covenant. While this chapter focusses its attention on the pastoral offices related to baptism rather than on baptism itself, telling the story of how we got these rites necessarily involves telling the story of how the rite of baptism itself evolved through the centuries.

The story has many twists and turns, but it is important to follow these twists and turns if we are to make sense of where we are today and how we got there. The provisions of the Book of Common Prayer 1979 and the *Book of Occasional Services* offer a creative response, deeply rooted in the liturgical and theological tradition, to the situation which faces the church today, but this response can only be understood and implemented if we survey the whole story. Those who interpret the present rites from the perspective of the various (and contradictory) rationales offered in the past century and a half for baptism and confirmation in earlier editions of the Book of Common Prayer will seriously misunderstand the rites which have now been adopted.

1. The Baptismal Journey for Adults in the Classic Rites of Initiation

In the New Testament and literature of the first two centuries of the common era, baptism followed immediately upon conversion or came after a very brief period of instruction, prayer, and fasting. In some regions (parts of Syria and Armenia according to recent research) a more extended period of preparation was very late in developing.[1] But by the beginning of the third century in most regions, the period of preparation for the baptism of adult converts had become much longer and more extensive and was generally divided into two stages:

1. **The catechumenate,** the initial period of preparation, which might last as long as three years;

2. **Candidacy,** the period of final preparation, which was of limited duration and immediately preceded baptism.

In the third century, the personalized catechesis of the first stage received strong emphasis, and the second stage — intense but relatively brief in duration — prepared the candidates for what would be expected of them in the rite of baptism itself. It is really only during the third century that we have evidence of the first stage as a time of serious and sustained preparation for baptism. Before that time preliminary instruction and preparation before the convert was accepted for baptism seems to have been relatively informal, and after the edict of toleration in the early fourth century there is little evidence of any sustained course of preparation until catechumens applied for baptism at the next baptismal feast.

By the middle of the fourth century, the church was faced with large numbers of applicants for baptism in a social environment where the Christian faith was suddenly an advantage rather than a risk which could cost people their lives. By the end of that century, the church had developed a new strategy for dealing with this situation. The personalized catechesis of the old catechumenate was not possible for so large a number of applicants. By this time bishops throughout the church were devoting the church's resources and energy to an intensive course of preparation during Lent for the large groups who sought baptism at the Easter vigil. For all intents and purposes, the extended catechumenate before candidacy as a time for serious instruction and formation had disappeared. By some time into the fifth century catechesis declined in importance, for most of the population had become at least nominally Christian and there were far fewer adult candidates from non-Christian families in the urban centers of the Roman empire.

The Catechumenate

In many regions converts to Christianity in the third century made formal application to be admitted as a catechumen to the authorities of the church, who required testimony on their behalf on the part of sponsors. In a time of sporadic legal persecution and of heretical sects, the church proceeded with more caution than it had in earlier times.[2] Admission of catechumens, according to Hippolytus, came only after a careful examination by the authorities into their motivation, their manner of life, and their profession.[3] The Christian faith found concrete expression not only in adherence to Christian doctrine but also in conduct, and the emphasis during the catechumenate fell primarily on the moral formation of the convert. Marital status was one issue in the examination which preceded admission as a catechumen: the concern was not so much with legal status, since social distinctions rendered some unions irregular in Roman law, but with whether the applicant led a chaste life as a single person or displayed fidelity within a relationship.

The list of professions which disqualified the applicant is more extensive than we might first expect. It is not surprising that prostitutes, pimps, officials in pagan cults, and those involved with the occult were excluded. It is likewise not surprising to find participants in the violence of the amphitheater or chariot races on the list of proscribed professions. But the list was more extensive than this. Teachers were suspect because their texts were pagan literature, actors because of the moral ambiguity of the roles they played, and sculptors and artists because their subject matter was pagan. Soldiers and civil magistrates were excluded because their official duties might involve taking human life: to do so was to "despise God."[4] These persons might also be called upon in the line of duty to officiate at pagan rites or to take part in such rites. The decision to become a Christian entailed the withdrawal from pagan society and consequently cut the convert off from much of the ordinary public life of the ancient world. It was not merely a private decision; it had significant public consequences.

In the *Apostolic Tradition* of Hippolytus, from which the description above is taken, this first stage of the baptismal journey receives considerable emphasis. Once admitted as a catechumen or "hearer," the applicant underwent a prolonged process of catechesis. Hippolytus stipulates three years, though the process might be shortened. The content of such catechesis, as far as we can discover, was more moral than doctrinal: the catechumens had to grow into a Christian way of life. According to Hippolytus, it was their conduct (*tropos*) that determined their readiness for baptism. This seems consistent with what we learn from such earlier works as the *Didache*, where instruction is on the "two ways," the way of life and the way of death. Sponsors probably played an important role during this period as guides and tutors for converts on their baptismal journey.

Catechetical instruction seems to have taken many forms. The instructor could be lay or ordained. Justin Martyr (a layman) established for himself a role as a teacher of philosophy in second century Rome, and his instruction no doubt served as catechesis for those who were considering baptism. Tradition lists Pantaenus and Clement as heads of the "catechetical school" in Alexandria as the second century drew to a close, though it is unclear exactly what the official relationship of this "school" was to the official structures of the church or to the instruction which the church required for baptism. Origen as a layman later took on the task of preparing catechumens for baptism at their request when most of the clergy of Alexandria had fled the city during a period of prosecution, and his "school" received episcopal recognition of sorts, though his relationship to the bishops of Alexandria was often strained and eventually broke down entirely.

In the *Apostolic Tradition* of Hippolytus instruction of catechumens has official status in the church. Every session of instruction was concluded with prayer and the laying on of hands by the catechist. The catechumens could attend the first part of the eucharist, but they could neither pray with the baptized nor exchange the peace with them: they were dismissed after prayer was offered for them and before the prayers of the faithful which ordinarily concluded the first part of the eucharist.

In Western traditions, this time was seen in very realistic terms as a time of struggle with the powers of evil. Although initially the stage of preparation which developed into the catechumenate was probably a time of relatively informal inquiry and instruction, as it took more formal shape it came to be seen as a time when the hold of pagan ways on the catechumen was broken. Though there is no explicit reference in Hippolytus to exorcism until the beginning of the period of candidacy,[5] in later witnesses in many traditions exorcism is an important part of preparation during the catechumenate as well. Exorcism might take a variety of forms. Formulas of exorcism might be addressed directly to evil spirits, or they might take the form of prayer to God to drive out the evil spirits. Associated ritual actions include "blowing" the evil spirit out of those being exorcized, signing them with the cross, and laying hands upon them. These words and actions were seen as ways of breaking the control which evil spirits exercised over catechumens so that they would be capable of renouncing these spirits before they made their formal profession of allegiance to Christ in baptism. There are some traditions, however, in which this exorcistic emphasis seems never to have become part of the preparation for baptism.[6] It should be noted that exorcism is not "native" to the process of baptismal preparation. In the New Testament, it is the possessed who are exorcized, not those who seek baptism. The incorporation of exorcism into the process of baptismal preparation undoubtedly arises out of the church's mission to pagans at a time when pagan gods were often interpreted as evil spirits who had captured the world for Satan.[7]

Admission to the catechumenate at first may have been a relatively informal matter. The catechist simply accepted the applicant for instruction. When the catechumenate received official status in the local church, admission took ritual form. Later Western sources speak of exorcism, the laying on of hands, signing the applicant with the cross, and the administration of salt.[8] These actions might be repeated at intervals during the catechumenate. Indeed as time went on they became so important that to "catechize" meant to exorcize rather than to instruct. By the late fourth century, however, admission to the catechumenate was no longer the beginning of a time of instruction and moral formation. It was becoming little more than a rite of loose affiliation with the church for adult converts and the children of Christian families. Serious preparation for baptism really began only with admission to candidacy, and catechumens often put off that step into the indefinite future.

Candidacy

Not long before the administration of public baptism, for which Easter was a privileged occasion, the church considered applications from catechumens for enrollment as candidates. Hippolytus gives these instructions:

> [L]et their life be examined, whether they lived piously while catechumens, whether "they honoured the widows," whether they visited the sick, whether they have fulfilled every good work.[9]

The way in which catechumens were examined reenforces what was said above about the nature of the catechumenate: this is an examination as to whether the catechumens have learned appropriate Christian conduct; the concern of the first stage of preparation was conduct more than doctrine. When the catechumenate began to disappear as a time of serious preparation for baptism, this examination before admission to candidacy became even more important. Egeria witnesses to how seriously it was taken in Jerusalem at the end of the fourth century.[10]

Later rites for enrollment of candidates (known as their "election" at Rome) included ritual actions characteristic of admission of catechumens, but also the public registration of the names of those accepted in a book kept for the purpose (sometimes known as "the book of life," with reference to such texts as Revelation 3:5, Exodus 32:32, Psalm 69:26, and Daniel 12:1). In liturgical texts that have come down to us from the fourth century on, it is not always easy to distinguish rites of enrollment from rites of admission to the catechumenate; indeed it appears that the texts given for the admission of catechumens in some cases were actually those used for the enrollment of candidates, and that the distinction between catechumens and candidates was disappearing.[11]

Hippolytus tells us that in the final period of preparation there should be daily instruction and exorcism with the laying on of hands.[12] The daily exorcism was evidently seen as the final, intense stage of the candidates' struggle against the powers of evil — a struggle which would come to a climax at baptism itself. It was closely associated with the "scrutinies" of later rites, which were originally — as their name indicates — examinations of the candidates' moral progress in the struggle against evil. Of the nature of the daily instruction during this final stage of preparation, Hippolytus says only that once admitted candidates are to "hear the gospel."[13] The reference is perhaps to the specific "good news" about God that baptismal candidates are asked to affirm before baptism — what Irenaeus had called somewhat earlier "the rule of faith." The actual formula used in baptism itself seems to be the core of this rule of faith. It is built around Matthew's command to baptize "in the name of the Father, and of the Son, and of the Holy Spirit."

In the Roman tradition the rule of faith took the form of three questions used in the administration of baptism In the *Apostolic Tradition* and in the Gelasian Sacramentary the three questions are associated with the threefold baptismal immersion.[14] In their declarative form these questions developed in the West into what we know as the Apostles' Creed. Some Eastern churches developed the baptismal creed in a somewhat different way. The rule of faith was seen as a contract entered into by the candidates. This contract was a prerequisite to baptism but distinct from the administration of baptism. The formula used in baptism itself in this case was the formula from Matthew recited by the minister of the sacrament while administering baptism to the candidate.[15] In either case, the candidates had to receive instruction in what we should call the creed to be able to make the affirmations required of them in order to be baptized. It appears likely that this was the principal content of the instruction once catechumens had been accepted as candidates for baptism. In the classical rites of the late fourth century, the last weeks of instruction before baptism continued to be devoted to the creed.

The change in the church's situation in the fourth century, when Christianity was granted legal toleration at the beginning of the century and then established as the legal religion of the empire after 380, called for new strategies to prepare the greatly increased numbers of those who were requesting baptism. Some kind of rough consensus seems to have emerged from the Council of Nicea on this issue. The consensus seems to have mandated a forty-day fast as the time of preparation for paschal baptisms.[16] In any case, shortly after the council a forty-day Lent (reckoned in a bewildering variety of ways) emerged as a season devoted to baptismal preparation. Robert Cabié speaks of this preparation as having three components: 1) ascetical, 2) catechetical, 3) liturgical.[17]

Ascetical Preparation for Baptism in Lent: Ascetically, preparation consisted primarily of the forty-day fast. Initially the baptismal fast had been understood less as a penitential exercise than as an intensive form of prayer. We find evidence of the association of a preparatory fast with baptism as early as the *Didache*, which probably dates to the beginning of the second century. The association of fasting with penitence became more prominent in those traditions which associate baptismal preparation with a struggle against the forces of evil and a renunciation of paganism. The association of Lent from the fourth century on with preparation of public penitents for reconciliation with the church during holy week also strengthened the association of fasting with penitence.

Catechetical Preparation for Baptism: The catechetical component of baptismal preparation during Lent took many forms. Throughout the fourth century we see various local churches devising different programs for this catechesis. Instruction could be integrated into the daily life of the church in various ways. A very common strategy seems to have been to begin with a general introduction to the biblical economy of salvation, using Genesis as a text,[18] and to conclude with instruction on the creed (and sometimes the Lord's Prayer). To a large extent, the general instruction took the place of the catechesis which had been given in the previous century before candidates were enrolled for baptism. In some traditions the general catechesis seems to have continued throughout Lent at one service, while catechesis on the creed was given in the last weeks of Lent at another service, so that there were two "tracks" of catechetical instruction going on simultaneously. That appears to be the case in Antioch at the time of John Chrysostom,[19] and it may be the reason that the lectionary of Constantinople integrated catechetical readings into both the late morning service of terce-sext and the late afternoon and evening service of vespers. While texts for Lenten catechesis later became fixed in lectionaries for the eucharist and the office, at least initially bishops seem to have used Lent for a course of homilies on whatever book of the Bible they themselves chose as appropriate for the purpose in a particular year.

Rome, unlike many other churches, shows no real evidence of a program of catechesis based on a sequential reading of Genesis. The lectionary provisions for Lenten gospel readings at Rome and elsewhere in the West were drawn largely from the gospel of John, which seems to have been used as the basis for teaching on the meaning of the initiatory sacraments and their relationship to the death and resurrection of Christ.[20] But the Roman program to which early documents bear witness seems to have been restricted to liturgies of the word on station days and the Sunday eucharist. There is no witness in the fourth century to the daily catechesis during candidacy of which Hippolytus speaks. And we have in Roman sources no extended series of catechetical lectures comparable to those which survive for other major sees.

This program of Lenten catechesis seems to have replaced in large measure the longer catechetical program of the third century. Frequently the admission of candidates came at the beginning Lent before the whole program of catechesis. But the association of candidacy with instruction on the creed seems often to have been strong enough to delay admission of candidates in many churches until mid-Lent, the time when catechesis on the creed began. We are accustomed to thinking of sacramental or mystagogical catechesis as a postbaptismal program of instruction during Easter week, but this could also be linked with catechesis on the creed as part of the Lenten curriculum. Chrysostom and Theodore both include some sacramental catechesis in their Lenten series, and we have already noted the use of readings from John for this purpose at Rome.

The intensive programs of Lenten catechesis which have come down to us date largely from the end of the fourth century. By the next century there were fewer adult candidates for baptism within the empire. Regular preaching was also beginning to decline. Systems of lectionary provisions for catechesis were now integrated into the daily office in the East and into the weekday liturgies of the word in the West, but it is not at all clear how often the readings were accompanied by actual catechetical instruction. The impression is often given by contemporary scholars that the golden age of baptismal catechesis lasted from the third century well into the sixth (the date of the earliest liturgical texts of the dominant ritual families). The fact that the greater part of the surviving homilies relating to this catechesis date from the last quarter of the fourth century and the early decades of the fifth ought to make us highly suspicious of such claims.

Liturgical Preparation for Baptism: The evidence which we have leads us to suspect that such catechesis as survived after the early fifth century took the form of fixed texts integrated into the lectionary for the Lenten liturgy, such as the homily at the rite of renunciation and allegiance on Good Friday in Constantinople and the exposition of the gospels and introductions (*praefationes*) of the creed and the Lord's Prayer in Roman sources.[21] What became increasingly more important was the role of liturgical texts and dramatic ritual actions as part of the final preparation for baptism. Initially texts of prayers and specific ritual actions such as exorcism and the "handing over" the creed and the Lord's Prayer to the candidates and the "return" of these texts by the candidates were closely integrated with the program of catechesis. But as catechesis declined, these texts and ritual actions took on a life of their own and tended to serve as a replacement for catechesis. Indeed, catechizing in later centuries often meant exorcizing and the ritual handing over and return of the creed and the Lord's Prayer. This becomes particularly problematic when the objects of these ritual actions are infants, whose experiential appropriation of what was done to them was subconscious at best.

Conclusions on the Baptismal Journey of Adults in the Classic Rites

One of the most important liturgical reforms which came out of the Second Vatican Council was the creation of a new *Rite of Christian Initiation of Adults* (usually known as the RCIA). This rite, adapted for the use of the Episcopal Church in *The Book of Occasional Services*, drew extensively on recent research by liturgical scholars into what we have called the baptismal journey of converts to Christianity in the third through the sixth centuries. The heart of the new rite is an extended catechumenate which culminates in a period of candidacy during Lent before baptism at the Great Vigil of Easter.

As the RCIA has been implemented, it has proved a very effective vehicle for preparing adults for baptism. Recent literature about the initiatory process in the early church tends to take the RCIA as its point of reference and to suggest that the RCIA is an adaptation to modern circumstances of a stable pattern of initiation which remained relatively constant and uniform in the Christian church from the time of Hippolytus (early third century) until early forms of the tradition which lies behind the Roman initiatory rites found in Ordo Romanus XI and the Gelasian Sacramentary (some time in the seventh century). That is, as we have seen, a much more problematic conclusion, for it fails to take account of the complexity of the developments. At the beginning of this period preparation for baptism took the form of an extended catechumenate which concluded with a brief but intense period of instruction on the creed. By the late fourth century, however, the catechumenate had become in most cases a period of only nominal association with the church. The real work of catechesis, the primary preparation for baptism, took place during the forty days of Lent, after the candidates had been enrolled. This catechesis was reenforced by being set in a liturgical context which dramatically heightened its impact on candidates. By the middle decades of the fifth century actual catechesis had disappeared, for there were few adult candidates in the urban centers of the Christian empire. Most candidates were infants or young children. As we shall see, various regions adapted the rites of the baptismal process to this new situation in different ways.

Some traditions (such as the East Syrian and the Armenian rites) seem never to have developed the extensive preparatory process which we know as the catechumenate and candidacy. Instruction during preparation in these traditions was relatively brief and informal, as it had been throughout the church in the early years of its existence. Exorcism and explicit forms of renunciation and affirmation appear late in these traditions. It is therefore impossible to sustain a claim of uniformity in the baptismal journey from the third to the sixth centuries or from region to region. It is also hard to sustain the claim that the church maintained for any significant time highly developed forms of both the catechumenate and candidacy. The third century was characterized by careful and personalized preparation during the catechumenate, but candidacy was relatively brief and focussed largely on creedal catechesis. By the late fourth century, the catechumenate had lost much of its significance and tended to be understood by many as a form of nominal affiliation with the church in view of baptism sometime in the indefinite future, while candidacy had been expanded to forty days of fasting, intensive catechesis, and a much fuller set of dramatically elaborated liturgical rites designed to serve as a crash course of preparation for the crowds seeking baptism. The impression at the end of this later period begins to grow that the very drama of the rites will create faithful Christians: the church was on the verge of a mechanical view of sacramental efficacy.

2. The Baptismal Journey of the Children of Christian Families Until the Breakdown of the Classic Rites

In recent literature on baptism there has been very little discussion of the baptism of children in the classic era of the baptismal rites. Indeed, recently it has not been unusual for scholars in denominations which practice the baptism of infants to suggest that the baptism of adults was the norm during this period. Aidan Kavanagh, perhaps the most influential Roman Catholic interpreter of the initiatory rites in this country after the Second Vatican Council, writes in his treatment of the issue in *The Shape of Baptism*:

> The data of neither scripture nor tradition can be made to support infant baptism as the pastoral norm. But those same data clearly support the practice as a benign abnormality in the life of a community whose ministry regularly focuses upon the evangelization, catechesis, and initiation of faith into its midst.[22]

Louis Weil, co-author of the book on liturgy in the Episcopal Church's semi-official Church's Teaching Series, has recently written in a thoughtful article on baptism in the Book of Common Prayer 1979 and the Anglican tradition,

> From a theological point of view, an adult is always the normative candidate for baptism.[23]

Weil is in fact explicitly drawing on Kavanagh in making this claim.

One would hardly suspect from these two statements and many others like them that the *Apostolic Tradition* of Hippolytus seems to take the baptism of children, even those too young to answer for themselves, as a matter of course requiring no special justification. In giving directions for the administration of baptism, the text of the *Apostolic Tradition* simply notes,

> . . . they shall baptize the little children first. And if they can answer for themselves, let them answer. But if they cannot, let their parents answer or someone from their family.[24]

Kavanagh and Weil have entered the wild goose chase initiated by the radical reformers in the sixteenth century — the quest for a single normative occasion for baptism in the course of human life. That one moment as Kavanagh describes it is mature conversion — a moment which obviously makes infant baptism abnormal.[25] All of this is in part a reaction to Western practice which has for years given the impression that the baptism of adults is abnormal. The pendulum has swung, and contemporary scholars are now speaking of the baptism of infants as abnormal, even if this is a "benign abnormality," in Kavanagh's words.

A careful reading of the few authors in the classical period who treat the issue does not suggest that most of them saw either the baptism of adults or the baptism of children as abnormal. Origen in the early third century, Cyprian at mid-century, and Augustine at the end of the fourth century all take the baptism of the children of Christian parents as a normal practice in the church: Origen considers it of apostolic origin and the title of Hippolytus' treatise might lead us to suspect that he did, too.[26] The North Africans Cyprian and Augustine in fact consider the delay of baptism for the children of Christian families abnormal — an abuse to be corrected. The lone dissenting voice is that of Tertullian, who knows the practice of infant baptism and disapproves of it. But Tertullian's well-known rigorism was soon to lead him into Montanism, and it is dangerous to take him as a representative voice for the church in his time. At the end of the fourth century, Gregory of Nazianzus recommends baptism as soon as children can speak for themselves — a practice that lasted for some time in the Byzantine tradition, as we shall see below.

Most contemporary authors who address the issue seem to ignore the possibility that the early church could establish different norms for baptism in different contexts. The baptismal journey of the adult convert to Christianity from paganism is very different from the baptismal journey of the child born to faithful Christian parents, and while there is no clear evidence as to how the New Testament church dealt with such children, there is evidence about how the church in certain regions was dealing with such children by the third century. When the Council of Carthage in the middle of the third century directs that children be baptized within eight days after birth and Augustine in the late fourth century preaches against delaying the baptism of infants, it is hardly accurate to say that the baptism of infants born to Christian families is *abnormal* in the tradition of the North African church. And similar canonical legislation in other regions of the West from the fourth century on established baptism of children shortly after birth as the norm throughout the West.

Canonical legislation on this matter certainly met resistance. But the grounds for delaying baptism in the third and fourth centuries have little if anything to do with the theological grounds advanced for adult baptism today. Edward Yarnold, who has retained a more balanced perspective than many contemporary authors who address the issue, sums up the grounds commonly advanced in the third and fourth centuries for delaying baptism very well:

> St. Augustine refers to the common belief that it is best to prolong the period before baptism, so that a person may sin with the assurance that he will receive forgiveness at baptism: "let him alone, let him do as he pleases; he is not baptized" (*Confessions* 1:18. Cf. Tertullian, *de Paenitentia* 6; J. Jeremias, *Infant Baptism*, pages 87-89). The less cynical would say that it was better to wait until the individual was prepared for total conversion of life; the passionate years of youth, or a position of civic authority which might involve the taking of life, were good reasons for postponing the sacrament.[27]

By the end of the fourth century, bishops throughout the church were arguing against such excuses for the delay of baptism.

Whether baptism was delayed or administered not long after birth, it seems to have become customary to make infants catechumens as soon as possible. In regions where baptism was reserved to the baptismal feasts except in emergencies,[28] there would be some lapse of time before the administration of baptism to a healthy child could be scheduled. In the West, insofar as we can tell from later witnesses, the same rite was used for making catechumens of both infants and adults. The Byzantine tradition, on the other hand, developed a distinctive rite for admitting children as catechumens, as we shall see.

The Baptismal Journey of Children in the West

We have no idea what portions of the rites of the baptismal process Hippolytus intended to be used for the initiation of children or how those rites were adapted when used with infants. By the late sixth or early seventh century in the West (the period in which the rites in the Roman tradition were taking the form found in the Gelasian Sacramentary and the Ordo Romanus XI), we find rites originally designed for adults being used for infants with minimal adaptation. Thus the infants are enrolled in Lent, exorcized frequently at the scrutinies, signed with the cross, given salt, instructed on the gospels, the creed, and the Lord's Prayer, and put through the paces of returning the creed, renouncing Satan, and making the creedal affirmations. The liturgical texts and ritual actions were adapted to infant candidates simply by having parent, sponsor, or cleric make required responses on their behalf. After baptism, children received the anointing and laying on of hands by the bishop and then were given communion. The Ordo Romanus XI even cautions that children are not to be nursed after baptism so that they may receive communion fasting! Infant candidates were of necessity purely passive participants in the baptismal process. The minimal adaptations reveal a relatively mechanical understanding of the sacramental process. This is true particularly of the "handing over" of creed, Lord's Prayer, and gospels and the return of the creed by proxy. What disappeared, of course, was functional prebaptismal catechesis. This was clearly impossible with infant candidates.

The Baptismal Journey of Children in the Byzantine Tradition

A careful examination of texts in the Byzantine tradition reveals a very different approach.[29] Gregory of Nazianzus recommended that children be baptized several years after their birth, when they were old enough to make the responses for themselves in the baptismal rites.[30] The rubrical tradition found in the typikon of the Great Church (Hagia Sophia in Constantinople) as late as the end of the first millennium shows that parents were expected to bring their children to church during the last weeks of Lent for catechetical instruction.[31] The euchological tradition of Constantinople gives us further information about baptismal practice in the Byzantine rite. The euchologies of that tradition preserve prayers for children on the eighth and fortieth days after their birth which serve to affiliate them with the church as catechumens. The biblical model behind these prayers is the naming of Jesus on the eighth day after his birth and his presentation in the temple on the fortieth day after his birth, as reported in Luke's gospel.[32] The text of the prayers makes it clear that they were for children before their baptism. The prayers and the rubrics indicate that the liturgical actions which were a part of these rites were the equivalent of those by which converts were made catechumens — signing the children with the cross and laying a hand upon them. Because the Byzantine church did not develop the doctrine of original sin in the way that the North African church did, it did not feel the urgency for baptism immediately after birth that we find articulated in the sermons of Augustine and in later Western authors. The baptismal practice of the Byzantine church thus developed a more coherent rationale for the baptism of children and a less mechanical sacramental theology for the practice than we see in the West. Except in emergencies, children were for centuries baptized after preliminary catechesis at an age when they were able to appropriate experientially the meaning of their initiation.[33] Furthermore, because the postbaptismal anointing was delegated to presbyters in the absence of a bishop, the sacraments of initiation were never separated as they were in the Roman tradition. From the time of their baptism children were fully initiated members of the church and their admission as communicants was not postponed. The baptismal journey of adults and infants was different, but its culmination was the same — entry by the same baptismal liturgy into the full sacramental life of the community of faith.

3. The Breakdown of the Original Initiatory Pattern in the West and the Emergence of Other Patterns

In the West, the baptismal journey of adults in the classic rites of the third and fourth centuries had been a journey of ascetical, catechetical, and liturgical preparation which reached its culmination in the baptismal liturgy of the paschal vigil (or the vigil of Pentecost). A shift in the process of initiation which made baptism the *beginning* rather than the *culmination* of the process started very early in the West and continued through a series of historical accidents which eventually generated their own theological rationale. As a result of those accidents, the initiatory journey started with the baptism of the child within eight days of its birth and usually culminated in confirmation at "the years of discretion."[34]

The church had developed by the late fourth century a carefully crafted series of rites which gave concrete and effective expression to the process of conversion from paganism to the Christian faith and incorporated converts into the disciplined life of the community of those who knew Christ and were committed to his service. This series of rites presupposed the conscious and active participation of both the convert and the members of the Christian community. The sacramental theology which undergirded these rites understood the rites to work by signifying what they achieved.

The situation of those who were born into this community was different. Theirs was not a journey from paganism to the Christian faith. Because they would grow up in the community of faith the goal of their initiation was growth into the full life of that community which knew Christ and was committed to his service. Their experiential appropriation of the Christian faith could not be the same as those who had come to that faith from paganism. The Byzantine tradition gives witness of the conscious effort to redesign the rites of the initiatory process with such children in mind. The rites of the baptismal journey in this tradition articulate the child's growth into the life of such a community.

The collapsing culture of the twilight of the empire in the Latin-speaking West was not equal to addressing the situation of children with similar creativity. Its initial approach was simply to put infants through the rites of a process designed for the baptismal journey of adult converts. There was no small measure of incongruity in the solution of the Western church, which presumed that the passive, largely unconscious participation of infants in this series of rites would achieve the same results as the active, conscious participation of adult converts. It was not long before this approach would break down as the process began to unravel in a chain of events that slowly unfolded over the course of the middle ages.

This chain of events was, for the most part, the result not of a conscious strategy for redesigning the process, but of historical accidents. The key changes were these:

1. the separation of the prebaptismal rites from their original setting in the corporate liturgy of Lent;
2. the separation of the baptismal liturgy itself from its original setting in the corporate liturgy of the baptismal feasts of Easter and Pentecost;
3. the disintegration of the rite of baptism itself into three separate sacraments — baptism (the baptismal immersions), confirmation (the final anointing, signation, and imposition of hands by the bishop in the original baptismal liturgy), and

communion (to which candidates were originally admitted at baptism);

4. the eventual association of post-baptismal catechesis with confirmation and admission to communion.

We shall now look at each of these events in somewhat more detail.[35]

The Separation of the Prebaptismal Rites from the Lenten Liturgy

It is evident that the catechetical components of the Lenten liturgy — the lessons of Lent and catechesis based on them — have no real function in preparing infants for baptism. Indeed, as Latin ceased to be the language of the people, it is hard to see how these lessons — still read in Latin — could even have functioned effectively for the catechesis of adults! The Western traditions (and the Byzantine tradition as well) eventually refocussed the Lenten lessons on penitence as a return of sinners to their baptismal status[36] in preparation for Easter communion. But the Western tradition, with its doctrine of original sin did find a use for the exorcistic components of the Lenten liturgy (the "scrutinies") in the baptism of infants. Since these exorcisms did not require a corporate context, they were eventually detached from the Lenten liturgy, along with the "return" of the Creed and the Lord's Prayer" which continued to be associated with baptism. These prebaptismal rites were then refashioned into a single prebaptismal service such as we find in the rites of the tenth-century Ordo Romanus L — the basis of the Romano-German Pontifical which became the Roman liturgical standard of the late middle ages.[37] Except in the case of baptisms at the corporate liturgy of the baptismal feasts, the prebaptismal rites came to be united with the baptismal liturgy itself, though the distinction between the two rites might be maintained by celebrating the prebaptismal rite at the door of the church and bringing the child into church at the beginning of the baptismal rite itself.[38]

The Separation of Baptism from the Baptismal Feasts

Roman tradition restricted baptism to the two ancient baptismal feasts of the West, Easter and Pentecost. As the control of the papacy spread throughout the West, this restriction spread throughout the Latin-speaking church. Canonical legislation continued to reenforce it throughout the first millennium, although provision was always made for pastoral emergencies, and the danger of infant mortality must have meant that exemptions from the restriction were common.[39] By the eleventh century, however, we note shifts in canonical legislation. Provision begins to be made for baptism of infants at any time, without reference to the danger of death. By the fourteenth century parents are being directed to present their children for baptism soon after birth. Indeed, baptism at the vigils of Easter and Pentecost was restricted in the late medieval Sarum manual to those born within eight days of the feasts. What had happened over the centuries was that clinical baptism had ceased to be the exception and had become the rule.

The Disintegration of the Baptismal Liturgy Itself

The baptismal liturgy of the classic initiatory rites of the fourth century was a liturgy at which the bishop himself presided, assisted by the presbyters and deacons of the diocese. A diocese in this era normally included the see city and its immediate environs. In such a situation the bishop could be the chief minister of the initiatory sacraments, and it was fitting that he himself should perform the ritual actions which completed baptismal initiation. In most rites, the final ritual act was a postbaptismal anointing with chrism, and in many traditions a signation and an imposition of hands were included in these concluding rites.

These ritual actions were so closely associated with baptism that in most traditions they were originally delegated to a presbyter when the bishop did not preside at the baptismal liturgy. Even in the fourth century, the bishop could not preside at every clinical baptism, and there were churches in many dioceses too remote from the cathedral for parents to bring their children to the cathedral for baptism at the principal diocesan celebration of the vigils of Easter and Pentecost. In the Roman tradition, however, authority to perform these concluding ritual actions was not delegated to presbyters. Those who did not receive the bishop's anointing and imposition of hands at baptism were to be brought to him as soon as possible after baptism so that he could complete their initiation. Nevertheless they were usually communicated at their baptism or at the first celebration of the eucharist after their baptism.

The ancient dioceses of Italy were geographically compact, and at first the absence of a bishop at baptism did not mean that any significant time would pass before the person baptized by others would receive the final baptismal anointing and the laying on of hands from the bishop. But in other regions of the Latin-speaking West bishops were responsible for vast expanses of territory, and years might pass before a bishop was available to complete the initiation of those baptized in his absence. Indeed, many might never receive this episcopal "confirmation" of their baptism. In many regions of the West the completion of the baptismal liturgy was therefore delegated to presbyters as it was in the East. But as the pope extended his jurisdiction over other churches, he imposed the baptismal tradition of the Roman tradition on those churches as well.

It was not long before a theological rationale began to be articulated for this accidental disintegration of the baptismal rite. The starting point for this rationale can probably be traced to the way the church in the third and fourth centuries decided to reconcile schismatic Christians to the communion of the church. In the East, they were reconciled by an anointing with chrism (myrrh). In the West the usual practice was to reconcile them by the laying on of hands. The somewhat dubious theological rationale developed for these rites of reconciliation was that schismatics were outside the church as the body in which God's Spirit worked, so that when a schismatic group baptized the baptism was valid but did not take effect until the person baptized received the Spirit upon reconciliation with the church. The close analogy between the laying on of hands and chrismation as acts which bestowed the Spirit on schismatics at their reconciliation and the use of these actions to articulate the gift of the Spirit in baptism itself led theologians to understand the postbaptismal anointing and laying on of hands as the sacramental means by which the Spirit was given in the baptismal liturgy rather than as actions which gave concrete expression to the bestowal of the Spirit by means of the baptismal immersions.[40] The laying on of hands and anointing were beginning to be understood as a sacrament distinct from baptism itself.

However, the Roman tradition was unique in the fact that it included two postbaptismal anointings — one by the presbyter and one by the bishop. By the late middle ages, theologians were arguing the Spirit was given in the first postbaptismal anointing, while the second postbaptismal anointing bestowed the spiritual gifts and strength necessary for Christian maturity. In confirmation an increase of the Spirit was given *ad robur*, for strengthening.[41] This theology suggested that the second anointing should not be conferred at baptism even when the bishop presided, but only when a person reached the undefined "age of discretion."[42]

Although baptism, "confirmation," and first communion follow one another in that sequence in the original baptismal liturgy, the absence of the bishop at most baptisms meant that the sequence of ritual acts was altered for most of those who were baptized in the middle ages. Ordinarily they would be admitted to communion immediately after baptism and then confirmed whenever the bishop was available. But eventually first communion also came to be associated with the age of discretion. This might mean that children were admitted to first communion once they had been confirmed. But at other times first communion was administered to children at a younger age, while confirmation was administered at the threshold of maturity. Confirmation and first communion were both delayed; however, the order in which the two sacraments were administered varied from region to region and from century to century. After the Council of Trent, the sequence of baptism, confirmation, and first communion was the norm in most regions of the Roman Catholic Church. In the United States, the Second Plenary Council of Baltimore had established seven as the minimum age for confirmation, and ten to fourteen as the normal age for first communion. The decree of Pius X in 1910 (*Quam singulari*) lowered the age for first communion, and as a result the sequence of confirmation and first communion has been reversed since that time in the American Church.[43]

The Association of Postbaptismal Catechesis with Confirmation and First Communion

The relation of catechesis and formation to baptism was not entirely forgotten once the majority of candidates for baptism were infants. But such catechesis as they received necessarily came after their baptism. The responsibility for such catechesis fell primarily on sponsors and parents. They were expected to instruct children on the texts which formed the basis of the catechesis of the last part of Lent in the original prebaptismal rites — the Creed and the Lord's Prayer. When confirmation and first communion began to be associated with the age of discretion, the completion of this elementary catechesis began to be linked with the administration of these sacraments. Regulations on this matter in the late middle ages began to make their way into the rubrics of the baptismal rite. We find such rubrics in the Sarum manual of the late middle ages, along with a vernacular exhortation to godparents which spells out this requirement:

> God faders and godmodyrs of thys chylde whe charge you that ye charge the foder and te moder to kepe it from fyer and water and other perels to the age of vii yere, and that he lerne or se yt be lerned the Our Father, Hail Mary, and I believe, after the lawe of all holy churche and in all goodly haste to be confermed of my lorde of the dyocise or of hys depute . . . .[44]

In order to reenforce this requirement, regulations such as those issued in England by Archbishop Peckham in 1281 were issued in many churches. Those regulations eventually found their way into the rubrics of the Book of Common Prayer at the time of the English Reformation:

> And there shal none be admitted to the holye communion: until suche time as he be confirmed.[45]

These developments are the material out of which churches in the West would construct a new pattern for initiatory rites in the Reformation era. What we need to note at this point is that the function of baptism has shifted within the process over the centuries. By the sixteenth century it had become the functional equivalent of the rite for making a catechumen in the classical initiatory liturgy. The question that needs to be asked about this shift, however, is a question that only the radical Reformers asked in the sixteenth century: Can baptism be used in this way without undermining the basic meaning of the sacrament?

4. The Book of Common Prayer and the Pattern of Initiation in England after the Reformation

The link between the catechesis of children and their confirmation and admission to communion had already been made some centuries before the Reformation. What the reformers did was to try to provide a coherent theological rationale for this link.[46] While the Council of Trent continued to insist that confirmation was a distinct sacrament, the reformers rejected this claim as unwarranted. Instead, they followed the lead of the followers of Jan Hus in the previous century and saw confirmation as the solemn ratification of the baptismal covenant made by those baptized in infancy at the conclusion of a period of systematic catechesis. Calvin in his Institutes quite correctly argues that the New Testament gives no warrant for confirmation as a sacrament distinct from baptism. But he goes on to make a claim entirely unwarranted by the historical evidence:

> It was an ancient custom in the church for the children of Christians, after they were come to years of discretion, to be presented to the bishop in order to fulfil that duty which was required of adults who offered themselves to baptism. For such persons were placed among the catechumens, till, being duly instructed in the mysteries of Christianity, they were called to make a confession of their faith before the bishop and all the people. Therefore those who had been baptized in their infancy, because they had not then made such a confession of faith before the church, at the close of childhood or the commencement of adolescence, were again presented by their parents, and were examined by the bishop according to the form of catechism which was then in common use. That this exercise, which deserved to be regarded as sacred and solemn, might have the greater dignity and reverence, they also practised the ceremony of imposition of hands. Thus the youth, after having given satisfaction respecting his faith, was dismissed with a solemn benediction. This custom is frequently mentioned by the ancient writers.[47]

It was on this basis that most of the churches of the Reformation that baptized infants eventually adopted a rite of confirmation (though they did not always use this name, and all except Anglicans delegated the rite to the parish pastor). They likewise made this rite or its equivalent a prerequisite for admission to communion. The problem here is that, despite Calvin's argument, the prayers and ritual gestures which came to be known as confirmation in the early middle ages were only linked to the completion of catechesis, a personal profession of faith, and admission to communion in the late middle ages. The historical basis which Calvin claims for them is fictitious.

In 1549 Archbishop Cranmer handled the Sarum rites for baptism and confirmation conservatively and with great sensitivity. In his baptismal service the prebaptismal rite, celebrated at the door of the church, remains distinct from baptism itself, celebrated at the font after the baptismal party has entered the church. While Cranmer did not think it pastorally feasible to reinstate the restriction of baptism to the ancient baptismal feasts, he did insist that — except in pastoral emergencies — baptism be administered during a public service (morning or evening prayer) on a Sunday or feast day. He retained the main components of the medieval rites, including a presbyteral anointing after baptism. It may be that in 1549 he saw this postbaptismal anointing as the equivalent of the second anointing in the Roman tradition — the anointing that some understood as the sacramental sign of confirmation.[48]

In any case the form for confirmation which he drafted in 1549 had no anointing associated with it. The ritual gestures used were the laying on of hands and the consignation. Confirmation in that book came after catechesis of the candidates on the creed, the Lord's Prayer, and the ten commandments. As soon as candidates knew these texts and the brief explanation of them provided in the short catechism prefixed to confirmation, they were to be confirmed and admitted to communion. Functionally, confirmation is understood here in a way characteristic of both the late middle ages and the sixteenth-century reformers and their precursors: as a solemn conclusion to catechesis and an admission to communion.

A comparison of the exhortation to godparents and the rubrics in the Sarum manual with similar materials in the 1549 Book of Common Prayer[49] shows the continuity in the way confirmation functioned in the life of the church:

Sarum Manual

Vernacular exhortation to godparents at baptism: God faders and godmodyrs of thys chylde whe charge you that ye charge the foder and te moder to kepe it from fyer and water and other perels to the age of vii yere, and that he lerne or se yt be lerned the *Our Father, Hail Mary*, and I believe, after the lawe of all holy churche

and in all goodly haste to be confermed of my lorde of the dyocise or of hys depute . . . .

Rubric at baptism: Also no one must be admitted to the sacrament of the body and blood of Christ save in danger of death, unless he has been confirmed or has been reasonably prevented from receiving the sacrament of confirmation.

1549 Book of Common Prayer

Exhortation to godparents at baptism: You must remember that it is your partes and duetie to see that these infantes be taught, so soone as they shalbe able to learne, what a solemn vowe, promyse, and profession, they have made by you. And that they maye knowe these thynges the better: . . . chiefly you shal prouide that thei may learne the Crede, the Lordes prayer, and the ten commaundmentes in thenglish tounge: and all other thinges which a christian manne ought to knowe and beleue to his soules health.

Rubric at baptism: The minister shall commaunde . . . that the children be brought to the Bushop to bee confirmed of hym, so soone as they can saye in theyr vulgare tounge the articles of the fayth, the Lordes prayer, and the ten commaundementes, and be further instructed in the Catechisme, set furth for that purpose, accordingly as it is there expressed.

Rubric at confirmation: So soone as the children can say in their mother tongue tharticles of the faith, the lordes praier, the ten commaundements, and also can aunswere to such questions as the Bushop (or suche as he shall appointe) shal by hys discrecion appose to them in: then shall they bee brought to the Bushop by one that shalbee his godfather or godmother, that euerye childe maye have a wittenesse of hys confirma-cion.

Rubric at confirmation: And there shal none be admitted to the holye commu-nion: until suche time as he be con-firmed.

But in 1549 Cranmer handled the actual text of the confirmation rite so conservatively that it still seemed to retain its status as a separate sacrament — even though it was probably Cranmer's intention that the rite be understood as a solemn seal and blessing at the conclusion of catechesis in preparation for admission to communion rather than as a sacramental act. Cranmer did eliminate the anointing at confirmation. In pre-Reformation debates most English bishops had conceded that Scripture provided no warrant for this anointing.[50] But Cranmer retained the two other gestures associated with the rite — the imposition of hands and the consignation. The principal prayer said over the confirmands in 1549 (based on Isaiah 11) had no significant variants from the earlier rites, and the formula used to confirm individual confirmands had only one significant variant: since the confirmand was no longer anointed, but had a hand laid on his head, the formula was changed accordingly (see the underlined text below):

> **Sarum manual:** N., I sign thee with the sign of the cross and <u>confirm thee with the chrism of salvation</u>, in the name of the Father and of the Son and of the Holy Spirit. Amen.

> **1549:** N., I signe thee with the signe of the crosse, <u>and laye my hande upon thee</u>, in the name of the father, and of the sonne, and of the holy gost. Amen.[51]

The medieval prayer (once separated from its original context in the baptismal liturgy itself) suggested that it was the ritual gestures associated with confirmation which effected the indwelling of the Holy Spirit. Cranmer was quite clear that the Holy Spirit was given in baptism, as the 1549 formula for the postbaptismal anointing by the presbyter made evident (compare the underlined text):

> Almighty God, the Father of our Lord Jesus Christ, who hath regenerated thee by water and the Holy Spirit and hath given thee remission of all thy sins himself anoints thee <u>with the chrism of salvation</u> in the same our Lord Jesus Christ unto eternal life.[52]

> Almighty God the father of our lorde Jesus Christ, who hath regenerate thee by water and the holy gost, and hath geuen unto thee remission of al thy sinnes: he vouchsafe to annoynte thee <u>with the unccion of his holy spirite</u>, and bryng thee to the inheritaunce of euerlasting lyfe. Amen.[53]

The Sarum text of this prayer had spoken of an anointing with "the chrism of salvation"; this prayer speaks of an anointing with "the unction of the Holy Spirit" and so seems to imply that the action conveys the gift of the Holy Spirit. But Cranmer's modest revision of the language of the prayer over the candidates at confirmation (which still asked God to send down upon them the Holy Spirit with manifold gifts of grace) made it possible to continue to interpret confirmation as a rite which bestowed the Spirit or the gifts of the Spirit. There is consequently a certain theological incoherence to the 1549 rites.

These rites for baptism and confirmation are probably best understood as an attempt to continue the traditional usages within a reformed perspective. In England there was no basic disagreement between the conservative and the reformed positions on the issue of catechesis before confirmation and admission to communion. There were differences on how the rite of confirmation itself was to be understood. What was bestowed on the candidate in confirmation? the Holy Spirit? the gifts of the Holy Spirit? a solemn blessing? Either of the first two answers could find support in traditional Catholicism. The continental reformers would give the third answer. Cranmer quite clearly believed that the Holy Spirit was given in baptism, not in confirmation. By using the traditional texts for the administration of confirmation, however, he created a rite which is difficult to interpret as nothing more than a solemn blessing. It is natural to interpret the gestures and the language of the rite as conferring the gifts of the Holy Spirit for strength, and this is exactly how Rabanus Maurus had understood confirmation. While Cranmer declined to give the rite sacramental status, it nevertheless functioned as a sacrament: the imposition of hands functioned as a sign of grace bestowed.

Cranmer further revised the rites for baptism and confirmation in 1552. The baptismal rite was simplified, so that the baptismal immersions stood out more clearly as the sacramental sign. The prebaptismal rite, performed at the door of the church in 1549, was fused with baptism itself and performed at the font. The postbaptismal anointing by the presbyter was eliminated: the only significant gesture other than the baptismal immersions was the consignation. Cranmer moved the consignation from before the immersions to after the immersions in such a way as to claim for baptism the meaning of confirmation in earlier rites:

> We receyue this child into the congregacion of Christes flocke, and doe signe him with the signe of the crosse, in token that hereafter he shal not be ashamed to confesse the fayth of Christ crucified, and manfully to fight under his banner agaynst synne, the world, and the deuyll, and to continue Christ's faythfull souldiour and seruaunt unto his lyues end. Amen.[54]

The strength (*robur*) that those who followed Rabanus Maurus saw as the sacramental gift received in confirmation was now ascribed to baptism. The anointing, for which no clear biblical warrant can be claimed, was now eliminated from baptism as well as from confirmation.

The key revisions are found, however, in the 1552 rite of confirmation. Cranmer revised the prayer over the confirmands and the formula used to confirm individual candidates to make it clear how the rite was to be understood. Note the difference in the underlined portions of the text:

1549	1552
Prayer over confirmands: Almighty and euerliuing God, who hast vouchsafed to regenerate these thy seruauntes of water and the holy goste: And hast geuen unto them forgeuenesse of all their sinnes:	Prayer over confirmands: Almightie and euerliuinge God, who haste vouchesafed to regenerate these thy seruaunts by water and the holy gost, and hast geuen unto them forgyuenes of all theyr sinnes:
Sende down from heauen we beseche thee, (O lorde) upon them thy holy goste the coumforter, with the manifold giftes of grace,	strengthen them, we besche thee, (O Lord,) with the holy goste the comforter, and daily encrease in them thy manifold giftes of grace,
the spirite of wisdom and understanding, the spirite of counsell and gostly strength; The spirite of knowledge and true godliness, and fulfil them, (o lord) with the spirite of thy holy feare. Aunswere. Amen.	the spirite of wisdom and understanding; the spirite of counsel and gostly strength, the spirite of knowledge and true godlynes; and fulfil them, (O lord,) with the spirit of thy holy feare. Amen.

Signe them (o lorde) and marke them to be thyne for euer, by the vertue of thy holye crosse and passion. Confirm them with the inward unccion of thy holy gost, mercifully unto euerlasting life. Amen.

Formula when signing candidates and laying a hand on them: N. I signe thee with the signe of the crosse, and laye my hande upon thee. In the name of the father, and of the sonne, and of the holy gost. Amen.[55]

Formula laying a hand on candidates: Defende, O lord, this child with thy heauenly grace, that he may continue thine for euer, and dayly encrease in thy holy spirite more and more, until he come unto thy euerlastyng kyngdom. Amen.[56]

The elimination of the consignation and the references to it in both the prayer and the formula heightens the meaning of the consignation in baptism. The text of the prayer over the candidates quite explicitly excludes the idea that the Holy Spirit is given in confirmation, which the "send" might have suggested in 1549. Confirmation in the 1552 texts is about the increase of grace and continual strengthening through the *gifts* of the Holy Spirit; it is not the rite which confers the *gift* of the Holy Spirit.

Although the rubrics of confirmation speak of the rite as the occasion at which children "ratify and confess" (1549) or "ratify and confirm" (1552) the promises made for them by their godparents, it was not until 1662 that such a ratification found expression in the text of the rite. Note the shift in emphasis on the meaning of the word confirm after 1552: In 1549 the bishop prayed that God would "confirm and strengthen" the candidates; these words disappear from the prayer in 1552, and the rubrics speak of the candidates "confirming" their baptismal vows. However, even the 1662 rite has the ritual shape of the pre-Reformation service of confirmation. The prayer, the formula, and the ritual gestures do not give the impression that this rite is primarily a ratification of baptismal promises before admission to communion. The texts and ritual gestures which according to this perspective are simply a bestowal of a solemn blessing in fact are the dominant components of the service and so undercut the Reformed understanding of the rite.

Roman Catholics and Anglicans alike had from the sixteenth century a rite whose language and ritual shape did not cohere with its real function. Whatever explanations the theologians gave, the practical consequence of the rite was admission to communion. Indeed, when admission to communion was granted before confirmation,[57] both churches found it difficult to make its members take confirmation seriously. "Increase of grace" or "strength to confess the faith" were gifts too intangible to be real to most members of the church, and the idea that the Spirit was not given in baptism was theologically incoherent.

Conclusions

Theoretically, there is a very significant theological difference between the understanding of confirmation in Catholic theology and the understanding of confirmation in the theology of the churches of the Reformation. For Catholic theology, the rite is a sacrament; for the continental reformers, it is a solemn blessing and does not objectively bestow a distinctive grace or confer an indelible character. But the theoretical difference should not blind us to the fact that the Reformation understanding of confirmation articulates the way that the rite already functioned in late medieval Catholicism and would continue to function in post-Reformation Catholicism. The distinctions between the sacramental rite of the Catholic tradition and the new rites of the churches of the Reformation were theoretical rather than real. In both cases confirmation functioned as the prerequisite for the admission of the baptized to communion.

But that meant that baptism itself had been evacuated of the meaning which it had in scripture and the early tradition of the church. It now functioned as the admission of catechumens had originally functioned — as a rite by which persons were enrolled for catechesis before they were incorporated into the eucharistic fellowship of the church. Baptism had once been the culmination of a journey in faith that began with admission as a catechumen. Over the course of the centuries it had been transformed so that it was the start of a journey in faith that ordinarily culminated in confirmation.

Two factors obscured for Christians in this era the fundamental incoherence of this shift in the function of baptism. 1) Catechesis was an issue of overriding importance to reformers, Catholic and Protestant alike, during this era. 2) Neither Catholic nor Protestant in this period succeeded in establishing the reception of communion as the characteristic observance of the Lord's Day: it remained for most at best a quarterly obligation. A flawed understanding of baptism was the end result of a flawed understanding of the church. As the church recovered its identity as a eucharistic community in the twentieth century the initiatory pattern which had emerged at the Reformation lost its credibility.

5. The Initiatory Reforms of the Twentieth Century: Baptism and the Affirmation of the Baptismal Covenant in the Book of Common Prayer 1979

The twentieth century has witnessed the gradual recovery of a more adequate eucharistic theology and practice, so that the eucharist is once again coming to be understood as the distinctive and proper service for the Lord's Day and the general communion of the congregation is becoming the rule rather than the exception. This in turn has facilitated the recovery of a eucharistic ecclesiology, in which the eucharist is understood as the epiphany of the church — the place where the true character of the church is revealed. In this context, the anomaly of a baptismal practice which made the newly baptized members of the church but not communicants became obvious, and the fragmentation of Christian initiation became intolerable.

The rites for baptism and confirmation in the Book of Common Prayer 1979 went through several drafts before the final form was worked out.[58] The continuing concern was to fashion a unified baptismal rite which was (in the words of the final rubrics) "full initiation by water and the Holy Spirit into Christ's Body the Church."[59] This entailed eliminating the ambiguity of prior rites for baptism and confirmation in the Anglican tradition. It was the probable intention of Archbishop Cranmer that baptism be understood as full initiation, but that was undercut by delaying admission to communion until the time of confirmation and by the resemblance of the texts and ritual actions of the rite of confirmation to the concluding rites of the ancient baptismal service.[60] The rite of confirmation in the Anglican tradition often continued to be understood in terms of its function when it was the conclusion of a unified rite of initiation — as the sacramental act which bestowed the Holy Spirit. The result was theological incoherence when confirmation was detached from baptism and used as a solemn blessing at the completion of catechesis.

The drafting committee for the Book of Common Prayer 1979 originally proposed the elimination of confirmation as a rite separate from baptism and the reintegration of all the components of the original rites of initiation, which could be administered by either a bishop or a presbyter. This rite, printed in *Services for Trial Use* in 1970, proved too drastic a change for the Episcopal Church, and the final 1979 book retains a separate rite known as "confirmation." What the revision attempts is a rethinking of what confirmation is. The baptismal rite of 1979, understood as full initiation, now includes the texts (the prayer for the sevenfold gifts of the Spirit and a formula for sealing) and ritual acts (laying on of a hand, consignation, and — optionally — chrismation) which once concluded baptism and were later split off as the separate rite of confirmation. A glance at the rite of confirmation in the current Roman Catholic tradition reveals that its texts and ritual acts are included in the baptismal rite of the Episcopal Church. A new rite was drafted for "Confirmation" in the Book of Common Prayer 1979: this rite is not initiatory but finds its focus in the laying on of hands by the bishop that the Spirit may strengthen the candidates for the commitments undertaken in the affirmation of the baptismal covenant (for the first time in maturity, on reception into the Episcopal Church, or on other occasions of renewal and recommitment). New texts were drafted for this service, since the traditional texts (except the 1552 formula during the laying on of hands) are now a part of the baptismal liturgy. The texts in the baptismal service are these:

After this action [the baptism] has been completed for all candidates, the Bishop or Priest, at a place in full sight of the congregation, prays over them, saying

Let us pray.

Heavenly Father, we thank you that by water and the Holy Spirit you have bestowed upon these your servants the forgiveness of sin, and have raised them to the new life of grace. Sustain them, O Lord, in your Holy Spirit. Give to them an inquiring and discerning heart, the courage to will and to persevere, a spirit to know and to love you, and the gift of joy and wonder in all your works. Amen.

Then the Bishop or Priest places a hand on the person's head, marking on the forehead the sign of the cross [using Chrism if desired] and saying to each one

N., you are sealed by the Holy Spirit in Baptism and marked as Christ's own for ever. *Amen.*[61]

The prayer over the candidates is a paraphrase of Cranmer's prayer over *confirmands* quoted above; the formula for the sealing opens with the words used in the Byzantine chrismation and post-Vatican II confirmation in the Roman rite.

The new texts for confirmation are as follows:

The Bishop says to the congregation

Let us now pray for these persons who have renewed their baptismal covenant.

Silence may be kept.

Then the Bishop says

Almighty God, we thank you that by the death and resurrection of your Son Jesus Christ you have overcome sin and brought us to yourself, and that by the sealing of the Holy Spirit you have bound us to your service. Renew in these your servants the covenant you made with them at their Baptism. Send them forth in the power of that Spirit to perform the service you set before them; through Jesus Christ your Son our Lord, who lives and reigns with you and the Holy Spirit, one God, for ever and ever. *Amen.*

For Confirmation

The Bishop lays his hand upon each one and says

Strengthen, O Lord, your servant N. with your Holy Spirit; empower him for your service; and sustain him all the days of his life. *Amen.*

or this

Defend, O Lord, your servant N. with your heavenly grace, that he may continue yours for ever, and daily increase in your Holy Spirit more and more, until he comes to your everlasting kingdom. *Amen.*

For Reception

N., we recognize you as a member of the one holy catholic and apostolic Church, and we receive you into the fellowship of this Communion. God the Father, Son, and Holy Spirit, bless, preserve, and keep you. *Amen.*

For Reaffirmation

N., may the Holy Spirit, who has begun a good work in you, direct and uphold you in the service of Christ and his kingdom. *Amen.*

Then the Bishop continues

Almighty and everliving God, let your fatherly hand ever be over these your servants; let your Holy Spirit ever be with them; and so lead them in the knowledge and obedience of your Word, that they may serve you in this life, and dwell with you in the life to come; through Jesus Christ our Lord. Amen.[62]

The 1552 formula is retained as an alternative for confirmation, but apart from that the texts are new compositions. The rubric directing the bishop to lay a hand on the candidates is ambiguous; by its placement it only requires this "for confirmation;" but subsequent practice has generally been to use the laying on of hands with the other formulas as well.

The most obvious reading of the rite with its three categories of formulas for administration is to understand it as a rite which, in the words of the catechism, bestows "strength from the Holy Spirit through prayer and the laying on of hands by a bishop" upon those who are ready to make "a mature commitment to Christ" in an affirmation of their baptismal covenant. The formulas articulate the context in which they are making the affirmation; the gift bestowed in each case is the same — strength to keep the commitment. From this perspective, the rite is repeatable and does not confer "character." Theologically, character is a new relationship to Christ, but this rite marks an intensification of the baptismal relationship, not a new relationship. It should be noted that the official formularies of Anglicanism have never committed it to the doctrine that confirmation confers a distinct character, though Anglicans in the Catholic tradition have often claimed that it did on the basis of Roman Catholic sacramental theology. The present catechism claims the status of a sacramental rite for confirmation, but in this case it is quite clear that the rite is not one of the "sacraments of the gospel" that are "given by Christ," but a rite "that has evolved in the Church under the guidance of the Holy Spirit."[63] For those who nonetheless insist that confirmation bestows a distinct "character," the canons recognize as "confirmed" any who receive the laying on of hands with any of these formulas, as well as adults who are baptized by the bishop and so have his hands laid on them there in the postbaptismal rites.

This rite is best understood as an "intensification" of the baptismal relationship with God, rather than as the completion of initiation.[64] The continued use of the title "confirmation" for this rite leads to a certain amount of confusion in the meaning and function of the rite and was a concession of the drafters to conservative pressure, but the rubrics and texts of the service make it clear that this is not an initiatory sacrament and that it is baptism, not confirmation, which bestows the Holy Spirit and admits to communion. The canonical expectation that an adult baptized by a presbyter in the Episcopal Church will make another affirmation of baptismal vows before the bishop and receive the laying on of hands by the bishop is a theological anomaly, however.[65] It suggests that baptism is not, as the rubric of the baptismal rite states, "full initiation by water and the Holy Spirit into Christ's Body the Church," and that it requires the laying on of hands by the bishop for its completion. The continuing canonical recognition of "confirmed" status also implies that confirmation imparts a "character" distinct from baptism — a position for which it is hard to find justification in the rites themselves. There is no question that Confirmation responds to a genuine pastoral need; however, the continued use of the name "confirmation" for the rite (not the original intention of the drafters) can mislead us into misunderstanding its purpose.

Preparation for Baptism and Confirmation in the Book of Occasional Services

The Book of Occasional Services sets both baptism and the affirmation of the baptismal covenant in the context of processes which resemble the catechumenate of the early centuries. Three parallel processes are provided: Preparation of Adults for Holy Baptism, Preparation of Parents and Godparents for the Baptism of Infants and Young Children, and Preparation of Baptized Persons for Reaffirmation of the Baptismal Covenant.[66] The Preparation of Adults for Holy Baptism is an adaptation of the ancient catechumenate, based on the work of the Roman Catholic Church in the *Rite of Christian Initiation of Adults* (RCIA). The other two processes are imaginative adaptations to the different baptismal journey of children of Christian parents and to the journey of deepened faith which culminates in the Reaffirmation of the Baptismal Covenant ("Confirmation"). In the case of children, the process works primarily with parents and sponsors and resembles in part the ancient provisions of the Byzantine tradition; in the case of candidates for confirmation, adaptation of the catechumenate is required because these candidates are already baptized. This process is shaped in part by the process of public penance during Lent in the early church, as is evident from the texts for use on Ash Wednesday and Maundy Thursday.[67] For this reason it may be more appropriate for those affirming their baptismal covenant after a lapse than for those making their first mature affirmation of their baptismal covenant or those being received from other churches. The stages and related rites are set out in the following tables:

PREPARATION OF ADULTS FOR THE HOLY BAPTISM	PREPARATION OF PARENTS AND GOD-PARENTS FOR THE BAPTISM OF INFANTS AND YOUNG CHILDREN	PREPARATION OF BAPTIZED PERSONS FOR REAFFIRMATION OF THE BAPTISMAL COVENANT
Stage 1: The Precatechumenal Period	**Stage 1:** Formation of parents at the beginning of pregnancy	**Stage 1:** Period of Inquiry
Rite 1: Admission of Catechumens (Sunday Eucharist)	**Rite 1:** The Blessing of Parents at the Beginning of Pregnancy (Sunday Eucharist)	**Rite 1:** Welcoming of Baptized Christians into a Community (Sunday Eucharist)
Stage 2: The Catechumenate	**Stage 2:** Formation of Parents and Godparents Until Birth	**Stage 2:** Preliminary Formation
Rite 2: Enrollment of Candidates for Baptism (First Sunday in Lent or Advent)	**Rite 2:** Thanksgiving for the Birth or Adoption of a Child and Enrollment for Baptism (Sunday Eucharist)	**Rite 2:** The Calling of the Baptized to Continuing Conversion (Ash Wednesday)
Stage 3: Candidacy for Baptism (Lent or Advent)	**Stage 3:** Preparation for Baptism of the Child	**Stage 3:** Preparation for the Reaffirmation of the Baptismal Covenant (Lent)
Rite 3: Holy Baptism (Easter Eve or Feast of Christ's Baptism)	**Rite 3:** Holy Baptism (at a baptismal feast)	**Rite 3:** Maundy Thursday Rite for Baptized Persons in Preparation for the Paschal Holy Days
		Rite 4: Reaffirmation of the Baptismal Covenant at the Easter Vigil (with the laying on of Hands if the Bishop is Present; otherwise, an additional reaffirmation with the laying on of the bishop's hands in Easter Season).
Stage 4: Postbaptismal Catechesis (Easter Season)	**Stage 4:** Catechesis of the Child	**Stage 4:** Continuing catechesis (Easter Season)

These parallel processes or journeys are perhaps best understood as apprenticeship in living the Christian faith. They reenforce the truth that catechesis is not to be understood as simply acquiring information, but is experiential in nature: candidates learn to become Christians by living like Christians. Sponsors are a key factor in each of the three processes: they share their experience of the Christian faith with those whom they sponsor, and — in the preparation for the baptism of children — share their experience of raising children in the Christian faith.

These provisions take seriously several aspects of baptism that have been lost sight of for centuries:

1. "Baptism is full initiation by water and the Holy Spirit into Christ's Body the Church."[68] As in the early church, baptismal initiation is complete: it does not require some further gift of the Spirit to complete it, and it admits the baptized (even infants) to communion in the church as the eucharistic assembly.

2. Baptism involves the ministry of the whole church. The processes related to baptism and the affirmation of the baptismal covenant entail the ministries of bishop (by sole right in "Confirmation," in person or by delegation in baptism), presbyters, deacons, sponsors, parents (in the case of children), catechists, and the other members of the congregation. It is the church in its diversified ministries that is the agent of Christ as the minister of baptism and the affirmation of the baptismal covenant.

3. Baptism itself is the culmination of the initiatory journey, not its beginning (as it was understood to be when it required completion by confirmation and when catechesis was required before admission to communion).

4. The baptismal journey of those who come to the Christian faith as adults will be distinctly different from the journey of children of Christian families, and it is appropriate that these different journeys be ritualized differently, though the baptismal rite in which each culminates is the same. The two different processes of preparation provided in the *Book of*

Occasional Services recognize this fact and provide different models for the two journeys.

5. The necessity of continuing conversion means that there may be occasions when a solemn affirmation of the baptismal covenant is appropriate as a rite of "intensification," and a period of catechesis like the catechumenate may be appropriate in preparation for such a solemn affirmation, but this renewal of the baptismal covenant is rooted in the baptismal status of the baptized, so that those affirming the baptismal covenant are not to be confused with catechumens. The process envisioned for this rite (with admission on Ash Wednesday and a solemn conclusion on Maundy Thursday and at the Easter Vigil) is in some ways similar to the process of public penance during Lent in the early church which culminated in reconciliation on Maundy Thursday — though the candidates are not here treated as excommunicate, as public penitents were.

The residual ambiguity of Confirmation in the Book of Common Prayer 1979 also creates anomalies in the Preparation of Adults for Holy Baptism. The refusal to delegate the episcopal "laying on of hands" and the continuing canonical standing of "confirmed" status mean that a certain incompleteness remains after the culmination of the catechumenate in baptism unless the bishop presides and lays on hands. The directions concerning the service for confirmation still articulate the expectation that the baptized "make a public affirmation of their faith and commitment to the responsibilities of their Baptism in the presence of a bishop and . . . receive the laying on of hands."[69] It is hard to see any compelling theological rationale for this expectation. It also makes little theological sense to treat the baptismal laying on of hands as having differing meanings, depending on who administers it and the age of the person baptized.

Other anomalies occur in the process known in the *Book of Occasional Services* as the Preparation of Baptized Persons for the Reaffirmation of the Baptismal Covenant. The initial rubrics appear to intend the process for those who are to be "confirmed" in the strict sense and for those who are to be received from another church, as well as for those already confirmed who wish to receive the laying on of hands in *reaffirmation* of their baptismal covenant (using the third of the formulas in this rite). The first problem is raised by the title for the process. For those baptized as infants, Confirmation is the first solemn affirmation of the baptismal covenant, not a *reaffirmation*. Further problems are raised by the fact that this process is modelled on the traditional process of *public penance*. Two of its distinctive rites are modelled on the ancient admission of public penitents on Ash Wednesday and their reconciliation on Maundy Thursday (see chapter 3 below). This may be appropriate for those who are making a reaffirmation of the baptismal covenant after a lapse in the practice of the Christian faith. It is not particularly appropriate for the "confirmation" of those who have been baptized as infants or children and are faithful Episcopalians who have now reached maturity. It is equally inappropriate for receiving those who have been faithful Christians in another tradition.[70] (Re)affirmation of the baptismal covenant in this process is seen as an aspect of the continuing conversion which is necessary for all Christians. This is indeed an aspect of the "intensification" of baptismal commitment which is the primary thrust of these rites. But modelling the process of preparation on the ancient discipline of public penances gives a penitential cast to confirmation.

Other anomalies are found in the two rites associated with the third stage of this process — the laying on of hands in absolution in the Maundy Thursday rite and the laying on of hands by the bishop at the affirmation of the baptismal covenant at the Easter vigil if the bishop presides, or at another time in Easter Season if the bishop is not present at the vigil. The ancient Western rites of public penance culminated in solemn reconciliation of the penitents through the laying on of hands on Maundy Thursday. Adding another laying on of hands at the vigil (or later) with a different meaning (strengthening by the Holy Spirit) creates confusion (intensified by the use of the same ritual gesture) about whether the goal of preparation is absolution and reconciliation or strength for intensified commitment. Even if we are comfortable with the two impositions of hands at the culmination of the process, the postponement of the second laying on of hands if the bishop is not present at the vigil is awkward. Here again, the refusal to delegate "confirmation" to presbyters creates bad liturgy.

The Preparation of Parents and Godparents for the Baptism of Infants and Children resembles in some ways the baptismal journey of children in the Byzantine rite. It might be worth considering conforming the process more closely to the Byzantine model. In this case the Thanksgiving for the Birth or Adoption of a Child might be used to enroll the children as *catechumens*, not as candidates for baptism, and the children might be enrolled as candidates at an age when they could be given elementary prebaptismal catechesis, could answer for themselves at baptism, and could experientially appropriate their initiation into the church.

A Form of Commitment to Christian Service

The Standing Liturgical Commission from the beginning of the revision process which culminated in the Book of Common Prayer 1979 consistently presented baptism as the one rite of sacramental initiation into the church. Every baptismal rite which it drafted included the texts and gestures associated with initiatory "confirmation" (that is, the concluding portion of the ancient baptismal rite — the prayer for the gifts of the Spirit and the laying on of hands with consignation and optional chrismation with a formula associating these acts with the seal of the Spirit). In the 1970 draft contained in *Services for Trial Use*, there was no rite identified as "Confirmation" and baptism itself was understood to admit to communion. For occasions when a Christian wished to make a solemn affirmation of the baptismal covenant, A Form of Commitment to Christian Service was drafted.[71] It was not restricted to the bishop and it conferred no special status on the person who made the commitment. It was designed to fulfill the *non-initiatory* functions associated with the rite of confirmation in earlier prayer books. The enabling resolution for the adoption of these texts for trial use did not give presbyters authority to lay on hands in baptism and left admission to communion before confirmation subject to regulation by diocesan bishops.[72] Pressure on the commission led to the preparation of an episcopal rite for "Confirmation," consisting of a "Profession of Faith and Commitment" (a solemn affirmation of the baptismal covenant) by the candidates and a "Dedication to Mission" with the laying on of hands by the bishop, which appeared in *Authorized Services* in 1973. New texts were drafted for the prayer to be said over the candidates by the bishop, as well as a new formula for use when he laid hands on them (whether in the first mature solemn affirmation of the baptismal covenant, a subsequent affirmation, or on reception into the Episcopal Church of other Christians),[73] the baptismal laying on of hands with the prayer for the gifts of the Spirit was retained, and the rubrics explicitly identified baptism as full initiation. In addition to this new rite of non-initiatory "Confirmation," the 1970 Form for Commitment to Christian Service was also retained in 1973 — for use on other occasions. Although texts were redrafted for the rites of baptism and confirmation for the 1979 book,[74] the principles behind the 1973 rites were retained intact, and the Form for Commitment was also retained. While this rite continues to be useful for commitment to special forms of service of Christ in the world, its use for making a general commitment to the service of Christ in the world duplicates one of the purposes for the rite called "Confirmation" (in particular, those occasions for which the third formula — "for reaffirmation" — would be used). It makes more sense to delegate the authority to "confirm" to presbyters than to create distinct presbyteral and episcopal (or "sacramental" and "non-sacramental") forms of what is essentially the same rite.

Conclusions

The baptismal journey is the response to the call to walk with Jesus the way of the cross, that we might know the power of the resurrection. Baptism does not sanctify any specified moment in our lives other than the moment when our feet are set on that path: there is no one age which is properly associated with the norm of baptism. Our response to that call makes us part of the church as the people whom God has "called out" of the world (for that is what *ekklesia*, "church," means), it incorporates us into the body of Christ and begins the process of our conformation to him in his death and resurrection, and it endows us with the Spirit which binds us together as the communion of saints.

As the exhortation on Ash Wednesday reminds us, all Christians have a continuing need "to renew their repentance and faith," that is, to turn to Christ again and again. It is often appropriate that this need leads to the solemn renewal of the baptismal covenant which the Episcopal Church calls confirmation (broadly understood as encompassing the different occasions for which provision is made in the formulas of the rite). This renewal properly understood confers no special status or "character," but is nonetheless an occasion of grace. For some, a steady life of faithful discipleship may give rise to no occasion when such a solemn renewal is called for. Others may find more than one occasion in the ebb and flow of their life of faith when such a solemn renewal seems appropriate. If the Episcopal Church finds the courage to abandon the theological anomaly of granting the confirmed a separate status and to authorize the delegation of "Confirmation" to presbyters, the provisions of the Book of Common Prayer 1979 and of the *Book of Occasional Services* will serve it well.

It is when we respond to God's call and set out with Christ on the way of the cross in baptism that we discover the truth which Thomas Traherne puts so eloquently:

> The Cross is the abyss of wonders, the center of desires, the school of virtue, the house of wisdom, the theater of joys, and the place of sorrows. It is the root of happiness, and the gate of heaven.[75]

Learning this truth is the goal of catechesis in each of the processes; making it the basis of our lives is the goal of the both baptism and "confirmation."

ENDNOTES

[1]See Gabriele Winkler, *Das armenische Initiationsrituale*, Orientalia Christiana Analecta 217 (Rome: Pont. Institutum Studiorum Orientalium, 1982).

[2]The *Canons of Hippolytus*, now considered one of the earliest derivatives of the *Apostolic Tradition*, warn that prospective catechumens "should be examined with all care, to know why they forsake their own religion, and lest by any chance they come in to jeer." For this text of canon 60, see E. C. Whitaker, *Texts of the Baptismal Liturgy* (London: SPCK, 1960), page 78.

[3]The description which follows is based on the *Apostolic Tradition* of Hippolytus. I cite from Gregory Dix, *The Treatise on the Apostolic Tradition of St. Hippolytus of Rome, Bishop and Martyr, Reissued with*

corrections, preface, and bibliography by Henry Chadwick (London: Alban Press, and Ridgefield, CT: Morehouse Publishing, 1992). Material on the catechumenate comes from chapters 16-19, pages 23-30. Readers should be warned that the text of this document is reconstructed from later documents which incorporate it, that it is a reform tract whose initial use may have been limited, and that, despite general consensus, its provenance is not undisputed. It nevertheless gives us in all probability an early third-century ideal.

[4]Hippolytus, *Apostolic Tradition* 16:17, Dix and Chadwick, pages 26-27.

[5]It may be that the prayer and laying on of hands with which each catechetical session during the catechumenate concludes in the Apostolic Tradition is to be understood as an exorcism. But Hippolytus does not say so explicitly.

[6]Cf. Gabriele Winkler, *Das armenische Initiationsrituale.*

[7]See Henry Ansgar Kelly, *The Devil at Baptism: Ritual, Theology, and Drama* (Ithaca, NY, and London: Cornell University Press, 1985). Kelly insists rightly, I believe, that we should not read the baptismal rites as suggesting that catechumens were possessed in the same sense in which those exorcized in the New Testament were possessed. The use of a rite created for adult converts for the baptism of infants gave rise among North African authors like Augustine to a doctrine of original sin, but that is a significant leap from the original function of exorcism as a means of breaking the hold of pagan gods on converts from paganism.

[8]The administration of salt is a particularity of Latin traditions, attested in North Africa and Rome. We do not find it in the East. Some rites also lack the exorcism.

[9]*Apostolic Tradition* 20:1, Dix and Chadwick, pages 30-31.

[10]Egeria, *Diary of a Pilgrimage*, translated and edited by George E. Gingras, Ancient Christians Writers 38 (New York: Newman Press, 1970), chapter 45, pages 122-123.

[11]Thus the prayers said over those accepted as candidates for baptism (the "elect"), § 30 in the Gelasian Sacramentary (E. C. Whitaker, *Documents of the Baptismal Liturgy*, pages 159-160), are subtitled "for making a catechumen." Similarly, the "prayer for making a catechumen" in the early euchology of Barberini MS 336 (Whitaker, Documents, page 65) seems to serve the same purpose in the Byzantine rite.

[12]*Apostolic Tradition* 20:3, Dix and Chadwick, page 31. There is, in fact, no clear reference to exorcism until candidacy in Hippolytus, although it is an important part of the first stage of the catechumenate in later Western tradition.

[13]*Apostolic Tradition* 20:2, Dix and Chadwick, page 31.

[14]Hippolytus, *Apostolic Tradition* 21:12-18, Dix and Chadwick, pages 36-37.

[15]See the rite of renunciation and allegiance in the text of the Byzantine rite in E. C. Whitaker, *Documents of the Baptismal Liturgy*, pages 60-64, and the baptismal formula on page 72. This parallels the Antiochene rite reflected in Chrysostom's homilies; see the excerpt from Chrysostom on pages 32-33.

[16]On this issue, see Thomas Talley, *The Origins of the Liturgical Year* (NY: Pueblo, 1986), pages 214- 222.

[17]"Christian Initiation," in Aimé Georges Martimort, *The Church at Prayer*, volume 3 (Collegeville, MN: Liturgical Press, 1988), pages 11-100, here pages 27-34.

[18]Fourth-century authors whose Lenten homilies on Genesis survive include Chrysostom, Basil of Caesarea, Augustine, and Ambrose.

[19]See the discussion in Rolf Zerfass, *Die Schriftlesung im Kathedraloffizium Jerusalems*, Liturgiewissenschaftliche Quellen und Forschungen 48 (Münster, Westfallen: Aschendorffsche Verlagsbuchhandlung, 1968), pages 132-137, particularly the discussion on page 136 of Chrysostom's reference in an afternoon sermon on Genesis to a sermon that morning for the baptismal candidates.

[20]A good overview of the Lenten lectionary in Western traditions is found in the charts of § 21 of Adrien Nocent, *The Liturgical Year*, volume 2, Lent (Collegeville, MN: Liturgical Press, 1977), pages 221-236. The reader should note the series of selections from John's gospel in the various traditions. Antoine Chavasse has suggested a reconstruction of the sequence of readings from John beginning on the third Sunday of Lent and continuing into Holy Week. His list makes sense, but it should not be tied to his theory of a three-week fast in fourth-century Rome, which has been seriously challenged. See his article, "La structure du carême et les lectures des messes

quadrigésimales dans la liturgie romaine," *Le Maison Dieu* 31 (1952), page 76-119. It may be the particularities of the Roman liturgy (such as Lenten ember week and mediana week) which resulted in the restriction of the Johannine readings to the later weeks of Lent. Elsewhere in the West, they are characteristic after the first Sunday. On the importance of John's gospel to catechesis for baptism, see Oscar Cullmann, *Early Christian Worship* (London: SCM, 1953), Part II.

[21]The earliest liturgical sources are the Gelasian Sacramentary, which has at least two strata of texts and dates in its present form to some time in the seventh century, and Ordo Romanus XI, which draws on the Gelasian Sacramentary and probably dates from later in the same century. A key witness to the earlier form of the Roman baptismal liturgy is the letter of John the Deacon to Senarius of about 500. English translations of the key texts may be found in E. C. Whitaker, *Documents of the Baptismal Liturgy*. Analyses of the texts may be found in Robert Cabié, "Christian Initiation," and Edward J. Yarnold, "Initiation: The Fourth and Fifth Centuries," in Cheslyn Jones, Geoffrey Wainwright, Edward Yarnold, and Paul Bradshaw, editors, *The Study of the Liturgy*, revised edition (London: SPCK, and New York: Oxford University Press, 1992), 129-144.

[22]Aidan Kavanagh, *The Shape of Baptism* (New York: Pueblo, 1978), page 108.

[23]Louis Weil, "Reclaiming the Larger Trinitarian Framework of Baptism," in Ralph McMichaels, ed., *Creation and Liturgy* (Washington, DC: Pastoral Press, 1993), pages 129-143, here page 134.

[24]*Apostolic Tradition* 21:4, Dix and Chadwick, page 33.

[25]Thus Kavanagh writes in his introduction to a collection of essays which he edited, *Made, not Born* (Notre Dame, IN: University of Notre Dame Press), "when we are discoursing about Christian initiation we are face to face with conversion in Jesus Christ dead and rising" (page 2).

[26]Robert Cabié gives a succinct summary of the evidence in "Christian Initiation" on pages 62-63.

[27]Edward J. Yarnold, "Initiation: The Fourth and Fifth Centuries," page 131.

[28]This would seem to be the case in most of the church after the fourth

century, though the list of baptismal feasts varied somewhat from region to region. Pope Leo in the fifth century makes Easter and Pentecost the only ordinary occasions for baptism except in emergencies. North African authors seem to have excepted infants from this rule.

29For the baptism of children in the Byzantine tradition, the key modern study is the critical text of the rite with French translation and commentary by Miguel Arranz published in *Orientalia Christiana Periodica* 48-55 (1982-1989) in a series of articles entitled "Les sacrements de l'ancien euchologe byzantin." Much insight into the texts can be found in Alexander Schmemann, *Of Water and the Spirit: A Liturgical Study of Baptism*, revised edition (Crestwood, NY: St. Vladimir's Seminary Press, 1974). A brief study which focusses on the way that the rite was adapted to children is found in Kenneth Stevenson, "The Byzantine Liturgy of Baptism," *Studia Liturgica* 17 (1987), pages 176-190. Most of the key texts may be found in E. C. Whitaker, *Documents of the Baptismal Liturgy*, but he unfortunately does not give the prayers for the eighth and fortieth days. The most convenient place to find these prayers in English translation is in Schmemann's book, although Schmemann is dealing with the present form of the rite, not the earlier form found in the euchologies.

30See Oration 49:28, "On Baptism," in Philip Schaff, ed., *A Select Library of Nicene and Post Nicene Fathers*, second series, volume 7, page 370.

31We should take Paul Bradshaw's cautions seriously here and recognize that the presence of the rubrics in manuscripts of this era does not mean that parents were still waiting until children were old enough for such instruction to present them for baptism. But the rubric does bear witness to the practice in the earlier stages of this tradition.

32The churching of *women* is only an apparent parallel in Western rites. In the Byzantine tradition, the early texts are concerned with the churching of the *child*; the purification of the mother after childbirth only appears in the prayers of later manuscripts. In the West, the sole concern of the prayers of the rite is the purification of the mother. The Western rite is concerned, as its title shows, with the churching of the *mother*. There is no indication at all that it has any theological relationship to the baptism of the *child*. The child is churched in baptism: the churching of the child in late medieval

Western rites marks the transition from the former rites of the catechumenate to the baptismal liturgy proper. In the Sarum manual, the child was brought into the church at this point with the formula, "N., enter into the temple of God, that thou mayest have eternal life and live for ever and ever. Amen." The 1549 Book of Common Prayer marks the entrance into the church with the words, "The Lord vouchsafe to receive you into his holy household, and to keep and govern you always in the same, that you may have everlasting life. Amen." After 1552 the entire baptismal rite was performed in the church and this formula disappeared.

[33]Eventually, as in the West, baptism was administered shortly after birth in a single continuous rite, without catechesis and no longer in the context of the corporate liturgy of the baptismal feasts. But the separation of "confirmation" and admission to communion from baptism never occurred in this tradition.

[34]The best study of the process is probably J. D. C. Fisher, *Christian Initiation: Baptism in the Medieval West: A Study in the Disintegration of the Primitive Rite of Initiation* (London: SPCK, 1965).

[35]See J. D. C. Fisher, *Christian Initiation: Baptism in the Medieval West*, for documentation and analysis of these developments.

[36]This very traditional understanding of the meaning of penitence is skillfully articulated in the first form for the Reconciliation of a Penitent in the 1979 Book of Common Prayer.

[37]The "handing over" of the gospels, the creed, and the Lord's Prayer disappeared from the Lenten liturgy and were not incorporated in the prebaptismal service. Instruction of infants on these texts struck even people in the middle ages as unreal!

[38]See note 30 above.

[39]For the history of this change, see J. D. C. Fisher, *Christian Initiation: Baptism in the Medieval West*, chapter 7.

[40]The fact that not all early rites have a postbaptismal anointing, imposition of hands, or consignation makes it theologically indefensible to argue that such gestures are necessary to bestow the Spirit on those being baptized.

[41]Faustus of Riez first interprets confirmation as strengthening for the

Christian "battle" in a sermon in the late fifth century, attributed to Pope Melchiades of the fourth century in the False Decretals of ca. 850. The name "robur" for this strength comes from Alcuin and Rabanus Maurus. See J. D. C. Fisher, *Christian Initiation: Baptism in the Medieval West*, pages 125, 134.

[42]See J. D. C. Fisher, *Christian Initiation: Baptism in the Medieval West*, page 123 and passim. The phrase the "age of reason" is also common. This rule became canonical with the catechism of the Council of Trent in the sixteenth century.

[43]See Tad Guzie, *The Book of Sacramental Basics* (New York: Paulist Press, 1981), pages 103-116 for a discussion of these developments and post-Vatican II Roman Catholic practice. Roman Catholic practice has been further muddied by the intrusion of first confession into the sequence.

[44]Text cited from A. J. Collins, *Manuale ad usum percelebris ecclesiae Sarisburiensis* (Henry Bradshaw Society, 1960) in J. D. C. Fisher, *Christian Initiation: Baptism in the Medieval West*, page 166. The exhortation is a translation of the Latin rubric of the same rite found on page 175.

[45]This rubric appeared in 1549 at the end of the confirmation service and was included in subsequent editions in substantially the same form until the liturgical revisions of the present century. In 1662 the following words were added: "or be ready and desirous to be confirmed." This clause made provision for those who had been duly prepared for confirmation, but were prevented for due cause (such as residence in the colonies where there were no bishops) from being confirmed.

[46]For careful documentation of Reformation developments, see J. D. C. Fisher, *Christian Initiation: The Reformation Period* (London: SPCK, 1970).

[47]Calvin, *Institutes of the Christian Religion* IV:19:4, cited in J. D. C. Fisher, *Christian Initiation: The Reformation Period*, page 258.

[48]On Cranmer's understanding of baptism and confirmation, see Marion J. Hatchett, "Thomas Cranmer and the Rites of Christian Initiation," unpublished S. T. M. thesis, General Theological Seminary, 1967. Hatchett summarizes his conclusions in the treatment of these rites in his *Commentary on American Prayer Book* (New York: Seabury, 1980), pages 261-265.

[49]The Sarum text may be found in J. D. C. Fisher, *Christian Initiation: Baptism in the Medieval West*, pages 166 (exhortation to godparents) and 178 (rubric at baptism). In the BCP 1549, the texts are found on pages 241-242 (exhortation and rubric at baptism); pages 250-251 (rubrics at confirmation).

[50]See the documents from the Convocation of 1537 and the Questionnaire of 1540 which record the views of the English bishops, in J. D. C. Fisher, *Christian Initiation: Baptism in the Medieval West*, pages 208-220, 223-227.

[51]The Sarum text may be found in J. D. C. Fisher, *Christian Initiation: Baptism in the Medieval West*, page 181. In the BCP 1549, the text is found on page 251.

[52]The Sarum text may be found in J. D. C. Fisher, *Christian Initiation: Baptism in the Medieval West*, page 174.

[53]BCP 1549, page 241.

[54]BCP 1552, page 398.

[55]BCP 1549, pages 250-251.

[56]BCP 1552, pages 408-409.

[57]This happened in Anglicanism during the Commonwealth and in colonial America — where confirmation was an impossibility for most people because bishops were not available. English-speaking Catholics generally maintained the discipline of confirmation before first communion until the early twentieth century. Early in the liturgical revision which culminated in The Book of Common Prayer 1979, the Episcopal Church began to admit children to communion before confirmation — initially (in 1970) at the same age as Roman Catholics, then from the time of baptism. In the Episcopal Church, as we shall see, the issue is clouded because the components of the rite of confirmation related to the completion of initiation were restored to the baptismal rite, while a new, non-initiatory rite for the affirmation of the baptismal covenant kept the name "confirmation."

[58]On the rites of initiation and confirmation in this book, see Daniel B. Stevick, *Baptismal Moments, Baptismal Meanings* (New York: Church Hymnal, 1987); Marion J. Hatchett, *Commentary on the American Prayer Book* (New York: Seabury, 1985), pages 251-188; and Leonel Mitchell,

Praying Shapes Believing: A Theological Commentary on the Book of Common Prayer (Minneapolis: Seabury/Winston, 1985), pages 68-127.

[59]BCP 1979, page 298.

[60]See the references in note 48 above.

[61]BCP 1979, page 308.

[62]BCP 1979, pages 309-310.

[63]For references to the catechism in this paragraph, see BCP 1979, page 860 (on confirmation), page 857 (on sacraments of the gospel), page 860 (on other sacramental rites).

[64]For an thoughtful discussion of affirmation of the baptismal covenant as a rite of intensification, see the section on "Occasions of Renewal" of Daniel B. Stevick, *Baptismal Moments, Baptismal Meanings*, pages 138-150. The discussion of "intensification" is on page 142.

[65]The issue is primarily canonical, but it also finds expression in the second rubric on page 412.

[66]These are found in the *Book of Occasional Services*, 2nd edition (New York: Church Hymnal, 1988), pages 112-126, 132-141, and 155-161. The title of the third process is misleading, for the process may also be used for candidates for "Confirmation" — which is a first solemn affirmation of the baptismal covenant made on their behalf at their baptism, and is therefore not a "reaffirmation."

[67]See the account of public penance and of the Ash Wednesday and Maundy Thursday rites in chapter 3 below.

[68]BCP 1979, page 298.

[68]BCP 1979, page 412.

[70]The laying on of hands was sometimes used in the West for the reconciliation of those baptized in schismatic or heretical groups, but this hardly seems the model for an appropriate way to receive other Christians into the Episcopal Church today.

[71]See the rationale articulated by the Standing Liturgical Commission in *Pastoral Offices*, Prayer Book Studies 24 (New York: Church Hymnal, 1970), pages 9-11.

[72]See the text of the resolution on page 21 of *Services for Trial Use* (New York: Church Hymnal, 1971). The house of bishops prepared guidelines on

admission to communion whose effect was to authorize admission of children to communion after catechesis, according to the current Roman Catholic pattern. This pattern continued in many places after the adoption of the BCP 1979. Current practice is in flux, with a movement toward admission at baptism or when a child begins to attend worship regularly. A formal rite of admission to communion is generally discouraged at present.

[73]A single formula was to be used on all occasions: "Strengthen your servant, N, with the riches of your Holy Spirit; sustain him and empower him for your service." The old confirmation formula (in the plural) then became the concluding prayer over all the candidates.

[74]In particular, the prayers and formulas associated with "Confirmation" were redrafted. In the 1979 book (which received its first reading in 1976) separate formulas are provided for the three occasions, and the old confirmation formula is provided as an alternative for the first mature affirmation, for which the name "confirmation" is retained.

[75]*Centuries* (Wilton, CT: Morehouse-Barlow, 1986), "First Century," no. 58, page 28.

CHAPTER 2

FOR THE SAKE OF THE KINGDOM

THE CELEBRATION AND BLESSING OF A MARRIAGE AND RITES OF RELIGIOUS PROFESSION

"Christians cannot be distinguished from the rest of the human race by country or language or customs . . . . They marry like everyone else," wrote an anonymous apologist in the *Letter to Diognetus*.[1] Had it suited his apologetic purpose, he could have added that some Christians also renounce marriage as others who are not Christian do. Marriage and celibacy are not distinctively Christian institutions. They are part of the fabric of human society and are ritualized in different ways in different cultures. Often they take on religious meaning, but at other times they are treated from the perspective of social and legal convention. For Christians, they are transformed by God's grace as ways of life in this world that anticipate the joy and fulfilment of the kingdom of God, the life of the world to come.

By their nature, they are rites of passage. Through them a person enters into a new and different constellation of social relationships. As rites of passage, they represent the transition from one relationship to society to another. In most cultures, they have the character of a process with rites marking their stages rather than a single rite. The beginning of the passage marks the beginning of the break with one relationship to society, the end of the passage marks the end of a period of transition and the entry into a new relationship to society. This is particularly true of marriage. In the ancient cultures in which Christianity was born, the rite of passage ordinarily began with engagement, which formalized the intention of two people to marry, and concluded with the marriage itself. The stages and rites in these cultures are as follows:[2]

Roman Society	Jewish Society
Betrothal	*Betrothal*
Exchange of promises	By money, contract, or cohabitation
Gift of ring and pledges by groom	Betrothal berakah
Kiss	
Marriage	*Marriage*
	All-day fast by bride and groom
Dressing of bride at her home	Dressing of bride and groom
crown of myrtle or orange	both in crowns of myrtle
veil (*flammeum*)	bride in veil
Presentation of the bride to groom	
Consultation of the oracles	
Contract (*tabulae matrimoniales*)	
Exchange of consents, joining hands	
Sacrifice and wedding feast	
Procession of all to groom's house	Procession of bride and attendants
Offering of fire and water to bride	to house of groom
	Contract (*ketubah*) written at
	threshold
	Wedding feast with seven
	berakoth

It should be noted that this table gives the full form for a patrician Roman marriage and uses later Talmudic sources for a Jewish wedding. Most

Romans would have had a simpler rite and other areas of the empire had their own customs, and we are not sure whether all Talmudic details date back to the time of Christian origins. In both cases, it is the contract which establishes the marriage, and other details of both betrothal and marriage are secondary.

In the same section of Matthew's gospel, Jesus not only recognizes the union of man and woman in marriage as a union brought about by God, but also recognizes that there are those who choose celibacy for the sake of the kingdom (Matthew 19:4-6, 12):

> "Have you not read that the one who made them at the beginning 'made them male and female,' and said, 'For this reason a man shall leave his father and mother and be joined to his wife, and the two shall become one flesh'? So they are no longer two, but one flesh. Therefore what God has joined together let no one separate."

> ". . . there are eunuchs who have made themselves eunuchs for the sake of the kingdom of heaven."

This dual affirmation of marriage and celibacy found a place in the life of the New Testament church as well. Marriage in Christ, Ephesians tells us (5:32) images forth the union of Christ and the church. Celibacy receives special honor from Paul, because (1 Corinthians 7:32-34)

> the unmarried man is anxious about the affairs of the Lord, how to please the Lord; but the married man is anxious about the affairs of the world, how to please his wife. And the unmarried woman and the virgin are anxious about the affairs of the Lord, so that they may be holy in body and spirit, but the married woman is anxious about the affairs of the world, how to please her husband.

The New Testament, in other words, affirms both the fulfilment of human sexuality in marriage and the renunciation of such fulfilment "for the sake of the kingdom" in celibacy.[3] Jesus' attitudes to both marriage and celibacy radicalized the ordinary Judaism of his day. He protested against the patriarchal domination of wives by his rejection of the husband's right to divorce at will; he recognized celibacy as a religious vocation in a way characteristic only of the more radical forms of Judaism in his day. His attitude to women finds subsequent expression in the declaration in Galatians 3:28 that in Christ there is neither male nor female, though patriarchal attitudes were beginning to regain standing by the end of the New Testament period.[4]

So far as we can discern, the New Testament knows no distinctive ritual or liturgical forms for marriage or for the profession of celibacy. Marriage was understood in both Judaism and Roman law as a legal contract,[5] though in both it might also find ritual expression which was religious in character. Christians from a Gentile background might enter marriage in the same ways as their pagan neighbors, while avoiding the ritual acts associated with paganism (consultation of soothsayers and offering of sacrifice); Christians of a Jewish background might continue to use the ritual forms of Judaism, though they might transform them by reference to Christ. But the issue was not of sufficient significance for New Testament authors to direct their attention to it in the literature which has come down to us.

1. Marriage in the Early Church and in the Early Middle Ages

A Survey

It is really not until the third century that we find unambiguous reference in Christian literature to the rite of marriage. Authors such as Ignatius in the second century speak of the bishop's involvement in the decision to marry, but what he says does not necessarily imply that the bishop presided at marriage itself. We also know very little about the ways in which Christians undertook vows of celibacy. Virgins and widows who undertook a celibate life receive more attention in early centuries than men who undertook such commitments, but that is due in part to the fact that they were under the special protection of the local church and its bishop.

The description of Christian marriage by Tertullian in the early third century has been the matter of considerable debate. The rites as they are portrayed by him can be understood as the Christian transformation of the traditional Roman ceremony:

> How shall we ever be able to describe the happiness of that marriage which the Church arranges, the Sacrifice strengthens, upon which the blessing sets a seal, at which angels are present as witnesses, and to which the Father gives his consent?[6]

We must be careful with this evidence, as Kenneth Stevenson reminds us: Tertullian may already have been a Montanist when he wrote it and we cannot presume that such a rite was the predominant form of marriage for Christians. But this passage suggests that already in some cases Christian marriage involved a blessing by the church, that it may have been solemnized in a Christian assembly, and that the eucharist was associated with it. While it was unlikely that most Christian marriages took this form in Tertullian's day, it does seems likely that the Church was beginning to give liturgical expression to the marriage of its members, and that this expression took the form of a nuptial blessing and participation in the eucharist. That is the most which we can say until after the peace of the church.

After the fourth century, we begin to have evidence of the liturgical form which marriage might take in both the Latin-speaking West and the Greek-speaking East.[7] In the West the rite is generally known as the *velatio nuptialis* (the veiling of the bride) and the liturgical text is the nuptial blessing; in the East the rite is generally known as crowning and the liturgical text is found in prayers for the blessing at the crowning. In both East and West it continued to be the consent which gave marriage legal status, but no liturgical texts incorporate the expression of consent into the marriage rite of the church.[8] We have no evidence that the betrothal originally took liturgical form. The commitment to marry formalized in the betrothal acquired legal status, so that breaking an engagement to marry had legal and financial consequences, and as a result the formal rite of betrothal later tended to be fused with the marriage rite itself. Indeed, domestic rites for marriage in some regions of the West took the ritual shape that rites of betrothal had elsewhere. The exchange of a ring or rings (with or without other pledges) was the key part of the betrothal. When rites of betrothal and marriage begin to merge, the distinction is usually maintained by performing the rite of engagement outside the church, most often at the church door (as in the Byzantine tradition and the later Roman tradition), but at times (as in the Visigothic tradition) in the home. In the West the exchange of rings often migrated into the marriage rite itself, and a distinction began to be made between engagement rings and wedding rings.

By the time of the early liturgical texts, there was a definite shift at Rome (but not in all regions of the Latin-speaking West) and in the East from a domestic to an ecclesial setting for the blessing of the marriage. In the West the early liturgical texts in the sacramentaries of the Roman tradition were set in the context of a nuptial eucharist with special propers and a blessing of the bride before communion. The most common title for the rite was "nuptial veiling," but how this title was understood is not clear: it may describe several different practices. In the Roman tradition itself it was the bride who was veiled,[9] just as it was the bride who was blessed. It may be that she was veiled at home before the rite, or perhaps she was veiled in the context of the rite itself. The veil in this case was the *flammeum*, the bridal veil. But elsewhere in the West both bride and groom were covered with a veil during the blessing. Sometimes they seem to be covered entirely and eventually the veil might take the form of a canopy, at other times the rubrics specify that the veil covers the bride's head but the groom's shoulders. Where both were veiled, both were usually blessed. Note that this rite was set in the context of the eucharist, but it appears to be a votive eucharist, not the parish eucharist on Sunday. As was also the case in the Byzantine rite, the marriage took place in the church, but the gathering was a gathering of the family rather than a gathering of the parish community.

In much of the West, it is likely that many marriages were not solemnized at a nuptial eucharist. Visigothic rites with a blessing of the marriage chamber and the exchange of rings and pledges in the context of a marriage banquet at the groom's house show the survival of a tradition of domestic rites of marriage, and we have evidence that such rites also survived in other parts of Western Europe. Note that the ring or rings, originally associated with the betrothal, now became wedding rings. The use of wedding rings was taken over into later traditions, although the exchange of an engagement ring as well (usually outside the context of the liturgy) might endure as a local custom. Visigothic texts provide for a eucharist for the newly-married the next day with a blessing of the couple in the context of the eucharist, but it seems likely that here and elsewhere many couples were married with only the domestic rite. The heart of the domestic rite was, as we have seen, the exchange of rings and other pledges — actions earlier associated with the rite of betrothal. Since Roman law recognized consent as the determining factor in marriage, not even these religious observances were absolutely necessary. But difficulty in resolving disputes over marriage made a domestic context problematic, and the church in the medieval West worked hard to require a public rite in the church and to suppress domestic rites in order to avoid clandestine unions. In the late middle ages, the domestic rites were associated with the nuptial eucharist, with the exchange of a ring or rings at the church door and with the blessing of the marriage chamber *after* the nuptial eucharist.

In the East it is unclear whether the crowning and the blessing had their original setting in the home or in the church. By the time that liturgical texts appeared, however, the rite took place in the church and was sealed with communion by the couple. Originally, the crowning was probably incorporated at the Sunday eucharist after the Great Thanksgiving, but in the earliest liturgical texts that have come down to us communion was administered from the reserved sacrament at first marriages.[10] This suggests that while the setting may still have been the church, the gathering was frequently a gathering of the family rather than the parish community.

A careful reading of the literature reveals how much the marriage liturgy was dependent on local tradition and custom. The focus on the veiling of the bride in the Roman sacramentaries as contrasted to the crowning of both bride and groom in the Byzantine East illustrates this. The Roman custom places the emphasis on the change in the bride's social status, ritualized by her change of clothes (the veil). The "giving away of the bride" in this tradition removes her from the authority of her father and places her under the authority of her husband, and the veiling signals this change. Marriage does not represent as significant a change in social relationships for the groom. The original Roman blessing of the bride *alone* reenforces this sense. The crowning of both in the East and the use of two rings represents a far greater emphasis on the mutuality of the marital relationship, although in other ways Eastern society remains strongly patriarchal in orientation.

The ambiguous relationship between marriage as a legal contract and marriage as a relationship which receives liturgical recognition in the church's blessing of the couple works out in different ways in the East and West. In the writings of Augustine we find references to the written contract of marriage, the *tabulae matrimoniales*, which is read out by the bishop. Though no evidence of this usage has come down to us in liturgical texts, this seems to have been an important feature of the rite in North Africa, where Roman legal tradition was especially strong and where the influence of Jewish customs was also felt. The contract apparently included reference to three purposes for marriage — *proles, fides,* and *sacramentum* (offspring, mutual fidelity, and a covenant which was a sign of Christ's love for the church). Explicit reference to such a written document in the context of the liturgical celebration of marriage does not reappear until many centuries later in the West, where the contract was understood as the contract to marry — i.e., a derivative of the original betrothal contract — and is read out as a preliminary before the nuptial mass. The general willingness of the Western church to settle for an implicit contract or later an oral contract gives rise to the ambiguous unions recognized as "common law marriages" and to clandestine marriages and the problems associated with such arrangements.

In the East legal developments took a different turn. Emperor Leo VI (reigned 886-912) legislated that only marriages crowned by the church would enjoy legal recognition; Alexos 1 Comnenos (reigned 1081-1118) extended this form of legal recognition to slaves as well as free citizens.[11] This forced the church to perform second marriages, which used a different rite and subjected those entering them to canonical penance. The original approach of the Eastern Church had been to recognize such marriages but not to give them sacramental status by crowning them. Before the collapse of the imperial administration and civil law in the West, we find a similar attitude on the part of Ambrose.[12] The later Western approach (when canon law regulated marriage after the collapse of the imperial legal system) was to recognize second marriages after the death of a spouse, but not after divorce (as opposed to annulment).

We should note a certain ambivalence about marriages after the death of a spouse in both East and West. In the West, the marriage contract was considered to be dissolved by the death of a spouse, although the nuptial blessing might be omitted in marriages where one of the couple had been widowed. In the East, the marriage contract was considered eternal; remarriage after the death of a spouse was treated as equivalent to marriage after divorce and subjected a person to a period of penance.

The Roman Rite for Marriage

We have already taken note of the Roman and Byzantine rites for marriage; these are the dominant rites in the Christian tradition and we will now look at them in greater detail as they appear in the early euchologies and sacramentaries. For most of the first millennium, the marriage rites in the tradition of Rome itself seems to have given liturgical expression only to the marriage, and not to the betrothal. Western rites for marriage exhibit far greater local diversity than the rites of the Byzantine tradition, which were relatively uniform. We will focus our attention on the Roman marriage rite, but we need to note that there were other quite different rites — rites which have survived in some form to the present day and which had their impact on the later rite in the Roman *rituale* itself. According to the early Roman sacramentaries, the blessing of the marriage took place in the context of a nuptial mass — that is, a special votive mass, not the Sunday eucharist of the parish. The three major sacramentaries provide the customary prayer texts for a mass — opening collect, prayer over the gifts, a proper preface (except in the Verona sacramentary), a proper insertion for the *hanc igitur*, and a postcommunion — as well as texts for a blessing between the end of the eucharistic prayer and communion. A special blessing at the end of the canon is an early tradition in the Roman rite, where the blessing was associated with the eucharistic prayer. Indeed, this prayer was often sung to the same tone as the canon, the preface tone. The Gregorian text of this prayer follows:

O God, who didst make all things out of nothing through thy mighty power; who after thou hadst set in order the elements of the world didst appoint for man, made in thine own image, woman as his inseparable helper, that from man's flesh she should take her origin, teaching that what thou didst graciously ordain from one beginning should not be separated;

O God, who hast consecrated the state of matrimony in so excellent a mystery that in the bond of marriage thou didst prefigure the union of Christ with the church;

O God, by whom woman is joined to man, and the union, instituted at the beginning, is endowed with a blessing that is taken away neither by the punishment of original sin nor the sentence of the flood:

Look with mercy, we pray, on this woman, thy servant, now to be joined in matrimony, who seeks to be defended by thy protection. May the yoke of love and peace be upon her. May she be a faithful and chaste wife in Christ and follow the pattern of holy women. May she be dear to her husband like Rachel, wise like Rebecca, long-lived and faithful like Sarah. May the author of deceit not prevail over her in her deeds. May she remain firm in faith and in keeping the commandments. May she be true to one husband, and avoid unlawful companionship. May she remedy her weakness with the strength of discipline. May she be decorous and grave, reverential and modest, well taught in heavenly doctrine. May she be fruitful in child-bearing, innocent and sinless. May she attain in the end to the peace of the blessed and the kingdom of heaven. May she see her children's children to the third and fourth generation, and reach the age which she desires;

through Jesus Christ thy Son our Lord, who lives and reigns with thee in the unity of the Holy Spirit, one God, for ever and ever. Amen.[13]

The noteworthy feature of the blessing in the ancient sacramentaries is that it is a blessing *of the bride alone*. This leads us to suspect that the nuptial veiling — which is the title of the rite in the Verona and Gregorian sacramentaries — referred originally to the veiling of the bride alone as well. It may refer to the fact that she came to church veiled (in the *flammeum*), or it may be that she was veiled immediately before the blessing — either with the *flammeum* or with another veil. The rite seems to be a deliberate parallel to the veiling of virgins which consecrated them to a celibate life — a rite which developed at the same time as the nuptial veiling. Outside Rome, there is evidence from as early as the fifth century that the veil used was extended (at least partially) over the groom as well, and the solemn blessing before communion (as well as other texts) was revised to include the groom when possible. But the classic Roman rite focusses almost exclusively on the bride.

This focus on the bride and on her change of status was characteristic of the majority of Western rites. In those rites, as they were further elaborated with ritual actions and liturgical texts (as we shall see below), the bride was given by her father to her husband, the bride promises obedience to her husband, and the bride alone receives a ring. This gave Western rites a distinctly different character from that of Eastern rites, whose prayers and ritual acts gave expression to the mutuality of marriage.

The Byzantine Rite for Marriage

While the Roman rite for marriage focussed on the veiling and blessing of the bride, the Byzantine rite focussed on the crowning and blessing of both bride and groom. The outline below gives the details of the Byzantine rite from the early euchologies (from the eighth century), with other probable elements of the rite noted in italics:[14]

Betrothal (Arrhas) at the church door
Initial benediction
Bidding and First Engagement Prayer
Bidding to bow the head and Second Engagement Prayer
  (with bowed heads)

Exchange of rings with formula

Marriage (Crowning) in the Church
Psalm 128 and procession into church with candles
Initial benediction
Litany and First Marriage Prayer
Crowning *with formula*
Proper Liturgy of the Word
Responsorial Psalm (Prokeimenon)
  Epistle (Apostle): Ephesians 5:20-33
  Alleluia
  Gospel: John 2:1-11
Bidding to bow the head and Second Marriage Prayer
Third Marriage Prayer
Communion from the Reserved Sacrament (Presanctified Gifts)

The formulas for the engagement and the crowning eventually took the passive form of formulas for the administration of the sacraments customary since the time of John Chrysostom: "The servant of God N. is betrothed to the servant of God M. in the Name of the Father, and of the Son, and of the Holy Spirit. Amen." "The servant of God N. is crowned for the servant of God M. in the Name of the Father, and of the Son, and of the Holy Spirit. Amen."

The two ancient prayers of the betrothal rite clearly look forward toward the future marriage of the couple; the first looks back to Isaac and Rebecca, the second draws on the nuptial imagery of Ephesians 5:

> O eternal God, who hast brought into unity those who were separated and hast ordained for them an indissoluble bond of love, who didst bless Isaac and Rebecca and make them heirs of thy promise: Bless also these thy servants N. and M., guiding them in every good work: for thou art a merciful God, who lovest humankind, and to thee we ascribe glory, Father, Son, and Holy Spirit, now and for ever and unto the ages of ages. Amen.

O Lord our God, who hast espoused the church as a pure virgin from among the nations: Bless this betrothal and unite and preserve these thy servants in peace and oneness of mind: for to thee are due all glory, honor, and worship, to Father, Son, and Holy Spirit, now and for ever and unto the ages of ages. Amen.[15]

The first marriage prayer refers to creation and asks God to unite husband and wife and to crown them; the second makes reference to the wedding in Cana of Galilee and prays for the future life of the married couple; the final prayer is related to the communion of the bride and groom (though now it is understood as a blessing of the common cup).

O holy God, who didst fashion man of dust and form his wife from his side, and didst yoke her to him as a helper, since it seemed good to thee that he should not be alone upon earth: now Lord, stretch forth thy hand from thy holy dwelling place, and yoke your servants, this man and this woman, that the woman may be yoked by thee to the man. Join them together in unity of mind; crown them in one flesh; graciously bestow upon them the fruit of the womb and gladness in their children: for thine is the majesty, and thine is the kingdom and the power and the glory, of the Father, and of the Son, and of the Holy Spirit, now and for ever and unto the ages of ages. Amen.

O Lord our God, who in thy saving providence didst graciously show marriage worthy of thy presence at Cana of Galilee: now preserve in peace and harmony these thy servants N. and M. whom thou hast graciously joined together. Show them that marriage is honorable, keep their marriage bed undefiled, make their life together blameless, and grant that they may reach abundant old age, walking in thy commandments with a pure heart: for thou art our God, the God who shows mercy and saves, and to thee we ascribe glory, to Father, Son, and Holy Spirit, now and forever and unto the ages of ages. Amen.

O God, who didst create all things by thy might and didst make sure the round world and didst adorn with a crown all things which thou hast made: Bless now, with thy spiritual blessing, this common cup which thou dost give to those who are now united in the communion of marriage: for blessed is thy name, and glorified is thy kingdom, of the Father, and of the Son, and of the Holy Spirit, now and for ever, and unto the ages of ages. Amen.[16]

The eventual fusion of the betrothal and the crowning make the integration of the rite into the eucharist awkward. When betrothal and crowning were celebrated separately the crowning and blessing seem to have come at the time of communion at the eucharist. Sunday remains a privileged time for the crowning in the Byzantine rite, but the marriage is now distinct from the eucharistic liturgy. The third marriage prayer in the present order is integrated into a set of litanies like those which come before communion in the liturgy of the presanctified gifts and is probably to be read as a prayer related to communion, for reception of the eucharist was understood as the seal of the marriage rite in the early centuries. Since the church placed those entering second marriages under penance, they would not have been given communion, and a cup of blessed wine was given them as a substitute. Eventually the administration of communion fell out of use even in first marriages.

The rites have remained remarkably stable since the eighth century, though they have been filled out somewhat, forms of consent were eventually added, and the distinction between the rite for first and subsequent marriages has blurred. Interpreters see the rite of espousal, performed originally at the church door, as the church's recognition of marriage as a natural state in human society; the distinctively Christian rite is the crowning and blessing, which comes after the entrance into the church and raises marriage to an expression of love which Christ transforms so that it mirrors his love for the church. The reception of communion seals the marriage by incorporating it into the life of the church, which draws its life from Christ himself.

Crowning is a local custom, for which both Jewish and pagan culture provided precedent. The Eastern churches developed a Christian interpretation of this rite, however, whereas veiling, the ritual focus of the Roman tradition, received relatively little emphasis in Western theological tradition. We find the interpretation of crowning in authors such as John Chrysostom and in the texts and hymnody of both the Byzantine and other Eastern rites. The contemporary Orthodox theologian Alexander Schmemann develops this tradition and explores three dimensions of the significance of this rite. The crowns are, first of all, a recognition of the bride and groom as king and queen of creation, fulfilling the royal role which they were assigned in paradise. The are, second, martyrs' crowns, for "the way to the kingdom is the *martyria* — bearing witness to Christ. And this means crucifixion and sacrifice. A marriage which does not constantly crucify its own selfishness and self-sufficiency, which does not 'die to itself' that it may point beyond itself is not a Christian marriage. . . . It is the cross of Christ that brings self-sufficiency to an end. But 'by the cross joy entered the whole world.' It is the joyful certitude that the marriage vow, in the perspective of the kingdom, is not taken 'until death part' but until death unites us completely." Finally, the crowns are "crowns of the Kingdom, of that ultimate reality of which everything in this world — whose fashion is passing away — everything has become a sacramental sign and anticipation."[17]

There is, as we have noted, a mutuality about the rites of betrothal and crowning which we do not find in Western rites. Here the betrothal involves the exchange of rings by both husband and wife, and the characteristic action of the marriage itself is the crowning of both husband and wife with prayers of blessing. There is also a note of joy and festivity in these rites which seems lacking in the more sober provisions of the Roman rite.

A Note on the Byzantine Rite of *Adelphopoiesis*: Another Kind of Domestic Partnership

The Byzantine euchologies include a rite known as *adelphopoiesis* ("making brothers") which gave to a household (or, in today's language, a domestic partnership) formed by two unrelated men as "brothers" social, legal, and religious recognition in the same way that crowning gave such recognition to a household formed by a man and a woman as husband and wife. This is the text of the rite in an early manuscript euchology:[18]

The Order for *Adelphopoiesis* (Making Brothers)
(MS Grottaferrata G B II)

The priest places the book of the holy gospels on the reading stand and the brothers place their hands upon it, holding lighted candles in their left hands, and the priest censes them.
And the deacon says
[The Litany][19]

In peace, let us pray to the Lord.
[R.   Lord, have mercy.]

For the peace from above, [for the loving-kindness of God, and for the salvation of our souls, let us pray to the Lord.
R.   Lord, have mercy.]

For the peace of the whole world, [for the welfare of the holy churches of God, and for the unity of all, let us pray to the Lord.
R.   Lord, have mercy.]

For this holy house [and for those who have entered it with faith, devotion, and the fear of God, let us pray to the Lord.
R.   Lord, have mercy.]

That these thy servants N. and M. may be blessed with a spiritual blessing, let us pray to the Lord.
[R.   Lord, have mercy.]

That their love may be preserved without hatred or scandal throughout their life, let us pray to the Lord.
[R.   Lord, have mercy.]

That the Lord our God would graciously bestow on them blameless faith and sincere love, let us pray to the Lord.
[R.   Lord, have mercy.]

That they and we may be delivered from all tribulation, [wrath, danger, and necessity], let us pray to the Lord.
[R.   Lord, have mercy.]

Have mercy upon us, O God, [according to thy great mercy. We beseech thee: hear us and have mercy upon us.][20]
R. Lord, have mercy. Lord, have mercy. Lord, have mercy.

The priest [concludes][21]
For thou art a merciful God and lover of humankind, [and to thee we give glory, to the Father and the Son and the Holy Spirit, now and for ever and unto the ages of ages. R. Amen.][22]

[First Prayer]

O Lord and Master, who didst make humankind after thine image and likeness, who wast pleased that thy holy apostles Philip and Bartholomew should become brothers, bonded according to the way not of nature, but of faith and spirit: As thou didst make thy holy martyrs Sergius and Bacchus worthy to become brothers, bless these thy servants N. and M., bonded not by the bond of nature but according to the way of faith and spirit, giving them peace and love and concord. Purge from their thoughts every stain and impurity, and grant that they may love each other without hatred and without scandal all the days of their life, through the intercessions of the holy bearer of God and of all thy saints: for to thee is due all glory, [honor, worship, and power, to the Father and to the Son and to the Holy Spirit, now and for ever and unto the ages of ages. R. Amen.]

A Second Prayer for Establishing the Bond of Brotherhood

O Lord our God, who hast graciously bestowed upon us all things necessary for salvation and who hast commanded that we should love each other and forgive each other our faults: O Master and Lover of good and Lover of humankind, bless and hallow these men who love each other with a spiritual love and come into this holy temple to be blessed and hallowed. Graciously give them irreproachable faith and sincere love, and as thou didst give to thy holy apostles and disciples thy peace and thy love, provide for them, O Christ our God, graciously giving them all their petitions for salvation and eternal life: for thou art the true light,[23] and to thee we give glory, [to the Father and to the Son and to the Holy Spirit, now and for ever, and unto the ages of ages. R. Amen.]

And they do obeisance to the book of the holy gospels and to the priest and to each other, and the dismissal is given.

Note: A variety of prayers for the rite are found in other manuscripts. The rite is sometimes concluded by reception of communion from the reserved sacrament and often includes readings from 1 Corinthians 12:27-13:8, and John 17:1, 18-16, as well as Psalm 133.

This rite, previously known to few except Byzantine liturgical scholars, has recently gained considerable attention because John Boswell cites it in *Same-Sex Unions in Premodern Europe* as the same-sex equivalent of the rite of crowning for heterosexual marriage. The rite itself uses different prayers and different readings from the rites for betrothal and crowning: in *adelphopoiesis* the significant act is the placement of hands on the gospel book; the ritual focus of the Byzantine rites for betrothal and crowning are the exchange of rings and the crowning of the bride and groom.[24] The bond of marriage is understood as both a physical bond (of sexual intimacy: the two "become one flesh") and a spiritual one. The prayers of *adelphopoiesis* speak of a spiritual bond, but not of a physical one. Neither canon law nor civil law exempted those united by the bond of *adelphopoiesis* from penalties prescribed for homosexual intimacy, although no doubt this was a dimension of the relationship in many cases. If the contemporary church adopts a rite for same-sex unions, the rite of *adelphopoiesis* provides a problematic precedent: one purpose of such a rite today should surely be to provide an appropriate context for sexual intimacy.

2. Developments of the Marriage Rite in the Medieval West

Before the collapse of the structures of imperial administration the church in the West did not need to concern itself with the legal aspects of marriage. But with the collapse of the empire, the effective oversight of matrimonial matters passed into the hands of the church. The consistent teaching of the church had been that it was consent that created a legitimate marriage, and the blessing of the marriage at a nuptial eucharist has never been required for marital legitimacy. But when the church took over responsibility for determining the legal aspects of matrimony in its courts, it was logical that it should begin to take more notice of the way in which consent was given and to give to this liturgical expression as well. At first, as we have seen, it did this in many regions by the priest's presence at domestic rites at the house of the groom when the groom gave the bride a ring and a pledge and the couple entered the marriage chamber to consummate the union after the marriage feast. A nuptial eucharist with its blessing might follow the next day, or the domestic rite might be the only liturgical form that the marriage took.

By the late middle ages, the elements of the domestic rite were redeployed, and the rite of consent (the distant descendant of the earlier betrothal) now took place at the church door. The couple then entered the church for the nuptial eucharist if it was to follow, and the blessing of the marriage chamber followed after the rite of consent at the church door (and the nuptial mass). The emphasis now tended to fall on the rite of consent as the principal requirement for a legal marriage, and the language of this rite of necessity was partly vernacular. The consent might be passive in form, with the bride and groom giving consent in response to the priest's questions; active forms of consent also developed, with vows which the couple spoke to each other. English rites were distinctive because they eventually included both passive and active forms of consent. The rite at the church door also acquired a changing variety of other elements — the "giving of the bride" and joining of hands,[25] the groom's gift of a ring and pledges to the bride and the blessing of the ring, a preliminary address to the congregation, often in the vernacular, by the priest, and a miscellany of other prayers and blessings. Indeed, the prayers become so numerous and so diffuse that it becomes nearly impossible to tell which are considered significant. The rite of the Sarum manual, for use in the diocese of Salisbury, is given in the following outline:[26]

Rite of Consent at the Church Door
Vernacular Exhortation
Vernacular consent of man and woman in passive form (questions)
Giving of the bride by the father to the man
Vernacular vows (active consent) by the man and woman
Blessing and giving of ring and pledges
Ring-giving formula
Suffrages, Kyrie, and Lord's Prayer
Prayers and blessings

Initial Rite at the Altar
Entrance to the church to Psalm 128
Suffrages, Kyrie, and Lord's Prayer
Prayers and Blessings

Nuptial Eucharist
Proper collect
Proper Epistle: 1 Corinthians 6:15-20
Proper Gospel: Matthew 19:3-6
Proper Prayer over the gifts
Prostration of couple under veil (pall) throughout canon and blessing
Nuptial blessing after the canon and Lord's Prayer
Proper postcommunion

Final Rites
Blessing of cup and bread for husband and wife
Blessing in the marriage chamber

The vernacular forms for the consent, the vows, and the giving of the ring in the Sarum manual are as follows:

N., wilt thou have this woman to thy wedded wife, wilt thou love her, and honour her, keep her and guard her, in health and in sickness, as a husband should a wife, and forsaking all others on account of her, keep thee only unto her, so long as ye both shall live? *Answer*: I will.

N., wilt thou have this man to thy wedded husband, wilt thou obey him, and serve him, love, honour, and keep him, in health and in sickness, as a wife should a husband, and forsaking all others on account of him, keep thee only unto him, so long as ye both shall live? *Answer*: I will.

I N. take the N. to my weddyd wyf to have et to holde from this day wafort bettur for wurs for richere, for porer: in sikenis and in helte tyll deth us departe, if holi chyrche wol it ordeyne: and ther to I plycht the my trouth.

I N. take te N. to my weddyd husbonde, tho have et to holde for ths day for bettur, for wurs, for richere, for powrer, in sykenesse and in helthe, to be bonowre et buxum, in bed et atbord, tyll deth vs departe, if holy chirche wol it ordeyne: et ther to I plyche te my throute.

With thys ryng I the wedde and tys gold and silver I the geue: and wyth my body I te worscype, and with all my worldly catell I the honore.[27]

The Western church's concern with the legitimacy of marriages led not only to the emphasis on consent, expressed in the rite at the church door, but to the requirement that banns be asked in church on three successive holy days to discover if there be any impediment to either party giving consent. The address which begins the rite at the church door includes a fourth and final asking about impediments. The question is asked of both the congregation and the man and woman. Impediments might include prior commitment to another (by marriage or engagement), insufficient age, psychological incapacity to give consent, undue influence, and relationship by blood or marriage of the man and woman.

In the Western church the focus on consent became so strong that the rite of consent rather than the nuptial blessing became the operative component of the marriage.[28] Here the concerns of canon law dominated in the formulation of sacramental theology and the solemn blessing before communion, the focal element of the liturgical texts of the early rites, receded in importance. With expanded rites like that of Salisbury in the late middle ages, the element of consent entered into the rites themselves and the liturgical witness itself became ambiguous.

In Latin theology, it becomes unclear what distinction can be made between a lawful marriage between Christians and a sacramental marriage. The minimum required for a sacramental union between two baptized Christians is informed consent. It becomes unclear, therefore, what function the nuptial blessing itself has. Part of the issue here is the teaching that the couple themselves are the "ministers" of this sacrament. In a more adequate sacramental theology, a sacrament is an action of Christ in the church with its diverse ministries, and it is inappropriate to single out the bride and groom as the ministers of this sacrament.[29]

3. Marriage in the Book of Common Prayer

In 1549 Cranmer provided a simplified vernacular version of the Sarum rite for marriage.[30]

Rite in the Body of the Church
Opening Exhortation, with purposes for marriage and banns
Consents of the bride and groom
Giving of the bride
Vows of the bride and groom with joining of hands
Prayer for the couple
Ring giving with formula
Matthew 19:16 and Declaration of Marriage
Blessing

Rite before the Altar
Psalm 128 or 67 in procession
Kyrie, Lord's Prayer, Preces
4 prayers of blessing

Nuptial Eucharist with Sermon or Biblical Catechesis

For the most part, Cranmer translated and paraphrased traditional material from the Sarum rite. The opening exhortation used the Sarum material and traditional teaching on the purposes of marriage drawn from the King's Book (a statement of Christian doctrine dating from this period) and ended with the final asking of impediments.[31] The question of the celebrant which initiates the giving of the bride is from the York tradition: in the Sarum tradition the rubrics prescribe the giving, but provide no liturgical text for the action. The consent in the form of passive vows[32] was taken from Sarum also, with the addition in the opening phrase of the words "after God's ordinance in the holy estate of matrimony." In the active consent, the vows, the words "according to God's holy ordinance" replaced the words, "if holy church will it ordain." While there may be a nuanced suggestion here that matrimony is an ordinance, not a sacrament, that may be reading more into the changes than Cranmer intended, since the word "ordain" — used in the older Sarum rite — is the verbal form of the noun "ordinance." The formula used for the ring giving was largely Sarum, though mention of "silver and gold" disappeared in 1552. The prayer and the blessing which concluded this part of the rite were adaptations of Sarum material; between them Cranmer has inserted the text from Matthew and the declaration of marriage, a reformed touch probably taken from the work of Hermann von Wied, reforming Archbishop of Cologne.

What was distinctive about the second part of the rite was the fact that Cranmer placed the material of the nuptial blessing before the eucharist. The prayers of this part of the rite were all derived from Sarum material — the third of the four prayers was a section of the ancient blessing of the sacramentaries. But, as Stevenson remarks, the element of blessing was now "spread like butter" throughout the rite,[33] so that the sharp focus of the original solemn blessing under the veil was lost. It was intended that the couple receive communion at the eucharist which followed. The wording of the rubrics suggests that Cranmer intended the rite to be used before the parish eucharist on Sundays. Nuptial communion became increasingly rare over the years, and the association with the parish eucharist was broken at the time of the Commonwealth out of Puritan dislike for marriage festivities on Sunday.

Very few changes were made in subsequent English revisions of the prayer book. But the long-standing ambiguity of what constituted a legal marriage was decisively resolved by Lord Hardwicke's marriage act of 1753, which required that all marriages be celebrated in buildings of the established church according to the formularies of the Book of Common Prayer.[34] Celebrations of marriage in domestic settings, which had long enjoyed favor among certain segments of the population, even though the rubrics of the Book of Common Prayer made no provision for them, were no longer possible. The American revision of 1789 drastically abbreviated the rite, removing the purposes for marriage from the exhortation and deleting in effect the entire second part of the rite (beginning with the procession to the altar).[35] These alterations reflect the reforms proposed by many in England during this period. The revision also permitted marriage in private houses — a provision which reflected an enduring custom only recently prohibited in England and which originally owed much to the conditions of colonial and frontier life. The 1928 revision of the American Book of Common Prayer deleted the word obey from the bride's vow and provided eucharistic propers for marriage (the nuptial eucharist was beginning to come back into use under the influence of the Oxford movement).

It is usually suggested that Cranmer has given us a traditional rite with reformed nuances, but that overstates the change. Cranmer did not account marriage a "sacrament" instituted by Christ, but the distinction between sacramental and non-sacramental rites is characteristic of theological language rather than liturgical texts.[36] His repositioning of the nuptial blessing was distinctive, but it was understandable when we remember that he placed marriage in the context of the regular services of the parish church on Sunday. Cranmer also abandoned the use of the veil held over the couple during the nuptial blessing, but this custom was also falling out of use among many Catholics and its meaning had long been obscure. Cranmer's rite was, in fact, a provision which was fuller than the minimum set out by the Roman Catholic Church after the Council of Trent, and much fuller than that of most other reformers (who were working with simpler Latin originals in most cases).

4. Marriage in the Book of Common Prayer 1979

The provisions of the 1979 rite of the American Episcopal Church represent a thorough rethinking of the marriage liturgy.[37] It skillfully integrates marriage into a nuptial eucharist in a fuller way than any of the traditional rites. It may be outlined as follows:

The Rite of Consent
Opening Exhortation
Rewritten consents (understood as a declaration of intention)
Commitment of the Congregation
[Optional presentation in marriage]

The Ministry of the Word [at the eucharist]
with a proper collect, a selection of readings and psalms, and sermon

The Marriage
Rewritten Vows
Blessing and giving of rings with rewritten formula
Declaration of Marriage concluding with Matthew 19:16
The Prayers (which serve as the prayers of the people for the eucharist)
The Blessing of the Marriage
  one of two prayers of blessing
  declarative blessing
The Exchange of the Peace

The Celebration of the Holy Communion (not required)
with a proper preface and postcommunion

What the 1979 rite does is to put in appropriate order elements of the marriage rite which accumulated somewhat accidentally and incrementally through the centuries in the West. Since the consents which constitute the legal contract and the blessing which articulates the transformation which God's grace bestows on the contractual relationship are the twin foci of the developed Western marriage rite, it makes sense to bring the two together as the heart of the rite. The opening rite of intention sets the context for the liturgy which follows, setting out the biblical basis for marriage, restoring a revised statement of the purposes of marriage, and establishing the freedom of the couple to enter into the covenant of marriage and their intentions as well as the commitment of the congregation to this covenanted relationship. The giving of the bride has been recast as a presentation, with the suggestion that both husband and wife may be presented. The liturgy of the word then establishes the biblical foundation of marriage.

The actual marriage itself follows before the altar, with the couple exchanging their vows and the pledges of their vows and joining hands. The declaration of marriage concludes the exchange of vows. Solemn intercessions, which draw skillfully on the traditional themes of marriage prayers, introduce the prayer of blessing, which may be either the traditional prayer from the American prayer book or a new composition based on Eastern themes (including crowning), and a declaratory blessing. The new prayer of blessing includes a subtle reference to both the non-Roman Western act of veiling both the bride and groom and the Eastern act of crowning: "Let their love for each other be a seal upon their hearts, a mantle about their shoulders, and a crown upon their foreheads."[38] The solemn nuptial blessing thus regains its proper focus. The peace follows, giving the liturgical rationale for the traditional exchange of a kiss by the couple. When the eucharist follows, it is suggested that the bridal couple present the bread and wine.

The additional provision in this book for the blessing of a civil marriage at a parish eucharist brings the development of the rite full circle. There is a certain anomaly in having the celebrant act as a minister of the state to register the legal contract in addition to his or her proper function as a minister of the church in bestowing God's blessing on the covenant of marriage. When a civil marriage is blessed, we are back to the understanding of marriage in the church's early centuries. In this case, the blessing follows a form of vows which establish the couple's commitment to the church's understanding of marriage and the solemn intercession and blessing of the fuller marriage rite. It is placed between the ministry of the word and the celebration of the holy communion at the parish eucharist.

* * * * *

At the end of this story, what can we say about the theology of Christian marriage? Human marriage, whether Christian or not, is possible because God has so ordered creation for the well-being of society and the continuation of the human race. The sexual attraction of a man and a woman finds the proper context for its full expression in this covenant, which is more than a legal contract. Marriage is the institution of God as the "creator and preserver of all life," who makes the two one flesh in this covenant. The legal contract is based on the order of creation.

But Christians place this contract as a covenant within the context of the covenant established by the saving action of God in Jesus Christ. This is a new dimension of the covenant of marriage. God's grace so transforms the covenant of marriage for the bride and groom, in the words of the solemn intercessions,

> that their wills may be so knit together in [God's] will, and their spirits in [God's] Spirit, that they may grow in love and peace with [God] and one another all the days of their life. . . .

> [that they may have] grace, when they hurt one another, to recognize and acknowledge their fault, and to seek each other's forgiveness and [God's]. . . .

> [that] their life together [may be] a sign of Christ's love to this sinful and broken world, that unity may overcome estrangement, forgiveness heal guilt, and joy conquer despair. . . .

[that they may have], if it is [God's] will, the gift and heritage of children, and the grace to bring them up to know [God], to love [God], and to serve [God]. . . .

[that they may find] such fulfillment of their mutual affection that they may reach out in love and concern for others.[39]

Put in summary form, in the order of salvation a Christian marriage is so transformed by God's grace that it becomes a tangible sign of the way in which Christ's sacrificial love heals the sin and sickness of the world within the community of the new covenant which is the church. Through Christ God has made, in the words of the first prayer of blessing, "the way of the cross to be the way of life." Couples who are unwilling to enter marriage in this spirit but understand marriage only as a dimension of the order of creation have no right to ask the church to bless their marriage, for it will not be a marriage "in Christ." Marriage can be an "occasion of grace," but only "in Christ." Here, as in all the pastoral offices, liturgy has the danger of slipping back from the transformation of the natural order to the mere affirmation of the natural order as it is. The church has no business simply affirming the order of creation, without reference to the other dimensions of Christian marriage. The dual role of the minister as both an agent of the state and a minister of the church sometimes obscures this truth.

There is a final, eschatological dimension to marriage which the Byzantine rite captures better than most Western rites. In the power of the Spirit those who enter the covenant of marriage in Christ, that is, within the community of the new covenant, embody the beginning of the transformation of all human relationships that culminates in the joy of God's kingdom, which Scripture speaks of as the messianic banquet, the marriage supper of the lamb. This spirit is captured by the last of the petitions in the solemn intercessions and by the conclusion of the first prayer of blessing:

Grant that the bonds of our common humanity, by which all your children are united to one another, and the living to the dead, may be so transformed by your grace, that your will may be done on earth as it is in heaven . . . .

Bless them . . . in their life and in their death. Finally, in your mercy bring them to that table where your saints feast forever in your heavenly home.[40]

When their marriage is sealed in communion, in the words of the postcommunion prayer, the bride and groom are given an earnest that they may "obtain those eternal joys prepared for all who love" God.[41]

As a sacrament, Christian marriage must be understood in relation to all these dimensions — the order of creation, rooted in the social contract; the order of redemption, redeemed by the sacrificial love of Christ; the order of eschatological fulfilment, known by anticipation in the life of the church but realized in its fulness only in the kingdom which is the end of all things. The Orthodox theologian John Meyendorff puts this very well:

> Marriage is a sacrament because in it the future kingdom of God — the marriage feast of the Lamb (Rev. 19:7, 9), the full union between Christ and the Church (Eph. 5:32) — is being anticipated and re-presented. Christian marriage finds its ultimate meaning not in fleshly satisfaction, or in social stability, or in securing posterity, but in the *eschaton* — the "last things" which the Lord prepares for his elect."[42]

It is the tendency to forget this perspective which makes Western sacramental theology of marriage so problematic: the overemphasis on consent as that which constitutes the sacrament threatens to reduce Christian marriage to the order of creation alone.

In marriage, as in all things, we walk by faith. The journey of the newly married, like the journey of every Christian, is the way of the cross, and marriage attains its Christian transformation only by God's grace and the sacrificial love of the man and the woman and reaches its perfection only in the kingdom of heaven. Some marriages die, and fail to achieve the dimension for which they were intended in the order of salvation. The eschatological dimension presents other difficulties. Is the bond of marriage lifelong, or is it eternal? The West has answered that it is lifelong. The Byzantine answer is that it is eternal. The West presently blesses second marriages after the death of a spouse without distinguishing them from first marriages. In the

Byzantine theology of marriage, a second marriage after the death of a spouse presents the same problems that marriage after divorce does. It violates the sense that the bond of marriage is not severed by death.

The Eastern church recognizes that in God's providence second marriages have a place as an expression God's mercy, even though they do represent only imperfectly the covenanted relationship of which marriage is intended as a sign. It therefore recognizes them, though it celebrates them in a penitential spirit. The present rite of the Book of Common Prayer 1979 makes no distinction between first marriages and others. The church would articulate the realities of Christian life more honestly if the intercessions and prayers of the rite provided adaptations for the realities of second marriages — though the careful preparation of the couple seems to make more sense than placing them under canonical penance after marriage, as the strict requirements of the Byzantine rite would do (provisions not now enforced).

5. Celibacy in the Early Church and in the Middle Ages

By the second century, we know that some men had undertaken a life of intentional celibacy in the early church, and also that women had renounced marriage and undertaken a life of consecrated virginity. Local churches in the third century had consecrated virgins who lived in their own family households or in households of consecrated virgins living together under the auspices of the bishop. Methodius wrote his treatise, *The Symposium,* as a theological tract on the meaning of the life of virginity.[43]

It is not until the middle of the fourth century, however, that we have evidence that consecration to celibacy in the church took liturgical expression. Our earliest evidence comes from the Roman tradition, where the rite for women undertaking a life of virginity — like Ambrose's sister Marcellina — came to be known as the *velatio virginum,* the veiling of virgins. This rite appears at about the same time as the rite of nuptial veiling for brides and is developed as a counterpart to that rite. In the Roman tradition, it was "veiling" in both cases which signified the woman's change in status and found liturgical expression.

The rite which appears in the sacramentaries in the following centuries is, like that for the veiling of brides, a solemn blessing which is sung, like the eucharistic prayer, to the preface tone. It develops a carefully thought out theology of virginity:

> O God, who dost graciously dwell in chaste bodies; O God, lover of uncorrupted souls; O God, who through thy Word by whom thou didst first make all things dost so heal human nature, weakened in the first humans by the deceit of the devil, that thou dost not only restore it to the innocence of its first beginning, but dost also bring it to the experience of those good things which are to be enjoyed in the new creation and dost transform those once limited by the condition of mortals into the likeness of angels:

> Look, O Lord, upon these women, thy servants, who, placing in thy hands their resolve to live a life of continence, offer their consecration to the one on whose behalf they undertook their vows. For how can a soul, constrained by mortal flesh, conquer the law of nature, the false freedom of licentiousness, the force of habit, and the temptations of age, unless thou dost mercifully kindle this flame, graciously foster its brightness, and sustain its strength?

> For having poured forth thy grace upon all peoples, thou hast among other excellences showered forth from the bounty of thy generosity this gift on those from every nation under heaven who, countless in number as the stars, are heirs of the new covenant by adoption, and whom thou didst reckon to be born, not by blood, nor by the will of the flesh, but by the Spirit.

> That their abstinence might in no way lessen the honor of marriage, and that thy first blessing might abide on this sacred union, the noble souls who renounce the bond of husband and wife desire the reality of which marriage is the sacramental sign, and make their model not the earthly reality but that which it prefigures.

Consecrated virginity recognizes its author, and devotes itself with an integrity like that of the angels to his bridal bed and wedding chamber, who has thus espoused himself, the son of the ever virgin one, to those who are ever virgins.

Grant to those who ask thine aid, O Lord, and desire to be strengthened by the blessing of thy consecration, the defense and discipline of thy protection. Let not the ancient enemy who subverts the more excellent pursuits with more subtle deceits creep in to tarnish the prize of perfect continence nor snatch away the purity of a quest which they also share with those who follow the path of marriage.

May they possess, O Lord, by the gift of thy Spirit, a reverent modesty, a wise generosity, a strong gentleness, a chaste freedom. May they be aflame with charity and love nothing more than thee; may they live praiseworthy lives, yet not seek for praise. May they glorify thee in the holiness of their bodies and the purity of their souls. May they fear thee in love, and serve thee in love.

Be thou their honor, thou their joy, thou their desire, thou their solace in sorrow, thou their aid in perplexity, thou their defense in harm, thou their patience in tribulation, thou their wealth in poverty, thou their sustenance in fasting, thou their medicine in weakness. May they find all things in thee whom they have chosen over all things.[44]

This carefully crafted prayer skillfully balances the fulfilment of human love in a marriage which is a tangible sign of Christ's love with the renunciation of such fulfilment for the sake of Christ's love. The fulfilment of human love and the renunciation of human love mirror the tension between affirmation of the world and renunciation of the world which characterizes the church of the fourth century and echoes the eschatological tension of the gospel itself. The use of the veiling metaphor, however, led to more dubious developments of the treatment of the consecrated virgin as a bride of Christ

— introducing because of the limits of the metaphor an unfortunate distinction between the status of women and men in the vocation to celibacy.

The theological balance between marriage and celibacy was already threatened in the fourth century, and it has seldom been maintained since that time. Jerome,[45] the militant advocate of celibacy, railed against Jovinian, who had placed the married and the unmarried on equal footing in the church. Jerome's blast against marriage was so vitriolic that it evoked protests from Rome and even from Augustine, whose view of original sin rendered all sexuality suspect. In the end, the church moderated Jerome's dark view of married love, but from this moment Catholicism would see sexual renunciation as the more excellent way and eventually would restrict ordination to celibates. For the faithful Christian marriage was now only a distant second-best. The Reformers, more than a millennium later, would reverse Jerome's judgment and repudiate celibacy even more vitriolically than he had denigrated marriage. The early fourth-century balance proved hard to maintain.

By the fifth century the life of consecrated virgins was giving way to new forms of the ascetic life. The fourth century had seen a flight to the desert, and by the fifth century the ascetical life was beginning to take the new form of cenobitic monasticism favored by Basil in the East and, later, Benedict in the West. The model here was a common life for those vowed to celibacy. Men and women were created for life in community, and the monastic household became the alternative to the family household of the married. As communities took on organized form, it was profession and clothing which marked the entry into the ascetical life.[46] In both East and West this often took on a sacramental status, and both Eastern and Western authors numbered monastic profession among the sacraments (or *mysteria* in the language of the Byzantine East). It came to be understood as a second baptism.[47] In the East taking the lesser habit was understood as a commitment to a life of penance, while taking the greater habit was understood as an assumption of the angelic habit. Both penitence and clothing in the angelic habit or "robe of righteousness" are baptismal themes. The same theology was also developed in the West, but it did not become so dominant, and the fourth Lateran Council did not include monastic profession in its list of sacraments.

The predominant rite of profession to the religious life in its various forms in the West takes it origin from the provisions for monastic profession in the Rule of Benedict.[48] The candidate, according to the rule, presents himself before the abbot in the presence of the community (at the eucharist in later usage), makes his commitment orally (the *promissio*) and presents it in written form on the altar (the *petitio*), sings as a prayer (the *oratio*) the verse (Psalm 119:116), "Sustain me according to thy promise, Lord, that I may live," which is taken up by the community, asks the prayers of the members of the community, is stripped of his own clothing, and puts on the monastic habit. Eventually the rite acquired its own set of prayers, including a solemn consecration of the monk.[49] Aidan Kavanagh notes that as the extensive catechumenate before baptism disappeared, the novitiate and monastic profession acquired something of the same meaning for serious Christians that the catechumenate and baptism had once had for all Christians.[50]

6. Profession to the Religious Life in the Episcopal Church

All religious orders were abolished in the Church of England at the Reformation. Apart from the life of the community at Little Gidding under Nicholas Ferrar, no attempt was made to revive the religious life until the nineteenth century, when various forms of religious life for men and women were established under the influence of the Oxford Movement. The revival of the order of deaconess at about the same time in many of the churches of the Reformation restored for women a way of life very similar to that of the consecrated virgins of the early church. Renunciation of married love found recognized status once again in these churches as a Christian vocation, though often in the face of considerable opposition. The most successful form of such a vocation to life in a religious order has been the twentieth-century community at Taizé in France — in origin a foundation within the Reformed tradition, but later an ecumenical religious community.

Most of these orders have devised liturgical rites for profession that draw on traditional Western forms. As in the Roman Catholic Church, the rites are proper to the orders rather than to the churches themselves. In the

Episcopal Church, the *Book of Offices* provided a form for setting apart deaconesses — traditionally, like the veiling of virgins, a rite at which the bishop presides. Because deaconesses were traditionally a minor order in the church, however, their blessing involved a laying on of hands. With the recognition that deaconesses were within the order of the diaconate in recent decades, the rite for setting them apart became redundant. *The Book of Occasional Services* (successor to the *Book of Offices*) now makes provisions for rites of Setting Apart for a Special Vocation. The provisions are meant for those not associated with the regular religious orders, but involve the traditional vows of poverty, chastity, and obedience made to the bishop. Temporary vows are made after the novitiate, vows of life profession are the final stage. The rites for temporary and lifelong vows are set in the context of the eucharist after the Prayers of the People and follow in general the traditional order. The service includes the following components:

1. Request for admission
2. Sermon or homily
3. Examination by the bishop
4. Appropriate promises or vows
5. Prayer or blessing
6. Presentation of clothing or other tokens of the vocation.

The churches of the Reformation have thus begun to recover the balance between the witness of celibacy and the witness of marriage; conversely, Roman Catholicism after Vatican II has ceased to treat marriage as second-best to celibacy.

John Meyendorff puts the vocation to celibacy, like the vocation to marriage, into an appropriate theological perspective. In comparing the two vocations he writes:

> Now celibacy — and especially monastic life — are justified in Scripture and Tradition by the same reference to the future Kingdom [as marriage]. The Lord himself has said that "when they rise from the dead, they neither marry nor are given in marriage, but are like the angels in heaven" (Mark 12:25). . . . [T]his passage should not be understood to imply that Christian marriage will not remain a reality in the future

Kingdom, but it certainly points to the fact that human relations will not be "fleshly" any more. Thus, the New Testament repeatedly praises celibacy as an anticipation of the "angelic life."[51]

It is by referring celibacy to Christ and to the Kingdom that we discover its true Christian meaning, just as we discover the true meaning of marriage by referring it to Christ and to the Kingdom.

Conclusions on Marriage and Celibacy in the Church

Although Western theology in the Catholic tradition accounts marriage a sacrament on the basis of Ephesians, the dominant emphasis of the rites for marriage in that tradition falls on the bride's change of status (the veiling in earlier rites, the "giving away" in later centuries) and on consent as the basis of legitimate marriage (an emphasis which comes to the fore in the early period in the *tabulae matrimoniales* and in the late middle ages in the vows at the church door). The tone of much that the Catholic tradition has to say about marriage focusses in fact, on marriage as "a remedy against sin"; in the words of the the 1549 Book of Common Prayer,

> Secondly it was ordeined for a remedie against sinne, and to auoide fornicacion . . . .[52]

This has little positive to say about marriage, and behind it lies the tendency to treat marriage as second-best to celibacy. Even the sacramentality of marriage has been defined by canon law rather than by the liturgical tradition of the church.

On the other hand, the tendency to treat marriage exclusively as an aspect of the order of creation — as God's holy ordinance — in the churches of the Reformation has led them to develop a theology of marriage without reference to its transformation in Christ and its fulfilment in God's kingdom — the orders of redemption and of eschatological fulfilment. In the bourgeois culture of Protestant society marriage becomes the sole norm and celibacy becomes "unnatural" — neither is referred to Christ or to the Kingdom and human life becomes earthbound.

In its 1979 rite for the Celebration of a Marriage and Blessing of a Marriage, the Episcopal Church has begun to learn much of what the Eastern tradition, with its far richer and more positive theology of marriage, has to teach. The task before us now is to translate the liturgical witness into our theology and to balance our theology of marriage with our theology of profession to celibacy. We have seen that, from the time of Chrysostom, the church compared the crowns of the bride and groom in the marriage rite to martyrs' crowns. Early authors also saw monasticism as a form of martyrdom — a new expression of the costly witness to which Christians are called, once the legal establishment of the church in society made it less likely that the cost of Christian witness would be death at the hands of a hostile state. The theology of marriage and monasticism as forms of *martyria* — costly witness — link both to the commitments of the baptismal commitment. Both are ways of living out the baptismal witness in the life of this world. As such, marriage and profession of celibacy are occasions of grace. The words of John Meyendorff are once again worth pondering:

> [B]oth marriage and celibacy are ways of living the Gospel, anticipating the Kingdom, which was already revealed in Christ and must appear in strength at the last day. It is, therefore, only a marriage "in Christ" sealed by the Eucharist, and celibacy "in the name of Christ" which carry this eschatological Christian meaning — not marriage concluded casually, as a contract, or as a satisfaction for the flesh, and not celibacy accepted by inertia, or worse, by egoism and self-protective irresponsibility. . . . Christian celibacy is unthinkable without prayer, fasting, and obedience, humility, charity, and constant ascetical effort.[53]

ENDNOTES

[1]*Letter to Diognetus*, chapter 5:1, 6, in Cyril Richardson, ed., *Early Christian Fathers* (Philadelphia: Westminster, 1953), pages 216-217. Another apologist, Justin Martyr, holds up celibate men and women as

models of virtue; see his *First Apology*, chapter 15, page 250 of *Early Christian Fathers*.

[2]See Kenneth Stevenson, *Nuptial Blessing: A Study of Christian Marriage Rites* (New York: Oxford, 1983), pages 5-9 (Jewish customs); J. Evenou, "Marriage," in A. G. Martimort, ed., *The Church at Prayer*, vol. III, (Collegeville, MN: Liturgical Press, 1988), trans. Matthew J. O'Connell, pages 186-187 (Roman customs); Marion Hatchett, *Commentary on the American Prayer Book* (New York: Seabury, 1980), pages 427-428.

[3]Note that in the New Testament, it is not an aversion to sexuality that leads to renunciation of marriage, but fear of entanglements with the present, unredeemed social order through family obligations. This is quite clear in Paul's advice to the Corinthians. The environing Greco-Roman society, on the other hand, saw sexuality as a threat to the ideal of self-control and freedom from passion (the Stoic ideal of *apatheia*, which later colors the attitudes of many Christian authors).

[4]On this, see Elizabeth Schüssler-Fiorenza, *In Memory of Her: A Feminist Theological Reconstruction of Christian Origins* (New York: Crossroads, 1985), esp. chapters 6-8.

[5]At times, the church recognized unions that were irregular under Roman law (largely because of disparity of social class). Hippolytus is said to have broken with the Roman church partly over this issue, but even he is willing to admit to baptism slave women whose union with their masters cannot receive legal recognition in Roman law.

[6]*Tertullian: Treatises on Marriage and Remarriage, To His Wife, Exhortation to Chastity, Monogamy*, trans. William Le Saint (London, 1951); here *To His Wife*, 2:8, 6-9, pages 35 f, as cited by Kenneth Stevenson, *Nuptial Blessing*, page 17. For an evaluation of Tertullian's evidence, see pages 16-19 of *Nuptial Blessing*.

[7]See Kenneth Stevenson, *Nuptial Blessing*, chapter 2 (for the Latin West) and chapter 3 (for the East); also *To Join Together: The Rite of Marriage* (New York: Pueblo, 1987), chapter 2 (the West) and chapter 3 (the East); J. Evenou, "Marriage," in A. G. Martimort, ed., *The Church at Prayer*, vol. III, pages 189-192, 198-200 (the West), 192-197 (the East). See also the entries for specific traditions s. v. "Marriage" in J. D. Davies, ed., *The New*

Westminster Dictionary of Liturgy and Worship (Philadelphia: Westminster, 1986), pages 349-364. For a careful study of the Byzantine tradition (rather than the liturgical texts themselves), see John Meyendorff, *Marriage: An Orthodox Perspective* (Crestwood, NY: St. Vladimir's Seminary Press, 1970).

[8]Some other Western witnesses do seem to indicate the inclusion of a written contract in the marriage liturgy. This is particularly true for North Africa. But the contract does not survive in any *liturgical formularies* that have come down to us.

[9]Some Roman authorities and early Christian authors (such as Tertullian) witness to the custom of veiling the bride *from the time of betrothal*. The shift to the assumption of the veil at the time of marriage gives evidence of the fluidity of the relationship between betrothal and marriage and of the tendency of formal recognition of betrothal to be fused with the marriage rite.

[10]Second marriages placed those who entered them under canonical discipline and could not be sealed by communion.

[11]See John Meyendorff, *Marriage: An Orthodox Perspective*, page 29-30.

[12]See Kenneth Stevenson, *Nuptial Blessing*, page 27 in a discussion of Ambrose *In I Cor. 7.40.138.*

[13]A freer English translation is found in Kenneth Stevenson, *Nuptial Blessing*, pages 245-246, and *To Join Together*, pages 31-32. I have preferred a more literal translation, based on the Latin text. For the Latin text, see J. Deshusses, *La Sacramentaire Gregorien I* (Fribourg: University Press, 1971), § 200, no. 838, pages 310-311. The earlier form of the blessing is found in the Verona Sacramentary. For the text, see L. C. Mohlberg, ed., *Sacramentarium Veronese*, Rerum Ecclesiarum Documenta, Series maior: Fontes 1 (Rome: Herder, 1956), § 31, no. 1110. The Gelasian form is a variant of the Verona blessing: see L. C. Mohlberg, ed., *Liber sacramentorum Romanae aeclesiae ordinis anni circuli*, Rerum Ecclesiasticarum Documenta, Series maior: Fontes 4 (Rome: Herder, 1960), no. 1451, pages 109-110.

[14]See the outlines in Kenneth Stevenson, *To Join Together*, pages 75 and 77-78.

[15]For the English text of the prayers of this rite, see Isabel Florence Hapgood, trans., *Service Book of the Holy Orthodox-Catholic Apostolic Church*, 5th edition (Englewood, NJ: Antiochean Orthodox Christian Archdiocese of New York and All North America, 1975), pages 291-305, as well as the translations of some of the prayers in Stevenson, *Nuptial Blessing* and *To Join Together*. The Greek texts are found in Jacobus Goar, ed., *Euchologion sive Rituale Graecorum* (Venice: Ex Typographia Bartolomaei Javarina, 1730; reprint, Graz: Akademische Druck-und Verlagsanstalt, 1960), pages 310-322 (here pages 311, 317, 318, 319); for a French translation of the prayers for the crowning and commentary on the administration of communion, see Miguel Arranz, "La liturgie des présanctifiés de l'ancien euchologe byzantin," *Orientalia Christiana Periodica* 47 (1981), pages 332-388, here, pages 376-388 ("Rite du couronnement nuptial"). The translations are my own revision of Stevenson and Hapgood on the basis of the Greek and Arranz's work. I have retained the use of the second person singular (unlike Stevenson) because its use allows a translation syntactically closer to the Greek text.

[16]See note 15.

[17]Alexander Schmemann, *For the Life of the World*, pages 90-91 passim. See also the interpretation of the Byzantine rite by Paul Lazor in J. D. Davies, *New Westminster Dictionary of Liturgy and Worship*, s. v. "Marriage," page 350.

[18]Translated from the Greek text printed in John Boswell, *Same-Sex Unions in Premodern Europe* (New York: Villard/Random House, 1994), pages 345-347. Bracketed material provides headings and completes formularies indicated only by their opening words. The manuscript dates from the eleventh century and is located today in Grottaferrata, Italy. This rite is already found in the earliest Byzantine euchology, Barberini MS 336. See also the variants of the rite printed in Goar, *Euchologion sive Rituale Graecorum*, pages 706-709.

[19]There are many variants of this standard litany, adapted to various occasions. See the text of the full form in F. E. Brightman, *Liturgies Eastern and Western* (Oxford: Clarendon Press, 1896), pages 362-363.

[20]In place of the customary conclusion of this litany, the text gives a peti-

tion and the concluding doxology of the prayer from the litany of fervent supplication. For these texts, see Brightman, *Liturgies Eastern and Western*, page 373, lines 14-15, and 374, lines 4-6.

[21]Note that the beginning of this doxology (the *ekphonesis* of the priest) is not part of the prayer which follows. The text is divided incorrectly.

[22]For the text of the doxology, see Brightman, page 374, lines 4-6.

[23]The text reads *alethikon* for *alethinon*.

[24]There is no evidence that those who were made brothers were crowned. Boswell has misread the two passages which he cites in support of his claim that they *were* crowned.

[25]The Sarum rite provides a rubric for the giving of the bride, but the verbal formula associated with it comes from York.

[26]A translation of the rite is found in F. E. Warren, trans., *The Sarum Missal in English, Part II* (London: De La More Press, 1911), vol. 1, pages 143-160. I have worked from that translation and from the outline in Kenneth Stevenson, *To Join Together,* page 211. Note the giving of the bride prescribed by the rubrics as ritual act in Sarum usage. The question associated with the action comes from the usages of York and is not found in the Sarum rite.

[27]Texts from F. E. Warren, ed., *The Sarum Missal in English, Part II,* pages 145-147. The vernacular text of the vows and consents is taken from the 1526 printing in Paris. The passive consents are given in the original text of the missal in Latin with the direction that they be asked in the vernacular, and the text given above is Warren's translation.

[28]This emphasis on consent as the constitutive factor of marriage as a sacrament has come under increasing challenge by Roman Catholic theology. See the contributions in K. Richter, *Eheschliessung: Mehr als ein rechtlich Ding?* (Freiburg, Basel, Vienna: Herder, 1989), Quaestiones Disputatae 120.

[29]This view is also gaining acceptance at present among Roman Catholic scholars. See James A. Schmeiser, s. v. "Marriage, Ministers of," in Peter E. Fink, ed., *The New Dictionary of Sacramental Worship* (Collegeville, MN: Michael Glazier/Liturgical Press, 1990), pages 801-803.

[30]The text of the rite of 1549 may be found in E. C. S. Gibson, ed., *The*

First and Second Prayer Books of Edward VI (New York: E. P. Dutton, 1910), pages 252-258. See Kenneth Stevenson's commentary in Nuptial Blessing, pages 134-146, and To Join Together, pages 91-99. A comparative table with sources, the 1549 text, and changes of 1552 and 1559 is found in To Join Together, pages 92-92.

[31]This is the equivalent of a fourth reading of the banns. Although it is found in the Sarum rite, Cranmer's wording conforms more closely to the text of the York rite.

[32]There is a persistent tendency in Anglican commentators to treat these as the betrothal vows, and the active vows as the marriage vows. The English rites were peculiar in having both passive and active vows (elsewhere we find one or the other, but not both), but when vows make their appearance in English rites in the middle ages, both forms do so as *marriage* vows.

[33]Kenneth Stevenson, Nuptial Blessing, page 140.

[34]This ruled out marriages by dissenting ministers as well as marriages in private houses. Nineteenth-century legislation modified the restrictions of the act of 1753 in various ways. See Kenneth Stevenson, Nuptial Blessing, page 158.

[35]Only the Lord's Prayer (which was moved to a position directly after the second set of vows) was retained. In practice, American Episcopalians eventually came to divide the service into two parts once again by introducing a procession to the altar immediately after the "giving" of the bride, so that the second set of vows and the prayers took place before the altar. But the rubrics made no provision for this division of the rite.

[36]Commentators note the description of marriage as an "ordinance" in Cranmer's revision of the vows. But as we have seen, the older vows contained the phrase, "if holy church will it ordain." The language of ordinance is not, therefore, new to the rite.

[37]BCP 1979, pages 422-438. For commentary on this rite, see Marion Hatchett, Commentary on the American Prayer Book, pages 427-443; Leonel Mitchell, Praying Shapes Believing: A Theological Commentary on the Book of Common Prayer (Minneapolis, MN: Seabury/Winston, 1985), pages 187-197; Kenneth Stevenson, Nuptial Blessing, pages 192-195, and To Join Together, pages 154-156.

[38]BCP 1979, page 430. The veil extended over both bride and groom in Western usage might be understood as "a mantle about their shoulders." Veiling in this sense does not focus the attention on the change in the bride's status, but gives an emphasis to mutuality, as does the crowning. The prayer was composed by Boone Porter, who speaks of Jeremy Taylor's work as one inspiration for the prayer.

[39]BCP 1979, page 429.

[40]BCP 1979, page 430.

[41]BCP 1979, page 432.

[42]John Meyendorff, *Marriage: An Orthodox Perspective*, page 57.

[43]A thoughtful study of asceticism in early Christianity is found in Peter Brown, *The Body and Society: Men, Women, and Sexual Renunciation in Early Christianity* (NY: Columbia University Press, 1988). On consecrated virgins, see chapter 13; on Methodius, see chapter 9. In Methodius we see that strand of early Christianity which favored sexual renunciation over marriage, rather than holding the two in balance.

[44]For a contemporary English translation of the greater part of this text, see International Commission on English in the Liturgy, *The Rites of the Catholic Church as Revised by Decree of the Second Vatican Ecumenical Council and Published by Authority of Pope Paul VI*, vol. 2, (NY: Pueblo, 1980), pages 143-145. My translation has been made from the text in the Verona Sacramentary, found in L. C. Mohlberg, ed., *Sacramentarium Veronese*, Rerum Ecclesiasticarum Documenta., Series maior: Fontes I (Rome, 1956), § 30, no 1104, pages 138-139 For a contemporary study, see Adrien Nocent, "The Consecration of Virgins," in A. G. Martimort, ed., *The Church at Prayer*, vol. III, pages 209-220.

[45]See Peter Brown, *The Body and Society*, chapter 18.

[46]For a study of the rites of profession, see Adrien Nocent, "Monastic Rites and Religious Profession" in A. G. Martimort, ed., *The Church at Prayer*, vol. III, pages 209-220.

[47]See the treatment of Byzantine monasticism in John Meyendorff, *Marriage: An Orthodox Perspective*. The treatment of monastic profession as a *mysterion* is usually traced back to the fifth or sixth century author known as Dionysius the Areopagite. However, while it seems clear that he

gives the rite what we would call "sacramental" status, the word *mysterion* appears only in the subtitles of his *Ecclesiastical Hierarchy*, which are probably the work of a later editor. See the notes on chapter six of this work in Colm Luibheid, trans., *Pseudo Dionysius: The Complete Works* (NY: Paulist Press, 1987), pages 243-249. Dionysius appears to give pride of place to the rites of initiation (baptism, chrismation, and the eucharist), for which his term is *teleiotes*. See note 3, page 195, and note 138, page 232, in *Pseudo-Dionysius*; the notes are by Paul Rorem. Lev Gillet, writing under the pseudonym of "A Monk of the Eastern Church" in *Orthodox Spirituality: An Outline of the Orthodox Ascetical and Mystical Tradition*, discusses other sacraments (including monastic profession) by relating them to the three rites of initiation — a modification of Dionysius's scheme.

[48]For the rite in the Rule of Benedict, see Claude Pfeiffer, "Monastic Formation and Profession," in Timothy Fry, ed., *RB 1980: The Rule of St. Benedict in Latin and English with Notes* (Collegeville, MN: Liturgical Press, 1981), Appendix 5, pages 437-466. In the Rule itself, the profession is treated in chapter 58, found on pages 266-271 of this edition.

[49]The consecration is first mentioned in the West in the canons of Theodore, Archbishop of Canterbury, in the seventh century.

[50]Aidan Kavanagh, *The Shape of Baptism: The Rite of Christian Initiation* (NY: Pueblo, 1978), pages 154-158. Claude Pfeiffer comments on the relation of the catechumenate and the novitiate before profession on page 441, "Monastic Formation and Profession," in Timothy Fry, ed., *RB 1980: The Rule of St. Benedict in Latin and English with Notes*.

[51]John Meyendorff, *Marriage: An Orthodox Perspective*, page 57.

[52]BCP 1549, page 152.

[53]John Meyendorff, *Marriage: An Orthodox Perspective*, page 58. It is to the Byzantine tradition that we must turn also if we seek some kind of precedent for a covenanted relationship between two men or two women. Byzantine tradition does provide a precedent here for the recognition of such relationships, though for contemporary Christians it is important that such relationships also be recognized as the appropriate context for sexual intimacy. A theology of such relationships needs (like the theology of marriage and celibacy) to be formulated in trinitarian terms with reference to the orders of creation, redemption, and eschatological fulfilment.

CHAPTER 3

THE RETURN OF THE PRODIGAL

THE RECONCILIATION OF A PENITENT

1. Public Penance

The First Three Centuries: The Emergence of Public Penance

The literature of the New Testament understands the forgiveness of sins as the heart of the saving work of Jesus: he proclaims the message of God's forgiveness, he embodies that forgiveness in concrete ways in his own ministry, and he dies on the cross for our justification. The primary way in which that message was mediated in the church was through baptism. The Nicene Creed acknowledges "one baptism for the forgiveness of sins," and the reference in the Apostles' Creed to "the forgiveness of sins" is likewise surely to be read as a baptismal reference. But it took the church centuries to determine how to deal with post-baptismal sin. The Epistle to the Hebrews (6:4) represents a rigorist strain that considered it unthinkable that reconciliation with God was possible for those guilty of serious sins after baptism, and this rigorism found much support in the first centuries of the church's life. *The Shepherd of Hermas* is a tract of a member of the

Christian community in Rome in the early second century whose principal purpose was to argue that such reconciliation was possible.

In early Christian communities, the rupture of relationships within the church which sin caused was understood as a visible manifestation of the rupture of the relationship between the sinner and God. In a hostile environment, the church considered it imperative to resolve disputes between Christians within the community, rather than in civil courts, and the bishop played a quasi-judicial role in this process. Serious sin brought expulsion from the community and from its eucharist, and tangible evidence of repentance and amendment of life was required before the sinner could be reconciled to the community and readmitted to communion. The church found warrant for its discipline in Christ's delegation of the authority to forgive — the power of the keys — to Peter (Matthew 16:19) and to the apostles (Matthew 18:18; John 20:23), as well as in the process of community discipline found in Matthew 18:16-17. We see Paul exercising such authority in 1 Corinthians 5. The purpose of the penitential process was the preservation of the community's health and the restoration of the sinner's health. But its quasi-judicial character could lead to misunderstanding.

In the course of the second and third centuries, during which the church was forced to deal with hard cases of lapse (apostasy) in time of persecution, consensus was reached that reconciliation was possible for those guilty of serious sin. In many regions (in most of the West and North Africa and in Alexandria in the East) such penance was considered unrepeatable.[1] *One* reconciliation was the analogue of *one* baptism. The catalogue of serious sins (later to be classified as mortal sins) usually included three — murder, adultery, and apostasy. But the way of reconciliation was arduous. It began with expulsion from communion and admission as a penitent, involved a period of penitential exercises (which might sometimes last a lifetime), and concluded with reconciliation to the communion of the church through the laying on of hands by the bishop and readmission to communion.[2] This process was ordinarily administered by the bishop. It should be noted that it was the *penance* itself which was public; confession was made privately to the bishop or his delegate before public admission to the ranks of the penitents.

One of the most complete early descriptions of public penance in this period comes from the North African Tertullian early in the third century. While we should treat his evidence with a certain amount of caution, since his rigorism eventually led him into Montanism, he is still an important witness to what he called "second penitence":

> God has permitted the door of forgiveness, although closed and locked by the bar of baptism, still to stand open. He has placed in the vestibule a second penitence so that it may open the door to those who knock; only once, however, because it is already a second time; never, again, because the last time was in vain. . . .
>
> Since this second and last penitence is so serious a matter, it must be tested in a way which is proportionately laborious. Therefore it must not be performed solely within one's conscience but it must also be shown forth in some external act. This external act, rather expressively designated by the Greek word for it in common use, is *exomologesis*. Herein we confess our sin to the Lord, not as though he were ignorant of it, but because satisfaction receives its proper determination through confession, confession gives birth to penitence and by penitence God is appeased.
>
> *Exomologesis*, then, is a discipline which leads a man to prostrate and humble himself. It prescribes a way of life which, even in the matter of food and clothing, appeals to pity. It bids him to lie in sackcloth, to cover his body with filthy rags, to plunge his soul into sorrow, to exchange sin for suffering. Moreover, it demands that you know only such food and drink as is plain; this means it is taken for the sake of your soul, not your belly. It requires that you habitually nourish prayer by fasting, that you sigh and weep and groan day and night to the Lord your God, that you prostrate yourself at the feet of the priest and kneel before the beloved of God making all the brethren commissioned ambassadors for your pardon.[3]

The primary concern here is the disciplined life of the Christian community. Herman Wegman argues,

> The holiness of the community was a centrally important aim in the exercise of penance and reconciliation; therein was expressed the faithfulness to the way of the Lord that one had taken on through the confession of faith at baptism. That is why the baptismal theme stood out so clearly in the celebration of reconciliation.[4]

The reconciliation of penitents, like the baptism of catechumens, was an important part of the community's life, and so prayer for penitents as well as for catechumens found a regular place in the church's intercessions at public worship.

Canonical Penance in the Imperial Church and Early Middle Ages

The life of the church as a disciplined and cohesive community disintegrated at least in part with imperial recognition. Like baptismal discipline, penitential discipline was threatened by the end of the fourth century. Just as the church had difficulty giving adequate formation to the crowds who sought baptism by the end of this century, so the church had difficulty maintaining discipline among the throngs now baptized but inadequately catechized, only partly converted, and seldom formed in Christian practices. Public penance in this new situation was more public, and the church seems to have made it more arduous. Its administration was left less and less to the pastoral discernment of the bishop and more and more regulated by canonical legislation: public penance became canonical penance.[5] Penance took on an increasingly legal rather than remedial character, particularly in the West.

We see a fully developed scheme for public penance in the East in the liturgy of the *Apostolic Constitutions*, usually dated sometime in the course of the fourth century. This document develops the related material of the *Didascalia*, dating perhaps a century and a half earlier. The provisions include liturgical rites for admission as a penitent, special areas reserved for penitents in churches, special prayers offered for them at the eucharist and at morning and evening prayer, and a special rite of reconciliation.

Elsewhere there is evidence that the period of public penance was subdivided into stages — weepers (who could not enter the church), hearers (who could enter the vestibule), kneelers (who could enter the church but were required to kneel while others stood), and standers (who could stand with the others but were not yet restored to communion). But by the end of the century public penance and the order of penitents had been abolished in the East.

In the West during the fourth and fifth centuries, Lent became the time of public penance, with penitents admitted at the beginning of Lent and reconciled to the church by the bishop on Maundy Thursday or Good Friday, so that they might receive communion at the paschal eucharist. Many of the weekday Lenten propers for the eucharist in the Roman tradition are related to the program of public penance. But increasingly few entered the order of penitents of their own accord as time went on, and public penance fell into disuse in the West as the empire collapsed. The time of penance was frequently spent in a monastery, but even after reconciliation, penitents lived under restrictions for the rest of their lives. This procedure was so arduous that few underwent its rigors willingly, though it was still imposed by the church on those guilty of notorious sins which caused public scandal. Canonical penance provided no way to deal with the issue of penitence for less serious sins (later classified as venial sins). During this period, however, the faithful in general began to treat the season of Lent as a season of communal penance, undertaking some of the penitential exercises required of public penitents.

Liturgical Provisions

The liturgies for the admission of penitents at the beginning of Lent and the reconciliation of penitents on Maundy Thursday have been preserved for us in the sacramentaries, though it is not always easy to disentangle the stages of the development of these rites. By the seventh century, the time of the earliest form of the Gelasian sacramentary extant, the officiant clothed the penitents with hairshirts, dismissed them from the church, and shut them up (presumably in a monastery) for the duration of Lent.[6] The blessing of ashes with which we are familiar is not found in any of the early Roman sacramentaries but developed elsewhere, and by the time it was incorporated in the Roman liturgy (in the twelfth century), ashes were imposed on all who desired them. A group of psalms (6, 32, 38, 51, 102, 130, 143) came to be identified as the penitential psalms and to be used liturgically on various occasions as prayers of personal penitence and as intercession for those undergoing public penance.

Reconciliation came after the gospel on Maundy Thursday. Much of the rite for this day survived until the time of the Reformation and may be found in the Sarum missal, from which the following translations of some of the more ancient texts are taken.[7] A deacon began the rite by addressing the bishop on behalf of the penitents, prostrate outside the church in later forms of the rite,[8] with the following words:

> The accepted time is come, O venerable pontiff, the day of divine propitiation and salvation of men; when death was abolished, and eternal life begun; when a planting of new vines is so to be made in the vineyard of the Lord of Sabaoth, that the blindness of the old man may be purged away. For, albeit no time is devoid of the riches of the goodness of God, yet now forgiveness of sins is more ample by reason of his indulgence, and the admission of those who are reborn [in baptism] is more numerous by reason of his grace. By those to be regenerated we are increased in numbers, by those who return [to the unity of the church] we are increased in strength. Waters wash [in baptism]; tears wash [in penance]; hence there is joy over the receiving of those who are called [to baptism], and there is joy over the absolution of penitents. Hence it is that thy suppliants, after they, by neglect of the divine commandments and by transgression of approved morals, have fallen into divers kinds of sin, [now] cry unto God, humble and prostrate, in the words of prophet, saying, "We have sinned with our fathers; we have dealt wickedly; we have commit-

ted iniquity; have mercy, O Lord, upon us, who turn not a deaf ear to the gospel words, 'Blessed are they that mourn, for they shall be comforted.'" They have eaten, as it is written, the bread of affliction; they have watered their couch with tears; they have afflicted their soul with grief and their body with fasting, that they might recover the health of their souls which they had lost. Accordingly, it is the singular privilege of penitence that it is both profitable to the individual and conduceth to the common welfare of all. Renew, therefore, in them, O apostolic pontiff, whatsoever hath been decayed by the suggestion, or rage, or ravage of the devil; by the merits and patronage of thy prayers on their behalf, make them men near to God, through the grace of divine reconciliation; so that they who were before displeasing in their perverse ways, may now get the victory over the author of their death, and rejoice that they please the Lord in the land of the living.

This carefully crafted address reveals the close relationship which the church of the time saw between baptism and penance and articulates a theology of penance as a second baptism.

After this the penitents were led into the church and prostrated themselves before the bishop. What appear to be the most ancient texts of the rite are a preparatory collect, a prayer perhaps used while the bishop laid hands on each penitent in reconciliation, and a solemn prayer for the reconciliation of penitents sung to the preface tone (similar sets of texts are found for blessing the font, for the nuptial blessing, and for ordinations).[9] This is the text of the solemn prayer:

O God, most gracious creator, and most compassionate restorer of mankind, who by the blood of thine only Son hast redeemed mankind, cast down by the envy of the devil from immortality, quicken these thy servants, whom thou desirest in no wise to die unto thee, and do thou, who dost not leave them to stray, receive them back after correction. Let the sorrowful sighings of these thy servants, O Lord, we beseech thee, move thy loving kindness. Do thou heal their wounds, and stretch out thy saving hand to them as they lie before thee. Let not thy church be robbed of any part of her body. Let not thy flock suffer loss. Let not the enemy rejoice over the injury to thy family. Let not a second death get possession of those who have been born again in the laver of salvation. To thee, therefore, O Lord, we humbly offer our prayers; to thee we pour out the sorrows of our heart. Spare thou them that confess; that by thy aid they may so weep over their sins in this mortal life, that in the tremendous day of judgment they may escape the sentence of eternal damnation, and may never know, most loving Father, the terrors of darkness and the gnashing of teeth in flames; but that returning from the errors of their way into the path of righteousness, they may be wounded no more; but let that which thy grace hath bestowed and thy pity hath reformed, be made whole and entire; through Jesus Christ thy Son our Lord, who liveth and reigneth with thee, in the unity of the Holy Spirit, one God, for ever and ever. *Amen.*

Here the goal of penance in reconciliation of the penitent to the church articulates the communal dimensions of the process and the concern with the holiness of the church. The bishop reconciled penitents by laying hands on them and then raised them up.

There were attempts to revive public penance in the Carolingian era, and Frankish and German rites elaborated the original Roman provisions with further material. The liturgy for Ash Wednesday in these regions was typologically interpreted to represent the expulsion of Adam from paradise[10] — a theme also represented by the *troparia* of the Sabaite form of the Byzantine office for the Sunday before Lent. The blessing of ashes with which we are familiar comes from these sources and did not enter the

Roman liturgy until the twelfth century by way of the Germano-Roman Pontifical.[11] By that time the ashes were imposed on all, not just public penitents. Reconciliation was also elaborated with further prayers and ritual actions in these traditions.[12]

2. Tariff Penance and Auricular Confession

Public penance by its very character was best suited to more serious sins. But this process was poorly suited to the primary need of most ordinary Christians — pastoral care which brought them to repentance for their daily sins and inculcated the need for continuing conversion. This was a need which Augustine had recognized in the Latin West. He speaks of three kinds of penitence — the penitence which leads to baptism, the penitence for serious sins which require public penance, and

> daily penance. Where in Scripture can we show this kind of daily penance? I have no better evidence than the daily prayer in which our Lord taught us what to say to the Father. He put it thus: "Forgive us our debts as we forgive our debtors" (Matthew 6:12).[13]

This kind of penitence did not find adequate expression in the liturgical formularies of the West in the early centuries, however. Not until some time in the middle ages did general confessions and absolutions enter the daily office and the eucharist. The Lenten provisions for public penance, as they came to be undertaken voluntarily by the whole church through fasting, prayer, and almsgiving, met this need in some ways. As the Lenten provisions for the preparation of candidates for baptism receded in importance, the provisions for public penance became more prominent, and Christians not subject to public penance began to associate themselves with these penitential exercises also.

The canons of the Council of Nicea had mandated that no one in danger of death be denied reconciliation to the church, and many Christians alienated from the church by their sin postponed doing penance as earlier

Christians had postponed baptism, so that penance became something of a last rite in many cases. The church could require public penance of those whose sins were notorious; it had no way of submitting to public penance those whose sins were serious but not public, however, or of dealing with the everyday sins of ordinary Christians. Public penance was not suited to the pastoral care of ordinary Christians, and the result was that many went through much of their lives cut off from the sacramental life of the church because they were unwilling to submit to the drastic disciplines which were the principal way which the church provided for resolving their relationship with God.

After the fall of the empire in the West, a variety of solutions were sought for this dilemma.[14] Carolingian bishops sought to encourage more widespread use of public penance — with little success. Deathbed penance, which brought immediate reconciliation without public penance, remained the practice of many; we find special provisions for it in the sacramentaries and ordines. In France it began to be customary to allow priests to supervise privately the penance of those whose sins were serious but not public, and then to present them to the bishop for reconciliation; sometimes bishops also allowed priests to reconcile them. The voluntary but communal penitential exercises of Lent served as means of dealing with less serious sins, and the reconciliation of penitents on Maundy Thursday was sometimes extended to those who had joined in the penitential exercises of Lent.

Another approach — which was ultimately to prevail, had its origin in the monasticism which had grown up after the fourth century. Monastic life was often understood as a life of penance and continuing conversion, and the movement grew because serious Christians found in monasticism a discipline of Christian formation not available in the ordinary life of the church. The very name given in the West to those who associated themselves with monastic communities in a life of penance, *conversi*, "those who have undertaken conversion," indicates the penitential emphasis of much monastic life.[15] In the life of a monastery, practical wisdom was developed for dealing with sin. This differed from public penance in at least four ways: 1) skill as a guide was unrelated to ordination, and few early monks were ordained;

2) emphasis was placed on matching penances as remedies to particular sins; 3) because the process was private, it concluded with the penitent's fulfilment of the remedy, rather than in public reconciliation with the church; 4) since conversion was an ongoing process, this kind of penance was not restricted to once in a lifetime. Monks who developed skills in such guidance were also sought out by lay persons who associated themselves with the monasteries.

Penitence under the direction of these monks, which was personal rather than public, was an important aspect in the life of Eastern Christianity. Similar practices evolved in Celtic Christianity, where monks devised from the sixth to the ninth centuries penitentials with penances "graded" according to the nature of sin as guides for directing penitents. As these monks spread across the European continent in their missionary zeal, they took their penitential practices with them. The type of penance which they instituted has come to be known as "tariff" penance because of these "schedules" of penances. By the seventh century, this was becoming the way in which ordinary Christians found pastoral remedy for their sins. In this situation, penitents made their confessions to the monks and were assigned appropriate penances. There was no formal and public entry into the order of penitents: the process was a private matter between the confessor and the penitent. The process found its conclusion in the fulfilment of the penance, after which the penitent returned to communion, rather than in an official act of reconciliation with the church.

Out of this variety of approaches a new form of penance emerged — that with which we are familiar today. Like tariff penance, it was private rather than public. But by the ninth century in the West, the church insisted that — except in emergencies — the confessor be a priest, and in ordinary circumstances one's parish priest. The priest might also use the occasion to instruct penitents on the basic elements of the Christian faith. Like tariff penance, this form was not a remedy available once in a lifetime, but part of ongoing pastoral care. Penances were imposed, but they eventually came to be performed after absolution, for as in deathbed penance reconciliation was pronounced at once. The penance was performed after absolution as an act of gratitude and contrition. Scholastic theologians gave new importance to absolution or official reconciliation; in the sacramental theology which they developed for penance, the "form" of the sacrament required to make it objectively effective were the words "I absolve you" and older liturgical formularies, where reconciliation was expressed by prayer rather than this declaratory phrase addressed to the penitent, were revised accordingly.

By the fourth Lateran Council in 1215, this had become ordinary means of the church's pastoral care for sinners. Although the communal dimension of reconciliation with the church had receded into the background, a sense of the necessity of reconciliation with God before communion remained strong, and confession before the principal festivals was often recommended, so that people could receive communion at the eucharist on the feast day. The council mandated an annual confession before Easter communion for all Christians who had reached the age of discretion. Although canon law only required absolution for mortal sins before receiving communion, most Christians came to communion each time only after they had made their confession, and the custom of receiving communion only after confession remained the ordinary practice of Roman Catholics until recent decades. Frequent confession became a means of grace and an act of devotion, even for those whose sins were venial rather than mortal.

Liturgical Forms

The confession of sins took place in three ways in the texts which have come down to us: the confessor might examine the penitent to determine the sins, the penitent might bring specific sins to the confessor, or the penitent might make a general confession which covered all sins. Eventually the customary form developed for the daily office and the eucharist was adapted for the purposes of auricular confession. Reconciliation was expressed at first by formulas borrowed from other services, but the need for a declarative absolution and for "applying" the church's treasury of merit led to the addition of other forms. The form issued by the Council of Trent had the following texts for the purpose of reconciliation. The first two are from texts used in the office and the eucharist. The third contains what scholastic theologians considered the "form" of penance as a sacrament. The fourth expresses the church's intercession for the penitent and articulates the theology of the "treasury of merits."

> May Almighty God have mercy upon you, forgive your sins, and lead you to eternal life. Amen.

> May the almighty and merciful God grant to you pardon, absolution, and remission of all your sins. Amen.

> May our Lord Jesus Christ absolve you, and I by his authority absolve you from every bond of excommunication and interdict, as far as I am able and you need it. And I absolve you from your sins in the name of the Father, and of the Son, and of the Holy Spirit. Amen.

> May the Passion of our Lord Jesus Christ, the merits of the blessed Virgin Mary and of all the saints, whatsoever good you do and evil you endure be to you for the remission of sins, the increase of grace, and the reward of eternal life. Amen.[16]

The Theology of Sacramental Confession

It was only in the middle ages that Western theologians formulated in a systematic way a theology of the sacraments. The Latin *sacramentum* translated the Greek *mysterion* and had its roots in the biblical idea of the secret purposes of God, revealed to the prophets and fulfilled in Christ. A typological reading of the process related the worship of the church to the salvation achieved in Christ and foreshadowed in the Old Testament. As definitions were sharpened and narrowed, sacraments came to be understood as outward and visible signs which were the instrumental means by which Christ's work is mediated to us. A theology was elaborated out of disputes about the eucharist and initiation and then applied to other rites. It needs to be noted that in this sense, sacrament is not a biblical word. The New Testament never speaks of sacraments in this sense: sacrament is a theological category defined by theologians and superimposed on the church's rites. Not until the fourth Lateran Council was the number of sacraments fixed in the West. Penance was a relatively recent addition to the list of sacraments, and it fits awkwardly into sacramental categories such as matter, form, and minister. Interpreting penance in this context brought the formula of absolution into new prominence as the "form" of the sacrament: the earlier emphasis had fallen on the laying on of hands by the bishop and restoration to communion. But ordinary Christians found the sacramental status of the rite pastorally reassuring, because it secured the objective offer of God's forgiveness.

It was the nature of penances in "tariff penance" and its descendants which created the greatest theological problems in the theology of this sacrament. While at first penances in both public penance and tariff penance were understood as remedies to restore the sinner and the Christian community to health, the legal spirit of Western theology soon led them to be understood less as appropriate remedies for particular sins than as legal satisfaction of the requirements of divine justice which had to be fulfilled in this life or in the life to come. We find this legal language of satisfaction as early as Tertullian; it also meshed with the ideas of Germanic law; and Anselm gave it powerful theological expression at the beginning the theological renaissance of the middle ages. As the theology of tariff penance evolved, the priestly absolution was understood to reconcile the penitent to God, but not to remit the penalty due for the sin: satisfaction must be made by penances in this life and — to the extent that this satisfaction is not completed in this life — in purgatory after one's death. Priestly absolution secured God's forgiveness and assured the sinner of ultimate salvation, but did not remit the penalties that must be paid before the sinner achieved union with God. So long as penances had been understood as remedies intended to restore the spiritual health of the penitent and the community, they had stayed within the intention of the New Testament. But when the language of satisfaction began to lead the church to understand them as penalties incurred by sin which must be "paid off" by penitents before they could "merit" salvation, abuses arose.

The "debt" incurred was quantified and could be redeemed in a number of ways. One might pay for masses to meet the debt, since the sacrifice of the mass was coming to be understood as having "merit" in its own right. One could undertake a pilgrimage or perform pious acts for which the church would issue an indulgence — a partial or full remission of the debt. When pious acts included donations to the church's enterprises (such as the building of the Vatican basilica), the impression was given that salvation could be bought, although strictly speaking it was remission of temporal punishments, not forgiveness of sins, that was granted by indulgences. In addition, the "merit" of prayers and masses for the departed was thought to help release them from purgatory by "paying off" their debt. For this reason, votive offices and masses for the dead grew to become a dominant part of the church's worship. The basis of all these transactions was the doctrine that the "surplus" merits of Christ and the saints were a treasury at the church's disposal.

Although a form of auricular confession evolved in the Byzantine tradition[17] as well, Eastern theology worked with neither this understanding of satisfaction nor with this legalistic perspective on the process of purification after death. The rite is seen as second baptism, a means of reconciliation with the church. The Western language of satisfaction is not to be found in the rite. Monks have continued to be important as spiritual directors in the pastoral care of Christians of the Byzantine rite in many churches, and their direction plays an important role in the continuing conversion of lay persons. The ordinary form of forgiveness remains a prayer in form, though some churches in the Byzantine tradition have adopted the declaratory form under the influence of Western sacramental theology. Alexander Schmemann captures very well the spirit of this rite:

> Baptism is forgiveness of sins, not their removal. It introduces the sword of Christ into our lives and makes it the real conflict, the inescapable pain and suffering of growth. It is indeed after baptism and because of it, that the reality of sin can be recognized in all its sadness, and true repentance becomes possible. Therefore, the whole life of the Church is at the same

time the gift of forgiveness, the joy of the "world to come," and also and inescapably a constant repentance. The *feast* is impossible without the *fast*, and the fast is precisely repentance and return, the saving experience of sadness and exile. The Church is the gift of the Kingdom — yet it is this very gift that makes obvious our absence from the Kingdom, our alienation from God. It is repentance that takes us again and again into the joy of the Paschal banquet, but it is that joy which reveals to us our sinfulness and puts us under judgment.

The *sacrament of penance* is not, therefore, a sacred and juridical "power" given by God to men. It is the power of baptism as it lives in the Church. From baptism it receives its sacramental character. In Christ all sins are forgiven once and for all, for He is Himself the forgiveness of sins, and there is no need for any "new" absolution. But there is indeed the need for us who constantly *leave* Christ and *excommunicate* ourselves from His life, to return to Him, to receive again and again the gift that has been given once and for all. And the absolution is the sign that this return has taken place and has been fulfilled. Just as each Eucharist is not a "repetition" of Christ's supper but our ascension, our acceptance into the same and eternal banquet, so also the sacrament of penance is not a repetition of baptism, but our return to the "newness of life" which God gave to us once and for all.[18]

3. Penance at the Reformation and in the Book of Common Prayer

The Approach of the Reformers

It was, in part, the abuses related to the penitential system of the middle ages — in particular, the sale of indulgences — which triggered the Reformation of the sixteenth century. The doctrine of justification by grace swept away the idea that penitents could make "satisfaction" for their sins, though the entire issue continued to be debated in juridical terms. The Reformed tradition and the Anglican reformers both made attempts to restore the ancient penitential discipline characteristic of public penance, though the Reformed tradition was not inclined to approve of the outward signs of penitence, such as sackcloth and ashes, characteristic of public penance in the early church. Reformation England and Calvinist Geneva were both characterized by the cooperation of church and state in enforcing this discipline, though civil and ecclesiastical authorities worked much more closely together in this effort in Geneva than in England, where the Puritan party was never able to institute the stricter ecclesiastical discipline characteristic of the Reformed tradition. Only the radical reformers aimed at the creation of a church community distinct from the world with its own discipline enforced by purely internal constraints rather than the compulsory force of civil law. For this reason the anabaptists and their heirs are the only reformers who really recaptured the spirit of the penitential discipline of the first three centuries, when the church was radically distinct from its environing society.

Luther, Calvin, and the English reformers were all concerned to make the weekly celebration of the Lord's Supper the heart of the life of the parish community. But they all had an equal concern to "fence the table" — to admit only serious Christians who approached the table with faith and repentance. One common technique was to preface the celebration with an exhortation which spelled out what was required of those who wished to receive communion. Reformed liturgies in particular made this exhortation a prominent feature of the eucharist. The most serious attempt to secure worthy communicants was probably the Reformed custom of communion tokens issued by the elders to those whom they found in good standing in the church. Luther and Cranmer made provision for auricular confession as a preparation for communion. Neither required it, though it remained a significant practice in Lutheran churches until the disruption of church life by the wars of religion. In both traditions, the theology of the rite was distinctly different from that of the middle ages, for in the Reformation traditions the idea that penitents could make adequate satisfaction for their sins was considered contrary to the gospel.

The Provisions of the Book of Common Prayer

Lent and Public Penance: The Anglican provisions are set out in the 1549 Book of Common Prayer and have remained substantially the same in subsequent revisions. Like all liturgies of the era, the eucharistic rite of the Book of Common Prayer included a general confession — a feature which was also included in the orders for morning and evening prayer in 1552. Cranmer's attitude toward public penance is set out in the service which he drafted for Ash Wednesday, known after 1552 as a "commination against sinners." Cranmer put an end to the imposition of ashes on this day, but he was well aware of the fact that the day in earlier centuries had marked the beginning of public penance and created a liturgy from that perspective. The service, which follows morning prayer and the litany on that day, begins with this opening exhortation, which sets out his intentions:

> Brethren, in the prymitiue churche there was a godlye disciplyne, that at the begynning of lente suche persones as were notorious synners, were put to open penaunce, and punished in this worlde, that theyr soules myght bee saued in the day of the lord. And that other admonished by theyr example, might be more afrayed to offend. In the steede whereof until the same disciplyne may bee restored agayne; (whiche thynge is muche to bee wyshed,) it is thoughte good, that at thys tyme (in your presence) shoulde bee read the general sentences of goddes cursyng agaynste impenitente sinners, gathered out of the xxvii Chapter of Deuteronomie, and other places of scripture. And that ye should aunswere to every sentence, Amen; to thentente that you beeyng admonished of the greate indignacion of God agaynst sinners: may the rather be called to earneste and true repentaunce, and maye walke more warely in these daungerous dayes, fleying from such vices, for the whiche ye affirme with your owne mouthes: the curse of god to be due.[19]

The exhortation is followed by the curses, and then a further exhortation to repentance. The office closed with the recitation of Psalm 51, a set of preces, and three prayers — all adapted from the traditional Ash Wednesday rite of the Sarum missal.

The full ancient discipline of public penance was never restored. But public penance was indeed enforced by both ecclesiastical and civil courts for notorious sins, as various church records bear witness. The discipline did not entirely die out until the nineteenth century. Sinners might be required to do penance by standing in church in linen gowns with a wand for specified periods of time, until they were publicly reconciled by the minister, upon due testimony of repentance, after the second lesson of morning prayer. It is far from certain that this public penance had the desired result: it did indeed serve as a warning against sin, but it was intensely unpopular and served to alienate many from the church.

Auricular Confession: We find reference to auricular confession in two places in the 1549 Book of Common Prayer — in the exhortation at communion and in the order for the visitation of the sick. In one of the exhortations with which the communion table was fenced, we find these words:

> And yf there bee any of you, whose conscience is troubled and greued in any thing, lackyng comforte or counsaill, let him come to me, or to some other dyscrete and learned priest, taught in the law of God, and confess his synne and griefe secretly, that he may receiue such ghostly counsaill, aduyse, and comfort, that his conscience may be releued, and that of us (as of the ministers of GOD and of the churche) he may receiue comfort and absolucion, to the satisfaccion of his mynde, and auoyding of all scruple and doubtfulnes: requiryng suche as shalbe satisfied with a generall confession, not to be offended with them that doe use, to their further satisfying, the auriculer and secret confession to the Priest: nor those also whiche thinke nedefull or conuenient, for the quietnes of their awne conscience, particuliarly to open their sinnes to the Priest: to bee offended with them that are satisfied, with their humble confession

to GOD, and the generall confession to the churche. But in all thinges to folowe the rule of charitie, not judgyng other mennes myndes or consciences; where as he hath no warrant of Goddes word to the same.[20]

Substantially the same advice is given in this exhortation in the subsequent English editions of the prayer book, although the concluding portion which commends the legitimacy of both general confession and auricular confession was omitted. Indeed, future prayer books ceased to use the term "auricular confession."

The reference in the visitation of the sick includes both encouragement for those who are seriously ill to make a special confession and the form of absolution to be used in all auricular confessions:

Here shall the sicke person make a speciall confession, yf he fele his conscience troubled with any weightie matter. After which confession, the priest shall absolue him after this forme: and the same forme of absolution shalbe used in all pryvate confessions.

Our Lord Jesus Christ, who hath lefte power to his Churche to absolue all sinners, which truely repent and beleue in hym: of his great mercy forgeue thee thyne offences: and by his autoritie committed to me, I absolue thee from all thy synnes, in the name of the father, and of the sonne, and of the holy gost. Amen.[21]

This provision too remained in subsequent prayer books, though the rubric was reworked in 1662 so that the priest absolved the penitent "if he humbly and heartily desire it," and the mention of other occasions for private confession was removed in 1552.[22] While this office gives a form for absolution, it provides no forms for the confession or for the administration of auricular confession in other circumstances. English clergy drafted such forms from time to time, but none was ever incorporated into the prayer book.

The authority of clergy to grant absolution was a matter of some debate at the Reformation, both in England and elsewhere, but the English formularies consistently affirmed it. From the beginning, the ordination of priests included as part of the charge during the laying on of hands, "whose synnes thou doest forgeue, they are forgeuen: and whose sinnes thou doest retain, thei are retained."[23] Provisions for both public penance and auricular confession were grounded in this "power of the keys."

Subsequent Developments: Some forms of public penance lasted until the nineteenth century, when the power of ecclesiastical courts was reduced, but the practice of public penance died out over the centuries.[24] It might legitimately be asked whether it ever successfully served the ends for which it was intended — the preservation of the church's holiness as a community. Auricular confession never became a general practice in the Church of England after the Reformation, though it was known in the sixteenth and seventeenth centuries and Anglican authors generally defended the practice. It was revived — with considerable opposition — in the nineteenth century during the Oxford movement.

In the American Episcopal Church, the English provisions were attenuated. The Ash Wednesday service was drastically abbreviated in 1789, and although subsequent books once again enriched these provisions, the commination exhortations were not restored. No form of public penance is envisaged by the American prayer books. The communion reference to auricular confession was likewise modified to remove the reference to absolution, and in the office for the visitation of the sick, there was no reference to a special confession until the revision of 1928. The only service to mention such a special confession and absolution was the 1789 office for visitation of prisoners. That revision did not use the absolution from the English book, but substituted the one from the eucharist.[25] It was the Oxford movement which introduced auricular confession to the American church, where it was as fiercely resisted at first as it was in England in the same period.

The Theology of the Provisions: John Gunstone in his study of penance argues that there are five chief features of Anglican teaching in classic authors on penance as it relates especially to auricular confession:

1. The meaning of repentance is understood to include all personal penitence in a life of continuing conversion; classical Anglican authors rejected the scholastic narrowing of the term to the context of auricular confession.
2. Although they strongly affirmed the biblical basis of ministerial authority to forgive the sins of the penitent ("the power of the keys"), they declined to include such absolution within the definition of a sacrament for lack of an outward sign.
3. Although they recognized the more serious nature of some sins, they generally denied the scholastic distinction between mortal and venial sins.
4. They rejected the scholastic doctrine of "satisfaction" out of their conviction that Christ had made the "full, perfect, and sufficient sacrifice, oblation, and *satisfaction* for the sins of the whole world."
5. They rejected the rule which obliged Christians to go to auricular confession once a year, though they made the ministry available to those who wished to avail themselves of it.[26]

4. The Provisions of the Book of Common Prayer 1979

Ash Wednesday and Lent as a Time of Public Penitence for the Whole Church

By the time the revision which led to the Book of Common Prayer 1979 was under way, the Episcopal Church was ready to rethink the ministry of reconciliation as that found expression in its liturgy. The new rite for Ash Wednesday sounds once again the penitential note of Lent, but carefully sets it in relation to Lent as a season of preparation for baptism. The rite is set in the context of the eucharist for the day, and begins with a carefully crafted exhortation after the sermon:

> Dear People of God: The first Christians observed with great devotion the days of our Lord's passion and resurrection, and it became the custom of the Church to prepare

for them by a season of penitence and fasting. This season of Lent provided a time in which converts to the faith were prepared for Holy Baptism. It was also a time when those who, because of notorious sins, had been separated from the body of the faithful were reconciled by penitence and forgiveness, and restored to the fellowship of the Church. Thereby, the whole congregation was put in mind of the message of pardon and absolution set forth in the gospel of our Savior, and of the need which all Christians continually have to renew their repentance and faith.

I invite you, therefore, in the name of the Church, to the observance of a holy Lent, by self-examination and repentance; by prayer, fasting, and self-denial; and by reading and meditating on God's holy Word. . . .[27]

The revisers, like Cranmer, took note of the ancient practice of public penance. But they call, not for the restoration of this discipline, but for the continuing conversion of the whole church (summoning Christians "to renew their repentance and faith").

If desired, this may be followed by a prayer over ashes, which are to be imposed as "a sign of mortality and penitence" on those who desire them.[28] The traditional sentence for the imposition of ashes follows. The service continues with the recitation of Psalm 51 (during the distribution of ashes, if they are imposed). The penitential rite concludes with a confession and a penitential litany, which carefully spells out the corporate as well as the personal dimensions of sin. The litany ends with the absolution — the old text from Morning and Evening Prayer put to a new use. The eucharist continues with the peace.

While the drafters of the 1979 book made no effort to restore public penance, those who know the history of the rites for Ash Wednesday and Maundy Thursday will be able to discern that the process in the *Book of Occasional Services* known as Preparation of Baptized Persons for Reaffirmation of the Baptismal Covenant is a skillful adaptation of public penance, interpreted as a particular expression of the need for continuing conversion. Since the candidates are already baptized, they should be regular communicants during the time of preparation as a means of growth in the faith. In the rite which is the analogue of admission to candidacy in the baptismal process, the candidates for reaffirmation are called to conversion. After an examination of their sponsors in the progress of the candidates in their preparation, the candidates first receive ashes and then join the celebrant in imposing them on the rest of the congregation.

On Maundy Thursday, the second form for the reconciliation of a penitent is used for a general confession, and the candidates are individually reconciled with the laying on of hands with the text of the first form of absolution. Then their feet are washed by the celebrant, and they in turn wash the feet of other members of the congregation. The process ends with the renewal of the baptismal covenant at the Easter vigil and (if the bishop is present) the laying on of hands. If the bishop is not present at the vigil, the candidates are to be presented to the bishop during Easter Season for the laying on of hands.

Skillful as the adaptation is, it presents some problems. Although it is specifically designated for those being confirmed and those being received into the Episcopal Church as well as for those reaffirming their baptismal vows, it is really best suited to those in the last category who are returning to the practice of the Christian faith after a lapse. It is for them that the solemn act of reconciliation on Maundy Thursday makes most sense. It seems inappropriate to suggest that those baptized in infancy who are making their first solemn affirmation of the baptismal covenant in confirmation or those being received from another church should be singled out from others for a solemn reconciliation. And it is perhaps unwise to associate so closely the Maundy Thursday laying on of hands in absolution with an Easter laying on of hands in strengthening. To do so makes the laying on of hands for strengthening in some ways anticlimactic. The problem becomes more acute if the second laying on of hands cannot take place at the vigil but is postponed until sometime later in Easter season. The decision of the 1979 book *not* to delegate the authority to presbyters to lay on hands in confirmation as other churches do is particularly problematic here. It would seem more apt to use the confession as a congregational text followed by a general absolution on Maundy Thursday and to let the laying on of hands by a presbyter at the vigil serve to reconcile as well as to strengthen.

The Ministry of Reconciliation and the Reconciliation of a Penitent

We noted above the attenuation of provisions in American prayer books for auricular confession. The 1979 book has reversed the process and strengthened the provisions considerably. The word absolution is restored in the exhortation from the eucharist. But the book goes considerably farther than that. For the first time it makes the rite for auricular confession into a distinct office, known as the Reconciliation of a Penitent, rather than simply including provisions for it in the ministry to the sick. Indeed, the office was intentionally separated from the ministry to the sick (though its use is suggested there), in order to avoid the suggestion that it should primarily be reserved for that situation.

The need for continuing conversion has been carefully articulated in many of the 1979 rites. A general confession and absolution is provided for both the eucharist and the daily office. On occasion, the eucharist may begin with the penitential order. A commitment to "persevere in resisting evil," and if we "fall into sin," to "repent and return to the Lord" is included in the baptismal covenant at baptism and whenever the covenant is renewed by the congregation and the individual Christian (at the baptismal feasts and baptism at other times, at the time when a solemn affirmation of the baptismal covenant is made before the bishop, and in the form of commitment to Christian service). The marriage rite includes a prayer for the couple that they may have "grace, when they hurt each other, to acknowledge their fault, and to seek each other's forgiveness and [God's]." Confession is one of the components of the ministry to the sick. Prayers at the time of death ask God to set the person "free from every bond" and to "acknowledge . . . a sinner of your own redeeming." The prayers of the people at burial (Rite I) ask "pardon and peace" for the congregation and that the departed may be received into "the arms of [God's] mercy." A new church is dedicated as a place "to ask [God's] forgiveness."

The opening sentences of the directions for the reconciliation of a penitent balance this emphasis on continuing conversion and repentance by setting the church's ministry of reconciliation carefully in a broad perspective. The ordination rites emphasize the role of the ordained in this ministry: the prayer for the consecration of a bishop speaks of the bishop's "ministry of reconciliation"; priests at the exhortation before their ordination are reminded of their task "to declare God's forgiveness to penitent sinners"; deacons are bidden to "make Christ and his redemptive love known." But this ministry of the ordained needs to be set in the wider context of the ministry of reconciliation of the whole church:

> The ministry of reconciliation, which has been committed by Christ to his Church, is exercised through the care each Christian has for others, through the common prayer of Christians assembled for public worship, and through the priesthood of the Church and its ministers declaring absolution.[29]

The next sentence carefully corrects the suggestion that the reconciliation of a penitent is appropriate only at the visitation of the sick:

> The Reconciliation of a Penitent is available for all who desire it. It is not restricted to times of sickness. Confessions may be heard at any time and anywhere.[30]

The ancient custom of lay confessors in explicitly recognized, though they are not authorized to pronounce absolution, which is reserved to priests:

> The absolution in these services may be pronounced only by a bishop or priest. Another Christian may be asked to hear a confession, but it must be made clear to the penitent that absolution will not be pronounced; instead, a declaration of forgiveness is provided.[31]

Finally, it is made quite clear that any "penance" assigned is not to be understood as "satisfaction":

Before giving absolution, the priest may assign to the penitent a psalm, prayer, or hymn to be said, or something to be done, *as a sign of penitence and act of thanksgiving.*[32]

The first form for the rite is an adaptation of the standard Western form of confession, with either the absolution from the prayer book or another (see below). The second form is far more imaginative. Drafted by Thomas Talley on the basis of Byzantine forms, it explicitly sets the rite in a baptismal context. In its original form (modified in the 1979 rite) it included a renewal of the baptismal covenant, as does the Byzantine form. The rite as a whole is set in the context of the parable of the prodigal son.[33] It begins with the recitation of a portion of Psalm 51, concluded by the trisagion, and continues with the blessing of the penitent. The confessor may then continue with a scriptural word of assurance (the comfortable words from the eucharist are suggested). The confession itself follows:

The Priest then continues

Now, in the presence of Christ, and of me, his minister, confess your sins with a humble and obedient heart to Almighty God, our Creator and Redeemer.

The Penitent says

Holy God, heavenly Father, you formed me from the dust in your image and likeness, and redeemed me from sin and death by the cross of your Son Jesus Christ. Through the water of baptism you clothed me with the shining garment of his righteousness, and established me among your children in your kingdom. But I have squandered the inheritance of your saints, and have wandered far in a land that is waste.

Especially, I confess to you and to the Church . . .

Here the penitent confesses particular sins.

Therefore, O Lord, from these and all other sins I cannot

now remember, I turn to you in sorrow and repentance. Receive me again into the arms of your mercy, and restore me to the blessed company of your faithful people; through him in whom you have redeemed the world, your Son our Savior Jesus Christ.

Here we note the theology of reconciliation as a second baptism and also a strong emphasis on its corporate dimensions. The confessor offers words of comfort and counsel and may (according to the opening rubrics) assign a prayer or action as a sign of penitence or thanksgiving to the penitent. The dialogue which follows (which originally included a renewal of the baptismal covenant) emphasizes the need for continuing conversion:

> *Priest* Will you turn again to Christ as your Lord?
> *Penitent* I will.
>
> *Priest* Do you, then, forgive those who have sinned against you?
> *Penitent* I forgive them.

The confessor then continues with a prayer for the penitent and gives absolution, using one of two alternative forms and laying hands on the penitent's head. The text of the prayer and of the first alternative for absolution are as follows:

> May Almighty God in mercy receive your confession of sorrow and of faith, strengthen you in all goodness, and by the power of the Holy Spirit keep you in eternal life. *Amen.*
>
> Our Lord Jesus Christ, who offered himself to be sacrificed for us to the Father, and who conferred power on his Church to forgive sins, absolve you through my ministry by the grace of the Holy Spirit, and restore you to the perfect peace of the Church. *Amen.*

The conclusion of the rite draws again on the parable of the prodigal son:

The Priest concludes

Now there is rejoicing in heaven, for you were lost, and are found, you were dead and are now alive in Christ Jesus our Lord. Go (*or* abide) in peace. The Lord has put away all your sins.

Penitent

Thanks be to God.

Conclusions

The Book of Common Prayer 1979 has successfully recovered the penitential theology of earlier centuries preserved in the Byzantine tradition. The Christian life is set in the context of continuing conversion and penitence — an emphasis which finds expression in all the rites of the book and has a particular focus in the celebration of Lent as a corporate renewal of baptismal conversion. The catechism gives recognition to the reconciliation of a penitent as a sacramental expression of the church's ministry of reconciliation, though it does not reckon reconciliation as a sacrament of the gospel in the same sense as baptism and the eucharist are:

Q. What are the sacraments?

A. The sacraments are outward and visible signs of inward and spiritual grace, given by Christ as sure and certain means by which we receive that grace.

Q. What is grace?

A. Grace is God's favor towards us, unearned and undeserved; by grace God forgives our sins, enlightens our minds, stirs our hearts, and strengthens our wills.

Q. What are the two great sacraments of the Gospel?

A. The two great sacraments given by Christ to his Church are Holy Baptism and the Holy Eucharist.

. . . .

Q. How do [other sacramental rites] differ from the two great sacraments of the Gospel?

A. Although they are means of grace, they are not necessary for all persons in the same way that Baptism and the Eucharist are.

. . . .

Q. What is the Reconciliation of a Penitent?

A. Reconciliation of a Penitent, or Penance, is the rite in which those who repent of their sins may confess theirs sins to God in the presence of a priest, and receive the assurance of pardon and the grace of absolution.[34]

The Reconciliation of a Penitent is indeed an occasion of grace. In this rite, as Schmemann says, we experience "the power of baptism as it lives in the church,"[35] for God's prodigal children are given the grace to return home, the lost are found, and the dead come to new life, for God has put away their sins through the cross of Christ.

ENDNOTES

[1]*One* penance became the rule in Rome and in North Africa and there is similar evidence for Alexandria. *The Shepherd of Hermas* is the key text in this strand of the tradition. Other Eastern literature does not treat penance as unrepeatable, however.

[2]On public penance, see chapters 1-3 in James Dallen, *The Reconciling Community* (New York: Pueblo, 1986; Collegeville, MN: Liturgical Press, 1991), and s. v. "Reconciliation, Sacrament of," in Peter Fink, ed., *The New Dictionary of Sacramental Worship* (Collegeville, MN: Liturgical Press, 1990), pages 1052-1064; Pierre Marie Gy, "Penance and Reconciliation," in A. G. Martimort, *The Church at Prayer,* vol. III, trans. Matthew J. O'Connell (Collegeville, MN: Liturgical Press, 1988), pages 97-115; Joseph A. Favazza, *The Order of Penitents: Historical Roots and Pastoral Future* (Collegeville, MN: Liturgical Press, 1988); John Gunstone, *The Liturgy of Penance* (London: Faith Press, 1966).

[3]*De poenitentia* 9, in *Tertullian: Treatises on Penance: On Penance and Purity*, trans. William Le Saint, Ancient Christian Writers 28 (Westminister, MD, 1959), pages 31-32. Tertullian's rigorism would later drive him after he became a Montanist to repudiate this stance (from his Catholic days) and adopt the more rigorist one of his later tract, *De Puditia*, where serious sins

require the church to impose penitence, but do not allow for reconciliation.

[4]Herman Wegman, *Christian Worship in East and West: A Study Guide to Liturgical History* (New York: Pueblo, 1985), page 47.

[5]With canonical legislation, the rule of one penance (which had earlier prevailed in most of the Latin West and North Africa and in Alexandria, but was seldom invoked in the East) became universal. In addition, certain restrictions were placed on those who had done penance even after their reconciliation. For the distinction between the earlier practice and canonical penance, see Joseph A. Favazza, *The Order of Penitents*, pages 247-253.

[6]For the rite in the Gelasian sacramentary, see L. K. Mohlberg, ed., *Liber sacramentorum Romanae aeclesiae ordinis anni circuli*, Rerum ecclesiasticarum documenta, Series maior, Fontes 4 (Rome: Herder, 1960), 15-17, nos. 78-83, pages 17-56. Being "shut up" was probably a later development. No doubt the earlier custom was temporarily to "shut" penitents "out" of the church. For the very complex development of the rites of Ash Wednesday, see Kenneth Stevenson, "Origins and Development of Ash Wednesday," in idem, *Worship: Wonderful and Sacred Mystery* (Washington, DC: Pastoral Press, 1992), pages 159-187. Stevenson carefully traces the evolution of the Ash Wednesday rite from admission to public penance to its later treatment as the beginning of Lenten penitential exercises for all Christians. It should be noted that it is probable that (self-administered) ashes were probably in use long before the custom of blessing was adopted.

[7]F. E. Warren, trans., *The Sarum Missal in English, Part II* (London: De La More Press, 1911), pages 236-240. I have emended the texts slightly for a closer rendition of the Latin, and have added words in brackets to bring out the sense. For the Latin texts of the Gelasian sacramentary, see L. K. Mohlberg, ed., *Liber sacramentorum Romanae aeclesiae ordinis anni circuli*, § 17, nos. 352-359, pages 56-58.

[8]In the Gelasian sacramentary, the rite began with this address while the penitents were prostrate before the bishop in the church. The Gelasian form of this text is found in L. C. Mohlberg, ed., *Liber sacramentorum Romanae aeclesiae ordinis anni circuli*, § 17, nos. 353-354, pages 56-57.

[9]For the text of these three prayers, see L. C. Mohlberg, ed., *Liber sacramentorum Romanae aeclesiae ordinis anni circuli*, § 17, nos. 357-359, page 57. A similar set is found in nos. 360-363 — perhaps these were originally

the texts from another tradition. The translation here is adapted from that found in *The Sarum Missal*.

[10]See the description of the rite in the Pontifical of Durandus of Mende found in Thomas Talley, "The Liturgy of Reconciliation" in idem, *Worship: Reforming Tradition* (Washington, DC: Pastoral Press, 1990), pages 59-73, here pages 64-66.

[11]The expanded rite of the later middle ages is found in Cyrille Vogel, *Le Pontifical romain-germanique au Moyen Age*, vol. 2., Studi e Testi 227 (Vatican City, 1963), § 99, nos. 44-80, pages 14-23.

[12]The Latin texts may be found in Cyrille Vogel, *Le Pontifical romain-germanique au Moyen Age*, vol. 2, § 99, nos. 224-251, pages 59-67. For an English translation of the rite in a similar pontifical, that of William Durand, see Adrien Nocent, *The Liturgical Year*, vol. 2, trans. Matthew J. O'Connell (Collegeville, MN: Liturgical Press, 1977), pages 206-213.

[13]Sermon 352:7 (PL 39:1556-1558), as cited by P. M. Gy, "Penance and Reconciliation," in A. G. Martimort, ed., *The Church at Prayer*, vol. III, page 104.

[14]The complicated question of the origins of tariff penance is treated most clearly in the short article by John Dallen, "Reconciliation, Sacrament of," in Peter Fink, ed., *The New Dictionary of Sacramental Worship*, pages 1052-1064. He treats the topic at greater length in *The Reconciling Community*, chapters 4-5, and the emergence of the modern form of penance in chapters 5 and 6. See also the treatment in John Gunstone, *The Liturgy of Penance*, and Pierre Marie Gy, "Penance and Reconciliation," in A. G. Martimort, *The Church at Prayer*, vol. III, pages 97-115.

[15]Later in the middle ages, *conversi* became a name for "lay brothers" who were subordinate to "choir monks." In the process the term lost its sharply penitential overtones. On the *conversi*, see James Dallen, *The Reconciling Community*, pages 82-85.

[16]Texts from James Dallen, *The Reconciling Community*, pages 177-178.

[17]Less work has been done on the evolution of auricular confession in this tradition. See G. Wagner, "Bussdisziplin in der Tradition des Ostens," in A. Pistoia and A. M. Triacca, eds., *Liturgie et rémission des péchès: Conférences St. Serge. XXe Semaine d'Études Liturgiques* (Rome: Edizioni Liturgichi, 1975).

[18]Alexander Schmemann, *For the Life of the World: Sacraments and Orthodoxy* (Crestwood, NY: St. Vladimir's Seminary Press, 1973), page 79.

[19]BCP 1549, page 280.

[20]BCP 1549, page 217.

[21]BCP 1549, page 162.

[22]BCP 1662, page 368.

[23]BCP 1549, page 311.

[24]On the history of public penance and auricular confession in Anglicanism, see John Gunstone, *The Liturgy of Penance*, chapter 9,

[25]See the comparative texts in Paul V. Marshall, *Prayer Book Parallels: The public services of the Church arranged for comparative study* (New York: Church Hymnal, 1989), pages 484, 489. See also Marion J. Hatchett, *Commentary on the American Prayer Book* (New York: Seabury, 1980), page 452.

[26]John Gunstone, *The Liturgy of Penance*, pages 72-74.

[27]BCP 1979, pages 264-265.

[28]The use of ashes had gradually become common in the American Church in the twentieth century. Note that the prayer is not described as a blessing and is optional.

[29]BCP 1979, page 446.

[30]Ibid.

[31]Ibid. The custom of lay confessors has roots in monasticism, as we have seen earlier, and it was affirmed in the Lutheran tradition. The Roman Catholic tradition recognizes its validity in emergency situations.

[32]Ibid. I have added italics for emphasis.

[33]The text of the rite cited below is found on pages 449-451 of the BCP 1979.

[34]BCP 1979, pages 857-858, 859, 860. It should be noted that the catechism works with a very narrow definition of grace. Grace as defined here is the grace of redemption. Grace as God's freely given love also includes the grace of creation and the grace of sanctification. One reason that churches of the reformation have declined to give reconciliation the status of a sacrament is that there is no dominical sign given in the gospels.

[35]Alexander Schmemann, *For the Life of the World*, page 79.

CHAPTER 4

THE VICTORY OF LIFE AND PEACE

MINISTRATION TO THE SICK

When John the Baptist sent disciples to ask Jesus whether he was "the one who was to come," Jesus gave this reply:

> the blind receive their sight, the lame walk, the lepers are cleansed, the deaf hear, the dead are raised, and the poor have the good news preached to them.[1]

Jesus here identified his works of healing as signs of the kingdom. His reply echoed the promise found in the Book of the prophet Isaiah:

> Then the eyes of the blind shall be opened,
> and the ears of the deaf unstopped;
> then the lame shall leap like a deer,
> and the tongue of the speechless sing for joy.[2]

In Jesus, God's reign had dawned and touched humankind in its suffering. His ministry of healing echoed other promises in Isaiah as well:

> The Spirit of the Lord is upon me,
> because the Lord has anointed me,

he has sent me to bring good news to the oppressed,
    to bind up the broken-hearted,
to proclaim liberty to captives,
    and release to the prisoners
to proclaim the year of the Lord's favor . . . .[3]

Indeed, Jesus opened his ministry, according to Luke, by reading this passage and declaring, "Today this scripture has been fulfilled in your hearing."[4]

His deeds gave substance to his words: acts of healing are characteristic of his ministry in all four gospels. Not only did Jesus heal, he sent forth his disciples to do the same. Mark reports, "He called the twelve and began to send them out two by two, giving them authority over unclean spirits. . . . So they went out and proclaimed that all should repent. They cast out many demons, and anointed with oil many who were sick and cured them."[5] The disciples' use of oil is not remarkable. Oil was a common medication in the ancient world. But in this context it had a larger significance: the strength which oil gave was understood, as in the anointing of a king, as mediating the strength of the Holy Spirit, and the work of the Spirit heralded the dawn of the new age of God's kingdom, God's reign.

1. Ministry to the Sick in the Early Centuries

In the literature of the New Testament, there are many accounts of the healing which Jesus' followers brought to the sick in his name. But only in the letter of James do we find further reference to anointing:

> Are any among you sick? They should call for the elders [presbyters] of the church and have them pray over them, anointing them with oil in the name of the Lord. The prayer of faith will save the sick, and the Lord will raise them up; and anyone who has committed sins will be forgiven.[6]

This is, as it were, the charter of the church's ministry of healing. In the early church orders, we find evidence that oil was still used for the church's ministry of healing. It appears, however, that oil blessed for this purpose was available to all the faithful, and that it was not necessarily only the clergy who administered it to the sick. It might be taken internally as medicine or applied externally.

In the early third century, for example, we find in the *Apostolic Tradition* of Hippolytus the following directions:

> If anyone offers oil, [the bishop] shall give thanks, not as at the oblation of the bread and wine [at the eucharist], but with similar effect, saying,

> O God, who sanctifiest this oil, grant to all who use it or receive it the holiness with which kings, priests, and prophets were anointed, and so give strength to all who taste it and give health to all who use it.[7]

We find another prayer for the blessing of oil for the sick in the euchology attributed to Sarapion of Thmuis in the middle of the next century.[8] The key texts in early centuries were the prayers for the blessing of the oil, not the formulas for its administration. Note the reference to the anointing of kings, priests, and prophets — a reference more commonly associated with chrism. In actual fact, early texts for the blessing of oils for anointing make little distinction between the use of oil in the anointing before and after baptism and in sickness, and we might suspect that holy oil blessed by any of the prayers was used for a variety of purposes.[9]

The traditional Roman prayer for blessing the oil for the sick on Maundy Thursday is found in the Gelasian sacramentary, where it is incorporated into the eucharistic prayer before the final doxology — the place where the blessing for various offerings occurred. Its text is similar to what we have already seen in Hippolytus:

> Send forth from heaven, we beseech thee, O Lord, the Holy Spirit the Advocate upon the richness of this oil, which thou didst graciously bring forth from the green tree for the refreshment of mind and body; and let it serve through thy blessing as a protection of mind and body, soul and spirit,

for all who anoint themselves with it, taste it, or touch it, to drive away all suffering, all infirmity, all sickness of mind and body — a chrism perfected and blessed by thee, O Lord, abiding within us, as that with which thou didst anoint kings, priests, and prophets:

in the name of our Lord Jesus Christ, [through whom thou dost ever create, sanctify, vivify, bless, and bestow upon us these good things]. . . .[10]

The oil was ordinarily blessed by the bishop, but might also at times be blessed by presbyters. It appears that it was not only used by bishops and presbyters in their ministrations, but also distributed to the faithful upon request for use when needed.

Anointing was not the only ministration that the sick received. Justin Martyr in the second century speaks of the distribution of communion by deacons to those who could not be present at the Sunday eucharist, so the sick might continue to receive communion even when they could not attend the eucharist. They might also expect the prayers of the church — both in public services and at visitations in their home. Later witnesses know of special forms of the daily office for the sick and celebrations of the eucharist on their behalf.

In the East, we find similar provisions in early church orders and in euchologies. In the euchology of the Byzantine rite, we find an order for "prayer oil" (*euchelaion*) which is consciously modelled on the letter of James. It requires the presence of seven priests, who join in the consecration of the oil, which is poured into a lamp. All the priests join in the anointing. The earliest form of this rite is set in the context of the eucharist; later the blessing takes place in the context of a form of the vigil — evening and morning prayer (*hesperinos* and *orthros*) — and the anointing in the context of the eucharist; eventually, material from the office was fused with a seven-fold liturgy of the word, with an anointing by one priest after each set of readings. The earliest form of the rite has the following prayers for the blessing of the oil and the administration:

Lord, who through the generous gifts which thou dost bestow with a merciful hand dost heal the weaknesses of our souls and bodies: Sanctify this oil, O Master, that it may avail for those who are anointed with it for healing and relief from all suffering, bodily sickness, defilement of flesh and soul, and every evil, so that in this too thy holy name may be glorified. . . .

Holy Father, physician of our souls and our bodies, who didst send thine only-begotten Son, our Lord Jesus Christ, to heal every infirmity and to deliver us from death: Now by the grace of thy Christ heal thy servant of the bodily sickness that hinders him, and give life in thy good pleasure to him that he may show his gratitude to thee through good works . . . .[11]

The close association of the anointing and the forgiveness of sins in the letter of James has given this rite a certain penitential overtone in the Byzantine tradition — a theme which goes back to Origen and John Chrysostom. At present the rite is often celebrated in holy week as a service of general absolution, although this would seem to be a use of the rite which overemphasizes its penitential function and pushes its relation to the healing of the sick too far into the background. The Byzantine tradition also associates the last anointing with preparation for death, without restricting unction to the moment of death or forgetting the association of the rite with healing. Upon death in the Byzantine tradition, the sanctified lamp oil that has been used for the last anointing of one of the faithful is poured upon that person's body in burial — a custom which appears to go back to Dionysius the Areopagite.[12]

2. Ministry to the Sick in the Middle Ages in the West

In the West, the reforms of Charlemagne at the end of the eighth century sought to make ministration to the sick an ordinary part of the daily ministry of the ordained, and it was from this time that the consecration of the oil of the sick was reserved to the bishop and the anointing of the sick began to be restricted to those in priestly orders. It is also in this era in the West that we begin to find fuller liturgical orders for ministry to the sick and formulas for the administration of unction. The text from James is used as the basis for this ministry. The earliest full order for the anointing has been analyzed by Boone Porter. It begins with an aspersion with holy water, six short collects, and a longer prayer which sets the context for the anointing:

> Lord God, who hast spoken by thine apostle James, saying: Is any one sick among you? Let him call in the presbyters of the Church, and let them pray over him, anointing him with oil in the name of the Lord; and the prayer of faith shall save the sick man, and the Lord will raise him up; and if he be in sins, they shall be forgiven him; cure, we beseech thee, our Redeemer, by the grace of the Holy Spirit, the weakness of this sick man; heal his wounds, and forgive his sins; drive out from him all pains of body and mind, and mercifully restore to him full health, both inwardly and outwardly, that, recovered and healed by the help of thy mercy, he may be strengthened to take up again his former duties to thee.

Then, as the sick person kneels, the priest lays hands upon him or her, while other texts are recited. The person is then anointed upon the neck, the throat, and on the breast between the shoulders, or on the afflicted area. This is the formula for the anointing:

> I anoint thee with holy oil in the name of the Father and of the Son and of the Holy Spirit, that the unclean spirit may not remain hidden in thee, nor in thy members; rather, through the working of this mystery, may there dwell in thee the power of Christ, all high, and of the Holy Spirit. And through this ointment of consecrated oil and our prayer, cured and warmed by the Holy Spirit mayest thou merit to receive thy former and even better health.

Finally, the rubrics direct that the person be communicated in both species, and that the same ministrations be repeated for seven days, if necessary.[13]

It is also at this time, however, that the anointing of the sick begins to be part of a cluster of ministrations that would become the "last rites" and the final anointing ("extreme unction") becomes the *only* anointing. This cluster of last rites initially included the reading of the passion, administration of communion as "food for the journey" (the *viaticum*), and the commendation of the departed. To this original core deathbed penance (noted in the last chapter) was added, as well as the final anointing. Documents from this period (canons of local councils, capitularies, episcopal regulations) give evidence of these changes. The Council of Chalon in 813 decreed:

> According to the teaching of St. James, with which the teaching of the Fathers is in accord, the sick should be anointed by a priest with oil blessed by the bishop.[14]

In 789, Theodolf of Orleans stipulated:

> Priests are to be reminded of their duty regarding the anointing of the sick and the administration to these of penance and viaticum, lest anyone die without viaticum.[15]

We shall turn to these last rites in the next chapter, but we need to note here the impact this use of the unction of the sick as a final rite and its association with penance had on the way in which it was understood. We should also note that when most Christians no longer received communion each week at the Sunday eucharist, the reception of communion itself under these circumstances tended inevitably to be understood as a last rite, the viaticum.

By this time, unction was so closely associated with penance and with death that it was coming to be understood as a sacrament of forgiveness which prepared the dying for death. Since in Western theology original sin is forgiven in the sacrament of baptism and mortal sin requires the sacrament of reconciliation, scholastic theologians began to associate the last anointing with the forgiveness of venial sins or removal of the "remnants of sin" and to interpret it as as a preparation for final glory. This associated it with a healing of the soul. They were hesitant to associate it with healing of the body, because by this period a sacrament was defined as a sign which conferred an objective gift, and it was apparent that most who were anointed were *not* restored to physical health. Those who did recover, however, were expected to live the life of a penitent until death.

The formularies used during the unction began to be fixed during this period, and they articulated this penitential understanding of unction. Antoine Chavasse identifies three kinds of formulas:

1. Several parts of the body were anointed, but the formula used for the anointing was not related to the part of the body anointed. The order cited above has a formula of this sort.
2. Several parts of the body were anointed, with a special formula for each anointing in the indicative mood. The penitential nature of the anointing was emphasized and the medicinal aspect was blurred.
3. Several parts of the body were anointed, and a standard deprecative formula focussed on forgiveness rather than healing was adapted to the part anointed.[16]

A formula of the third type eventually prevailed: "By this anointing and by his great mercy may the Lord forgive thee whatever sin thou hast committed by *seeing* [or the action of other parts anointed]." A laying on of hands usually preceded the anointing. One formula which came down in the Roman tradition was this:

> In the name of the Father and of the Son and of the Holy
> Spirit may all power of the devil be extinguished in thee by
> the laying on of my hands.[17]

The rites for the visitation of the sick in rituals of the late middle ages and the Counter-Reformation usually included the following components when used with the seriously ill:

1. aspersion with holy water, the seven penitential psalms (and other psalms), lessons, prayers, and instruction;
2. confession and absolution (deathbed penance);
3. laying on of hands and unction;
4. communion from the reserved sacrament.

But the desire to make the anointing the last act before death led to a reversal of elements 3 and 4 above — a reversal which makes sense only when one remembers the scholastic theology of the anointing, which had lost the relationship of anointing to the healing of the sick. The Council of Trent on the whole endorsed the new understanding of unction, but it refused to break the original link with sickness. It declared

> this anointing is to be administered to the sick, *especially* to those who are so dangerously ill that they seem near to death.[18]

The "especially" permitted the gradual recovery within the Roman Catholic Church of an emphasis on anointing as part of the ministry to the sick (not just the dying) and meant that the sacrament could be administered more than once. All of this made possible the return at the second Vatican Council to the theology of the sacrament as the anointing of the sick rather than as "extreme unction," intended only for the dying.

3. Ministry to the Sick at the Reformation and in the Book of Common Prayer

Luther in his *Babylonian Captivity* and Calvin in his *Institutes* took violent exception to the rites for the sick and dying in the middle ages — particularly to the way in which unction was understood. Both were inclined to admit, grudgingly, the basis for the rite in the New Testament, but to argue that the rite was appropriate to the apostolic age and that superstitious use of the rite in their day warranted its abandonment.[19] They were also inclined to argue that the spirit of the medieval rite led Christians, to their souls' peril, to put off repentance to their deathbed. Nonetheless, they encouraged a renewed ministry to the sick with prayer, renewal of faith and repentance, and reception of holy communion. Their approach to the administration of communion to the sick varied. A few Lutheran church orders provided for what we should call extended communion, with the elements taken to the sick from the church on the day of celebration, but Carlstadt had abolished the practice and the usual custom was a full celebration in the home. This cohered better with Luther's insistence that it is proclaiming of the words of Christ at the last supper to the communicants which renders Christ present for them, and that this presence was not an abiding one but ceased at the conclusion of the public service. Reformed practice varied, with some preferring extended communion, some a celebration at the home, and many avoiding either.[20]

The provisions of Cranmer in the 1549 Book of Common Prayer included rites for both the visitation of the sick and the communion of the sick and also allowed for a continuous rite including both.[21] The rites included the following:

Visitation of the Sick

Items marked with an asterisk may be omitted when this office is combined with communion.

*Greeting: Peace be in this house, and to all that dwell in it.

*Psalm 143 with *Gloria Patri*.

Anthem: Remember not Lord our iniquities, nor the iniquities of our forefathers. Spare us good Lord, spare thy people, whom thou hast redeemed with thy most precious bloud, and be not angry with us for ever.

Threefold Kyrie and Lord's Prayer (without doxology)

*Preces

Two collects

Exhortation
  Opening section
  *Final section (omitted if necessary)

*Renewal of baptismal vows

*Exhortation to forgiveness and charity and disposal of goods by will

*Special confession if desired and absolution (see chapter 3)

*Prayer

Psalm 71 with *Gloria Patri*

*Anthem: O Saveour of the world saue us, which by thy cross and precious blood hast redeemed us, helpe us we besche thee, O God.

*Blessing: The almighty Lord, whiche is a most strong tower to all them that put their trust in hym, to whom all thynges in heauen, in earth, and under earth, doe bowe and obey: be now and euermore thy defence, and make thee knowe and fele, that there is no other name under heauen geuen to man, in whom and through whom thou mayest receyue saluacion, but only the name of our Lorde Jesus Christe. Amen.

*Administration of unction if desired (signing the person on the forehead or breast): As with this visible oyle thy body outwardly is annoyted: so our heauenly father almyghtie God, graunt of his infinite goodnesse, that thy soule inwardly may be annoynted with the holy gost, who is the spirite of al strength, coumforte, reliefe, and gladnesse. And vouchesafe for his greate mercy (yf it be his blessed will) to restore unto thee bodely helth, and strength, to serue him, and sende thee release of al thy paines, troubles, and diseases, both in body and minde. And howsoeuer his goodnesse (by his diuyne and unserchable prouidence) shall dispose of thee: we his unworthy ministers and seruaunts, humbly beseche the eternal maiestie, to doe with thee according to the multitude of his innumerable mercies, and to pardon thee all thy sinnes and offences, committed by all thy bodily senses, passions, and carnal affecions: who also vouchsafe mercifully to graunte unto thee gostely strength, by his holy spirite, to withstand and ouercome al temptacions and assaults of thine aduersarye, that in no wise he preuaile against thee, but that thou mayest haue perfit victory and triumph against the deuil, sinne, and death, , through Christ our Lord: Who by his death hath ouercomed the Prince of death, and with the father, and the holy gost euermore liueth and reigneth God worlde without ende. Amen.

*Psalm 13 with *Gloria Patri.*

Communion of the Sick

Either Extended Communion from the public celebration
    Confession, absolution, comfortable words
    Communion
    Postcommunion collect [and remainder of eucharistic rite]
Or a celebration if there be no public celebration that day
    Psalm 117 with Gloria Patri
    Threefold Kyrie
    Collect: Almightie euerlyuing god, maker of mankynde, which doest
      correcte these whom thou doest loue, and chastiset euery one

whome thou doest receyue: we beseche the to haue mercy upon this thy seruaunte visited with thy hande, and to graunte that he may take his sickenesse, paciently, and recouer his bodily helth (if it be thy gracious will), and whansoeuer his soule shall departe from the body, it may without spotte be presented unto thee: through Jesus Christe our Lord. Amen.

Epistle: Hebrews 12:5

Gospel: John 5:24

Full eucharistic prayer [and remainder of eucharistic rite]

The office for the visitation is Cranmer's adaptation and translation of the rite from the Sarum manual. The anthem had been used in the earlier rite with the seven penitential psalms (of which Psalm 143 is retained). These psalms were originally recited on the way to the sick person's home and were followed by the salutation of peace, the Kyrie, the Lord's Prayer, the preces, and nine collects. The first two collects are two of a series of nine in the Sarum rite (the last and the third). The absolution to the special confession is an adaptation of the Sarum form, and the prayer which follows is the old precative form of reconciliation for a penitent before the use of the declarative form was introduced. Psalm 71 and the anthem which follows are from the Sarum rite for unction. The blessing and the formula for administering unction are Cranmer's compositions. The various rubrics for the ministration and the exhortation are adapted from traditional usage. Note that the older sequence of confession, unction, and communion is restored when the offices of visitation and communion of the sick are used together.

The provisions for communion of the sick allow for either extended communion (taking the sacrament to the sick after the parish service on days when the eucharist was celebrated in the parish church), or a full celebration. They do not explicitly allow for reservation of the sacrament for communion of the sick. Cranmer composed the new propers for the celebration of the eucharist for the sick. A rubric for communion instructs the minister to assure the sick that if they be unable to receive the sacrament, they still receive its benefits through faith. By separating provisions for communion from those for the visitation of the sick, Cranmer may have been attempting to secure more frequent communion of the sick: though the theology of these propers is subject to criticism, they do not necessarily imply — as the visitation office still does — that the sick person is in imminent danger of death.

In these rites Cranmer is endeavoring to return to the practice of the early church, and he has restored unction as a sacrament of healing, but the tone is still very much one of "last rites." Note the language of the exhortation at the visitation, which reads in part:

> . . . there should be no greater coumfort to christian persons, then to be made lyke unto Christ, by sufferyng paciently aduersities, troubles, and sickensses. For he himselfe wente not up to ioy, but first he suffered payne: he entred not into his glory, before he was crucified. So truely our waye to eternall life: is gladly to dye with Christe, that we may ryse againe from death, and dwell with him in euerlasting life.[22]

The rubrics which follow the exhortation, for example, direct the minister to admonish the sick to set their affairs in order and to make a will, if they have not already done so. The ambiguous theology of the rites is tellingly revealed in the three ways in which the words "visit" and "visitation" are used in them. First of all, the office itself is entitled "the *visitation* of the sick," and here the word refers to the visitation made by the minister. Second, the initial collects of the rite ask that God "*visit* and relieve" the sick or "*visit* . . . and . . . restore unto this sick person his former health." But, third, the word is also used in a more ominous way. The sick person is instructed in the exhortation that sickness is "God's *visitation*," and the collect at communion speaks of the sick person as one "*visited* by [God's] hand." This theology of sickness as God's visitation — which directly relates all sickness to the sin of the person afflicted — contradicts the words of Jesus in John's gospel and can scarcely be said to be theologically defensible. Massey Shepherd says of the propers provided for the communion of the sick that they articulate "the notion, now universally abandoned, that sickness is a 'visitation' of God for correction and punishment, which the afflicted must patiently bear . . . . Furthermore, the . . . Epistle and Gospel have wrested the Scriptural passages from their context and given them a meaning they were never intended to bear."[23] A more careful reading of what the New Testament has to say about sickness suggests that we might best "regard sickness as a general sign of the fallenness of humanity, but not a specific sign of the sin of the individual who has fallen ill."[24] It also suggests that there are times when sinful behavior brings on sickness, although we might not wish to consider the resulting illness a direct visitation from God. Cranmer sought to encourage frequent and regular communion by the opening rubric of the rite for the communion of the sick and in other ways as well, but communion of the sick continued to be understood primarily as a "last rite" in the Anglican tradition until the present century.

In 1552 the offices for the visitation and communion of the sick were revised by Cranmer.[25] The offices were shortened somewhat,[26] but the primary change was the removal of the provision for the unction of the sick — a usage which, as we have seen, the continental reformers disliked as superstitious and Bucer had criticized in his critique of the 1549 book. As a result the portion of the office with the most hopeful note disappeared. In addition, the provision for extended communion disappeared, and communion of the sick was generally understood to require a full celebration of the eucharist.

4. Ministry to the Sick in the American Church and the Book of Common Prayer 1979

The American Prayer Book of 1789 removed all mention of a special confession from its provisions for ministry to the sick, replaced Psalm 71 with Psalm 130, and appended other prayers which might be used as appropriate.[27] Like the English book of 1662, it concluded the office for the visitation with the Aaronic blessing. The 1892 revision made provisions for use of the office for the communion of the sick with the aged and the bedridden, allowing the use of the propers for the day rather than the special propers for the sick.

The 1928 revision of the American book[28] represents a serious attempt to adapt the rites for the visitation and communion of the sick in such a way that they are suitable for all the sick, not just those who are in danger of death. The rite for the visitation is in some ways a return to the 1549 provisions, but it attempts to provide a rite suitable for a variety of circumstances. After the greeting and the anthem, one of the penitential psalms may be used. The Kyrie, Lord's Prayer, preces, and the first of the collects follows. The 1928 book then provides a series of psalms suitable for various occasions, each with its own antiphon and collect. In place of the exhortation, a series of rubrics directs the minister to "address the sick person on the meaning and use of the time of sickness, and the opportunity it affords for spiritual profit," to inquire as to his or her faith, to move the person to reconciliation with others, and to suggest a special confession, if conscience requires. Confession is restored to the visitation rite once again, but no form of absolution is given. The rite continues as in earlier American books.

A new provision follows this office, however. Following various prayers and material for use with the dying, the book made these provisions for unction of the sick or the laying on of hands:

> *When any sick person shall in humble faith desire the ministry of healing through Anointing or the Laying on of Hands, the Minister may use such portion of the foregoing Office as he shall think fit, and the following:*
>
> O Blessed Redeemer, relieve, we beseech thee, by thy indwelling power, the distress of this thy servant; release *him* from sin, and drive away all pain of soul and body, that being restored to soundness of health, *he* may offer thee praise and thanksgiving; who livest and reignest with the Father and the Holy Ghost, one God, world without end. *Amen.*
>
> I anoint thee with oil (*or* I lay my hand upon thee), In the Name of the Father, and of the Son, and of the Holy Ghost; beseeching the mercy of our Lord Jesus Christ, that all thy pain and sickness of body being put to flight, the blessing of health may be restored unto thee. Amen.[29]

No provision was made, however, for blessing oil for use in unction. It is unclear whether it was the intention of the revisers to use ordinary oil or whether the omission was an oversight. It became common in the following decades for bishops to bless oil for use in their dioceses. We might note that these forms, unlike the medieval ones or Cranmer's 1549 provisions, are not well suited for use with the dying, for they *presume* the recovery of the sick person.

For communion of the sick, the 1928 book added a second set of special propers, besides continuing the 1892 permission to use the propers of the day. The second set of propers avoided the suggestion of the first set, that sickness is a visitation by God. Like the forms for unction, however, its collect and epistle speak so strongly of healing that it might be inappropriate for use with those with whom there seems little chance of recovery.[30] The rubrics of the rite for communion provided appropriate ways for shortening the full eucharistic rite. A brief form of general confession and absolution were also provided. Although the rubrics authorized neither extended communion nor reservation of the elements for communion of the sick, both became common practices as it became customary to take communion to the sick and shut-in on a regular basis, particularly at Christmas and Easter.

Although the provisions for the visitation of the sick were an enormous theological improvement over previous Anglican rites, the office as a whole proved difficult to use, for its provisions were so elaborate that they required too much active participation on the part of the sick. In actual practice, clergy tended to use such prayers as seemed appropriate from the office, to administer unction when the sick requested it, to take communion to the sick and shut-in regularly, and to use the provisions for the dying when circumstances required. The office for the visitation as a whole, however, was seldom used.

The nineteenth and twentieth century had seen a growing interest among Anglicans and other Christians in the ministry of healing, and the 1928 revisions were in part a result of this movement, which had led to a report commissioned by the Lambeth Conference in 1920 and issued in 1924. That report had recommended the restoration of unction and the laying on of hands as "a form of treatment more immediately directed [than confession and absolution] to the complete restoration of the patient."[31] Here we see the "tilt" toward treating unction as a sacrament of healing which lies behind the 1928 American book. It was characteristic of most Anglican revisions of the period.

The 1979 revision completely reworks the provisions for the ministry to the sick, including separate rites for communion under special circumstances, for reconciliation of a penitent, for ministration at the time of death, and for ministration to the sick. The first two provisions take into consideration the fact that there are occasions other than serious illness in which private communions and reconciliation may be appropriate. The provision of a separate rite for ministration at the time of death clearly distinguishes ordinary ministrations to the sick from the "last rites." There are four basic components to the rite for ministration to the sick (although the enumeration in the headings groups the first two as one):[32]

Greeting
Part I: Ministry of the Word
a. 4 alternative sets of lessons (epistle, psalm, gospel)
b. confession and absolution
  either general confession and absolution
  or the reconciliation of a penitent
Part II: Laying on of Hands and Anointing
Part III: Holy Communion
  either full celebration from the peace
  or administration from the reserved sacrament

We will now look at the rite as a whole, and then examine each component in more detail. Each component in the rite may be used separately, but when two or more are used, they are to be used in the order listed.

The book makes possible a comprehensive program of ministration to the sick and the shut-in in every parish, utilizing the ministries of both clergy and lay persons. Such a ministry begins with regular communion for the sick and the shut-in who cannot attend the parish eucharist. Parish priests, deacons, and lay eucharistic ministers can all be involved in this ministry. Weekly communion, if desired, is possible even in large parishes with the assistance of lay eucharistic ministers, using the rite for communion under special circumstances or other authorized forms. That rite begins with either a brief passage of scripture or all or part of the eucharistic propers for the Sunday or feast and an appropriate prayer or prayers. This is followed by a confession and absolution (or prayer for forgiveness if the officiant is not a bishop or priest). The rite continues with the peace, the Lord's Prayer, communion in one or both kinds from the reserved sacrament or the parish celebration, a special postcommunion prayer, and the blessing or dismissal. For regular ministrations, the propers are probably preferable to the briefer lessons given in the rite. The clergy of the parish should be involved in this ministry on a regular basis, as well as lay eucharistic ministers, and at times a full celebration may be desirable, although extended communion or communion from the reserved sacrament is a way of including persons in the parish's worship and is preferable on most occasions.

Many parishes now schedule regular parish services of healing on a weekly or monthly basis — ordinarily a celebration of the eucharist according to the prayer book with the laying on of hands and/or anointing, or a service according to the rite found in the *Book of Occasional Services*. At such services those involved in ministering to the sick sometimes come forward for the laying on of hands or anointing also, but there is a certain theological incoherence to this healing by proxy, and it would be better to have them come forward specially for a laying on of hands to strengthen them for their ministry with a special blessing. Laying on of hands or anointing as a kind of all-purpose absolution (a custom which also occurs at times in the Roman Catholic and Orthodox traditions as well) is best avoided as an unwarranted generalization of the purpose of the sacrament.

At times of serious illness, the officiant would ordinarily be a parish priest, but when no priest is available, deacons and lay persons may officiate at all components of the office: all may officiate at the ministry of the word, a deacon or lay person substitutes a prayer for forgiveness for the absolution after a general confession or at the reconciliation of a penitent, a deacon or lay person may anoint a sick person with oil blessed by a bishop or priest, and a deacon may administer communion from the reserved sacrament, and a deacon or lay eucharistic minister may bring communion from a parish celebration. At the time of death, it is ordinarily a parish priest who will officiate, but in cases of necessity, a deacon or lay person may lead the prayers appointed for the occasion.

The first component of the particular provisions for the ministry to the sick is a ministry of the word. The purpose of these readings is to set the ministration to the sick through prayer and sacrament in its biblical context. Four sets of propers are provided, a general one and one related to each of the other components of the rite — penitence, anointing, and communion. The propers provided for the sick in "Various Occasions" in the eucharistic lectionary are also suitable:

General
2 Corinthians 1:3-5	God comforts us in affliction
Psalm 91	He will give his angels charge over you
Luke 17:11-19	Your faith has made you well

Penitence
Hebrews 12:1-2	Looking to Jesus, the perfecter of our faith
Psalm 103	He forgives all your sins
Matthew 9:2-8	Your sins are forgiven

When Anointing is to follow
James 5:14-16	Is any among you sick?
Psalm 23	You have anointed my head with oil
Mark 6:7, 12-13	They anointed with oil many that were sick

When Communion is to follow
1 John 5:13-15	That you may know that you have eternal life
Psalm 145:14-22	The eyes of all wait upon you, O Lord
John 6: 47-51	I am the bread of life

Various Occasions 20: For the Sick
2 Kings 20:1-5	Hezekiah prays and the Lord heals him
Psalm 13	The Lord has dealt bountifully with me
or Psalm 86:1-7	In the day of my trouble I call on you
James 5:13-16	Is any among you sick?
Mark 2:1-12	Jesus forgives a paralytic and heals him

In any ministration to the sick these propers may be used; in regular ministrations the propers of the day may be preferable. There is an additional table of lessons and psalms for a public service of healing in the *Book of Occasional Services*. The rubrics of the rite permit the use of one or more of these readings and a brief comment after any of them. Ordinarily, the officiant would choose a set which fits the focus of the particular components to be used. The wide variety of selections assures that the readings will be appropriate to the circumstances. Prayers ordinarily follow the readings as appropriate, though when communion is administered, an appropriate collect might be used before the readings. Confession and absolution follow. When circumstances warrant, the reconciliation of a penitent is used. Otherwise a general confession and absolution is appropriate.

Part II provides for the laying on of hands and unction. The following provisions are made:

If oil for the Anointing of the Sick is to be blessed, the Priest says
O Lord, holy Father, giver of health and salvation: Send your Holy Spirit to sanctify this oil; that, as your holy apostles anointed many that were sick and healed them, so may those who in faith and repentance receive this holy unction be made whole; through Jesus Christ our Lord, who lives and reigns with you and the Holy Spirit, one God, for ever and ever. *Amen.*

The following anthem is then said
Savior of the world, by your cross and precious blood you have redeemed us;
Save us, and help us, we humbly beseech you, O Lord.

The Priest then lays hands upon the sick person, and says one of the following
N., I lay my hand upon you in the Name of the Father, and of the Son, and of the Holy Spirit, beseeching our Lord Jesus Christ to sustain you with his presence, to drive away all sickness of body and spirit, and to give you that victory of life and peace which will enable you to serve him both now and evermore. *Amen.*

or this

N., I lay my hand upon you in the Name of our Lord and Savior
Jesus Christ, beseeching him to uphold you with his grace, that
you may know the healing power of his love. *Amen.*

*If the person is to be anointed, the Priest dips his thumb in the
holy oil, and makes the sign of the cross on the sick person's
forehead, saying,*

N., I anoint you with oil in the Name of the Father, and of the
Son, and of the Holy Spirit. *Amen.*

The Priest may add

As you are outwardly anointed with this holy oil, so may our
heavenly Father grant you the inward anointing of the Holy
Spirit. Of his great mercy, may he forgive you your sins, release
you from suffering, and restore you to wholeness and strength.
May he deliver you from all evil, preserve you in all goodness,
and bring you to everlasting life; through Jesus Christ our Lord.
Amen.

*In cases of necessity, a deacon or lay person may perform the
anointing, using oil blessed by a priest or bishop. If Communion
is to follow, the Lord's Prayer is now said. The Priest concludes*
The Almighty Lord, who is a strong tower to all who put their
trust in him, to whom all things in heaven, on earth, and under
the earth bow and obey: Be now and evermore your defense, and
make you know and feel that the only Name under heaven given
for health and salvation is the Name of our Lord Jesus Christ.
Amen.[33]

We now turn to look at these provisions in more detail, and to compare
them to provisions in 1549 and 1928.

Although the books of 1549 and 1928 provided for unction, this is the
first book to provide a prayer for blessing the oil for anointing the sick. The
intention of the rubrics is that it be blessed by a priest in the course of the
ministration, though reference in the rite to blessing by a bishop indicates
that the custom of a bishop blessing oil for the sick for use in the diocese

may also be followed. The prayer includes appropriate references to the practice of the apostles and asks for wholeness for those who receive the anointing with faith and repentance — a petition which fits theologically with unction in a variety of circumstances.

For the laying on of hands, two formulas are given as alternatives. Both look toward relief from suffering for the sick person through God's grace — for that "victory of life and peace which will enable [the sick person] to serve [God] both now and evermore." The first is oriented primarily toward relief from suffering through restoration of physical health, the second speaks only of "the healing power of [Christ's] love," but the wording of both is general enough to be suitable in circumstances where restoration of health is likely and those when relief from suffering is more likely to come through death.

Anointing may follow. A brief formula is given, which may be expanded with an abbreviated version of the form given by Cranmer in 1549. This recognizes the anointing with oil as an instrumental sign of an inward anointing with the Holy Spirit which seals our reconciliation with God (and so appropriately comes after confession and absolution) and brings wholeness, strength, and relief from suffering. As with the formulas for the laying on of hands, this text is inclusive enough to be used in the administration of unction both to those whose recovery is likely and to those who appear to be near death. We will reflect below on the theology which lies behind these uses.

The final component of the rite is the administration of communion, either from elements already consecrated, or as part of a celebration. We have already noted provisions for such communion above. The proper postcommunion prayer articulates the theology of communion under these circumstances: it is "the pledge of our redemption," and it is appropriate to pray

> that it may bring us forgiveness of our sins, strength in our weakness, and everlasting salvation. . . .[34]

The rite is followed in the book by prayers which may be useful in ministry to the sick, and prayers which are appropriate for the sick themselves to use.

Conclusions

The provisions of the Book of Common Prayer 1979 and the *Book of Occasional Services* provide the Episcopal Church with a wide range of resources for ministry to the sick and the dying under a similarly wide range of circumstances. This makes possible ministry to Christians who are chronically ill or shut-in, the aged who are unable to attend public worship on a regular basis, those whose circumstances are life-threatening or who face serious surgery, and those who are on the point of death. These provisions represent a certain ecumenical convergence: the revised rites of the Roman Catholic Church and other American churches of the Reformation are quite similar.

The church ministers to Christians at the time of illness with a full ministry of word, sacrament, and prayer. Communion as the bread of life is understood as a part of the ongoing liturgical life of Christians, and the church seeks to make communion regularly available to its members when circumstances prevent them from attending the parish eucharist on Sundays and major feasts. It takes on special meaning when it is administered to the sick — it is not only the bread of life, but the pledge of our redemption which brings strength in weakness and assures us of the hope of everlasting salvation, as the postcommunion prayer states. It gives concrete expression to the solidarity of Christians within the body of Christ which is broken neither by sickness nor death. It is not itself a "last rite," but it is appropriately included in the last rites as *viaticum*, "food for the journey" as the dying Christian completes the passover with Christ begun at baptism.

The rite of reconciliation was in the early centuries administered only in the case of serious sin and only once in a lifetime. As the centuries went on, Christians frequently sought the status of a penitent on their deathbed, that they might be restored to perfect peace with God and the church before their death. By the late middle ages, reconciliation in the form of auricular confession had become a part of the ongoing discipline of church life in the West and was expected once a year of all Christians before their Easter communion. By the end of the middle ages, priestly absolution to assure penitents of God's forgiveness was available whenever Christians felt the need of it in a life of ongoing conversion. But reconciliation at the time of serious illness retained a privileged place in the church's ministry to the seriously ill for two reasons: it prepared the sick for their final union with God in the case of death, and it also brought about the unburdening of conscience which was sometimes necessary before the sick could recover health. The 1979 provisions carefully reenforce the fact that the rite of reconciliation is not appropriate only when we are in danger of death by giving the rite a distinct place in the Prayer Book apart from the ministry to the sick. They also reenforce the fact that reconciliation is especially appropriate at times of serious illness by suggesting use of the rite in Part I of the ministry to the sick. While Form I of the rite of reconciliation is particularly useful for those who make regular use of the sacrament, Form II is particularly suited to the circumstance of those who are seriously ill and wish reconciliation and the recovery of their baptismal status after a review of their past life.

The sacraments of reconciliation and communion are appropriate in the church's ministry to the sick, but they are not unique to it. The unique form for the church's ministry to the sick is the laying on of hands and unction. The catechism of the 1979 speaks of these sacramental actions in this way:

> Q. What is unction of the Sick?
> A. Unction is the rite of anointing the sick with oil, or the laying on of hands, by which God's grace is given for the healing of spirit, mind, and body.[35]

We have already seen that we need to speak of the sacramental grace of this rite very carefully, for a sacrament is a sign of an objective gift of God's grace, and it is evident that restoration of physical health does not always follow the administration of unction. Reflecting on the Byzantine tradition, Sergei Bulgakov speaks of unction in this way:

> Anointing may bring either return to health or the increase of spiritual strength necessary to a Christian death; hence this one sacrament has two faces: one turns toward healing, the other toward liberation from illness by death.[36]

Any adequate account of the sacrament must take account of both faces. In the course of history, various periods have placed the emphasis on one or the other of these faces. In the early centuries, the emphasis seems to have been on the restoration of health. By the middle ages, unction was coming to be understood as a last rite which perfected the reconciliation brought about by the priestly absolution, and it came to be seen as a preparation for death. Cranmer once again began to restore balance, but unction disappeared from the prayer book in 1552. With the recovery of the healing ministry in this century, most of the emphasis at first fell on the restoration of health once again, as is evident from the language of the 1928 provisions for unction. The language of the 1979 rite is more carefully nuanced.

A distinction is perhaps appropriate between the sacramental administration of unction and the charismatic ministry of healing within the church, and failure to make this distinction may be the cause for some of the difficulty we have with the theology of unction, as Thomas Talley suggests in a thoughtful article which is cited by both Charles Gusmer and Leonel Mitchell. Talley argues that extraordinary cures that we encounter in the church's ministry to the sick are part of the "charismatic" gift of healing with which God endows some members of the church. Such charismatic, extraordinary healing cannot be "sacramentalized" — made the objective result of a rite of the church. It is indeed part of the life of the church and deserves more attention than it has often received, but it merits very careful treatment. It is sometimes suggested that lack of faith is all that prevents our recovery of health — a pastorally and theologically disastrous approach to ministering to the sick. It is also inappropriate to speak of such cures as "miraculous" or "supernatural": both of these words suggests that grace subverts rather than perfects the order of nature. Donald Baillie long ago suggested that even the cures effected by Christ are those which God works through human nature, not in contravention of it.[37]

The church's sacramental ministry to the sick, while in some cases it may effect a cure, has a different orientation. Talley writes:

> The object of the rite of anointing can be understood as renewal of the baptismal anointing by which each of us is *christos* so that the suffering and separation of sickness become identified as participation in the *pascha Christi*. By such anointing, *anamnesis* is made of the passage of Christ through death to life and of the patient's consecration in that

mystery. By such anointing, further, the suffering of the illness is oriented to a reopened future, a sense of movement in Christ through the present passage toward the kingdom.[38]

It is appropriate in concluding our reflections to look back at the text of James as the charter for this rite. The sick are instructed to

> call for the elders [presbyters] of the church and have them pray over them, anointing them with oil in the name of the Lord. The prayer of faith will save the sick, and the Lord will raise them up; and anyone who has committed sins will be forgiven.[39]

The ministration of the church in prayer and anointing "will save the sick, and the Lord will raise them up." "Saving" and "raising up" here have a double reference. Salvation may mean being raised up to physical health; it may also refer to our ultimate salvation, when we are raised up to eternal life with Christ. What is ultimately suggested here is conformation to Christ crucified and risen: the anointing is part of the process by which we are united with Christ in his victory over death and make his passover our own — the reason that Dionysius can suggest that a final anointing at death brings to completion the work begun in the first anointing at baptism.[40]

It is for this reason that this anointing, whether it raises us to physical health once more or prepares us to bring to completion our baptismal death to sin, that we may rise with Christ to new life, is a true "sign of the kingdom." Alexander Schmemann speaks of it in this way:

> . . . healing is a sacrament because its purpose or end is not *health* as such, the restoration of physical health, but the *entrance* of man into the life of the Kingdom, into the "joy and peace" of the Holy Spirit. In Christ everything in this world, and this means health and disease, joy and suffering, has become an ascension to, and entrance into this new life, its expectation and anticipation.

> In this world suffering and disease are indeed "normal," but their very "normalcy" is abnormal. They reveal the ultimate

and permanent defeat of man and of life, a defeat which no partial victories of medicine, however wonderful and truly miraculous, can ultimately overcome. But in Christ suffering is not "removed"; it is transformed into victory. The defeat *itself* becomes victory, a way, an entrance into the Kingdom, and this is the only true *healing*.

. . . The Church comes to take this man into the Love, the Light, and the Life of Christ; it comes not merely to "comfort" him, but to make him a *martyr*, a *witness* to Christ in his very suffering. A martyr is one who beholds "the heavens opened, and the Son of man standing on the right hand of God" (Acts 7:56). A martyr is one for whom God is not another — and the last — chance to stop the awful pain; God is his very life, and thus everything in his life comes to God, and ascends to the fullness of Love.[41]

It is the witness to a "victory of life and peace" which unction makes possible that makes this rite a sign of the kingdom.

ENDNOTES

[1]Matthew 11:5

[2]Isaiah 35:5-6; cf 29:18-19.

[3]Isaiah 61:1-2.

[4]Luke 4:18-21.

[5]Mark 6:7, 12-13.

[6]James 5:14-15.

[7]Gregory Dix, *The Treatise on the Apostolic Tradition of St. Hippolytus of Rome, Bishop and Martyr, Reissued with corrections, preface, and bibliography by Henry Chadwick* (London: Alban Press, and Ridgefield, CT: Morehouse Publishing, 1992), § 5:1-2, page 10. I have not used Dix's translation, but provided my own rendition of the Latin text. Most later church orders depend on Hippolytus, and so continue or expand his provisions.

[8]See John Wordsworth, *Bishop Sarapion's Prayer-Book* (Hamden, CT: Archon Books, 1964), pages 77-78.

[9]In the Byzantine tradition, the prayers for blessing oils at baptism and on Maundy Thursday each refer to the oil being blessed as an "oil of gladness" and the oil with which priests, kings, and prophets were anointed. In traditions in which the prebaptismal anointing has a distinctly exorcistic meaning, the oil used remains distinct from the oil used for other purposes, but even in these traditions, as we shall see below, the oil for anointing the sick is not always clearly distinguished from the oil of chrism.

[10]Gelasian Sacramentary, L. K. Mohlberg, ed., *Liber sacramentorum Romanae aeclesiae ordinis anni circuli*, Rerum ecclesiasticarum documenta series maior, Fontes 4 (Rome: Herder, 1960), Book I, § 40. My translation.

[11]Elie Mélia, "The Sacrament of the Anointing of the Sick," in Achille M. Triacca, ed., *Temple of the Holy Spirit: sickness and death of the Christian in the liturgy: the twenty-first Liturgical Conference Saint-Serge*, trans. Matthew J. O'Connell (New York: Pueblo, 1983), pages 127-160, here page 152. Translation adapted. Mélie gives a history of the rite in the euchology on pages 151-157. He considers the earliest form of the rite to be that found in Coislin MS 213, dated 1027. The rite in the earlier Barberini MS 336 has already developed beyond the rite in Coislin 213. A translation of the present rite (which includes a form of these two prayers) may be found in Isabel Florence Hapgood, trans., *Service Book of the Holy Orthodox-Catholic Apostolic Church*, 5th edition (Englewood, NJ: Antiochean Orthodox Christian Archdiocese of New York and All North America, 1975), pages 332-359. The final doxologies show considerable variation.

[12]Anointing the body for burial was a widespread custom in late antiquity. It is only in the East, however, that this preparation of the body becomes associated with consecrated oils. For Dionysius, there appears to be no clear distinction used for oils in the various anointings, and the anointing at the time of burial is associated with the prebaptismal anointing. Later Byzantine tradition generally used oil of unction ("lamp oil") to anoint the body for burial. See the treatment of burial in the *Ecclesiastical Hierarchy* in Colm Luibhead, trans., *Pseudo-Dionysius: The Complete Works* (New York: Paulist Press, 1967), pages 249-259, and the notes by Paul Rorem given with the text.

[13]Translation of texts from Paul F. Palmer, ed., *Sacraments of Forgiveness* (Westminster, MD: Newman, 1939); see the analysis in H. B.

Porter, "The Origin of the Medieval Rite for Anointing the Sick or Dying, *Journal of Theological Studies* 7(1956), pages 211-225.

[14]*Collectio conciliorum* 4:1040, as cited by Elie Mélia, "The Sacrament of the Anointing of the Sick," in Achille M. Triacca, ed., *Temple of the Holy Spirit*, page 141 (note 29, page 312).

[15]Cited by Elie Mélia, "The Sacrament of the Anointing of the Sick," in Achille M. Triacca, ed., *Temple of the Holy Spirit*, page 141 (the note number is missing, but the reference given in the notes appears to be PL 97:124, in note 30, page 312).

[16]A. G. Martimort, "Prayer for the Sick and Sacramental Anointing," in idem, ed., *The Church at Prayer,* vol. III, page 130. He is presumably citing A. Chavasse, *Étude sur l'onction des infirmes dans l'Église latine du IIIe au XIe siècle* 1: *Du IIIe siècle au reforme carolignienne* (Lyons: Librarie du Sacré-Coeur, 1942).

[17]Formula from the ritual of Pope Paul V (1615), as cited by A. G. Martimort, "Prayer for the Sick and Sacramental Anointing," in idem, ed., *The Church at Prayer,* vol. III, page 133. Note that this formula is exorcistic in nature. The earlier association with the Holy Spirit has disappeared from the formulas for both the laying on of hands and unction.

[18]Translation from J. Neuner and J. Dupuis, *The Christian Faith,* pages 441-442, from the Latin text in H. Denziger and A. Schönmeister, eds., *Encheiridion Symbolorum,* nos. 1695-1999, cited by Charles W. Gusmer, *And You Visited Me: Sacramental Ministry to the Sick and Dying* (New York: Pueblo, 1984), page 32 (note 50, page 46). The original draft had *only* instead of *especially.*

[19]This is reflected in Martin Bucer's criticism of the use of unction in the BCP 1549. See E. C. Whitaker, ed., *Martin Bucer and the Book of Common Prayer* (Great Wakering, UK: Alcuin Club/Mayhew McCrimmon, 1974), pages 124-127.

[20]Bucer voices no objection to either usage in the BCP 1549 in his review of the book. See note 19 above.

[21]BCP 1549, pages 259-265, 266-268

[22]BCP 1549, page 261. In the American BCP 1928, these words have become the basis for one of the collects used in Holy Week. We now find this as the collect for Friday at Morning Prayer in the BCP 1979.

23Massey Hamilton Shepherd, Jr., *The Oxford American Prayer Book Commentary* (New York: Oxford University Press, 1950), commentary for page 321.

24I owe the phrasing of this sentence to the Rev. Robert Prichard, who suggested it in a personal communication dated August 9, 1994.

25BCP 1552, pages 417-421, 422-423.

26Primarily by the removal of Psalms 143 and 13.

27For the history of the rites in the American BCP, see Paul V. Marshall, *Prayer Book Parallels: The public services of the Church arranged for comparative study* (New York: Church Hymnal, 1989), pages 474-503. Unfortunately, Marshall has omitted most of the material from provisions for the communion of the sick in his arrangement of the material before the present book.

28The revised rites are found on pages 308-323 of the BCP 1928. See Massey Shepherd, *The Oxford American Prayer Book Commentary* (New York: Oxford University Press, 1950), for a commentary on these rites.

29BCP 1928, page 320. See Massey Shepherd's commentary on this page in his *Oxford-American Prayer Book Commentary.*

30The book did, in its additional prayers, however, provide for a variety of circumstances, and provisions for ministry to the dying were expanded by the addition of a litany for the dying.

31Cited by Charles W. Harris, "The Visitation of the Sick: Unction, Imposition of Hands, and Exorcism," in W. K. Lowther Clarke, ed., *Liturgy and Worship: A Companion to the Prayer Books of the Anglican Communion* (London: SPCK, 1932), pages 472-540, here page 473. See also *Prayer Book Studies III: The Order for the Ministration to the Sick* (New York: Church Pension Fund, 1951).

32The rites for ministration to the sick are found on pages 453-457 of the BCP 1979, followed by prayers for the sick on pages 458-460 and prayers for use by a sick person on page 461. The separate services for communion under special circumstances, the reconciliation of a penitent, and ministration at the time of death are found, respectively, on pages 396-399, 446-453, and 462-467. For a more detailed discussion of the reconciliation of a penitent, see chapter 3; for ministration at the time of death, see chapter 5. For commentaries on these rites in the BCP 1979, see Marion J. Hatchett,

Commentary on the American Prayer Book (New York: Seabury, 1980), pages 459-471, and Leonel Mitchell, *Praying Shapes Believing: A Theological Commentary on the Book of Common Prayer* (Minneapolis, MN: Seabury/Winston, 1985), pages 207-215,

[33]BCP 1979, pages 455-456.

[34]BCP 1979, pages 399, 457.

[35]BCP 1979, page 861.

[36]Sergei Bulgakov, *The Orthodox Church*, translation revised by Lydia Kesich (Crestwood, NY: St. Vladimir's Seminary Press, 1988), page 114.

[37]D. M. Baillie, *God Was In Christ: An Essay on Incarnation and Atonement* (London: Faber and Faber, 1961), pages 13-14.

[38]Thomas J. Talley, "Healing: Sacrament or Charism?," in idem, *Worship: Reforming Tradition* (Washington, DC: Pastoral Press, 1990), pages 47-58, here page 55. Talley is cited by Leonel Mitchell, *Praying Shapes Believing*, pages 210-211, and by Charles Gusmer, *And You Visited Me*, particularly in the discussion beginning on page 154.

[39]James 5:14-15.

[40]Hence the possibility that the church may at times have used the same oil — chrism or myrrh — for both the baptismal anointing and the unction of the sick, as the text of some of the ancient prayers for the consecration of chrism seem to suggest. There is a close relation between our baptismal victory over sin and death, the victory over sin and death in the reconciliation of a penitent, and the completion of the process in the unction of the dying that is sometimes overlooked. They are all the work of the Holy Spirit, and the same sacramental signs have at times been used for all of them — the laying on of hands and anointing. In the case of reconciliation, the laying on of hands is a sacramental sign that is clearly part of the tradition, but was lost in the late middle ages; anointing was also a sign in some cases, as we see in Eastern rites for the reconciliation of schismatics and heretics.

[41]Alexander Schmemann, *For the Life of the World: Sacraments and Orthodoxy* (Crestwood, NY: St. Vladimir's Seminary Press, 1973), pages 102-103.

CHAPTER 5

TRAMPLING DOWN DEATH BY DEATH

MINISTRATION AT THE TIME OF DEATH AND THE BURIAL OF THE DEAD

The characteristic rite at the time of death is a rite of passage — the funeral procession.[1] As Christians took over the burial customs of other cultures, they gave a paschal interpretation to this rite of passage by setting it in the context of Christ's passover from death to life. Christians accompanied the departed from their dying moments to their burial with a continuous series of ritual acts, psalmody, and prayers. The liturgy began even before death with the church's ministration at the time of death and the preparation of the body for burial at the station at home. The classical Christian liturgy for the dead took on the character of a procession — beginning with a station at the home and concluding with final station at the place of burial while the body was lowered into the earth or sealed in the burial chamber. At times there was an intermediate station at the church.

What was distinctive about the Christian liturgy was not the rites themselves, which did not differ markedly from the rites of the environing culture, but the new meaning which the rites took on when interpreted in the light of Christ's resurrection. The pagan *viaticum* — the coin to pay the ferryman on the journey — was replaced by the ministration of communion before death as food for the journey and a pledge of the resurrection. The washing, anointing, and clothing of the body echoed the washing, anointing, and clothing of the Christian in baptism. The funeral procession was a triumphal procession celebrating the victory of life over death with psalms and alleluias, rather than a typical pagan funeral procession with cries of mourning and lament. The characteristic funeral and memorial meals or *refrigeria* at the grave were reinterpreted and eventually replaced by the celebration of the eucharist. The times for memorial observances on the third, ninth, and fortieth days (or third, seventh, and thirtieth days) were often reinterpreted in terms of paschal themes — especially with reference to Christ's resurrection on the third day and his ascension on the fortieth day.[2] Christians celebrated annual memorials not on the day of birth, but on the day of death — the day of rebirth into eternity.

The *Apostolic Tradition* of Hippolytus gives us no information about burial, but we find some information in the *Apostolic Constitutions*. In book 6, we find the following provisions:

> . . . assemble in cemeteries, reading the holy books, and singing for the martyrs who are fallen asleep, and for all the saints from the beginning of the world, and for your brothers and sisters who are asleep in the Lord, and offer the acceptable eucharist, the representation of the body of Christ, both in your churches and in the cemeteries; and in the funerals of the departed, accompany them with singing, if they were faithful in Christ. For "precious in the sight of the Lord is the death of his saints" (Psalm 116:15). And again, "Return, O my soul, return unto thy rest, for the Lord has dealt bountifully with thee" (Psalm 116:7). And elsewhere, "The memory of the righteous is a blessing" (Proverbs 10:7). And, "The souls of the righteous are in the hand of God" (Wisdom of Solomon 3:1). For those that have believed in God, although they are asleep, are not dead. For our Savior says to the Sadducees,

"As for resurrection of the dead, have you not read what is written, 'I am the God of Abraham, the God of Isaac, and the God of Jacob'? Now God is God not of the dead, but of the living; for to him all of them are alive" (Luke 20:38 and parallels, citing Exodus 3:6). Therefore, even the remains of those that live with God are not without honor. . . . You also, O bishops and others, who without [rites of ritual purification] come in contact with the departed, ought not to think yourselves defiled. Do not shun the remains of such persons, but avoid such [purificatory] observances, for they are foolish. And adorn yourselves with holiness and chastity, that you may become partakers of immortality and heirs of the kingdom of God, and may rest for ever, through Jesus Christ our Savior.[3]

In book 8, the author goes on to give the biddings of the diaconal litany and the concluding prayer of the celebrant for the departed. As is customary, the biddings are grouped together, without the response, which was "Lord, have mercy," as we know from elsewhere in the work.

The deacon shall add these biddings [to those of the great litany]:

Let us pray for our brothers and sisters who are at rest in Christ, that God, the lover of humankind, who has received his soul, may forgive him every sin, voluntary and involuntary, and be merciful and gracious unto him, and give him his lot in the land of the pious who have been received into the bosom of Abraham, and Isaac, and Jacob, with all those who have pleased him and done his will from the beginning of the world, the land from which all sorrow, grief, and lamentation have been banished.

Let us arise, and commend ourselves and one another to the eternal God, through the Word who was in the beginning.

And let the bishop say,

O thou who art by nature immortal and hast no end to thy being, from whom every creature, whether immortal or mortal is derived; who didst make thy human creature rational, the citizen of the world, in constitution mortal, and didst add the promise of a resurrection; who didst not suffer Enoch and Elijah to taste of death; the God of Abraham, the God of Isaac, and the God of Jacob, who art God of the living and not of the dead, for all human souls live with thee, and the spirits of the righteous are in thy hand, so that no torment can touch them, since they are all sanctified under thy hand: Do thou now also look upon this thy servant, whom thou hast chosen and received into another state, and grant him an angel of mercy, and place him in the bosom of the patriarchs and prophets and apostles and of all those who have been pleasing unto thee from the beginning of the world, the place where there is no grief, sorrow, or lamentation, the peaceable region of the godly, and the undisturbed land of the righteous and of those who there see the glory of thy Christ: by whom glory, honor, worship, thanksgiving, and adoration be unto thee, in the Holy Spirit for ever.

And let the deacon say,

Bow down and receive the blessing.

And let the bishop give thanks for them, saying,

O Lord, save thy people and bless thine inheritance, which thou hast purchased with the precious blood of thy Christ. Feed them under thy right hand, and cover them under thy wings, and grant that they may fight the good fight, and finish their course, and keep the faith immutably, unblameably, and unreprovably, through our Lord Jesus

Christ, thy beloved Son, with whom glory, honor, and worship be unto thee and unto the Holy Spirit for ever. Amen.

Let the third day of the departed be celebrated with psalms, and lessons, and prayers, on account of him who arose within the space of three days; and let the ninth day be celebrated in remembrance of the living and of the departed; and the fortieth day according to the ancient pattern: for so the people lamented Moses, and the anniversary day in memory of him.

And let alms be given to the poor out of his goods for a memorial to him. . . . Now when you are invited to their memorials, feast with good order and the fear of God, as disposed to intercede for those who are departed.[4]

Note that Christians rejected the idea, common in the ancient world, that contact with the departed rendered them ritually impure. Burial customs varied from region to region, but Christians followed the customs of the region, rejecting only associations with pagan mythology and the signs of mourning which would contradict their confident hope in the resurrection.

There are variants in Christian eschatology which were to have an impact on the way death was interpreted and the petitions which were made for the departed. In general, Christians understood the departed to rest in paradise (in the bosom of the patriarchs) after death, awaiting resurrection at the final advent of Christ. In this two-stage eschatology lie the origins of the later doctrine of purgatory. The seeds of this doctrine lie in the teaching of such early Christian authors as Origen and Gregory of Nyssa that the interim period was a time when the dead were made ready for their final union with God — a time when they were purged, if necessary, from the sin which had flawed their relationship to God during their lives. Eventually the *time* of purgation became a *place* of purgation — purgatory.

Because of the strong sense of the solidarity of all the faithful, living and departed, it seemed appropriate both to pray for the departed and to ask their prayers. Early Christians were also confident, however, that the martyrs by their conformity to Christ in his death also achieved conformity to him in his resurrection, so that they had already achieved union with Christ at the time of their death. In their case a paschal interpretation of death predominated, and the two-stage eschatology fell into the background. In the first three centuries (the church of the martyrs), a paschal interpretation of the death of all Christians was not uncommon. But after the time of the church's establishment in the fourth century, the character of the majority of Christians during their lives made such an interpretation of Christian death more problematic, and prayers for pardon and for mercy took on greater importance. During the middle ages these prayers overshadowed the paschal theme of the earlier centuries, and the fear of God's judgment began to dominate the liturgy for the dead.

1. Rites of Commendation and Burial in the Roman West

Early manuscripts of the Gelasian Sacramentary give the first concrete provisions for the rites associated with the time of death and burial. The earliest strata of these provisions furnish us only with prayers of commendation and prayers at the eucharist for the departed. Later manuscripts begin to fill the picture out for us. According to early manuscripts, the following rite is observed as death approaches:

> Reading of the Passion according to John
> Litany and prayers
> Communion as the *viaticum*, food for the journey (sometimes
>   before the Passion)
> Psalms and Responsories while the body is washed and prepared
>   for burial

This is the station at the home of the departed.[5] The funeral procession and the burial rites follow:

> Psalmody in procession to the church
> Station at the church with psalms and responsories
> Burial at the church

In some manuscripts, there is a station at the church and then the procession continues to the final station at the place of burial.

The following are among the ancient texts in early manuscripts, which vary considerably. Provisions for the various stations and processions are fluid, and draw on a stock of antiphons, psalms, and responsories which may be used in various contexts.

Prayers of Commendation

Roman

O God, in whom all mortal things have their life, and in whose sight our bodies, when we die, do not perish but are changed to a better state, we beseech thee to receive the soul of thy servant. Let the angels take it in their hands to the bosom of the patriarch Abraham thy friend, and let it rise to new life on the final day of the great judgment. In thy goodness forgive and wash away whatsoever stain it may have contracted at the devil's prompting while it sojourned in the mortal world; through Jesus Christ thy Son our Lord, who lives and reigns with thee in the unity of the Holy Spirit, one God, for ever and ever. *Amen.*[6]

Gallican

Go forth, O Christian soul, from this world
in the name of God the Father who created thee,
in the name of Jesus Christ, the son of the living God, who
    suffered for thee,
in the name of the Holy Spirit, who has been poured out
    upon thee,
in the name of the angels and archangels,
in the name of the thrones and dominations,

in the name of the principalities and powers and all the
   heavenly virtues,
in the name of the cherubim and seraphim,
in the name of the patriarchs and prophets,
in the name of the apostles and martyrs,
in the name of the confessors and bishops,
in the name of the priests and deacons
   and the whole hierarchy of the Catholic Church,
in the name of the monks and hermits,
in the name of the virgins and the faithful widows.
May *his* dwelling place be established in peace this day
   and *his* home in the heavenly Jerusalem. *Amen.*

Lord, receive thy servant into blessedness. *Amen.*
Deliver the soul of thy servant from all the dangers of hell,
   and from the snare of punishment, and from all tribulation. *Amen.*
Deliver the soul of thy servant
   as thou didst deliver Noah by the deluge. *Amen.*
Deliver the soul of thy servant
   as thou didst deliver Enoch and Elijah
   from the death common to all in this world. *Amen.*
Deliver the soul of thy servant
   as thou didst deliver Moses
   from the hand of Pharaoh, king of the Egyptians. *Amen.*
Deliver the soul of thy servant
   as thou didst deliver Job from his sufferings. *Amen.*
Deliver the soul of thy servant
   as thou didst deliver Daniel from the lion's den. *Amen.*
Deliver the soul of thy servant
   as thou didst deliver Jonah from the belly of the whale.
   Amen.

Deliver the soul of thy servant
   as thou didst deliver the three young men from the fiery
   furnace and the hands of the wicked king. *Amen.*
Deliver the soul of thy servant
   as thou didst deliver Susanna from false witnesses.
   Amen.
Deliver the soul of thy servant
   as thou didst deliver David from the hand of King Saul,
   from Goliath, and from all his difficulties. *Amen.*
Deliver the soul of thy servant
   as thou didst deliver Peter and Paul from their imprison-
   ments. *Amen.*
Graciously deliver the soul of thy servant
   and grant that *he* may dwell with thee in heavenly
   blessedness. *Amen.*[7]

Responsories Most Frequently Used

Come to assist *him*, O saints of God;
come forth to meet *him*, Angels of the Lord:
Receiving *his* soul, presenting *him* before the face of the
   Most High.
May Christ who has called thee receive thee;
and may angels bear thee into the bosom of Abraham:
Receiving *his* soul, presenting *him* before the face of the
   Most High.
Rest eternal grant unto *him*, O Lord;
And let light perpetual shine upon *him*:
Receiving *his* soul, presenting him before the face of the
   Most High.[8]

Thou knewest me before I was born, O Lord,
for thou didst make me in thine image:
now I return my soul to thee, for thou art my creator.

My sins make me afraid, O Lord, and bring me shame;
Do not condemn me when thou comest in judgment:
now I return my soul to thee, for thou art my creator.[9]

Antiphons in Common Use

Thou hast formed me from the earth and clothed me with
    flesh:
Lord, my redeemer, raise me up on the last day. [10]

Into paradise may the angels lead thee;
at thy coming may the martyrs receive thee,
and take thee to Jerusalem, the holy city.[11]

May the choir of angels welcome thee,
and with Lazarus, once poor, mayest thou have eternal
    rest.[12]

Rest eternal grant unto them, O Lord:
And let light perpetual shine upon them.[13]

Psalms Most Commonly Used

114; 120; 25; 4; 116; 143; 139; 23; 93; 33; 43; 132; 51; 42;
65; 15; 22; 121; 146; 118[14]

Station at the House: The most important ministration to the dying was the administration of communion as the viaticum; by the time of the Council of Nicaea this rite had become normative. Charles Gusmer describes the rite in this way:

> The emergence of the eucharist as viaticum, the sacrament of the dying, is another instance of cultural adaptation by Christian antiquity. There were, however, marked dissimilarities from pagan rites. Pagans gave "viaticum" to those already

dead, to corpses; Christian viaticum is for the living. Pagans provided the dead with an inanimate coin as viaticum; Christians provided the living with life as viaticum. Christian viaticum was not intended to pay for the journey of the soul to the place of eternal rest, but was a provision for passage to eternity, being itself a pledge of eternal life.[15]

The association of communion in John 6 with the bread in the wilderness during the exodus underscored the paschal associations of the rite; Ignatius had described the eucharist as the "food of immortality."[16] Associated with the administration of the viaticum was the reading of the passion, which linked the death of the Christian with Christ's own passover from death to life. The frequent use of Psalm 114 and the antiphon, "May the choir of angels welcome thee," further reenforced the paschal associations.

The commendation of the soul likewise made use of paschal and baptismal themes. The prayer, "Depart, O Christian soul," echoed the baptismal creed, and the prayers for deliverance are rich in the foretypes of paschal deliverance found in the lessons of the Easter vigil and cited in exorcisms before baptism. The preparation of the body for burial with washing, anointing, and clothing echoed the rite of baptism. The physical death of the Christian fulfilled the baptismal death to sin and completes the transition to new life begun at baptism. The cortege of saints and angels summoned in the commendation and in the responsory, "Come to assist him," marked the goal of the paschal pilgrimage of the Christian.

Procession and Final Station: The funeral procession then set out from the initial station at the house for the precincts of the church, where the burial would take place, with further psalmody. After a final station at the church, for which the earliest manuscripts prescribe psalms and responsories,[17] burial in the church itself or within its precincts followed, with further psalmody and final prayers. As the station in the church developed into a vigil or wake, the procession to the grave also grew in importance as the principal funeral procession. Perhaps the most important psalms for the funeral procession or processions were the paschal psalms — 114, with the antiphon, "May the choir of angels," and 118, with verse 19, "Open for me the gates of righteousness; I will enter them; I will offer thanks to the Lord," as its antiphon. At the close of the procession Psalm 132, with verse 15, "This shall be my resting place for ever; here will I dwell, for I delight in it," as its antiphon, was also noteworthy.

From these beginnings in the eighth and ninth century, the rites continued to develop in the books of the monastic orders and local dioceses. Richard Rutherford traces the following stages of the formation of an official rite until the promulgation of a standard rite in the seventeenth century:

1. The publication of the rite of the Roman curia as an appendix to the Franciscan breviary in 1260. The rite shows the influence of monastic liturgy on the ritual and became a model for other rites.[18]

2. The publication by Alberto Castellano (de Castello, Castellani) of a pastoral handbook for priests — the *Liber sacerdotalis* (Venice, 1523); after 1537 the *Sacerdotale iuxta Sanctae Romanae Ecclesiae ritum*. This had a fuller rite for clergy and a simpler rite for ordinary Christians.[19]

3. The compilation by Giulio Santori (Sanctorio) of the *Rituale Sacramentorum Romanum Gregorii XIII* (1584-1612). Santori resisted the distinction of rites for clergy and laity.[20]

4. The promulgation for recommended use in 1614 of the *Rituale Romanum Pauli V. P. M.*[21]

The later middle ages saw the station in the church develop into a wake which eventually took the form of vespers, vigil (matins), and lauds. This came to be followed by a eucharist, of which there was no mention in the provisions of the earliest Roman orders. In some rites, the eucharist followed the vigil (matins) in the church, and the service at the grave seems to be a form of lauds, with the canticle *Benedictus* and the antiphon, "I am the resurrection and the life. Those who believe in me, even though they die, will live, and everyone who lives and believes in me will never die"

(John 11:25-26), being recited during the actual burial.[22] By the end of the middle ages, the eucharist before burial would grow in importance to become the principal focus of the funeral rite. The ritual provisions of the middle ages that have come down to us developed in a monastic environment, and it is probable that the funeral of ordinary Christians was less elaborate.

2. Shifts in the West during the Middle Ages

In the early centuries, the dominant note of rites for the dying and the dead had been paschal triumph. During the middle ages in the West, the ordeal of the final judgment became predominant. This affected both the ministry to the dying and the rites of burial. In the early centuries, the viaticum had been the sacrament of the dying. But during the middle ages, penitence came to be seen as the appropriate preparation for death, and two other sacraments came to take on increasing importance as "last rites." The first was deathbed penance, at first as a survival of the early public penance and then as the last confession. The second was anointing. What had earlier been administered at the beginning of a serious illness and interpreted as a sacramental rite oriented toward strength for the recovery of health or for the struggle of death now acquired a distinctly penitential character related to the forgiveness of sins and so came to be interpreted as a preparation for glory; consequently, it eventually came to be administered after the viaticum at the moment of death.

The rites of burial themselves also took on a distinctly penitential character. After the fourth century, the Western understanding of the intermediate state before the final resurrection came to emphasize this as a time when Christians made satisfaction for the sins committed during their lives. Prayers for the forgiveness of the departed became the dominant theme of the burial rites, penitential psalms began to overshadow paschal psalms, and the eucharist came to be understood as an offering to assist the departed in purgatory. A final rite after the burial eucharist, eventually known as the "absolution," took on new significance. In early manuscripts this is simply a final commendation, with an aspersion and censing of the corpse accompanied by one of the traditional responsories and one of the commendations originally used at the moment of death. But in the late middle ages, the responsory used emphasized the note of judgment and the prayer was an absolution, seeking pardon for the sins of the departed.

The shift can be seen particularly in the texts of the prayers, psalmody, and responsories of the burial rites. The prayers at the time of death and at the grave now focussed on judgment and forgiveness. The prayer over the gifts and the postcommunion prayer pleaded the offering of the eucharistic sacrifice on behalf of the departed, that they might be cleansed and forgiven. Of the propers, the tract after the gradual psalm and the offertory in particular illustrate the shift in focus:

> Absolve, O Lord, the souls of all the faithful departed from every bond of sin; and by the help of thy grace may they be enabled to escape condemnation at judgment and enjoy the blessedness of everlasting light.

> O Lord Jesus Christ, King of glory, deliver the souls of all the faithful departed from the pains of hell and from the deep pit: deliver them from the mouth of the lion, that hell may not swallow them up, that they may not fall into darkness; but let thy holy standard-bearer Michael bring them to the holy light, which thou didst once promise to Abraham and his seed. We offer to thee, O Lord, sacrifices and prayers of praise: receive them on behalf of those souls whom we remember this day. Grant that they, O Lord, may pass from death to that life which thou didst once promise to Abraham and his seed.[23]

The note of judgment dominates in particular in the sequence hymn which came into general use for funerals at the very end of the middle ages and was incorporated in the liturgy after the Council of Trent. This is the *Dies irae*, a hymn derived from the responsory used at the absolution at the conclusion of the burial mass and inspired by Zepheniah 1:14-15. A translation was included in earlier editions of the Episcopal hymnal. Its opening stanza sets the tone:

Dies irae, dies illa,	Day of wrath!
	O day of mourning!
solvet saeclum in favilla,	See fulfilled the prophets' warning,
teste David cum Sibylla.	heaven and earth in ashes burning.[24]

These texts set a very different tone for the rites of burial than the paschal joy characteristic of earlier usage.

The note was underscored by the brief rite of absolution of the corpse which came at the end of the eucharist while the body was aspersed and censed before being taken to the grave for burial. By the end of the middle ages a responsory which sounded the note of judgment had come into use for this rite and the prayers were those of absolution.

> Enter not into judgment with thy servant, O Lord; for unless thou grant forgiveness of all his sins, no one shall be justified in thy sight. Do not allow, therefore, we beseech thee, the sentence of judgment upon one whom a true supplication in Christian faith commends to thee to crush *him*, but assist *him* with thy grace, that *he* who in *his* lifetime was sealed with the seal of the holy Trinity may escape the judgment of condemnation, O thou who livest and reignest for ever and ever. *Amen.*

> Deliver me, O Lord, from everlasting death in that dreadful day, when heaven and earth shall be shaken, when thou shalt come to judge the world by fire. Trembling comes upon me and I am afraid of the time when judgment and the coming wrath shall come, when heaven and earth shall be shaken. O that day, a day of wrath, of woe and tribulation, a great and exceedingly bitter day, when thou shalt come to judge the world by fire. Rest eternal grant unto them, O Lord; and let light perpetual shine upon them.

Deliver me, O Lord, from everlasting death in that dreadful day, when heaven and earth shall be shaken, when thou shalt come to judge the world by fire.

Threefold Kyrie and Lord's Prayer
Preces

Absolve, we beseech thee, O Lord, the soul of thy servant N. from every bond of sin, that *he* may be raised up in the glory of the resurrection and be refreshed among thy saints and thine elect: through Christ our Lord. Amen.

V. Rest eternal grant unto *him*, O Lord.
R. And let light perpetual shine upon *him*.

May he rest in peace. *Amen.*[25]

No longer was the dominant note of the burial eucharist the entry of the departed into the paschal victory of Christ. The theme which now prevailed was the offering of the eucharistic sacrifice as satisfaction for the sins of the departed. The shift from white vestments to black signals the change of tone very dramatically.

This markedly penitential approach to death and this fear of purgatory affected not only the burial rites, but the whole character of liturgy in the medieval West. It led to the *daily* recitation of the office for the dead in addition to the daily office in many religious communities and to a proliferation of masses for the dead, so that the most frequent celebration of the eucharist in the middle ages was not the mass of the parochial or religious community, but the "private" mass on behalf of the departed purchased by either stipend or endowment. It was for this purpose that most monks came to be ordained in the late middle ages, and chantries employed priests without pastoral responsibilities for the sole purpose of reciting the office of the dead and offering mass for the dead. The result was a distorted theology of the eucharist, a distorted theology of death, an overloaded burden of daily prayers, and a distorted theology of the ordained ministry.[26] As we shall see, this never happened in the East, where eucharistic theology did not countenance "applying" mass intentions and so made no provision for celebrations of the eucharist as private masses rather than as communal liturgies.

We can trace the beginning of these developments in the theology of Augustine, who distinguished sharply between the martyrs, whose prayers we need, and the rest of the departed, who need our prayers.[27] Augustine argued that prayers, celebrations of the eucharist, and charitable works availed to relieve the suffering of those under purgation.[28] It was, however, Gregory the Great who set out the popular rationale for the celebration of masses for the dead in his *Dialogues*.[29] There he tells the story of Justus, a monk who died and languished in purgatory until mass had been said on his behalf for thirty days. The offering of the eucharist, Gregory suggests, freed his soul from purgatory.

3. Burial Rites in the Byzantine Tradition

The rites of burial in the Byzantine tradition developed out of the pattern which we saw earlier in the *Apostolic Constitutions*.[30] The provisions which became standard toward the end of the middle ages take the form of a vigil (*pannychis*) and — in the case of priests — morning prayer (*orthros*). The celebration of the eucharist at burials fell out of general use. The rites begin with the preparation of the body for burial in the home, continue with the procession to the church and the burial office there, and conclude with the procession to the grave and burial. Distinct services for lay persons, monks, and priests appear only at the end of the middle ages (that for children is even later). The principal elements of the office at the church in the common rite and the rites for monks and priests are these:

Psalm 91 (omitted in the rite for priests)
Psalm 119, divided into three antiphons
    Refrain to first and third antiphons, "Alleluia"
    Refrain to second antiphon, "Have mercy upon thy servant"
    Troparia (*eulogitaria*) at the conclusion of the third antiphon

Psalm 51

Canon by Theophanes (except in the rite for monks)

Kontakion, "Give rest, O Christ"

(after sixth ode; without odes in rite for monks)

> with only one *oikos* ordinarily

> with 24 *oikoi* in rite for priests

Troparia by John of Damascus in eight tones

> before final kiss for priests

> lacking in rite for monks

Beatitudes with *troparia* (except in rite for monks)

Prokeimenon, epistle, alleluia, gospel

> One in common rite

> Five in rite for priests

> None in rite for monks

Psalms 148-150, *Gloria in excelsis, kataxioson* (cento of texts from scripture, and conclusion of orthros (in rite for priests)

Rite of the last kiss and dismissal

What we find is in fact elements of the daily office in the Byzantine tradition utilized as a vigil before burial. Proper *troparia*, a proper *kontakion*, and the litany and prayer for the departed relate the rite to burial. Into this framework other components are added in the different offices — sets of proper readings, the beatitudes, and psalm verses with special *troparia*. The most important *troparia* for the office are attributed to St. John Damascene and, with the *kontakion*, they provide a meditation on the shortness and uncertainty of life — a monastic shift from the paschal themes of earlier burial rites.

Among the oldest proper provisions for the service are the prayer for the dead, which is the standard prayer throughout the course of the rite, and the *kontakion* of the dead (reduced to the *proiomion* and the first *oikos* except in the rite for priests, which retains all 24 *oikoi*):

> O God of the spirits and of all flesh, who hast trampled
> down death and overthrown the devil: Do thou, the same

Lord, give rest unto the soul of thy departed servant, N., [in the bosom of Abraham, Isaac, and Jacob,] in a place of verdure, a place of repose, whence all sickness, sorrow, and sighing have fled away. Pardon every transgression which *he* has committed, whether by word, or deed, or thought. For thou art a good God, and lovest humankind, because there is no one who lives and does not sin: for thou only art without sin, and thy righteousness is to all eternity, and thy word is true: for thou art the resurrection and the life, and the repose of thy departed servant, N., O Christ our God, and to thee we ascribe glory, together with thy Father who is from everlasting, and thine all-holy, good, and life-giving Spirit, now and for ever, and unto the ages of ages. Amen.[31]

Give rest, O Christ, to thy servant with thy saints,
where sorrow and pain are no more,
neither sighing, but life everlasting.

Thou only art immortal, the creator and maker of mankind; and we are mortal, formed of the earth, and unto earth shall we return. For so thou didst ordain when thou createdst me, saying, "Dust thou art, and unto dust shalt thou return." All we go down to the dust; yet even in the grave we make our song: Alleluia, alleluia, alleluia.[32]

Other distinctive features of the rite include the giving of the last kiss to the dead at the conclusion of the service in the church (a pagan custom assimilated to the exchange of the peace in Christian usage) and the pouring of lamp oil (oil of unction) from the last anointing on the body — a custom which goes back, as we have seen, to Dionysius. Like Western liturgies for the dead, the Byzantine rite has overlaid the early elements of the rite with later elements which are more penitential in tone. Yet Eastern Christians, while they prayed for the departed, did not develop the doctrine of purgatory in the way that the West did, and so the liturgy of the dead did not come to overwhelm the entire liturgy of the church the way that it did in the West.

4. Rites for the Dying and for Burial at the Reformation and in the Book of Common Prayer

Rites for the Dying

In 1549 the office for the visitation of the sick included the three sacraments which had become "last rites" in the Western tradition — the reconciliation of a penitent, unction, and communion. Unction in that book was handled in such a way as to be appropriate to those for whom recovery was possible and those who sought strength as they faced death. After 1552 the provision for unction was eliminated, but later English prayer books continued to encourage a special confession and communion for those near death — although the treatment of communion as a viaticum received no particular emphasis. American books until 1928 removed the reference to a special confession. In 1662 two prayers were added to the rite for the visitation of the sick — a prayer for a person near death and a commendation. American revisions of the prayer book included both of these, and a third prayer of a similar nature was added in 1892.

The Catholic revival in the nineteenth century led to a renewed emphasis on the traditional ministry to the dying. The 1928 prayer book restored provision for a special confession, and reservation of the sacrament for the purpose of administering communion to the sick and dying became common. Unction was also restored, as we saw in the last chapter, and was used as a "last rite," although the emphasis on unction as a sacrament of healing made its use with the dying problematic. This book made separate provision for ministration to the dying, with the following components:

> A Prayer for a Sick Person, when there appeareth but small hope of Recovery
>
> A Prayer which may be said by the Minister in behalf of all present at the Visitation

A Commendatory Prayer for a Sick Person at the point of Departure

A Litany for the Dying

An Absolution to be said by the Priest

A Commendation

A Commendatory Prayer when the Soul is Departed[33]

The first and third prayers are those added in 1662. The second, taken from the writings of Jeremy Taylor, was added to the American book in 1789. The litany for the dying is adapted from a form composed by William Bright from various ancient sources and published in his *Ancient Collects* in 1861. It follows the form of the Great Litany, but focusses on petition for someone who is dying. In this litany, the response to the invocations of the Trinity and the deprecations is, "Have mercy upon the soul of thy servant." The litany continues as follows:

> We sinners do beseech thee to hear us, O Lord, God; That it may please thee to deliver the soul of thy servant from the power of the evil one, and from eternal death;
> *We beseech thee to hear us, good Lord.*
>
> That it may please thee mercifully to pardon all *his* sins;
> *We beseech thee to hear us, good Lord.*
>
> That it may please thee to grant *him* a place of refreshment and everlasting blessedness;
> *We beseech thee to hear us, good Lord.*
>
> That it may please thee to give *him* joy and gladness in thy kingdom, with thy saints in light;
> *We beseech thee to hear us, good Lord.*
>
> *Agnus Dei*, threefold Kyrie, Lord's Prayer

O Sovereign Lord, who desirest not the death of a sinner: We beseech thee to loose the spirit of this thy servant from every bond, and set *him* free from all evil; that *he* may rest with all thy saints in the eternal habitations; through Jesus Christ our Lord, who liveth and reigneth with thee and the Holy Ghost, one God, world without end. *Amen.*[34]

The litany, which was included in the revised books of other churches of the Anglican communion at the time, met a need for prayer at the time of death for which earlier prayer books had made inadequate provision. It was not, strictly speaking, prayer for the departed, and so it fell within the limits for prayer set at the Reformation. Its petitions are for pardon, peace, and admission into paradise for the dying person at death. The concluding collect ultimately derives from a Byzantine prayer for a dying person, from which it draws its key phrases.[35]

The absolution which follows is more questionable, for absolution is properly pronounced only after confession of sins. It inclusion here probably is to be traced to the Roman Catholic custom of giving the apostolic pardon before death. In form, however, it is unexceptionable as a prayer for forgiveness. Two commendations follow:

Depart, O Christian soul, out of this world,
　In the Name of God the Father who created thee.
　In the Name of Jesus Christ who redeemed thee.
　In the Name of the Holy Ghost, who sanctifieth thee.
May thy rest be this day in peace, and thy dwelling-place
　in the Paradise of God.

Into thy hands, O merciful Saviour, we commend the soul of thy servant, now departed from the body. Acknowledge, we humbly beseech thee, a sheep of thine own fold, a lamb of thine own flock, a sinner of thine own redeeming. Receive *him* into the arms of thy mercy, into the blessed rest of everlasting peace, and into the glorious company of the saints in light. *Amen.*[36]

The reader will recognize the first commendation as an adaptation of that found in the early sacramentaries. The second was a composition of John Cosin. With these provisions, the Episcopal Church made possible a ministry to the dying which bears strong resemblance to the rites of the early Western sacramentaries.

Burial Rites

The theology of purgatory and satisfaction which undergirded the medieval burial rites and votive offices and masses for the dead was fiercely attacked by the reformers. The corruption to which this theology had given rise led reformers to curtail burial rites and to abolish entirely the votive office and mass for the dead. Indeed, most reformers concluded that prayer for the dead had no biblical warrant. In the reformed tradition, burial became at times an entirely secular observance and there were no liturgical provisions at all, even at the grave.

Cranmer's reform of the rites in the Book of Common Prayer 1549 was much more conservative, although the votive offices and masses were eliminated and the doctrine of purgatory was eliminated. The following provisions were given in 1549:[37]

Procession from the Church Gate to the Church or Place of Burial
3 anthems (John 11:25-26; Job 19:25-27; 1 Timothy 6:7 with Job 1:21)
Office at the Grave
2 anthems (Job 14:1-2; responsory with trisagion)
Prayer of committal as earth is cast on the body by the priest
Anthem (Revelation 14:13)
2 prayers

Office in the Church before or after burial
Psalms 116, 139, 146
Lesson: 1 Corinthians 15:20-58
Threefold Kyrie and Lord's Prayer

Preces
Prayer

Eucharist
Psalm 42 as introit
Collect
Epistle: 1 Thessalonians 4: 13-18
Gospel: John 6:37-40

Cranmer worked largely with the provisions of the Sarum rite (and also of some of the continental reformers), drawing on materials from them to produce a greatly simplified rite at the grave and an office in the church. The office in the church resembles the daily office, and in later editions of the prayer book its propers seem often to have been intended for use in the daily office. A celebration of the eucharist is retained, but there is no suggestion that it is offered on behalf of the departed. Of interest to us is the style of prayer adopted, both for the burial office and for the eucharistic intercession. Cranmer provides prayers for the dead, but avoids anything which could suggest the doctrine of purgatory. The text of the prayers is as follows, with the key phrases underlined:

At the Grave

We commende into thy handes of mercy (most mercifull father) the soule of this our brother departed, N. And his body we commit to the earth, besechyng thyne infinite goodnesse, to geue us grace to lyue in thy feare and loue, and to dye in thy fauoure: that when the judgmente shall come which thou haste commytted to thy welbeloued sonne, both this our brother, and we, may be found acceptable in thy sight, and receiue that blessing, which thy welbeloued sonne shall then pronounce to all that loue and feare thee, saying: Come ye blessed children of my Father: Receyue the kingdome prepared for you before the beginning of the worlde. Graunt this, mercifull father, for the honour of Jesu Christe our onely sauior, mediator, and aduocate. Amen.

Almightie God, we geue thee hertie thankes for this thy seruaunte, whom thou haste delyuered from the miseries of this wretched world, from the body of death and all temptacion. And, as we trust, hast brought his soule whiche he committed into thy holye handes, into sure consolation and reste: Graunte, we beseche thee, that at the daye of iudgement his soule and all the soules of thy electe, departed out of this lyfe, may with us and we with them, fully receiue thy promisses, and be made perfite altogether thorow the glorious resurrection of thy sonne Jesus Christ our Lorde.[38]

Suffrages and Prayer at the Office in the Church

Priest.	Entre not (o lorde) into iudgement with thy seruaunt.
Aunswere.	For in thy sight no liuing creature shalbe iustifyed.
Priest.	From the gates of hell.
Aunswere.	Deliuer theyr soules, o lorde.
Priest.	I beleue to see the goodnes of the lorde.
Aunswere.	In the lande of the liuing.
Priest.	O lorde, graciously heare my prayer.
Aunswere.	And let my crye come unto thee.

Let us pray.

O Lorde, with whome lyue the spirites of them that be dead: and in whome the soules of them that bee elected, after they be deliuered from the burden of the fleshe, be in ioy and felicitie: Graunte unto thy seruaunte, that the sinnes whiche he committed in this world be not imputed unto him, but that he, escaping the gates of hell and paynes of eternall darknesse: may euer dwel in the region of lighte, with Abraham, Isaac, and Jacob, in the place where is no wepyng, sorowe, nor heauinesse: and when that dredeful day of the generall resurrection shall come, make him to ryse also with the iust and righteous, and receiue this bodie agayn to glory, then made pure and incorruptible, set him on the right hand of thy sonne Jesus Christ, among thy holy and elect, that then he may heare with them these most swete and coumfortable wordes: Come to me ye blessed of my father, possesse the kingdome whiche hath bene prepared for you from the beginning of the worlde: Graunte thys we beseche thee, o mercifull father: through Jesus Christ our mediatour and redemer. Amen.[39]

Collect at the Eucharist

O mercifull god the father of our lorde Jesu Christ, who is the resurreccion and the life: In whom whosoeuer beleueth shall liue thoughe he dye: who also hath taughte us (by his holye Apostle Paule) not to bee sory as men without hope for them that slepe in him: We mekely beseche thee (o father) to raise us from the death of sin, unto the life of righteousness, that when we shall departe this lyfe, we maye slepe in him (as our hope is this our brother doeth), and at the general resurreccion in the laste daie, bothe we and this oure brother departed, receiuyng agayne oure bodies, and rising againe in thy moste gracious fauoure: may with all thine elect Saynctes, obteine eternall ioye. Graunte this, o Lorde god, by the meanes of our aduocate Jesus Christ: which with thee and the holy ghoste, liueth and reigneth one God, for euer. Amen.[40]

Petition in the Eucharistic Prayer

We commend unto thy mercye (O Lorde) all other thy seruauntes, which are departed hence from us, with the signe of faith, and nowe do reste in the slepe of peace: Graunt unto them, we beseche thee, thy mercy, and euerlasting peace, and that, at the day of the generall resureccion, we and all thy which bee of the misticall body of thy sonne, may altogether be set on his right hand, and heare that his most ioyful voyce: Come unto me, O ye that be blessed of my father, and possesse the kingdom, whiche is prepared for you from the begynning of the worlde.[41]

What is asked for the departed is rest and peace until the time of judgment, mercy and forgiveness on the day of judgment, and a share in the joyful inheritance of the saints at the time of the general resurrection. Prayers for mercy and forgiveness focus on deliverance from damnation in hell, not from punishment undergone in purgatory. They echo themes which we find in the first Christian centuries. Cranmer shows particular partiality to themes drawn from the parable of judgment in Matthew 25. The result is a rite which is too much influenced by medieval themes to return entirely to the paschal and baptismal focus of the early rites, but which does moderate the fear of judgment that dominated the rites of the late middle ages and which eliminates the various abuses associated with the doctrine of purgatory.

Martin Bucer in his critique of the 1549 book argued, according to the customary teaching of the continental reformers, that scripture offered no warrant for prayers for the departed.[42] He therefore called for their removal from both the burial rite and the intercession at the eucharist. Cranmer's 1552 revision took account of this critique on the part of Bucer and others.[43] Reference to the departed was removed from intercessions at the eucharist, and the burial rite was extensively reworked. The entire office was now to take place at the grave and provisions for a celebration of the eucharist were removed. Only two prayers were retained for burial. The closest that these prayers come to petition for the departed is one which agrees with Bucer's suggested language:

that we with this our brother, and al other departed in the

true faith of thy holy name, maye haue our perfect consumma-
cion and blisse, both in body and soule, in thy eternal and
euerlastyng glory.[44]

The 1552 rite, though sparing, was retained in 1559, although Latin editions of the prayer book provided for an office in the church and a celebration of the eucharist. The 1662 book once again made provision for a
service in the church, restoring psalms and directing that the lesson be read
there. The psalms were not those of 1549, but psalms 39 and 90, apparently
drawn from proposals of Jeremy Taylor, and the psalms with the lesson
from 1 Corinthians 15 may have been intended for use with the daily office.
At the eucharistic intercession, the 1662 book restored reference to the
departed, but in the form of a thanksgiving for them and a petition that we
might follow their good examples:

> And we also bless thy holy Name for all thy servants
> departed this life in thy faith and fear; beseeching thee to
> give us grace so to follow their good examples, that with
> them we may be partakers of their heavenly kingdom.[45]

The principal alteration made in the rite in American prayer books in
1789 and 1892 was to replace the full psalms with selected verses from
each. The formula for the committal underwent a variety of changes in various editions of the book.

The American Book of Common Prayer 1928 included both a restoration
of prayer for the departed and a provision for a burial eucharist. In the burial office itself,[46] the provisions for psalms and lessons was expanded by the
inclusion of selections from Psalms 27, 46, 121, and 131, and from Romans
8 and John 14. The office in the church was filled out by rubrics permitting
the use of a hymn or anthem, the Creed, the Lord's Prayer, and other
prayers, concluding with the Aaronic blessing. For the 1549 anthems at the
grave the 1928 book provided an alternative set with a somewhat more
hopeful focus, consisting of John 6:37, Romans 8:11, and Psalm 16:10, 12.

The following provisions were made for petitions for the departed in the
eucharistic intercession, the prayers of the burial office, and the eucharistic
propers for a burial in 1928. Key phrases are underlined.

Eucharistic Intercession

And we also bless thy holy Name for all thy servants departed this life in thy faith and fear; beseeching thee to grant them continual growth in thy love and service, and to give us grace so to follow their good examples, that with them we may be partakers of thy heavenly kingdom.[47]

Burial Office

Remember thy servant, O Lord, according to the favour which thou bearest unto thy people, and grant that, increasing in knowledge and love of thee, *he* may go from strength to strength, in the life of perfect service, in thy heavenly kingdom; through Jesus Christ our Lord, who liveth and reigneth with thee and the Holy Ghost ever, one God, world without end. *Amen.*[48]

O God, whose mercies cannot be numbered; Accept our prayers on behalf of the soul of thy servant departed, and grant *him* an entrance into the land of light and joy, in the fellowship of thy saints; through Jesus Christ our Lord. *Amen.*[49]

O Almighty God, the God of the spirits of all flesh, who by a voice from heaven didst proclaim, Blessed are the dead who die in the Lord; Multiply, we beseech thee, to those who rest in Jesus, the manifold blessings of thy love, that the good work which thou didst begin in them may be perfected unto the day of Jesus Christ. And of thy mercy, O heavenly Father, vouchsafe that we, who now serve thee here on earth, may at last, together with them, be found meet to be partakers of the inheritance of the saints in light; for the sake of the same thy Son Jesus Christ our Lord. *Amen.*[50]

At a Eucharist at the Burial of the Dead

O eternal Lord God, who holdest all souls in life; <u>Vouchsafe, we beseech thee, to thy whole Church in paradise and on earth, thy light and thy peace</u>; and grant that we, following the good examples of those who have served thee here and are now at rest, may at the last enter with them into thine unending joy; through Jesus Christ our Lord. *Amen.*[51]

or the prayer from the burial office, "O God, whose mercies cannot be numbered."

For an Anniversary of One Departed

Almighty God, we remember this day before thee thy faithful servant [N.], and we pray thee that, <u>having opened to *him* the gates of larger life, thou wilt receive *him* more and more into thy joyful service, that *he* may win, with thee and thy servants everywhere, the eternal victory</u>; through Jesus Christ our Lord. *Amen.*[52]

Memorial Days

Almighty God, our heavenly Father, in whose hands are the living and the dead; We give thee thanks for all those thy servants who have laid down their lives in the service of their country. <u>Grant to them thy mercy and the light of thy presence, that the good work which thou hast begun in them may be perfected</u>; through Jesus Christ our Lord. *Amen.*[53]

Notice besides the traditional petitions for mercy, light, and peace and for a share in Christ's victory a new theme — growth in God's love and service and increase in knowledge and love. This is a recovery of a theme which we find in such Eastern fathers as Gregory of Nyssa and represents a positive statement of the purpose which is generally expressed in the West as purgation. The recovery of prayer for the departed in the 1928 book was facilitated by a widespread sense after the experience of World War I that some kind of prayer for the departed was appropriate. This sense overrode the hesitance of Episcopal evangelicals about such prayer.

5. The Provisions of the Book of Common Prayer 1979

In the process of revision which culminated in the Book of Common Prayer 1979, the provisions of the 1928 book for ministry at the time of death and the burial of the dead were completely reworked. The new rites were as follows:

Ministration to the Sick (see chapter 4)

Ministration at the Time of Death
A Prayer for a Person near Death
Litany at the Time of Death
A Commendation at the Time of Death
A Commendatory Prayer
Petition for the Departed

Prayers for a Vigil

Reception of the Body

The Burial of the Dead (Rites I and II)
Liturgy of the Word
    Entrance Anthems
    Collect(s)
    Readings from the Old Testament, Epistles, and Gospels
    Psalms for Use between the Readings
    Homily
    Apostles' Creed
Proper Prayers of the People
The Celebration of the Holy Communion
    Proper Preface
    Proper Postcommunion Prayer

The Commendation
  Anthem (Byzantine *kontakion*)
  Commendation
  Dismissal and/or Blessing with Anthems for the Procession

Committal (Rites I and II)
Anthems
[Blessing of the Grave]
Committal
Lord's Prayer
Prayers
Dismissal

Undergirding these various provisions is a theology which places the death of a Christian in a paschal, baptismal, and eucharistic context. The paschal context is set by the opening prayer of the rite for the ministration to the dying, which asks that God comfort the dying person "with the promise of life everlasting, given in the resurrection of your Son Jesus Christ our Lord."[54] It finds its fullest expression, however, in the note appended to the burial office:

> The liturgy for the dead is an Easter liturgy. It finds all its meaning in the resurrection. Because Jesus was raised from the dead, we, too, shall be raised.
>
> The liturgy, therefore, is characterized by joy, in the certainty that "neither death, nor life, nor principalities, nor things present, nor things to come, nor powers, nor height, nor depth, nor anything else in all creation, will be able to separate us from the love of God in Christ Jesus our Lord."
>
> This joy, however, does not make human grief unchristian. The very love we have for each other in Christ brings deep sorrow when we are parted by death. Jesus himself wept at

the grave of his friend. So, while we rejoice that one we love has entered into the nearer presence of our Lord, we sorrow in sympathy with those who mourn.[55]

The 1979 provisions thus represent a recovery of the Christian perspectives toward death in the early centuries.

Ministration at the Time of Death

By taking the provisions for the ministry at the time of death out of the context of the ordinary ministry to the sick, the 1979 revision has distinguished more sharply than earlier prayer books did between the focus on the restoration of health in the ministry to the sick and the focus on preparation for death in this rite.[56] The initial rubric in 1979 directs that the minister of the congregation be notified when someone is near death, that the ministrations of the church may be provided. It would certainly be appropriate that the dying person make a special confession at this time, if this has not been done earlier in the illness, and that communion be administered. The Episcopal Church has not, however, developed a strong theology of communion as viaticum. The language of the forms for unction make it possible to administer it in these circumstances, although it is not treated in this book as primarily a last rite.

The first prayer in this rite owes some of its language to the 1662 prayer for use "when there appeareth but small hope of recovery," but its brevity makes it far more appropriate at a time when a dying person's attention and vitality are ebbing. The litany has been recast in contemporary language and revised to avoid suggesting a body-soul dualism that is Greek rather than Christian in origin. The two commendations are retained, but the absolution has been removed. A final prayer for the departed brings the office to an appropriate close at death.

Prayers for a Vigil and the Reception of the Body

Although prior American prayer books have made no provision for them, "wakes" or vigils before the burial office — in the home, the funeral home, or the church — have long been customary, and in some areas it has also been customary to ask clergy to take prayers during these wakes. The 1979 provisions allow the use of psalms, lessons, and prayers from the burial office at this time and the use of the litany at the time of death.[57] The following is provided as an alternative set of intercessions on such occasions. It may also be used with the Rite II Burial Office.

Dear Friends: It was our Lord Jesus Christ himself who said, "Come to me, all you who labor and are burdened, and I will give you rest." Let us pray, then, for our brother (sister) N., that *he* may rest from *his* labors, and enter the light of God's eternal sabbath rest.

Receive, O Lord, your servant, for *he* returns to you.
Into your hands, O Lord, we commend our brother (sister) N.

Wash *him* in the holy font of everlasting life, and clothe *him* in *his* heavenly wedding garment.
Into your hands, O Lord, we commend our brother (sister) N.

May *he* hear your words of invitation, "Come, you blessed of my Father."
Into your hands, O Lord, we commend our brother (sister) N.

May *he* gaze upon you, Lord, face to face, and taste the blessedness of perfect rest.
Into your hands, O Lord, we commend our brother (sister) N.

May angels surround *him*, and saints welcome *him* in peace.
Into your hands, O Lord, we commend our brother (sister) N.

The Officiant concludes

Almighty God, our Father in heaven, before whom live all
who die in the Lord: Receive our *brother N.* into the courts
of your heavenly dwelling place. Let *his* heart and soul ring
out in joy to you, O Lord, the living God, and the God of
those who live. This we ask through Christ our Lord.
Amen.[58]

The rubrics are sufficiently flexible to permit the vigil to take the form of a
liturgy of the word, one of the daily offices, or informal devotions. The
intercession is paschal in spirit and includes baptismal and eucharistic allusions as well.

The prayers at the reception of the body at the church[59] may take place
before a vigil (if that is held at the church), when the body is brought to the
church for the burial office, or at the beginning of the burial office (if that
office begins with the procession into the church). It is suggested that the
paschal candle go before the body into the church — a reminder that in
death Christians make Christ's passover their own. The provisions include
prayer for both the departed and the bereaved.

The Burial Office

From the early centuries, a station in the church before burial has been customary at the death of a Christian. There is precedent for both a form of the
daily office and a burial eucharist at this station. We have witnesses to the
eucharist in the early centuries. Some form of the office is the predominant
liturgy at this station in the East. In the Catholic West, early medieval rites
give witness to an office at this station; in the late middle ages, both the
office and the eucharist were often celebrated in the church; and since the
late middle ages the eucharist has been the predominant liturgy for this station in the Catholic tradition. A liturgy which took the general form of a
daily office has been the predominant rite in Anglicanism, but there was
provision for a burial eucharist in 1549 and this provision was restored in
the American church in 1928. In the twentieth century the burial eucharist
became increasingly common, and the 1979 rite for the burial office is

placed in the context of the eucharist rather than the daily office (though the celebration of the holy communion may be omitted).[60] The initial rubrics direct that a baptized Christian is properly buried from the church and that the service take place at a time when the congregation has opportunity to attend. The coffin is to be closed before the service and covered with a pall or other suitable covering.

The rite begins with a revised set of anthems for the procession into the church. The first two anthems are those of the 1549 book; the last anthem is replaced by two others — Romans 14:7-8 (new) and Revelation 14:13 (formerly used at the committal). Unfortunately, attention was not given to the concerns of inclusive language, so that the anthems are unsuited for the burial of a woman. Rite II gives a responsorial version of the 1549 anthem at the grave, "In the midst of life," and also allows the use of a hymn in place of these anthems. Rite I retains the 1928 collect for a burial eucharist and provides a collect for the burial of a child; Rite II adapts a collect for Eastertide, gives the 1928 collect as an alternative, provides a new alternative, gives a collect for the burial of a child, and allows the addition of a collect for the bereaved. A wide selection of proper lessons and psalms is provided for the liturgy of the word, providing appropriate propers for a variety of circumstances. A homily may follow. The liturgy of the word is appropriately concluded by the Apostles' Creed, which is given an introduction in Rite II which links the rite of burial with baptism.

Each rite has a proper set of intercessions for the prayers of the people. Rite I has a series of petitions (drawn largely from traditional prayers) which highlight the paschal and baptismal themes of the liturgy. It may also be used with Rite II. Rite II has adapted a litany from the Roman Catholic *Ordo Exsequiarum*:

> For our brother (sister), let us pray to our Lord Jesus Christ, who said, "I am Resurrection and I am Life."
>
> Lord, you consoled Martha and Mary in their distress; draw near to us who mourn for N., and dry the tears of those who weep.
> *Hear us, Lord.*

You wept at the grave of Lazarus, your friend; comfort us in our sorrow.
Hear us, Lord.

You raised the dead to life; give to our brother (sister) eternal life.
Hear us, Lord.

You promised paradise to the thief who repented; bring our brother (sister) to the joys of heaven.
Hear us, Lord.

Our brother (sister) was washed in Baptism and anointed with the Holy Spirit; give *him* fellowship with all your saints.
Hear us, Lord.

He was nourished with your Body and Blood; grant *him* a place at your table in heaven.
Hear us, Lord.

Comfort us in our sorrows at the death of our brother (sister); let our faith be our consolation, and eternal life our hope.
Hear us, Lord.

. . .

Lord Jesus Christ, we commend to you our brother (sister) N., who was reborn by water and the Spirit in Holy Baptism. Grant that *his* death may recall to us your victory over death, and be an occasion for us to renew our trust in your Father's love. Give us, we pray, the faith to follow where you have led the way; and where you live and reign with the Father and the Holy Spirit, to the ages of ages.
Amen.

or this

Father of all, we pray to you for N., and for all those whom we love but see no longer. Grant to them eternal rest. Let light perpetual shine upon them. May *his* soul and the souls of all the departed, through the mercy of God, rest in peace. *Amen.*[61]

Note the allusions to baptism and the baptismal anointing and to the eucharist in the litany. The first alternative for the concluding collect picks up these themes. The second alternative simply joins two short traditional intercessions for the departed. This version of the prayers of the people is obviously only appropriate for a regular communicant. When there is no celebration of the holy communion, the officiant may select other prayers in place of those in the rite.

The celebration of the holy communion begins with the peace. It is appropriate for the family or friends to present the bread and wine at the offertory. A proper preface and postcommunion prayer are provided. The text of the postcommunion prayer is worth examining more closely:

Almighty God, we thank you that in your great love you have fed us with the spiritual food and drink of the Body and Blood of your Son Jesus Christ, and have given us a foretaste of your heavenly banquet. Grant that this Sacrament may be to us a comfort in affliction, and a pledge of our inheritance in that kingdom where there is no death, neither sorrow nor crying, but the fullness of joy with all your saints; through Jesus Christ our Lord. *Amen.*[62]

Here the eucharist at a burial is understood not as a sacrifice for the departed, but as a consolation for the living, which unites them in eucharistic communion with the departed and gives them a pledge of Christ's final victory.

A commendation of the departed follows — a new feature of this book which serves the same function as what is called the final commendation and farewell in the present Roman Catholic rites (an adaptation of the old absolution of the body). The anthem suggested for this is the Byzantine kontakion cited above. The commendation is the commendatory prayer by John Cosin found in the ministration to the dying. This rite serves as an appropriate farewell for those who cannot be present at the committal. The commendation is omitted if the body is not present during the service in the church. After the blessing, the final anthems give a reprise of the paschal themes of the burial office:

> Christ is risen from the dead, trampling down death by death, and giving life to those in the tomb.

> The Sun of Righteousness is gloriously risen, giving light to those who sat in darkness and in the shadow of death.

> The Lord will guide our feet into the way of peace, having taken away the sins of the world.

> Christ will open the kingdom of heaven to all who believe in his Name, saying, Come, O blessed of my Father; inherit the kingdom prepared for you.

> Into paradise may the angels lead you. At your coming may the martyrs receive you, and bring you into the holy city Jerusalem.[63]

The first anthem is the Byzantine troparion for Easter; the last is one of the chief antiphons for burial in Western tradition. The second and third anthems, based on the *Benedictus*, recall the traditional use of that canticle at the grave in the later Roman rite. The fourth anthem is adapted from Matthew 25, a favorite reference of Cranmer in texts for funerals. The *Benedictus*, the *Nunc dimittis,* and the *Pascha nostrum* are also suggested as canticles for the procession. We have already noted the use of the *Benedictus* at burial in the Roman tradition; the *Nunc dimittis* is found in some liturgies of the continental Lutheran churches and is fitting for its eschatological themes; the *Pascha nostrum*, Cranmer's Easter invitatory, reprises the paschal theme of the burial liturgy.

The Committal

The service at the grave utilizes traditional Anglican materials.[64] The two sets of alternative anthems from the 1928 book[65] open the service in Rite I; in Rite II only the second set is used, since the first was employed as an alternative set of entrance anthems at the burial office in the church. The form of committal makes skillful use of the Aaronic benediction. The prayers which close the office are drawn from the prayer book tradition and older Western sources. A consecration of the grave is provided for use when appropriate.

Other Provisions

The 1979 book provides in addition to the two rites for burial an order for the burial of dead which may be used when neither of the two rites is deemed appropriate for pastoral reasons.[66] The order is analogous to orders provided for the eucharist and marriage in the 1979 book. The pastoral considerations involved might be the desire to use the burial rite of a prior edition of the prayer book, or circumstances in which a Christian family wishes to arrange for the burial of someone who is not baptized, does not profess or has repudiated the Christian faith, or has died in circumstances which make prayers for God's mercy more appropriate than prayers of paschal victory. *The Book of Occasional Services* provides appropriate materials to use with the order on such occasions.

The 1979 book also provides a set of eucharistic propers for memorial eucharists (Various Occasions 8) and lists the Commemoration of All Souls on November 2 as a lesser feast in the calendar. While a memorial celebration of the eucharist fits appropriately within the theology of the 1979 book, it is perhaps unfortunate that this book abandons the older Anglican tradition of commemorating the departed on All Saints' Day. Massey Shepherd wrote in his commentary on the 1928 Book of Common Prayer:

> The Reformers eliminated All Souls' Day from the Calendar
> . . . because they recognized that the New Testament pro-
> vides no warrant for the distinction of 'all saints' and 'all

souls.' . . . It was only after the Church began to develop the cult of the martyrs that the distinction between saints and other less noteworthy Christians was made. The Prayer Book propers for All Saints' Day are intended as a commemoration of all faithful departed souls.[67]

A similar distinction between the saints and the rest of the departed appears in the Prayers of the People in the Rite I Eucharist of the 1979 book:

And we also bless thy holy Name for all the servants departed this life in thy faith and fear [especially ___], beseeching thee to grant them continual growth in the love and service; and to give us grace so to follow the good examples of [___ and of] all thy saints, that with them we may be partakers of thy heavenly kingdom.[68]

The 1979 book does not mandate, however, the observance of All Souls' Day, and it is possible to continue to follow the sounder instincts of earlier Anglican prayer books and to remember *all* the departed on All Saints' Day.

There have been three major strands of theology in the burial rites of the various editions of the Book of Common Prayer: 1) in the theology which predominated at the Reformation, the only appropriate prayers for the departed are thanksgiving, a plea for rest after death, and a plea for mercy at the day of judgment, since the destiny of a Christian to damnation or salvation is fixed at the time of death; 2) in the theology which predominated in the West in the middle ages, prayers and the offering of the eucharist may alleviate the suffering in purgatory of those who are not damned but also are not yet fit for the immediate presence of God; and 3) in the theology which is rooted in the practice of the first Christian centuries, the context of burial is paschal, baptismal, and eucharistic, prayer for growth in God's love and service is appropriate for all the departed, and the burial eucharist gives expression to the communion between the living and the departed within the body of Christ which not even death can break. In reviewing the various provisions of the Book of Common Prayer 1979, we note that options make possible a rite which expresses any of these theologies. The rites are really designed to articulate the third theological strand, but texts may be used which are rooted in the first strand. The eucharist is presented as the ordinary context of the rite, but the Celebration of the Holy Communion may be omitted. Even the offering of prayer and the eucharist to alleviate the purgatorial sufferings of the departed is not ruled out, although this is not the most natural interpretation of the texts of the rite.

Conclusions

In all cultures burial rites are liminal — moments of transition for the departed and the bereaved from one constellation of relationships to another.[69] But Christ has changed the face of death for us, so that it becomes the gateway to eternal life. For Christians, however, the threshold of this transition is not physical death but our baptismal death to sin. The earthly journey which a Christian begins with preparation for baptism is completed in death. Burial rites are not sacramental in the same sense as the other pastoral offices, for the grace required for this journey has been given in baptism, renewed as necessary in reconciliation, sustained by the eucharist, and strengthened by unction. The prayers of the people for Rite II skillfully recapitulate the stages of this sacramental journey. All that remains is for Christians to enter into the joy of their Lord as they consummate by their deaths the task of making his passover their own.

The texts and rites of Christian burial therefore echo those of baptism and the eucharist, and like baptism and the eucharist they are rooted in the paschal mystery of Christ's death and resurrection. They also echo the liturgy of the feast of All Saints, for Christians by their deaths make the triumph of the saints over death their own. The 1979 rites echo all of these themes. The commendation at the time of death bids Christians to set out on the last stage of their journey in the name of the Trinity in which they were baptized; the use of the Apostles' creed at the burial eucharist echoes this baptismal orientation of the rites. The death of Christ and the death of the martyrs have classically been celebrated in the eucharistic feast; the same is true of the death of ordinary Christians. The postcommunion prayer is a reminder that the eucharistic banquet is a pledge of the solidarity of Christians living and departed in the body of Christ — a solidarity not broken even by death and a solidarity which will find its ultimate expression in the messianic banquet of which eucharistic communion is a pledge. All of this is made possible because Christ has transformed the nature of death by his resurrection, "trampling down death by death, and giving life to those in the tomb."

ENDNOTES

[1]For a comparison of pagan and Christian rites, see Cyrille Vogel, "The Cultic Environment of the Deceased in the Early Christian Period," in Achille Triacca, ed., *Temple of the Holy Spirit: sickness and death of the Christian in the liturgy: the twenty-first Liturgical Conference Saint-Serge*, trans. Matthew O'Connell (New York: Pueblo, 1983), pages 259-276. For the history of funeral rites in the Latin tradition, see the articles in that work and the following English articles and works: Damien Sicard, "Christian Death," in A. G. Martimort, *The Church at Prayer*, vol. III, trans. Matthew O'Connell (Collegeville, MN: Liturgical Press, 1988), pages 221-240; and Richard Rutherford, *The Death of a Christian: The Rite of Funerals* (New York: Pueblo, 1980).

[2]The ultimate origin of these observances is the understanding of death in what Cyrille Vogel calls the "human physiology" of late antiquity. See his article, "The Cultic Environment of the Deceased in the Early Christian Period," in Achille Triacca, ed., *Temple of the Holy Spirit: sickness and death of the Christian in the liturgy*, pages 259-276, here pages 267-270.

[3]*Apostolic Constitutions*, Book 8, § 30. Translation adapted from James Donaldson, ed., *Constitution of the Holy Apostles*, in A. Cleveland Cox, ed., *The Ante-Nicene Fathers*, vol. 7 (Buffalo, NY: Christian Literature Company, 1886), page 464.

[4]Book 8, §41-42, 43. Translation adapted from James Donaldson, ed.,

Constitution of the Holy Apostles, in A. Cleveland Cox, ed., *The Ante-Nicene Fathers,* vol. 7, pages 497-498.

[5]See here Charles Gusmer, *And You Visited Me: Sacramental Ministry to the Sick and Dying* (New York: Pueblo, 1984), chapter 3; idem, s. v. "Viaticum," in Peter Fink, ed., *The New Dictionary of Sacramental Worship* (Collegeville, MN: Michael Glazier/Liturgical Press, 1990), pages 1314-1316; Damien Sicard, "Christian Death," in A. G. Martimort, *The Church at Prayer,* vol. III, 221-240, here, pages 221-236; idem, "Preparation for Death and Prayer for the Dying," in Achille Triacca, ed., *Temple of the Holy Spirit,* pages 239-246; idem, *La liturgie de la mort dans les Églises latines, des origines à la réforme carolingienne* (Münster, Westfallen: Aschendorffsche Verlagsbuchhandlung, 1978). The last work is presently the definitive study.

[6]This is the authentic prayer of commendation in the Roman rite, found in the Gelasian Sacramentary. I have adapted the translation found in Damien Sicard, "Christian Death," in A. G. Martimort, *The Church at Prayer,* vol. III, pages 221-240, here page 234.

[7]The two texts above are found in the sacramentary of Gellone, a version of the Gelasian sacramentary. The types cited in the second text vary from manuscript to manuscript. The translation is adapted from the study of the texts in Damien Sicard, "Preparation for Death and Prayer for the Dying," in Achille Triacca, ed., *Temple of the Holy Spirit,* pages 239-246.

[8]This responsory was first used at the time of death. It was later used at the reception of the body in the church for the vigil and also for the absolution of the body. Early versions do not have the final verse, "Rest eternal." This is my translation of the current text in the present Roman rite, found in the *Ordo Exsequiarum* (no. 47). See Richard Rutherford, *The Death of a Christian,* pages 43 and 66 (use at the time of death), pages 60-62, 67, and 79-80 (at the absolution of the body), page 66 (at the entry into the church).

[9]This is another responsory used for the absolution of the body. This is my translation of the current text in the present Roman rite, found in the

Ordo Exsequiarum (no. 188) For its use here, see Richard Rutherford, *Death of a Christian,* pages 61-62 and 79-80.

[10]This antiphon was frequently used with psalm 93 at the time of the preparation of the body. We also find it used with Psalm 139. I have adapted the translation in Robert Rutherford, *The Death of a Christian,* page 45. On its use see Rutherford, pages 44-45, and pages 82-83.

[11]On the origin of this antiphon, see Bernard Botte, "The Earliest Formulas of Prayer for the Dead," in Achille Triacca, ed., *Temple of the Holy Spirit,* pages 17-31, here pages 19-21. This text originally had only two members and read, "Into paradise may the angels lead thee, and at thy coming may the martyrs receive thee in glory." It was used in the rite of Milan with Psalm 73 and echoes the language of verse 24 of the Vulgate version of that psalm. It was later used responsorially with Psalm 114 in that rite. In the standard Roman ritual after the Council of Trent it was joined with the following antiphon — even though they were set to two different modes. For its use with Psalm 25 in this tradition, see Richard Rutherford, *The Death of a Christian,* page 48; for its use with Psalm 114, see the same work, page 81.

[12]This text was frequently used as an antiphon with Psalm 114. In the standard Roman ritual after the Council of Trent it was joined with the prior antiphons — even though they were set to two different modes. For the text, see the *Ordo Exsequiarum,* no. 153.

[13]This text from 2 Esdras 2:34-35 seems at first to have been employed as an antiphon, then as a text used in place of the *Gloria Patri* (as in the first responsory above). See the discussion in Bernard Botte, "The Earliest Formulas of Prayer for the Dead," in Achille Triacca, ed., *Temple of the Holy Spirit,* pages 17-31, here pages 21-22.

[14]This list of psalms is taken from Damien Sicard, "Christian Death," in A. G. Martimort, *The Church at Prayer,* vol. III, 221-240, here, page 237, note 50.

[15]Charles Gusmer, *And You Visited Me: Sacramental Ministry to the Sick and Dying* (New York: Pueblo, 1984), page 110.

[16]*Epistle to the Ephesians,* § 20.

[17]Antiphons were used with different psalms in different rites, and psalms, antiphons by themselves, and responsories migrated, from place to place and age to age, from one station or procession in the rites to another.

[18]The rite is described by Richard Rutherford, *The Death of a Christian*, pages 65-69.

[19]See the discussion in Richard Rutherford, *The Death of a Christian*, pages 69-77.

[20]See the discussion in Richard Rutherford, *The Death of a Christian*, pages 77-87.

[21]See Richard Rutherford, *The Death of a Christian*, pages 87-102.

[22]See Richard Rutherford, *The Death of a Christian*, pages 68-69, for this rite at the grave. It first appears in the curial rite appended to the Franciscan breviary in 1260.

[23]Latin texts with an English translation in Ferdinand Cabrol, ed., *The Roman Missal in Latin and English for Every Day in the Year*, 12th edition (New York: J.P. Kenedy and Sons, n.d.), pages 1374-1397. The English translation for these two texts is adapted from pages 1376 and 1379.

[24]For the Latin text, see Ferdinand Cabrol, ed., *The Roman Missal*, pages 1376-1378. For the translation see *The Hymnal 1940*, Hymn 468.

[25]The Latin text of the rite as established in the Roman ritual promulgated after the Council of Trent is given with an English translation in Ferdinand Cabrol, *The Roman Missal*, pages 1397-1399. I have adapted the English translation slightly. The opening prayer was in its original form a bidding to prayer.

[26] See Joseph Jungmann, *The Mass of the Roman Rite: Its Origins and Development (Missarum Sollemnia)*, vol. 1, trans. Francis A. Brunner (Westminster, MD: Christian Classics, 1986), pages 127-141 for the way in which votive masses, particularly masses for the dead, distorted Christian liturgy, theology, and practice at the end of the middle ages.

[27]See Sermon 285:5 (*Patrologia Latina* 38, column 1295): "ut not sint suscepti nostri sed advocati" — the saints are not our clients but our advocates or patrons.

[28]On the influence of Augustine, see Richard Rutherford, *The Death of a Christian*, pages 17-18.

[29]For Gregory the Great, see Richard Rutherford, *The Death of a Christian*, pages 26-28. For the story of Justus, see Gregory's *Dialogues*, Book 4:55 (*Patrologia Latina* 77, columns 420-421 C).

[30]For the Greek text of the rites, see Jacobus Goar, ed., *Euchologion sive Rituale Graecorum* (Venice: Ex Typographia Bartolomaei Javarina, 1730; reprint, Graz: Akademische Druck und Verlagsanstalt, 1950), pages 421-478. English translations of the current rites for laity (the common rite), priests, and children are found in Isabel F. Hapgood, trans., *Service Book of the Holy Orthodox-Catholic Apostolic Church*, 5th edition (Englewood, NJ: Antiochean Orthodox Christian Archdiocese of New York and All North America, 1975), pages 368-393, 394-423, 242-434. The rites are modified in Easter Season. A brief structural analysis of the rites is found in Miguel Arranz, "Les prières presbytérales de la 'Pannychis' de l'ancien Euchologe byzantin et la 'Panikhida' des défunts," *Orientalia Christiana Periodica* 40 (1974), pages 314-343 and 41 (1975), pages 119-139. The funeral form of pannychis is treated in the second part, pages 127-139. The following articles in Achille Triacca, ed., *Temple of the Holy Spirit,* treat the Byzantine funeral rites: Alexis Kniazeff, "The Death of a Priest According to the Slavic Trebnik," pages 65-94; Pierre Kovalevsky, "Funeral Rites in the Easter Season and Prayers for the Dead from Easter to Ascension," pages 95-106; Alexandre Nélidow, "Rite for the Funeral of Children," pages 161-173. Kniazeff provides the most substantial analysis.

[31]The translation of this prayer is adapted from that in Isabel F. Hapgood, trans., *Service Book of the Holy Orthodox-Catholic Apostolic Church*, page 369. The phrase inserted in brackets seems to have been included in early forms of the prayer. See the discussion in Bernard Botte, "The Earliest Formulas of Prayer for the Dead," in Achille Triacca, ed., *Temple of the Holy Spirit*, pages 17-31, here pages 24-27 and notes 10, 11, and 18, page 304.

[32]Translation from the BCP 1979, page 482.

[33]BCP 1928, pages 316-320.

[34]BCP 1928, pages 317-319

[35]See the prayer in Isabel F. Hapgood, *Service Book of the Holy Orthodox-Catholic Apostolic Church*, pages 365-366.

[36]BCP 1928, pages 319-320.

[37]The rite is found in the BCP 1549, pages 269-277. For a commentary on the rites in the various editions of the BCP, see Marion J. Hatchett, *Commentary on the American Prayer Book* (New York: Seabury, 1980), pages 477-482 (general) and 483-500 (comparison of 1979 with provisions of prior rites).

[38]BCP 1549, page 270.

[39]BCP 1549, pages 275-276.

[40]BCP 1549, page 277.

[41]BCP 1549, page 222.

[42]See E. C. Whitaker, ed., *Martin Bucer and the Book of Common Prayer* (Great Wakering, UK: Alcuin Club/Mayhew McCrimmon, 1974), pages 50-53, 126-129.

[43]BCP 1552, pages 424-427.

[44]BCP 1552, page 427.

[45]The rite may be found in the appropriate column of Paul V. Marshall, *Prayer Book Parallels: The public services of the Church arranged for comparative study* (New York: Church Hymnal, 1989), pages 530-573. See this for the American rites of 1789 and 1892 as well.

[46]BCP 1928, pages 324-337. A separate rite is provided in this book for the burial of a child on pages 338-342. Massey Hamilton Shepherd, Jr., *The Oxford American Prayer Book Commentary* (New York: Oxford University Press, 1950), provides a commentary on the rite in the texts associated with these pages.

[47]BCP 1928, pages 74-75. See Massey Shepherd's commentary on this text in *The Oxford American Prayer Book Commentary*.

[48]BCP 1928, page 332.

[49]BCP 1928, page 334.

[50]BCP 1928, pages 335-336.

[51]BCP 1928, page 268.

[52]BCP 1928, page 598

[53]BCP 1928, page 42.

[54]BCP 1979, page 462.

[55]BCP 1979, page 507.

[56]BCP 1979, pages 462-467. For commentary, see Marion J. Hatchett, *Commentary on the American Prayer Book*, pages 472-475; Leonel Mitchell, *Praying Shapes Believing: A Theological Commentary on the Book of Common Prayer* (Minneapolis, MN: Seabury/Winston, 1985), pages 215-216.

[57]BCP 1979, pages 465-466. See the commentary by Marion Hatchett, *Commentary on the American Prayer Book,* page 475, and Leonel Mitchell, *Praying Shapes Believing*, pages 217-218.

[58]BCP 1979, pages 465-466. Marion Hatchett identifies the source of this litany as Gethsemani Abbey. See his *Commentary on the American Prayer Book*, page 475.

[59]BCP 1979, pages 466-467. See Marion Hatchett, *Commentary on the American Prayer Book*, page 476.

[60]Rite I is found in the BCP 1979 on pages 468-484; Rite II on pages 490-500. See Marion Hatchett, *Commentary on the American Prayer Book*, pages 483-491, and Leonel Mitchell, *Praying Shapes Believing*, pages 218-227.

[61]BCP 1979, pages 497-498. The original is no. 56, suggested for use at the station at the grave. The English version may be found in International Commission on English in the Liturgy, *The Rites of the Catholic Church as Revised by Decree of the Second Vatican Ecumenical Council and Published by Authority of Pope Paul VI*, vol. 1. (New York: Pueblo, 1983), pages 780-781. The BCP version shortens the citation of the opening bidding, adds a petition, and slightly alters the wording of some of the other petitions. The concluding collects are not part of the original Roman Catholic text.

[62]BCP 1979, pages 482 and 498.

[63]BCP 1979, pages 483-484 and 499-500.

[64]BCP 1979, pages 484-487 and 501-503. Additional Prayers are found on pages 487-489 and 503-505. See Marion Hatchett, *Commentary on the American Prayer Book*, pages 491-500, and Leonel Mitchell, *Praying Shapes Believing*, pages 227-232.

[65]In the first set, only the responsory "In the midst of life" from the 1549 book is used; Job 14:1-2 is omitted.

[66]BCP 1979, page 506. See Marion Hatchett, *Commentary on the American Prayer Book*, page 500.

[67]Massey Shepherd, *Oxford American Prayer Book Commentary*, commentary for page 256.

[68]BCP 1979, page 330.

[69]Philippe Aries has traced the shifting attitudes in Western culture to death in his work, *Western Attitudes Toward Death: From the Middle Ages to the Present* (Baltimore, MD: Johns Hopkins University Press, 1974). The early desire to be buried *ad sanctos*, near the bodies of the saints, represented a radical shift from pagan attitudes toward the dead, as Peter Brown also notes in *The Cult of the Saints* (Chicago: University of Chicago Press, 1981). By the sixteenth century, some pagan attitudes were beginning to reassert themselves in Christian guise.

PART II

EPISCOPAL
SERVICES

CHAPTER 6

THE MINISTRY OF THE NEW COVENANT

THE ORDINATION OF BISHOPS, PRIESTS, AND DEACONS

1. Ministerial Office and Ordination in the New Testament

The Royal Priesthood

At Sinai, God entered into covenant with the people of Israel and constituted them as a "treasured possession out of all the peoples of the earth, . . . a priestly kingdom and a holy nation."[1] This identity as a priestly people later found expression in a hereditary priesthood and a sacrificial cultus, eventually restricted to the temple in Jerusalem first erected under Solomon. In the literature of the New Testament, the cultic structure of Judaism was seen as reaching both its fulfilment and its end in Christ.

Christ's body was the temple which was to be raised on the third day after its destruction (John 2:19-22), for it is in the encounter with him that Christians worship the Father in Spirit and in truth (John 4:23-26); and Christians are the living blocks out of which he was to build the temple indwelt by God's Spirit (1 Peter 2:5). The sacrificial cultus was both abolished and fulfilled in the offering which Christ consummated on the cross

(Hebrews 9-11) and prefigured at the last supper (Matthew 11:26-29), and the sacrificial self-offering of Christians (Romans 12:1) finds its focus at the eucharistic meal which the church celebrates as Christ's anamnesis until he come again (1 Corinthians 11:23-26). Christ was also the end and the fulfilment of the priesthood through this offering (not a levitical priest, but a high priest after the order of Melchisedek: Hebrews 7-9), and Christians share in that priesthood as members of the body of Christ through baptism (1 Peter 2).

Alexander Schmemann writes eloquently of what this transformation of Israel's religious life through Christ means:

> . . . Christ is the one true priest because he is the one true and perfect man. He is the new Adam, the restoration of that which Adam failed to be . . . . He died the last victim of priestly religion, and in His death priestly _religion_ died and the priestly _life_ was inaugurated. He was killed by the priests, by the "clergy," but His sacrifice destroyed them as it abolished "religion." And it abolished religion because it destroyed the wall of separation between the "natural" and the "supernatural," between "the profane" and the "sacred," the "this-worldly" and the "other-worldly" — which was the only justification and _raison d'etre_ of religion.[2]

In other words, he abolished the distinction between "religion" and "life" which the introduction of the cultic priesthood into Israel's life had caused.

Ministerial Office

For this reason, the structure of ministerial office in the Christian church as the Israel of God (Galatians 6:16)[3] does not derive from the hereditary priesthood of the temple. It derives rather from the structure of Israel as a nation and as a local community, for — as we have seen — Israel as a whole is a "priestly people." Of the church as the people of God, the author of 1 Peter declared:

But you are a chosen race, a royal priesthood, a holy nation,
God's own people, in order that you may declare the mighty acts
of him who called you out of darkness into his marvelous light.[4]

And he bade them, as a holy priesthood, "to offer spiritual sacrifices acceptable to God through Jesus Christ."[5] No office of ministry was identified as
priestly in the New Testament because the whole church is priestly and
shares in Christ's priestly task of reconciling the world to God.[6]

According to the literature of the Old Testament, Israel had originally
been constituted as a nation of twelve tribes under the twelve patriarchs, the
sons of Jacob. Jesus began his ministry by appointing the twelve — a para-
bolic act which signifies the recreation of God's people, for the twelve are to
inherit in God's reign the function of Israel's original patriarchs (Luke
22:28). After Christ's resurrection, they were to exercise a universal authority in the church as the people of God — but it was an authority unique to
them, and not transmissible to later generations. The twelve were sometimes
known as "apostles," but the term also had a broader reference to the itinerant missionaries of the new church, including Paul and Barnabas and others
as well.[7] Apostles such as Paul exercised a ministry of supervision over the
local churches which they founded. In the *Didache*, probably to be dated
toward the beginning of the next century, we still find itinerant missionaries
known as apostles, prophets, and teachers, but this itinerant ministry was
already beginning to disappear.

On a local level, the church was organized differently. In the earlier literature of the New Testament, such as the letters of Paul, we find a variety of
terms used to describe those who ministered and their functions. It appears
from the later literature of the New Testament that local communities soon
began to organize themselves under boards of elders (presbyters) or over-
seers (bishops). These collegial bodies appointed ministers (deacons) to
assist in the charitable and financial affairs of the church and in its worship.
The late New Testament churches thus appear to have a twofold structure
to their local ministerial offices: 1) a collegial body of bishops or presbyters
and 2) assistants known as deacons. In the Jerusalem church the structure
was more complex: the Acts of the Apostles speaks of the ministry of the
presbyterate, the seven appointed for ministry to Greek-speaking Christians,

and the special role exercised by James, the brother of Jesus. The literature of the New Testament does not address the issue of the relationship of ministerial office to liturgical and eucharistic presidency in local communities.

Ordination in the New Testament

The twelve were chosen by Jesus and empowered by the Spirit after his resurrection: the gospels give no evidence that they received ordination. In the literature of the New Testament, however, we find evidence of an emerging rite for induction to ministerial office — what would later be known as ordination. Persons were chosen for ministerial office by lot (as in the case *choosing* of Matthias, Acts 1:26), by apostles (as in the case of presbyters appointed by Paul and Barnabas, Acts 14:23), by other ministers (by Titus as an apostolic delegate, Titus 1:5), or by election of the church (as in the case of the seven, Acts 6:1-6). All of these forms of appointment or election were seen as the prophetic discernment of God's choice of persons to exercise leadership in the church. The person who took on a ministry without any explicit *commis.* commission of the church seems to be the exception in the literature of the New Testament. The laying on of hands and prayer invested the persons chosen with authority for ministry. The laying on of hands is a multivalent action in biblical literature — it can be a gesture of blessing, as when Jesus blesses children (Mark 10:13; see the blessing given by Jacob in Genesis 48:14); a means of imparting the Spirit, as when the apostles lay hands on those who had received only the baptism of John (Acts 8:18-19, 19:6); and a sign of reconciliation and forgiveness (as it apparently is in 1 Timothy 5:22). It is also a sign of commissioning to an office, as it was when Moses commissioned Joshua (Numbers 27:18-23; Deuteronomy 31:14-15; 23). In the New Testament, the twelve lay on hands to appoint seven for ministry to Greek-speaking Christians (Acts 6:1-6), the church in Antioch lays hands on Paul and Barnabas to set them apart for the work to which they are called as missionaries (Acts 13:1-3); and Timothy was given a gift for ministry by prophecy and the laying on of hands by the elders (1 Timothy 4:15) and by Paul (2 Timothy 1:6). It is a gesture which was understood at times to recognize the gift of the Spirit in someone (in Joshua, Numbers 27:18; in the seven, Acts 6:3), and at times to "call down" the gift of the Spirit upon someone (upon Joshua, Deuteronomy 34:9; upon Timothy, 2 Timothy 1:6-7). The basic meaning seems to be that through the instrumentality of human agents, God has touched a person by the Holy Spirit to commission and empower that person for a task.

2. The Emerging Pattern of Ministry and Ordination in the Early Centuries

The Emergence of the Threefold Ministry

With the death of the apostolic generation, we find the beginning of a shift in the structure of ministerial office in the church. A single leader began to emerge at the head of the collegial presbyterate of local churches, and eventually the title bishop was reserved for him, while the title presbyter was reserved for other members of the collegial leadership. The bishop may at times have risen to authority locally as the chief presbyter and at other times have been an appointed delegate of the founding apostle. However the shift occurred, the result was a threefold structure for ministerial office in the local church, with the bishop exercising a local ministry as the head of the college of presbyters and a universal ministry as a member of the college of bishops. Eucharistic presidency was now vested in the bishop and in presbyters by delegation from the bishop. Such a pattern of ministry was first articulated in the letters of Ignatius of Antioch in the early second century. Ignatius saw the bishop as the guarantor of unity in the church. Somewhat later in this century, Irenaeus of Lyons would emphasize the role of the bishop in the preservation of the apostolic witness to Christ. By the end of the century, the threefold ministry seems to have been in place throughout the church. Irenaeus and *1 Clement* were concerned with succession in apostolic ministry — though they do not identify such succession in terms of ordination as the church was later to do. *1 Clement* also saw prototypes for the Christian ministry in the priesthood of the Old Testament — an idea explicitly rejected in earlier literature.[8]

Ordination

It is the *Apostolic Tradition* of Hippolytus, dating from the early third century, which first gives us a clear picture of ordination to the threefold ministry.[9] There the context of ordination was the eucharistic assembly of the local church on the Lord's Day. The following elements[10] were important in the rite of ordination in this document:

1. Election by the church, with the assent of clergy and laity;
2. Prayer by the congregation and the bishop who presided;
3. The imposition of hands (by the bishops in the ordination of a bishop; by bishop and presbyters in the ordination of a presbyter; by the bishop alone in the ordination of a deacon).

Election by the church was understood as the way in which God's call to ministry became manifest; it was the church which articulated the call to ordained ministry. The idea of the interior call does not loom large in early literature; indeed, some candidates were ordained with great reluctance on their part.

Election: Election might be initiated in a variety of ways. It appears that it was the whole church which elected a bishop in the *Apostolic Tradition*; the ordaining bishops confirmed the election by their participation in the ordination. At other times, it was the presbyters of the diocese who elected, and the election was confirmed by the people and by the ordaining bishops. In still other cases, the provincial bishops made the choice, which was ratified by the clergy and laity of the local church present at the ordination. After Constantine, it might even be the secular ruler who had the dominant voice in the choice of a bishop. Whoever took the initiative, other parties must give their consent. We have less certain evidence about the selection of presbyters and deacons. At times they may also have been elected by the local church; more frequently it appears that the bishop (or the bishop and the presbyters) made the choice, which was confirmed by the people.

Prayer: Prayer included the common prayer of the congregation (either in silence or in response to litanic biddings) and the solemn prayer of the presiding minister. It asked God to equip the candidate with the qualities necessary for the ministry undertaken. It was often, but not always, a solemn invocation of the Spirit. The prayers found in Hippolytus are these:

The Ministry of the New Covenant   237

For Bishops

God and Father of our Lord Jesus Christ, Father of mercies and God of all comforts, who dwellest in the heights and hast respect to the lowly, who knowest all things before they come to be, thou who hast set bounds within the Church through the word of thy grace, preordaining from the beginning the race of the just people of Abraham, establishing princes and priests and not leaving thy sanctuary without a ministry, thou since the beginning of the world hast been pleased to be glorified in those whom thou hast chosen. Pour forth now that power which is from thee, the governing Spirit, which thou gavest to thy beloved Son, Jesus Christ, which he gave to the holy Apostles, who established in every place thy Church, thy hallowing, to the glory and unceasing praise of thy name.

Father, who knowest the heart, grant to this thy servant, whom thou hast chosen for the episcopate, to feed thy holy flock; and to exercise high priesthood for thee without rebuke, serving night and day, to propitiate thy countenance unceasingly and to offer the holy gifts of thy Church; by the Spirit of high priesthood to have the power to remit sins according to thy commandment; to assign ministries according to thy directions; to loose also every bond according to the power which thou gavest to the Apostles; to please thee too by gentleness and a pure heart, offering to thee an odor of sweet savour; through thy Servant Jesus Christ, through whom be glory and power and honor to thee, to Father and Son with the Holy Spirit, both now and world without end. Amen.

For Presbyters

God and Father of our Lord Jesus Christ, look down upon this thy servant and impart to him the Spirit of grace and counsel for presbyters, so that he may support and govern thy people with a pure heart, as thou didst look down upon the people of thy choice and didst command Moses that he select presbyters whom thou didst fill with thy Spirit, which thou didst give to thy servant.

And now, O Lord, grant that the Spirit of thy grace may without fail be preserved among us, and make us worthy, in believing, to minister to thee, praising thee in simplicity of heart; through thy Servant Jesus Christ, through whom be glory and power and honor to thee, to Father and Son with the Holy Spirit, both now and world without end. Amen.

For Deacons

God who hast created all things and set them in order by thy Word, O Father of our Lord Jesus Christ, whom thou sentest to minister thy will and to make known to us thy desire, give the Holy Spirit of grace and care and diligence to this thy servant, whom thou hast chosen to minister to thy Church and to bring forward in thy holy of holies the gifts which are offered to thee by thine appointed high priests, so that serving blamelessly and with a pure heart, he may be counted worthy of serving this high office and glorify thee through thy Servant Jesus Christ, through whom be glory and power and honor to thee, to Father and Son with the Holy Spirit, both now and world without end. Amen.[11]

We should notice how the work of bishops, presbyters, and deacons is described in these prayers. Hippolytus works primarily with Old Testament foretypes of the episcopate and the presbyterate — thus giving expression to the church's claim to be the true heirs of Israel as the people of God. The bishop is compared to the patriarchs and high priests. No distinction is made here between leadership in the community and leadership in the cult. Similarly, presbyters are compared to the seventy elders empowered by the Spirit to assist Moses in governing the people of Israel: they are associated with the bishop in their task of governance. As for deacons (whose title means "minister" in Greek), no foretype from the Old Testament is presented for them. Instead, they are compared to Jesus, who came not to be ministered unto but to minister (Mark 10:41-45). What is noteworthy here is that there is no reference to the levitical priesthood of the Old Testament. Indeed, cultic language is used in the prayers only for bishops and deacons. Bishops were compared to high priests, perhaps echoing the language of Hebrews where Jesus is a high priest "after the order of Melchisedek" — that is, not in the levitical succession. The prayer for deacons refers to their assistance to bishops in presenting the gifts to be offered.

Boone Porter remarks on the allusive, typological character of the language of early ordination prayers:

> A typological and allusive manner of expression provides that degree of ambiguity which liturgical language must have. When we pray we express our needs to God and seek assistance from him. On the other hand, we cannot enlighten his understanding or define the exact ways in which he should assist us. The very essence of prayer is the recognition of God's sovereignty and commitment to the carrying out of his will. Ideally, therefore, Christian prayer *designates* what is being prayed for *without precisely defining it.*
>
> . . . these ancient ordination prayers are noble expression of this classic conception of Christian prayer. They scrupulously avoid any suggestion that we, in the course of our pilgrimage, can comprehend exactly what episcopate, presbyterate, or diaconate is. These orders are gifts from God, and like his other supernatural gifts they transcend earthly understanding. Yet the Church is also certain that its Lord bequeathed a ministry to it. With solemn prayer and the laying on of consecrated hands, the Church entreats in unhesitant faith that the Holy Spirit would bestow whatever gifts are necessary for the ministers of Christ to carry on whatever is God's will.[12]

The principal church orders which followed (except for that of Sarapion) were all dependent on the *Apostolic Tradition*, and the prayers of ordination which they provided were, for the most part, expansions of the prayers which we find in the *Apostolic Tradition*. Through these channels the prayers above passed in one form or another into many of the Eastern rites of ordination. The Western tradition which emerged in later centuries, however, makes no use of these prayers (until the restoration of Hippolytus' prayer for the episcopate by the Roman Catholic Church and some other Western churches after the second Vatican Council).[13]

The Imposition of Hands: The Greek version of the *Apostolic Tradition* uses the word *cheirotonia* for the action by which bishops, presbyters, and deacons are admitted to their office, and distinguishes this action from the *katastasis*, "institution," by which persons are admitted to other offices, such as subdeacon and lector, in the church. What distinguishes *cheirotonia* from *katastasis* is the laying on of hands, for which the Greek word is *cheirothesia*. *Cheirotonia* originally meant admission to an office by "raising of hands" — that is, it referred to election. *Cheirothesia* means "imposition" or "laying on of hands." What Hippolytus does is to equate the two words by reserving *cheirotonia* as the name for admission to office by *cheirothesia*.

The Latin version of the Apostolic tradition translates the Greek *cheirotonia* by the Latin word *ordinatio*, which was taken over from secular usage and means admission or induction into an *ordo*.[14] In secular usage *ordo* or "order" designated either the governing class as a whole or one of the ruling classes of Rome (the *senatores* and the *equites* — the senators and the knights). In Christian usage, the meaning was analogous. Tertullian could speak of the church as consisting of *ordo* and *plebs*, "clergy" and "laity," and the episcopate and the presbyterate were also understood as distinct *ordines* in the church. The gesture of laying on of hands by members of the the episcopate or the presbyterate as a collegial body was understood as induction or admission into these two orders, while the accompanying prayer asked God to equip, through the gift of the Holy Spirit, those being admitted with the requisite qualities. In the ordination of a presbyter, the bishop and presbyters as the presbyteral college of a diocese laid hands on a candidate for the presbyterate. In the ordination of a bishop, the chief bishop of the province and his fellow bishops as the provincial episcopal college laid hands on the candidate for the episcopate. The diaconate was not understood as a collegial ministry, but as a ministry of assistance to the bishop (and later to presbyters): hence it was the bishop alone who laid hands on a deacon; other deacons did not participate.

It is this understanding of ordination as induction into a responsibility (in the case of deacons) or a collegial body (in the ordination of bishops and presbyters) that lies behind the very careful directions in the *Apostolic Tradition* in regard to the laying on of hands for ordination of a bishop, presbyter, or deacon:

> . . . let [the bishops] lay their hands on [the one to be ordained bishop], and let the presbytery stand in silence.

> When . . . a presbyter is ordained, let the bishop lay his hand on his head, while the presbyters also touch him. . . .

> When a deacon is ordained, let the bishop alone lay on his hands, for the reason that he is not ordained for the priesthood, but for serving the bishop, to do those things which are commanded by him. For he is not a member of the council of the clergy, but attends to responsibilities and makes known what is necessary to the bishop; not receiving that common spirit of the presbytery, but that which is entrusted under the power of the bishop. Therefore let the bishop alone make him a deacon; on a presbyter, however, the presbyters also lay on their hands because of the common and like spirit of the clergy. For the presbyter has only the power to receive; he does not on the other hand have power to give. Because of this he does not ordain clergy; he rather is to put his seal on the ordination of a presbyter while the bishop ordains.[15]

Here it appears that the laying on of hands was understood primarily as an act of induction into office — *cheirotonia* is equated with *cheirothesia*, the imposition of hands with *ordinatio*. In the case of bishops and presbyters, this was understood as a collegial act and their orders are designated as those of priesthood, while the diaconate is understood as service or ministry.

The prayer said during this ritual action asks God to give the requisite gifts for the office through the Holy Spirit.

In places where the bishop was seen primarily as the chief presbyter, it may originally have been the local presbytery that laid on hands in the ordination of their bishop. The presbyteral ordination of bishops appears to have persisted longest at Alexandria, a region with a strong presbyteral tradition. Jerome, ardent advocate of presbyteral prerogative, remarks upon the custom there.[16] Hippolytus may here signal the shift to a different understanding of the episcopate, in which the bishop's role as a member of the episcopal college takes precedence over his role as the chief presbyter of the diocese. It may even be the case that the rubrics for the ordination of a bishop in the *Apostolic Tradition* represent a new custom at Rome. We note that the extended explanation of why presbyters join in the laying on of hands at the ordination of a presbyter is concerned to minimize the meaning of presbyteral participation in the act of ordination.[17]

The regulations regarding who lays on hands for ordination in each order were scrupulously preserved in later rites in the West, except in the case of the pope, who had the privilege of ordaining candidates for both the episcopate and the presbyterate alone.[18] The regulations from the *Apostolic Tradition* were embodied in a document known as the *Statuta Ecclesiae Antiqua*, which perhaps dates to Gennadius of Marseilles, c. 490, and passed from there as rubrics into later ordination rites.[19] In the East, however, from the time of the *Apostolic Constitutions* in the fourth century, it was generally only the bishop presiding at an ordination who laid on hands for each of the orders.

As we noted earlier, the laying on of hands is a multivalent sign. Not only was it understood as a gesture of appointment and induction, it was also frequently understood as a gesture "calling" the Holy Spirit "upon" the candidate, not only in ordinations but in other blessings. In Western sacramental theology this gesture might be understood as an instrumental sign, although we should note that when the Spirit is bestowed by this sign, it is God — not the bishop — who is the giver of the gift. Indeed, some of the Eastern prayers of ordination were concerned explicitly to deny that the bishop possesses the gift to bestow. One of the prayers in the Byzantine rite declared, "not by the imposition of my hands but by the descent of thine abundant mercies is grace given to those worthy of thee."[20]

In the ordination of bishops, many rites substitute for the imposition of hands or add to it the imposition of the gospel book. We find this curious substitute for the laying on of hands first in the rites of ordination in the *Apostolic Constitutions*, where the deacons hold the gospel book over the person being ordained. In the later rites of the East, it was usually accompanied by the imposition of hands by the presiding bishop. In the the traditions of Rome and Alexandria, the patriarch of these sees was ordained by the imposition of the gospel book without the laying on of hands, but he ordained other bishops by the imposition of his hands; in other Western traditions the imposition of the gospel book was an adjunct to the laying on of hands by the bishops present. The ultimate origin of this action has never been discovered, but as an icon of Christ the Word it would appear to be intended to signify that it is Christ himself who ordains the bishop. It the case of the patriarchs of Rome and Alexandria, the use of the gospel book appears to be intended to avoid the impression that subordinate bishops could bestow the episcopate on the one who was to assume the patriarchal see.

Assumption of Ministerial Function: Since ordination took place in the context of the eucharist of the local community, those ordained could immediately assume the duties for which they had been ordained. Hippolytus explicitly tells us that the newly ordained bishop presided by saying the eucharistic prayer. Although he does not explicitly say so, we may presume that newly ordained deacons took part in presenting the gifts at the offertory, and that newly ordained presbyters stood with the bishop at the table and laid hands with the rest of the presbyters on the offerings before the eucharistic prayer. Since the newly ordained took their place at the celebration with others of their order, the seating of the bishop in the *cathedra* from which he presided would in later rites take on greater prominence.

There is a simplicity and directness to the rites as we find them in the *Apostolic Tradition*. The process of election by which God's choice of ministers was discerned culminated in induction in the new ministry with the laying on of hands by appropriate persons and the prayer of the people and the bishop who presided at the ordination. Then the newly ordained ministers assumed their roles in the eucharistic assembly of the church. Rites in later centuries would place less emphasis on the election and confirmation of the candidates, would give increased emphasis to the prayer of the bishop who presided, and would highlight the assumption of ministerial function by bestowal of vestments and insignia, by the use of imperative formulae authorizing the performance of the duties of the ministry, by the addition of anointing as a sign of spiritual endowment, and by supplementing the rites with the bestowal of appropriate utensils of ministerial function (the scriptures, the bishop's pastoral staff, chalice and paten). While the elaborated rites gave clearer expression to the understanding of the ministry bestowed, they tended in their profusion to obscure the essential core of the rites and also to emphasize the cultic functions of the new ministers to the detriment of other functions.

3. Ordination in the Middle Ages in the Latin West

Roman Rites in the Early Middle Ages

By the seventh and eighth centuries, sacramentaries appeared which give us a relatively clear picture of the early rites of ordination in the Latin West.[21] By this time, the voice of the people in the selection of presbyters and deacons had been reduced to the opportunity to voice objection. In the Roman rite, the Sunday vigil eucharist of ember weeks was the ordinary occasion for ordinations to the diaconate and the presbyterate, and candidates for ordination were presented to the people at the eucharist on the prior Wednesday and Friday by the the pope or a notary speaking on his behalf with these words:

> With the assistance of the Lord God, Jesus Christ our Savior, we have chosen for the order of deacon (or presbyter) the subdeacon N. (or the deacon N.) of the parish of M. If anyone, however, has anything to allege against these men, let him step forward confidently for the sake of God and in obedience to God and speak. Let him, nevertheless, be always mindful of his communion.[22]

On the day of ordination, they were publicly called forward by the pope by name and title before he proceeded to ordain them. In the case of a bishop, *Ordo Romanus XXXIV* stipulates that the candidate be chosen by the people of the city and a certificate of election be made by the presbyters, clergy, and people. This certificate and a petition for ordination were then sent to the pope in Rome. The pope examined the credentials and the candidate before proceeding to ordain him.

The rites of ordination took place in the context, as we have noted, of a Sunday eucharist. The ordination followed the epistle and gradual responsory and may be outlined as follows:

> Entrance of candidates vested for the order to be received
> Bidding and Litany concluded by the bishop with a collect
> Laying on of hands
> Prayer of consecration (ordination)
> Assumption of functions in the eucharist

The candidates, vested for the order into which they were to be ordained, were presented to the ordaining bishop after the gradual psalm. The bishop bade the prayers of the people for them and the litany followed. In the earliest of the sacramentaries, the rite for each order had a proper collect to conclude the litany.

The laying on of hands originally took place during the principal prayer of the rite, known as the prayer of consecration in the Roman tradition, but the rubric was printed before the prayers in the later rites, so that this action eventually took place in silence. The provisions set out by Hippolytus as to who laid hands on candidates for each order were followed, except — according to some late documents — when the pope ordained. He had the privilege of laying on hands alone.

The prayers of consecration in the Roman tradition were probably sung, like all solemn prayers in that rite, to the preface tone. In later Gallican usage, in fact, they acquired a preliminary dialogue like that found before the eucharistic prayer. The texts for each order of ministry are as follows:

Consecration for Bishops

God of all the honors, God of all the worthy ranks, which serve to thy glory in hallowed orders; God who, holding familiar private converse with thy servant Moses, hast also given instruction, among the other patterns of heavenly worship, in regard to priestly vesture; and didst command that Aaron thy chosen should wear a mystical robe during sacred rites, so that the posterity to come might have an understanding of the meaning of the former things, lest the knowledge of thy teaching be lost in any age; and as the very outward sign of these symbols obtained reverence among thy people of old, also among us there might be a knowledge of them more certain than types and shadows. For the adornment of our mind is as the vesture of that earlier priesthood; and the dignity of robes no longer commends to us the pontifical glory, but rather the splendor of spirits, since even those very things, which then pleased fleshly vision, depended rather on these truths which in them were to be understood.

And therefore, to these thy servants, whom thou hast chosen for the ministry of high priesthood, we beseech thee, O Lord, that thou wouldst grant this grace: that whatsoever it was that those veils signified in radiance of gold, in sparkling of jewels, in variety of diverse workmanship, this may show forth in the conversation and deeds of these men. Complete the fullness of thy mystery in thy priests and hallow them, equipped with all the adornments of glory, with the dew of heavenly unction. May it flow down, O Lord, richly upon their head; may it run down below the mouth; may it go down to the uttermost parts of the whole body, so that the power of thy Spirit may both fill them within and surround them without. Let there abound in them constancy of faith, purity of love, sincerity of peace. Grant to them an episcopal chair to rule thy Church and the entire people. Be thou their strength; be thou their might; be thou their stay. Multiply upon them thy benediction and grace, so that, fitted by thine aid always to obtain thy mercy, they may by thy grace be devoted unto thee; through Jesus Christ . . . .

Consecration for Presbyters

O Lord, holy Father, almighty, everlasting God, bestower of all the honors and of all the worthy ranks which do thee service, thou through whom all things increase, through whom everything is made firm, by the ever-extended increase to the benefit of rational nature by a succession arranged in due order; whence the priestly ranks and the offices of the levites arose and were inaugurated with mystical symbols: so that, when thou didst set high priests to rule over thy people, thou didst choose men of a lesser order and secondary dignity to be their companions and to help them in their labor. Likewise in the desert thou didst spread out the spirit of Moses through the minds of seventy wise men, so that he, using them as helpers among the people, governed with ease countless multitudes. Likewise also thou didst impart to Eleazar and Ithamar, the sons of Aaron, the richness of their father's plenty, so that the benefit of priests might be sufficient for the salutary sacrifices and the rites of a more frequent worship. And also by providence, O Lord, thou didst add, to the Apostles of thy Son, teachers of the faith as companions, and they filled the whole world with these secondary preachers.

Therefore, we beseech thee, O Lord, to grant these assistants to our weakness also, for we who are so much frailer need so many more. Grant, we beseech thee, O Father, the dignity of the presbyterate unto these thy servants. Renew in their inward parts the Spirit of holiness. May they obtain and receive of thee, O God, the office of second dignity, and by the example of their conversation may they commend a strict way of life. May they be virtuous colleagues of our order. Let the pattern of all righteousness show forth in them, in order that, rendering in time to come a good account of the stewardship committed unto them, they may obtain the rewards of eternal blessedness; through Jesus Christ . . . .

Consecration for Deacons

Assist us, we beseech thee, Almighty God, giver of honors, distributor of orders, and bestower of offices; who abiding in thyself, dost make all things new, and disposest everything through thy Word, Power, and Wisdom, Jesus Christ thy Son our Lord; by thine everlasting providence thou dost prepare and apportion to each particular time what things are needful. His body, thy church, thou dost permit to grow and become large, diversified by a variety of heavenly graces and knit together in the distinction of its members, united through the wondrous law of the whole structure unto the increase of thy temple, establishing the service of sacred office in three ranks of ministers to do battle in thy name: the sons of Levi having been chosen first, that they might obtain by a perpetual apportionment an inheritance of everlasting blessing, by remaining in faithful vigilance over the mysterious functions of thy house.

We beseech thee, O Lord, also to look favorably upon these thy servants whom we humbly dedicate to do service within thy holy places in the office of deacon. And although indeed we, being human, are ignorant of divine thought and of highest reason, we judge their life as best we are able: things unknown to us, however, do not slip by thee, O Lord; hidden things do not escape thee. Thou art the witness of sins, thou art the discerner of spirits; thou mightest verily bring heavenly judgment upon them or else grant to the unworthy what we ask. Send upon them, O Lord, we beseech thee, thy Holy Spirit; through whom, faithfully accomplishing the work of ministering, they may be strengthened by the gift of thy sevenfold grace. Let the pattern of every virtue abound in them: discreet authority, unfailing modesty, purity of intention, and the observance of spiritual discipline. Let thy commandments be reflected in their conversation, so that by the example of their chastity they may win the imitation of thy holy people, and having the testimony of a good conscience may they continue strong and stable in Christ, and by fitting advancements from a lower rank may they be worthy, through thy grace, to take up higher things; through Jesus Christ . . . .[23]

By contrast, admission to the only minor orders which had not fallen into disuse — those of acolyte and subdeacon — was made during the distribution of communion by the delivery of the utensils of their office (a linen bag for carrying the eucharistic bread for acolytes and a chalice for subdeacons) and a generic blessing:

> At the intercession of the blessed and glorious and only ever-virgin Mary and of blessed Peter the apostle, may the Lord save and keep thee. Amen.[24]

The description of the ministries of bishop, presbyter, and deacon in these prayers is typological and highly allusive. The episcopate and presbyterate are understood as priestly orders: bishops are described as high priests, presbyters as priests of the second order. Their cultic functions are given preeminence, but their task of governance is not forgotten. In the prayer for bishops, we find reference to the episcopal chair (a sign of governing authority); and in the prayer for presbyters, the bishop is compared to Moses and the presbyters to the elders appointed to help Moses govern the people. The Old Testament allusions to priestly vestments and anointing in the prayer for bishops are meant as descriptions of the virtues required for the office, though in later ages they would be understood literally and lead to increased attention to vesting and anointing in the rites of ordination. The prayer for deacons gives little by way of description of their office: it is a general prayer for Christian virtues. The concluding reference to advancement from a lower rank to higher offices probably was not originally intended to refer to the presbyterate but to the administrative functions of the more important Roman deacons or even to the episcopate, for Roman bishops were quite frequently elected from the ranks of deacons.

The Early Gallican Rites of Ordination

We can get some idea of the Gallican rites by removing the Roman biddings, collects, and prayers of consecration from the early Gallican sacramentaries that have come down to us — the Gelasian sacramentary and the *Missale Francorum*.[25] Though the Gallican rite had its own proper prayers, its original structure was similar to that of the Roman tradition. The most notable difference was the fact that it provided an opening address for each rite which concluded with the final approval of the candidate by the congregation in the words, "He is worthy."[26] The equivalent prayer in the Gallican tradition to the consecration in the Roman tradition is entitled the blessing.

Blessing for Bishops (interpolation in Roman Prayer)

. . . May their feet, by thine aid, be beautiful for bringing good tidings of peace, for bringing thy good tidings of good. Give them, O Lord, a ministry of reconciliation in word and in deeds and in power of signs and wonders. Let their speech and preaching be not with enticing words of human wisdom, but in demonstration of the Spirit and of power. Give them, O Lord, the keys of the kingdom of heaven; let them use what thou hast given for edification, not for destruction, neither let them glory in power. Whatever they bind on earth, let it be bound also in heaven; and whatever they loose on earth, let it also be loosed in heaven. Whose sins they may retain, let them be retained; and whose sins they may forgive, do thou forgive. Whoever blesses them, may he be blessed; and whoever curses them, may he be filled with curses. May they be faithful and wise servants, whom thou, Lord, hast set over thy household that they may give them meat in due season, in order that they may show forth an entire perfect man. May they be unwearied in watchfulness; may they be fervent in spirit; may they hate pride; may they love truth, nor may they ever be so overcome by faintness or fear as to abandon it. May they never put light for darkness nor darkness for light; may they never say evil is good nor good evil. May they be debtors to the wise and to the unwise, and may they have the fruit of the benefit of all. . . .

Blessing for Presbyters

Author of all sanctification, of whom is true consecration, full benediction: do thou, O Lord, spread forth the hand of thy blessing upon this thy servant, N., whom we set apart with the honor of the presbyterate; so that he may show himself to be an elder by the dignity of his acts and the righteousness of his life, taught by these instructions which Paul presented to Titus and Timothy: that meditating day and night upon thy law, O thou Almighty, what he reads, he may believe; what he believes, he may teach; what he teaches, he may practice. May he show in himself justice, loyalty, mercy, courage; may he provide the example and demonstrate the exhortation, in order that he may keep the gift of thy ministry untainted; and with the consent of thy people may he transform, by an untainted benediction, the body and blood of thy Son. And in unbroken love, may he reach unto a perfect man, unto the measure of the stature of the fullness of Christ, in the day of the justice of eternal judgment with a pure conscience, with full faith, full of the Holy Spirit; through Jesus Christ. . . .

Blessing for Deacons

Holy Lord, bestower of faith, hope, grace, and increase, who dost pour forth thy good will through all the elements by the services of angels constituted everywhere in heaven and earth, graciously also shed the light of thy countenance particularly on this thy servant, N., that by thy favor he may grow as a pure and able minister at thine altars, and by thy indulgence being more pure, may he become worthy of the rank of those whom thy apostles, at the direction of the Holy Spirit, chose in a sevenfold number, with blessed Stephen as their chief and leader, and may he find favor as one equipped with all the virtues necessary for those who serve thee; through Jesus Christ. . . .[27]

These Gallican prayers present a somewhat different conception of the ministry than the one found in the Roman prayers. The Gallican portion of the prayer for the episcopate presents bishops as missionaries and emphasizes their role in community discipline. The prayer for presbyters emphasizes their role as teachers and their cultic function of presiding at the eucharist. Presbyters had by now acquired a greater independence as chief ministers of rural churches than they had in the urban dioceses of the Roman tradition. Their presbyteral role is set out with reference to the pastoral epistles rather than to the elders appointed by Moses. The prayer for the diaconate compares deacons to angels and finds their New Testament prototype in Stephen. The principal ministerial function assigned to them is service at the altar. Old Testament types play a much less important role in these prayers than they did in the Roman ones: the threefold ministry is set forth largely in New Testament terms.

Later Composite Rites

As Charlemagne rose to power, he sought to unify his realm ecclesiastically by making the Roman rite the norm for worship within its boundaries. The resulting usages were not, however, the unaltered Roman tradition, but a fusion of the older Roman rite with Gallican usages.[28] The Gallican prayers cited above were preserved only in sacramentaries which fused them with the prayers of the Roman tradition — the earliest of which were the Gelasian Sacramentary, the *Missale Francorum*, and the sacramentary of Angoulême. By the ninth century, ordination in the realm of Charlemagne followed a composite rite, in which the Gallican bidding and blessing followed immediately after the Roman collect, bidding, and prayer of consecration (now set out as a preface). The *Missale Francorum* added other elements, and the rites continued to be elaborated through the Middle Ages. Sacramentaries vary from each other in matters of detail, so that no two rites of ordination are exactly the same, but there is broad agreement on the overall structure of the rite. By way of illustration, the table below gives the rites for the ordination of a presbyter in the Gelasian Sacramentary, the *Missale Francorum*, and the Romano-German Pontifical, which might be said to represent three stages in the developing tradition:[29]

Gelasian Sacramentary	Missale Francorum	Romano-German Pontifical
		Litany
		Examination
	Gallican address	Gallican address
		Imposition of hands
Roman bidding	Roman bidding	Roman bidding
Roman collect	Roman collect	Roman collect
Roman consecration	Roman consecration	Roman consecration
		Adjusting of stole
		Vesting in chasuble
Gallican bidding	Gallican bidding	Gallican bidding
Gallican blessing	Gallican blessing	Gallican blessing
	Unction of hands	Unction of hands
		Giving of chalice/paten

In the composite rites for deacons and presbyters, candidates are in effect ordained twice — once according to the Roman prayers and once according to the Gallican ones. Note that the place of the litany has shifted in the latest rite. In the Roman tradition, it originally came after the bidding and was concluded by a collect. The prayer of ordination followed. However, both presbyteral orders and diaconal orders were often conferred in the same rite at the Sunday eucharist in ember weeks. It was therefore simpler to begin the rite with the litany, so that it did not need to be recited twice — once for each order. We have no way of knowing whether the people's prayer which followed the bidding in the Gallican tradition took the form of a litany. Most of the additions to the rite of the Romano-Germanic pontifical expressed an understanding of ordination as a delegation of authority by the bishop to the ordinand. This accounts for the emphasis on vesting. In earlier centuries, ministers wore the dress garments customary in the society of their day. But by the time of this pontifical, the garments had gone out of ordinary fashion and were vestments of office. Likewise the delivery of the book of the gospels to deacons, of the paten and chalice to presbyters, and of the ring and staff to bishops were understood to convey authority to carry out certain functions — for deacons to read the gospels, for presbyters to celebrate the eucharist, and for bishops to preside over the affairs of the diocese with the authority of spiritual and temporal power. A profusion of imperative formulas and prayers accompanied these actions. When the chalice and paten were delivered, the bishop said to the presbyter: "Receive power to offer sacrifice to God and to celebrate mass for both the living and the dead."[30] The laying on of hands would later come to be understood in much the same way. Thus in the ordination of presbyters, the imposition of hands would eventually come to be accompanied by the charge: "Receive the Holy Spirit. If thou forgive the sins of any, they are forgiven them, and if thou retain the sins of any, they are retained."[31] In some rites this came during the initial imposition of hands (which had originally taken place during the prayer of consecration to the presbyterate and later took place in silence before this prayer); later rites generally associated this formula with a second imposition of hands after communion.

Another feature which the composite rite took over from Gallican usage was that of anointing. Most commonly it was the hands of the presbyter that were anointed as a means of blessing them for sacramental actions; various formulas were provided for this. Bishops at their ordination were anointed on the head: this was done during the ordination prayer, at the words "hallow them . . . with the dew of heavenly unction," now understood literally rather than typologically. In some early English rites presbyters also had their heads anointed; and in many rites bishops received an anointing of the hands as well. We also begin to find another addition to the rite for presbyters and bishops — the singing of the hymn *Veni Creator* (in some rites the *Veni Sancte Spiritus*) as an invocation of the Holy Spirit upon the ordinand during the anointings in the rites for the presbyterate and episcopate.

A final addition to the rites of ordination in some rites was an examination of the candidate by the bishop. This brings into the rites of ordination a procedure which had once preceded it. In the provisions of the early Roman *ordines*, candidates for ordination to the diaconate and presbyterate had to swear to the pope during the eucharist on Monday in ember week that they were not guilty of a serious sin which barred access to ordination, and bishops sent to the pope for ordination were carefully examined by him on the day prior to their ordination.

The minor orders, many of which had fallen into disuse in the early middle ages, were restored in the later middle ages under the influence of the notices in the *Statuta Ecclesiae Antiqua.* While early Roman use had understood the various orders to be distinct from each other, later usage ranked them in a strict hierarchical order and required each order to be received before reception of the next. They constituted, in other words, a kind of career ladder within the church. By now admission to the lower orders was being understood as ordination, although it did not involve the laying on of hands. The orders of ministry were also grouped differently. The episcopate was often understood as the priesthood in its fullness rather than as a separate order; in later pontificals, rites for the consecration of a bishop are not found with those for ordination to other orders, but with those for the coronation of a king or emperor. The other orders were ranked as follows: doorkeeper, reader, exorcist, acolyte, subdeacon, deacon, priest; it was the last three that were often understood as the "major orders," because they were the primary orders involved in the celebration of the eucharist, and major orders were now defined primarily in terms of their relation to the eucharist. The minor orders each had its own distinctive blessing now as well as a presentation of the utensils of ministry (keys for the doorkeeper, lectionary for the reader, book of exorcisms for the exorcist, and cruet and torch for the acolyte). The rite for the ordination of the subdeacon, which included a blessing and the giving of a chalice, was elaborate, but never involved the laying on of hands. Despite the ceremonial elaboration of admission to minor orders, they were an archaizing restoration and had no genuine function in the life of the church.

Ministerial order in the later middle ages had become a hierarchy set over the church, rather than a genuine ministry within the church. In every age, the ordering of the life of the Christian community has been assimilated to some degree to the ordering of life in the environing society. During the middle ages, the ministerial order of the church reflected in large measure the feudal system of medieval society and was understood in those terms. Ordination was understood in terms of delegation of power and of jurisdiction, given ritual expression in the presentation of utensils of office with their accompanying formulas. The close link in the early church between ordination and the exercise of ministry in a local congregation ("title") was broken, and ordination was for practical purposes "absolute": title was now understood to mean a benefice which provided financial support for the person ordained rather than a community in which ministry was exercised.

The scholastic theology of ordination was developed largely in terms of sacramental theology, which was heavily influenced by legal and juridical concerns. Augustine's theology of ministerial "character" was rediscovered and elaborated to describe an objective and indelible change in status conferred by ordination. Making ordination a single sacrament posed certain problems, for a person received ordination for each order. Eventually this was addressed by understanding all ministerial office as participation in Christ's priesthood, so that ministry was now understood as priesthood, defined in terms of ability to offer the eucharistic sacrifice. In the terminology of sacramental theology, the question of the "form" and "matter" of ordination also arose. In early rites, it is clear that entry into ministerial office is by imposition of hands and prayer, but in the complex rites of the late middle ages this original core was not easily discernible. Many, including Thomas Aquinas, tended to define matter and form in terms of the presentation of the utensils or instruments of ministry and the accompanying formulas. For others, the anointing was a key part of the sacramental structure of the rite. Finally, this increasingly sacralized view of priestly ministry led in the West to the gradual imposition of celibacy on those who were ordained — an obligation never required of parish clergy in the East.

4. Ordination in the Byzantine Rite

Ordinations in the Eastern traditions all place their emphasis on the imposition of the bishop's hand (for all orders) and prayer.[32] There is not the profusion of secondary rites which we find in the later traditions in the West. There was, however, a profusion of ordination prayers in most traditions, as one tradition borrowed the prayers of others. Some rites have as many as four prayers of ordination. As in the West, the gospel book is imposed on a bishop during his ordination. The rite of ordination is introduced in all traditions by a formula announcing the appointment or election and asking the prayers of the congregation. As found in the Byzantine tradition, this proclamation and bidding takes the following form:

> The divine grace, which always heals that which is infirm and supplies what is lacking, selects the subdeacon (deacon, presbyter) N., beloved by God, as deacon (presbyter, bishop). Let us therefore pray that the grace of the Holy Spirit may come upon him.[33]

This seems originally to have been followed by a diaconal litany, but in the Byzantine rite the first ordination prayer has been intruded before the litany. The sequence in the Byzantine tradition for each order is as follows:

Proclamation/Announcement
First Ordination Prayer
Diaconal Litany with petitions for candidate
Second Ordination Prayer (said in silence)

In Eastern practice, the bishop lays his hand on the candidate throughout, beginning with the proclamation. In Byzantine usage, the sign of the cross is also made on the candidate — a kind of sealing in some ways parallel to the Western anointing.

The second ordination prayer in the Byzantine rites seems to be the original one. It is related to ordination prayers in several of the other Eastern rites. The texts are as follows:

For Bishops:

> O Lord our God, who, since human nature cannot sustain the essence of thy deity, hast established by thy dispensation teachers subject to the same passions as we are, that they may approach thy throne to offer thee sacrifice and oblation for all thy people: O Lord, make the one who has been made a dispenser of high-

priestly grace to be an imitator of thee, the true shepherd, giving his life for thy sheep, a guide to the blind, a light to those in darkness, a corrector of the ignorant, a lamp in the world, so that, after having formed in this present life souls who have been entrusted to him, he may stand before thy judgment seat without shame and receive the great reward which thou hast prepared for those who have striven for the preaching of thy gospel: for thine it is to show mercy and to save, O our God, and to thee do we ascribe glory, to the Father, the Son, and the Holy Spirit, now and for ever and unto the ages of ages. Amen.

For Presbyters

O God, great in power and unsearchable in understanding, wonderful in thy counsels beyond the children of men: Lord, fill this man, who thou hast chosen to undertake the rank of the presbyterate, with the gift of thy Holy Spirit, so that he may be worthy to stand blamelessly at thine altar, to proclaim the gospel of thy salvation, to exercise the sacred ministry of the word of thy truth, to offer thee gifts and spiritual sacrifices, and to renew thy people by the baptism of regeneration, so that, being present at the second coming of our great God and Savior Jesus Christ thine only Son, he may receive the reward of the good stewardship of his office through the abundance of thy goodness: for blessed and glorified is thy most honorable and magnificent name, of the Father, the Son, and the Holy Spirit, now and for ever and unto the ages of ages. Amen.

For Deacons

O God our Savior, who with an incorruptible voice didst prophesy to thine apostles and proclaim that he who fulfilled the work of a servant [deacon] should be first among them, as it is written in thy holy gospel, "Whoever would be first among you, let him be thy servant [deacon]": O Lord of all, fill this thy servant, whom thou hast counted worthy to undertake the ministry of a deacon, with all faith and love and power and holiness by the coming of thy life-giving Spirit, for not by the imposition of my hands but by the descent of thine abundant mercies is grace given to those worthy of thee, so that, free from all sin, he may stand blameless before thee on the dreadful day of judgment and receive the unfailing reward of thy promise: for thou art our God, the God of mercy and salvation, and to thee we ascribe glory, to the Father, the Son, and the Holy Spirit, now and for ever and unto the ages of ages. Amen.[34]

Like the Gallican prayers, but unlike the Roman ones, the Byzantine prayers do not draw on the Old Testament in their description of the Christian ministry. The bishop is high priest and shepherd; the presbyter is presented primarily as a teacher; the deacon's role is that of service. In the Roman prayer presbyters were described as priests of the second rank; here the title priest is not given to the presbyter.

Ordinations were set in the context of the eucharist in such a way that the candidate when ordained could exercise his ministry. This meant that the bishop was ordained at the entrance rite, so that he could preside; the presbyter after the transfer of the gifts to the altar, so that he could concelebrate with the bishop; the deacon before communion (at the eucharist or even at the liturgy of the presanctified), so that he could distribute communion. After ordination, candidates were clothed in the vestments of their order and acclaimed as worthy. This acclamation once came as the formal assent of the people to the selection of the candidate, as in the Gallican rites; with the decline of the participation of the people in the selection of clergy in the East, the acclamation generally was transferred to this new position. The bishop's role as a teacher of the faith was emphasized by having him make a threefold profession of the faith before his ordination.

In the East, the bishop also laid hands on candidates for minor orders. The distinction between major and minor orders is expressed in Eastern traditions by the restriction of the proclamation and bidding, "The divine grace . . . ," to the orders of bishop, presbyter, and deacon. By this standard, women deacons are within the major orders. They are ordained at the same place in the service as male deacons, although a different prayer is used for them. But their ordination, like that of male deacons, begins with the proclamation and bidding. Women deacons had an important part in anointing the bodies of women at baptism, which propriety made difficult for male ministers. The fact that the rubrics still specify that they be given chalices may mean that they once assisted in the administration of communion, though they no longer do so.

5. Ordination at the Reformation and in the Book of Common Prayer

The Preface to the Ordinal and the Intention of the Church of England at the Reformation

Archbishop Cranmer set out the intentions of the Church of England in regard to ordination and ministerial office in the first portion of the preface to the rites of ordination issued in 1550 and bound up with the 1549 Book of Common Prayer:

> It is euident unto all men, diligently readinge holye scripture, and auncient aucthours, that from the Apostles tyme, there hathe bene these orders of Ministers in Christes church, Bisshoppes, Priestes, and Deacons, which Offices were euermore had in suche reuerent estimacion, that no man by his own priuate aucthoritie, might presume to execute any of them, except he were first called, tried, examined, and knowen, to haue such equalities, as were requisite for the same. And also by publique prayer, with imposicion of handes, approued, and admitted thereunto. And therfore to the entent these orders shoulde bee continued, and reuerently estemed in this Church of England, it is requysite, that no man (not beynge at thys presente Bisshop, Priest, nor Deacon) shall execute anye of them, excepte he be called, tryed, examined, and admitted, accordynge to the forme hereafter folowinge.[35]

Here, as elsewhere in the Book of Common Prayer, Cranmer articulates the note of continuity.[36] It is the intention of the Church of England that the orders of bishop, priest, and deacon "should be continued and reverently esteemed in this Church of England," because these orders have existed in the church "since the apostles' time." The rites of ordination which follow are meant to preserve this traditional form of ministry.

On the continent, reformers generally dealt more radically with the ministry.[37] For Luther certain persons were called by the church to a ministry of word and sacrament for the good order of the church, but he argued that those so called were simply given authority to exercise the ministerial powers that all Christians possessed through baptism. Calvin — by rather selective exegesis — found four offices in the New Testament churches (minister or pastor, doctor or teacher, elder, and deacon), but strictly speaking only the pastor was a "minister," and later Reformed authorities would insist on the parity of ministers. Neither Lutheran nor Reformed traditions saw reason for a distinction in orders of ministry. Neither considered the episcopate distinct from the presbyterate. Luther did not reject the supervisory role of bishops, and some Lutheran churches continued the episcopate, but Lutherans did not consider the episcopate a distinct order of ministry or a necessary part of church order. Calvin considered episcopal government of the church acceptable, but his successors in the Reformed tradition insisted on a presbyterian polity. The diaconate, which had ceased to be a functional order in the middle ages, was restored in the Reformed tradition but treated as an office rather than an order of ministry. In the Lutheran tradition, the diaconate disappeared at the time of the Reformation. Both Lutheran and Reformed traditions thus worked with the concept of a single order of ministry, rather than three orders of ministry. Rites for ordination varied widely. The continental reformers in general considered the laying on of hands with prayer a fitting manner of ordination which was in accordance with Scripture, but they did not treat the laying on of hands as a *necessary* component of the rite. Bishops presided at ordinations in those Lutheran churches which retained or restored the office. Some Lutheran churches retained episcopal succession (that is, their bishops were ordained by those who had been ordained bishops before the Reformation), while others retained the office of bishop or restored it but did not maintain episcopal succession. from the pre-Reformation church.

The English reformers, on the other hand, had no intention of reorganizing the ministerial order of the church: as the preface to the ordinal states, their intention was to continue the orders of ministry which had come down to them. Unlike most of the continental reformers, they continued to use the word "priest" for the presbyteral order, thus maintaining a link with the understanding of ministry current in the middle ages which the continental reformers on the whole rejected. There was considerable debate among them as to whether bishops and presbyters constituted distinct orders or only degrees within a single order, but in this they were raising no new issue, but only continuing the debate among theologians of the middle ages. There is no clear consensus on the issue among sixteenth-century Anglicans, though by the seventeenth century Anglicans generally favored the position which the preface to the ordinal appears to set out — that bishops, presbyters, and deacons are distinct orders.

The Rites of Ordination in the Anglican Ordinal

Ordination according to the traditional manner was the means by which the English reformers intended to continue these orders. The preface to the ordinal of 1550 sets forth how the rite of ordination is understood: those who have been chosen for the ministry after due examination are to be admitted to their ministry "by public prayer, with the imposition of hands." In the imposition of hands, the rites stipulate the procedure customary in the West from the time of Hippolytus: bishops impose hands in the ordination of a bishop, the bishop and priests in the ordination of a priest, and the bishop alone in the ordination of a deacon.

To reform the rites of ordination which the Church of England inherited at the Reformation was no easy matter, for — as we have seen — medieval rites of ordination had been elaborated to so large an extent that it was very difficult to distinguish what were the primary elements of the rite and what were secondary embellishments. In the task of reforming the rites, Cranmer worked from the Reformation consensus that the key elements were public prayer and the imposition of hands. To an extent only recently discovered, Cranmer's rites of ordination are dependent on the rites sets out by the Strassburg reformer Martin Bucer in a work entitled *De Ordinatione*

Legitima,[38] though Cranmer modified Bucer's single rite into three distinct rites for deacons, priests, and bishops. Bucer provided a rite for presbyters, which he intended to be expanded for bishops and simplified for deacons, working with the idea that the episcopate and the diaconate are "orders" of the presbyterate.[39] Bucer's rite follows the general structure of the medieval rites, but highlights the imposition of hands and the prayer of ordination by removing most of the secondary elements in the service.

The best way to understand the Anglican rites for ordination is to begin with Bucer's rite and to see how Cranmer modified it. The following aspects of the rites are worthy of note:

1. The general shape of the rites;
2. Prayer;
3. The Imposition of hands;
4. The Presentation of Instruments of Ministry;
5. Vesture.

The 1550 rites were modified in detail in later editions of the Book of Common Prayer for various reasons. After 1552 the rites had a somewhat more Reformed cast to them. Some adjustments in the rite for priests were made in 1662 to make it easier to ordain deacons and priests in the same service. The principal modifications, however, were the changes made in 1662 in order clearly to distinguish the priesthood and the episcopate as separate and distinct orders.

1. The Shape of the Rites: Bucer retained the structure of the medieval rites of ordination, but simplified them to focus on what he considered the key elements of ordination — prayer and the imposition of hands. In accordance  with tradition, he set the rite in the context of the celebration of the eucharist on Sunday. The rite begins with a sermon, in which the preacher sets forth the duties of the ministry, and the common prayers of the church, in which intercession is offered for those to be ordained. The eucharist then follows. A selection of proper lessons is provided, and the rite of ordination itself is placed between the gospel and the creed. A final prayer proper to the rite is provided for use at the end of the service.

The following comparative table, adapted from Paul Bradshaw, shows how Cranmer adapted Bucer's single ordination rite to create three separate rites for the ordination of deacons, priests, and bishops. Components added by Cranmer are indicated by bold-faced type.[40]

BUCER	DEACONS (1550)	PRIESTS (1550)	BISHOPS (1550)
Sermon	Sermon	Sermon	Sermon
Common Prayers		Introit: Ps. 40, 132, or 135	Introit: Ps. 40, 132, or 135
Eucharist begins		Eucharist begins	Eucharist begins
Veni Sancte		Proper Epistle	Proper Epistle
Spiritus		Proper Gospel	Proper Gospel
Introit: Ps. 40, 132, or 135		*Veni Creator*	Creed
Proper Epistle			
Proper Gospel			
Presentation	Presentation	Presentation	Presentation
Inquiry	Inquiry	Inquiry	**King's Mandate**
Exhortation			**Oath of Supremacy**
			Oath of Obedience
			Bidding
	Litany & Collect	Litany & Collect	**Litany & Collect**
	Eucharist begins		
	Proper Epistle		
	Oath of Supremacy	**Oath of Supremacy**	
		Exhortation	
Examination	Examination	Examination	Examination
Silent Prayer		Silent Prayer	*Veni Creator*
Prayer		**Prayer**	**Prayer**
Imposition of hands	Imposition of hands	Imposition of hands	Imposition of hands
with Blessing	**with Formula**	**with Formula**	**with Formula**
Creed			**Imposition of Bible**
			with formula
	Delivery of New Testament with formula	**Delivery of Bible, Chalice, Paten with formula**	**Delivery of Staff with formula**
	Gospel of the Day	Creed	
Eucharist continues	Eucharist continues	Eucharist continues	Eucharist continues
Appropriate final prayer	**Prayer after postcommunion**	**Prayer after postcommunion**	**Prayer after postcommunion**

Cranmer's 1550 rites for priests and bishops closely resemble Bucer's rite. Cranmer has reordered the sequence of components in the rite for deacons so that one of the newly ordained deacons can read the gospel at the service. In place of Bucer's common prayers after the sermon Cranmer used the litany (placed after the presentation and inquiry — at the beginning of the service for the ordination of deacons, after the gospel in the rite for priests, and after the creed in the rite for bishops). In 1662 the presentation, inquiry, and litany were shifted in the rite for priests to the same position as in the rite for deacons in order to facilitate the ordination of deacons and priests in the same service. When this shift was made in 1662, the proper collect of the litany was shifted in these two rites to be used as the proper collect at the eucharist. In the rite for bishops, the proper collect for the litany was retained, and another proper collect was added for the eucharist.

Bucer had placed the *Veni Sancte Spiritus,* a hymn to the Holy Spirit originally associated with the anointing, at the beginning of his rite, after the sermon and common prayers. Cranmer omitted such a hymn in the rite for deacons. He made use of such a hymn (in this case *Veni Creator Spiritus*) in the other two rites, but assigned them to different places in the two rites — after the gospel and before the presentation in the rite for priests, and after the examination of the ordinand in the rite for bishops. In 1662 the hymn was moved in the rite for priests to the same position as in the rite for bishops. These are the principal alterations which Cranmer made in the sequence of components in Bucer's rite. The principal addition which he made to the rite was the presentation of the instruments of ministry with appropriate formulas. This served to set out the distinctive functions of each order of ministry and was taken over, with modifications, from the Sarum tradition. The various oaths which Cranmer added may best be seen as adapting Bucer's inquiry to the circumstances of the Church of England.

2. *Prayer:* Cranmer, like Bucer, thought that what was essential in ordination was the imposition of hands and prayer. In Bucer's rite, the key prayer was a solemn prayer of ordination which asked God to pour forth the Spirit on those about to be ordained. It came immediately before the laying on of hands. Cranmer made use of this prayer in the ordination of priests and bishops, but modified it. This is the text of that prayer:

Almighty God, the Father of our Lord Jesus Christ, we give thanks for thy divine majesty, and for thine infinite love and goodness towards us, through him thine only Son, our redeemer and teacher unto blessed and everlasting life. And it has been thy will that after he had perfected our redemption by his death and sat down at thy right hand in heaven, he should renew all things in heaven and earth and give to us lost and unhappy mortals Apostles, Prophets, Evangelists, Doctors, and Pastors, sending them to us as thou didst send him to us, that by their ministry he might gather unto thee thy children scattered throughout the world, and that manifesting thee to them in his own self he might restore and renew them unto thee to the perpetual praise of thy holy name.

<u>And through the same thy Son we humbly pray and beseech thee that in the name of thy Son thou pour out thy Holy Spirit richly upon these thy ministers: and that by him thou teach and govern them, that they discharge their ministry faithfully and usefully to thy people, the flock of thy Son and our good shepherd.</u>

To all those for whose salvation thou dost desire them to minister, give minds that can receive thy word. And to us all who here and in all places call upon thy name, grant that we may ever show ourselves grateful to thee for these and all his other benefits, and that through thy Holy Spirit we may so advance daily in the knowledge and faith of thee and of thy Son, that through these thy ministers, through those to whom thou hast desired us to give ministers, and through all of us, thy holy name may be for evermore fully glorified, that thy blessed kingdom may be more widely spread, and hold more powerful sway wherever it may come. Through the same thy Son Jesus Christ our Lord, who liveth and reigneth with thee in the unity of the same Holy Spirit, world without end. Amen.[41]

The Ministry of the New Covenant 267

The key petition in Bucer's prayer (underlined in the text above) asks that God pour out the Holy Spirit upon the ordinands to equip them for ministry.

A comparison of the text of Bucer's ordination prayer with the texts of the prayers found in Cranmer's rites for the ordination of priests and bishops may be found in Appendix 2. The most surprising modification that Cranmer made in Bucer's rite was the way that he handled this prayer. In the rite for deacons he eliminated it altogether. In the rite for priests he eliminated its central petition, transforming the prayer from a prayer for the ordinands to a prayer that the church might benefit from their ministry. In the rite for bishops he kept the first part of the prayer, weakened its central petition by making it a prayer for the bestowal of grace rather than for the outpouring of the Spirit, and concluded the prayer with wording which echoes some of the medieval prayers for the ordination of bishops. Only in the rite for the ordination of bishops, therefore, is there a prayer which might be construed as analogous to the ordination prayer in Bucer's rite.

What are we to make of this? Without a solemn prayer for ordination, how do Cranmer's rites for deacons and priests fulfil the requirement set out for ordination in the preface of "public prayer, with the imposition of hands"? Bradshaw in his study of Cranmer's rites comes to the following conclusion:

> In view of the fact that the central petition for the candidates in Bucer's prayer before the imposition of hands has been deleted in the Anglican rite for priests, turning it into a prayer for the congregation instead, and in view of the complete absence of any such prayer in the service for deacons, it would seem that in all three rites the litany with its special suffrage and concluding collect for the candidates was regarded as the essential 'publique prayer' of ordination.[42]

Insofar as any prayer within the rite is to be understood as the essential one, Bradshaw is no doubt correct. It is also possible, however, that the entire service with its various prayers is to be understood as the "public prayer" to which the preface refers.

In the rite for marriage the blessing of the couple, which was concentrated in a single solemn prayer in the rite found in early sacramentaries, was "spread like butter" throughout the rite in Cranmer's revision of 1549. Cranmer seems to have treated prayer for the ordinands in the same way in the ordination rites. Such prayer is no longer concentrated in a prayer associated with the laying on of hands, but is found at various places in the rite — in the suffrage added to the litany, in the concluding collect for the litany (which, after 1662, was used as the proper collect at the eucharist), and in the proper prayer for each rite which Cranmer added after the postcommunion collect. These prayers, which may be found in Appendix 3, are Cranmer's own compositions, although the final collect for deacons uses some of the language of the solemn Roman ordination prayer for that order.

3. The Imposition of Hands: As was usually the case in the late middle ages, both Cranmer and Bucer separated the imposition of hands from any particular prayer for ordination and provided another formula for this action. Cranmer's 1550 rites are distinguished from Bucer's rite by the distinctive formulas for each order during the laying on of hands. Here Bucer simply has a blessing:

> The hand of Almighty God, the Father, the Son, and the Holy Spirit, be upon you, protect and govern you, that you may go and bring forth abundantly from your ministry: and that it may remain unto eternal life. Amen.[43]

Cranmer retained wording from the medieval rites which Bucer eliminated, but he retained it in modified form. The formulas used at the laying on of hands for all the orders are imperative in form; those for priests and bishops incorporate citations from the New Testament which had been used during one of the impositions of hands in various medieval rites. The formulas serve to distinguish the orders from each other. In 1662 the formulas for priests and bishops were modified somewhat to make the distinction between these two orders clearer, largely in response to Puritans who argued that priests and bishops did not constitute distinct orders of ministry. The following table gives the original 1550 version of these formulas and the expanded version adopted in 1662, with significant additions underlined:

1550	1662

Deacons: Take thou aucthoritie to execute the office of a Deacon in the Church of God committed unto thee: in the name of the father, the sonne, and the holy ghost. Amen.[44]

Deacons: Take thou Authority to execute the Office of a Deacon in the Church of God committed unto thee: In the Name of the Father, and of the Son, and of the Holy Ghost. Amen.[47]

Priests: Receiue the holy goste, whose synnes thou doest forgeue, they are forgeuen; and whose sinnes thou doest retaine, thei are retained: and be thou a faithful despensor of the word of god, and of his holy Sacramentes. In the name of the father, and of the sonne, and of the holy gost. Amen.[45]

Priests: Receive the holy Ghost for the Office and Work of a Priest in the Church of God, now committed unto thee by the Imposition of our hands. Whose sins thou dost forgive, they are forgiven; and whose sins thou dost retain, they are retained. And be thou a faithful Dispenser of the Word of God, and of his holy Sacraments; In the Name of the Father, and of the Son, and of the Holy Ghost. Amen.[48]

Bishops: Take the holy gost, and remember that thou stirre up the grace of god, whiche is in thee, by imposicion of handes: for god hath not geuen us the spirite of feare, but of power, and loue, and of sobernesse.[46]

Bishops: Receive the holy Ghost, for the Office and Work of a Bishop in the Church of God, now committed unto thee by the Imposition of our hands; In the Name of the Father, and of the Son, and of the Holy Ghost. Amen. And remember that thou stir up the grace of God which is given thee by this Imposition of our hands: for God hath not given us the spirit of fear, but of power, and love, and soberness.[49]

Note that after 1662 the order conferred was named in the formulas used for priests and bishops as well as that used for deacons, and that the formula used for the order of bishops made it explicit that the grace of the episcopate was conferred by *this* imposition of hands, not the imposition of hands when the candidate had been ordained priest. The preface to the 1550 Ordinal and the other texts of the rite made it clear that the priesthood and the episcopate as understood in the Ordinal were distinct orders of ministry, but the 1662 rite was designed to remove any ambiguity.

In the ordination of priests, some medieval authors had attributed great importance to the use of the imperative formula from John 19:22-23. Although the preface to the ordinal did not treat this as essential to the rite, all Anglican rites retained it until the revisions of the twentieth century. Later Anglican authors have sometimes treated the formula as essential and have interpreted it as if it were the prayer intended when the preface speaks of imposition of hands with public prayer. Since the formula is addressed to the ordinands, however, and not to God, this interpretation is impossible to sustain. The first part of the citation was also used (before 1662 with the variant translation, "Take") in the ordination of a bishop, as it had been in some medieval uses; the formula for the ordination of a bishop concludes with a citation of 2 Timothy 1:6-7.

Bucer's rite specified that all the ministers present lay on hands in ordination to any order. Cranmer maintained the distinction between orders by specifying (in accordance with Western custom) that bishops lay on hands at the ordination of a bishop, the bishop and priests lay on hands at the ordination of a priest, and the bishop alone lay on hands at the ordination of a deacon.

4. Presentation of Instruments: The presentation of the instruments of office was also retained by Cranmer in 1550 in modified form. This was further modified in 1552. The presentations for the various orders were as follows:

1550	1662

Deacons (Delivery of New Testament): Take thou aucthoritie to reade the Gospell in the Church of God, and to preache the same, yf thou bee thereunto ordinarely commaunded.[50]

Deacons (Delivery of New Testament): Take thou Authority to read the Gospel in the Church of God, and to preach the same, if thou be thereto licensed by the Bishop himself.[53]

Priests (Delivery of Bible and Chalice and Paten): Take thou aucthoritie to preache the word of god, and to minister the holy Sacramentes in thys congregacion, where thou shalt be so appointed.[51]

Priests (Delivery of Bible): Take thou Authority to preach the Word of God, and to minister the holy Sacraments in the Congregation, where thou shalt be lawfully appointed thereunto.[54]

Bishops (Imposition of Bible and Delivery of the Pastoral Staff): Geue hede unto reading, exhortacion, and doctrine. Thinke upon these things conteined in this boke, be diligent in them, that the encrease comyng therby, may be manyfest unto all men. Take hede unto thyselfe, and unto teaching, and be diligent in doing them, for by doing this thou shalt saue thyselfe, and them that heare thee: through Jesus Christe our Lorde.

Bishops (Delivery of Bible): Give heed unto reading, exhortation, and doctrine. Think upon the things contained in this Book. Be diligent in them, that the increase coming thereby may be manifest unto all men. Take heed unto thyself, and to doctrine, and be diligent in doing them: for by so doing thou shalt both save thyself and them that hear thee. Be to the flock of Christ a shepherd, not a wolf; feed them, devour them not. Hold up the weak, heal the sick, bind up the broken, bring again the outcasts, seek the lost. Be so merciful, that you be not too remiss; so minister discipline, that you forget not mercy: that when the chief Shepherd shall appear you may receive the never-fading crown of glory; through Jesus Christ our Lord. *Amen.*[55]

Be to the flocke of Christ a shepeheard, not a wolfe: feede them, deuoure them not; holde up the weake, heale the sicke, binde together the broken, bryng againe the outcastes, seke the lost. Be so mercifull, that you be not to remisse, so minister discipline, that ye forgeat not mercy; that when the chief shepheard shal come, ye may receyue the immarcessible croune of glory, through Jesus Christ our lord. *Amen.*[52]

Here again, in order to distinguish the orders of ministry Cranmer adapted from the medieval rites uses which Bucer had eliminated. With a Reformation emphasis on the ministry of the word, the presentation of the scriptures took on new importance in the presentation of instruments. The deacon's gospel book became the whole New Testament; the book of the gospels held over the bishop became the full Bible (and after 1552 it was delivered to him, rather than held over him); and a presentation of the Bible to priests was added. Of the other instruments, the chalice and paten for priests and the pastoral staff for bishops were retained in 1549. They were, however, eliminated in 1552 and in subsequent books. The formulas used during the delivery of instruments were adapted in various ways by Cranmer. That for deacons expanded on the traditional form. That for priests served as a substitute for the late medieval form used at the delivery of the chalice and paten, which spoke (as we have seen above) of the authority to offer sacrifice. For this Cranmer substituted a general authorization to preach the word and minister the sacraments. The form for the delivery of the pastoral staff included some echoes of the words used for this in the Sarum rite, but the words for the imposition of the Bible seem to be largely Cranmer's composition.

5. Vesture: Bucer's rite did not specify the vesture of candidates for ordination. From his *Censura* it is clear that he rejected the use of eucharistic vestments, but his attitude toward the alb and surplice is less certain. In Cranmer's 1550 rite candidates for the diaconate and priesthood were presented in albs; candidates for the episcopate were presented in surplice and cope. In neither case did the rubrics specify further vesting in the course of the rite. In 1552, all references to vestments were eliminated because of Puritan objections. After 1662, the rubrics specified that candidates for the diaconate and priesthood be "decently habited," which appears to mean vested in surplices; candidates for the episcopate were presented in rochets and assumed the rest of their "episcopal habit" after their examination and before their ordination — the only case in which vestments were assumed in the course of the service of ordination. While investiture with the vestments of a particular order had become customary during the middle ages, this was originally in preparation for the assumption of the functions of the order in the course of the service. In the Anglican rites, the only time when a newly ordained minister assumed the functions of his order at the ordination eucharist was when a deacon read the gospel, for by the time of the Reformation the custom of concelebration by priests and bishops at their ordination had fallen out of use (though in attenuated form it survived elsewhere).[56]

Other Revisions in 1662: Besides the additions to the formulas for the imposition of hands, the 1662 Book of Common Prayer made two other changes to emphasize the episcopate as a separate order from the priesthood. The title of the rite for bishops was altered to read, "The Form of Ordaining or Consecrating of an Archbishop or Bishop." The underlined words were added to make clear that the rite was ordination to a distinct order, rather than simply the assignment of additional authority to those who were already priests. A collect for the eucharist was also added to the rite for bishops which explicitly identified bishops (rather than priests) as the pastors of the church, and other references to pastors in the rite were altered accordingly:

> Almighty God, who by thy Son Jesus Christ didst give to thy holy Apostles many excellent gifts, and didst charge them to feed thy flock: Give grace, we beseech thee, to all Bishops, the Pastors of thy Church, that they may diligently preach thy Word, and duly administer the godly discipline thereof; and grant to the people, that they may obediently follow the same; that all may receive the crown of everlasting glory; through Jesus Christ our Lord. *Amen.*[57]

Note the emphasis here on the bishop as the one who administers discipline — an emphasis designed to counter the Puritan emphasis on the presbyterian model of church discipline.

Summary: The intention of the Church of England as articulated in the formulas for the laying on of hands, the presentation of instruments of ministry, and vestments seems clear: traditional customs were preserved but modified to exclude the definition of the priesthood in terms of the sacrificial understanding of the priest's role at the eucharist rejected at the Reformation.[58] The English reformers intended to continue the traditional order of ministry (unlike most continental reformers), but to reform them. The lack of consensus on what constituted the proper "form and matter" of ordination has led to a variety of judgments on how successfully they did this. While subsequent historical research has made it evident that in the early church ordination involved the laying on of hands during an ordination prayer, later Western rites separated the prayer from the laying on of hands, and many treated the formula used during the laying on of hands as the requisite form. While during the middle ages the imperative formulas for the laying on of hands and the presentation of instruments were considered important, as was the anointing of presbyters and bishops, scholarship today considers them and the vesting of the candidates secondary elements in the rite of ordination. Moreover, when the prayer is considered the requisite "form" for ordination, it is difficult to specify this "form" any more precisely than prayer for those being ordained, for the wording of the prayers in the different traditions which have come down to us varies enormously.

The only significant revisions of the rites in the American church before 1979 were the provision of a proper litany for ordinations in 1928 and the provision of an alternative formula for the laying on of hands in the ordination of priests in the first American ordinal. This formula was modelled on the one for the diaconate, and its inclusion occasioned strong protest, but William White, the first Presiding Bishop, treated the two formulas as equivalent to each other.

6. The Reform of the Rites of Ordination in the Book of Common Prayer 1979

By the mid-twentieth century, historical scholarship had made available to the church a much clearer idea of how ordination "by public prayer, with the imposition of hands" was understood in the early centuries of the church's life. It had become clear that the core of the ancient rites was the imposition of hands while the bishop who presided recited a solemn prayer of ordination. That was not the understanding of prayer at ordinations in Anglican rites, where prayer for the candidates is spread like butter throughout the service, and the most clearly identifiable prayer for them is the litany and its concluding collect (which became the collect of the day in the rite for deacons and presbyters after 1662). Paul Bradshaw concludes his study of the Anglican ordinal with this assessment:

> Cranmer's attempts to construct simple ordination rites to replace the complex ceremonies of the Middle Ages were in part successful; they restored the imposition of hands to its central position and gave greater emphasis to the prayer of the people, but in other ways they left much to be desired, particularly in the absence of an ordination prayer in close association with the imposition of hands in the rites for the priesthood and the diaconate. . . .
>
> In spite of the importance attached by many Anglicans to the imperative formulas at the imposition of hands in the Anglican rites, particularly in the rite for the priesthood, their continued use can really no longer be defended. They have no place in the primitive pattern of ordination, and they serve only to detract from the ordination prayers and induce erroneous ideas about ordination; they suggest, for example, that the grace of order can be bestowed by command rather than sought in prayer.[59]

Some attempt to remedy this was made in the proposed rites of 1928 in the Church of England, but since this book never secured parliamentary assent, its revisions exercised their influence only on other churches of the Anglican communion which followed its lead.

That book provided a solemn prayer of ordination for the diaconate and prefaced the prayers for all orders with a eucharistic dialogue (on the model of the form that the Roman prayers had taken since the Gelasian sacramentary). At the last minute it restored an invocation of the Spirit on the candidate in the prayer for the priesthood. It also continued to separate the prayer from the imposition of hands, which was still accompanied by the traditional imperative formulas. Some other adjustments were made in the rite, but its basic shape was not altered.

The model for all future revisions of the ordinal was created in the rites prepared for the union of several denominations which resulted in the Church of South India (issued in 1958 and revised in 1962). It returned once again to the use of an ordination prayer during the laying on of hands rather than an imperative formula. It sets forth the principles on which the rite is constructed in a carefully crafted preface:

> . . . The Church as a whole is a priestly body, since it is the body of Christ the great High Priest. All its members, according to the measure of the gift of Christ, share in its priestly nature. Yet from the beginning God has entrusted particular ministries to particular persons within in it, and these have, through the Church, received the commission of Christ. . . . An ordination service is the rite by which one of these ministries [of Bishops, Presbyters, and Deacons] is conferred. . . . [I]n all ordinations and consecrations the true Ordainer and Consecrator is God, who, in response to the prayers of His Church, and through the words and acts of its representatives, commissions and empowers for the work and office to which they are called the persons whom it has selected.

> In the earliest ordination of which we have record, that described in Acts 6:1-6, the following parts appear: election by the people, prayer, and the laying on of apostolic hands. In accordance with this pattern . . ., the same three parts form the basis of the services [of the Church of South India]:

> (1) the presentation of the candidates to the presiding Bishop, this being the last step in the process of choice of them by the Church;
> (2) prayer for those about to be ordained or consecrated, that they may receive the gift of the Holy Spirit for their ministry; and
> (3) the laying on of hands of at least three Bishops (in an episco-

al consecration), of the Bishop and Presbyters (in an ordination f Presbyters), or of the Bishop (in an ordination of Deacons).

To these have been added an examination of the candidates concerning their beliefs and duties, the delivery to them of the instruments of their office (Bible, pastoral staff), and the giving of the right hand of fellowship. These ceremonies, however valuable for their symbolism, are not essential elements in the rites of ordination.[60]

The structure of the rite is the same for each order and may be outlined as follows:

The Ordination Rites of the Church of South India

Presentation, Inquiry, and Assent of the Congregation
Proper Ministry of the Word
Address and Examination of the Candidate
Ordination
    Bidding to Silent Prayer
    Veni Creator
    Ordination Prayer, with central petition for the Holy Spirit
    Laying on of Hands during central petition
Delivery of Bible as token of ministry
Right hand of fellowship (and delivery of pastoral staff to new bishop)
Declaration of Ordination
Continuation of the Eucharist with the Prayers of the People (litany)

Note that the litany is not used for the prayer for the ordinand in these rites, but follows the ordination in its usual place in the eucharist. The people's prayer for the ordinand is the silent prayer, followed by the hymn *Veni creator*. This hymn, originally associated with the anointing of bishops and presbyters, is now understood as a prayer to the Holy Spirit and included in the rite for deacons as well.

The revisions of the rites of ordination in the Roman Catholic Church after the second Vatican Council are quite similar to the South Indian rites, except that the presentation comes after the ministry of the word, the litany retains its traditional place before the ordination prayer, anointing of bishops and priests is retained, and the *Veni Creator* (at the presentation of a bishop and at the vesting of the priest) is optional.[61] The Roman Catholic rites have boldly returned to a single ordination prayer, revising the prayers for presbyters and deacons and returning to a version of the ordination prayer of the *Apostolic Tradition* for the ordination of a bishop. The revisions also abolished the subdiaconate and retained only the minor orders of acolyte and lector, treating them as "instituted" ministries — ministries to which one is appointed rather than ordained. The orders of presbyters and bishops, which in the past were often treated as degrees of the priesthood rather than as distinct orders, are clearly distinguished.

The revision process which began at the end of the 1960s in the American Episcopal Church produced a rite, published in 1970 and authorized for trial use in that year, that had the same basic structure as the South India rite.[62] With minor revisions, this rite was adopted as part of the Book of Common Prayer 1979. The drafting committee for the rite was chaired by H. Boone Porter. The committee took as the starting point for its work the results of recent scholarship, the South Indian rites and their derivatives, and the Roman Catholic reforms.

The 1979 preface to the rite, from a draft by Boone Porter, is a revision of the 1550 preface on the basis of contemporary scholarship and shows affinity to the South Indian preface:

> The Holy Scriptures and ancient Christian writers make it clear that from the apostles' time, there have been different ministries within the Church. In particular, since the time of the New Testament, three distinct orders of ordained ministers have been characteristic of Christ's holy catholic Church. First, there is the order of bishops who carry on the apostolic work of leading, supervising, and uniting the Church. Secondly, associated with them are the presbyters, or ordained elders, in subsequent times generally known as priests. Together with the bishops, they take part in the governance of the church, in the carrying out of its missionary and pastoral work, and in the preaching of the Word

of God and administering his holy Sacraments. Thirdly, there are deacons who assist bishops and priests in all of this work. It is also a special responsibility of deacons to minister in Christ's name to the poor, the sick, the suffering, and the helpless.

The persons who are chosen and recognized by the Church as being called by God to the ordained ministry are admitted to these sacred orders by solemn prayer and the laying on of episcopal hands. It has been, and is, the intention of this Church to maintain and continue these three orders; and for this purpose these services of ordination and consecration are appointed. No persons are allowed to exercise the offices of bishop, priest, or deacon in this Church unless they are so ordained, or have already received such ordination with the laying on of hands by bishops who are themselves duly qualified to confer Holy Orders.

It is also recognized and affirmed that the threefold ministry is not the exclusive property of this portion of Christ's catholic Church, but is a gift from God for the nurture of his people and the proclamation of his Gospel everywhere. Accordingly, the manner of ordaining in this Church is to be such as has been, and is, most generally recognized by Christian people as suitable for the conferring of the sacred orders of bishop, priest, and deacon.[63]

The claims made for the threefold ministry made in the preface are a contemporary restatement of those in the 1550 Ordinal. It must be admitted that, while the diversity of ministries in the New Testament is acknowledged, the explicit description of the threefold ministry in the first paragraph is more characteristic of second-century church order than of what we find in the literature of the New Testament, where the distinction between bishops and presbyters is not so clear. The description of presbyters as associates of the bishop in the work of ministry and of deacons as assistants gives clear expression to the collegial relation of the bishop and his presbyterate which developed in the second century.[64] The appropriate rite of ordination is carefully described in the second paragraph, and the intention of the Episcopal Church to continue the historic ministry of the church in this way is reaffirmed. The final paragraph works from an ecumenical perspective and makes a commitment to shape the rites of ordination according to the consensus emerging in the twentieth century about the appropriate elements of the rite of ordination.[65]

The general structure of the rite is very similar to that of the Church of South India:

The Ordination Rites of the Book of Common Prayer 1979

Presentation, Inquiry, and Assent of the Congregation

Litany and Collect

Proper Ministry of the Word

Address and Examination of the Candidate

Consecration (Ordination)

    Veni Creator (or *Veni Sancte Spiritus*)

    Silent Prayer

    Ordination Prayer, with central petition for the Holy Spirit

    Laying on of Hands during central petition

    Vesting according to order (with stole; other vestments if desired)

    Delivery of Bible (other symbols of ministry if desired for bishops and
      priests)

    Peace

Continuation of the Eucharist at the offertory (special postcommunion
  prayer)

Blessing by new bishop or priest; dismissal by new deacon

Differences from the South Indian rite include the retention the litany in its traditional place, the reversal of the order for the *Veni creator* and silent prayer, the elimination of the declaration of ordination, and the use of the peace rather than the right hand of fellowship (a difference of terminology rather than ritual act). The explicit reference to assumption of vestments is also not found in the South Indian rite. In older Anglican rites, the assumption of vestments occurs only in the rite for bishops after 1662 (where the rest of the episcopal habit is put on *before* the laying on of hands). A final difference from the South Indian rite is the decision to use contemporary rather than traditional language.

Many details are worthy of note. A serious attempt is made to set out the orders as distinctive ministries, not simply steps on a career ladder as they had become in the late middle ages. This is worked out in the new material in the preface, in the description of the ministries in the new addresses before the examinations and in the ordination prayers, and in the provision for the newly ordained to exercise their distinctive functions in the ordination eucharist. The distinction of each order from the others is displayed in the requirement that candidates for each order be presented in alb, rochet, or surplice, without vestments or insignia of present orders: baptism is (from a liturgical if not from a canonical standpoint) the only prerequisite status for ordination to any order. The rubrics placed before each service and incorporated in its text also carefully spell out the functions proper to each order and to lay persons in the rites of ordination: the diversity of the church's ministries is to be made evident in the service itself, in which the functions appropriate to each order are carefully assigned by rubric. We should note particularly the affirmation of the ministry of Christian laity by virtue of their baptism in the new rites. Bucer's exhortation before the examination of candidates, the basis of Cranmer's exhortation in the 1550 ordinal, took a relatively passive view of the role of lay persons in the church.[66] That address was drastically revised in the new rite, and the rubrics themselves give lay persons significant roles in the rite of ordination.

The sequence of orders is the sequence found in the more ancient documents and starts with the bishop — the reverse of the sequence found from the middle ages to the present century. It intends to "indicate the centrality of the episcopate" in the ministry of the church and to avoid the impression that the three orders are "an ascending scale of promotion."[67] The rites are in the singular (though they may be adapted for more than one candidate), giving precedence to locating the rite in the local church where the person ordained will exercise his or her ministry.[68] In the presentation, the people are given the active role of speaking their consent, rather than the passive one of silence unless they have an impediment to allege. Although the original proposal was to use the ancient acclamation that the candidate is worthy, the possible misinterpretation of this as moral worthiness led to the rephrasing of the people's response.

The title of each service is "Ordination"; "Consecration" is the heading used for the actual ordination to each order (as in the early Roman tradition). In these rites, all prayer specific to the order being conferred is concentrated in the prayer of consecration itself, not spread through the service as in older rites. The collect at the ministry of the word and the postcommunion prayer are common to all three rites, rather than specific to each order. The prayer of consecration for bishops is a modern adaptation of the prayer in the *Apostolic Tradition*. The prayers for priests and deacons are adaptations of those of the Church of South India. The South Indian prayer for deacons was a new composition (but echoes in some ways the language of the prayer in the Byzantine rite); the American version incorporates phrases from the ancient Roman prayer (once found in the prayer after the postcommunion in Anglican rites). The South Indian prayer for presbyters was a revision of Bucer's original prayer, with the final portion revised to express more adequately the distinctive functions of that order. As in the South Indian prayers, the central petition of the prayer invokes the Holy Spirit upon the candidate and is said during the laying on of hands. The prayers for the three orders are as follows:

> **Bishops:** God and Father of our Lord Jesus Christ, Father of mercies and God of all comfort, dwelling on high but having regard for the lowly, knowing all things before they come to pass: We give you thanks that from the beginning you have gathered and prepared a people to be heirs of the covenant of Abraham, and have raised up prophets, kings, and priests, never leaving your temple untended. We praise you also that from the creation you have graciously accepted the ministry of those whom you have chosen.
>
> Therefore, Father, make N. a bishop in your Church. Pour out upon *him* the power of your princely Spirit, whom you bestowed upon your beloved Son Jesus Christ, with whom he endowed the

apostles, and by whom your Church is built up in every place, to the glory and unceasing praise of your Name.

To you, O Father, all hearts are open; fill, we pray, the heart of this your servant whom you have chosen to be a bishop in your Church, with such love of you and of all the people, that *he* may feed and tend the flock of Christ, and exercise without reproach the high priesthood to which you have called *him*, serving you night and day in the ministry of reconciliation, declaring pardon in your Name, offering the holy gifts, and wisely overseeing the life and work of the Church. In all things may *he* present before you the acceptable offering of a pure, and gentle, and holy life; through Jesus Christ your Son, to whom, with you and the Holy Spirit, be honor and power and glory in the Church, now and for ever. *Amen.*[69]

Priests: God and Father of all, we praise you for your infinite love in calling us to be a holy people in the kingdom of your Son Jesus our Lord, who is the image of your eternal and invisible glory, the firstborn among many brethren, and the head of the Church. We thank you that by his death he has overcome death, and, having ascended into heaven, has poured his gifts abundantly upon your people, making some prophets, some evangelists, some pastors and teachers, to equip the saints for the work of ministry and the building up of his body.

Therefore, Father, through Jesus Christ your Son, give your Holy Spirit to N.; fill *him* with your grace and power, and make *him* a priest in your Church.

May *he* exalt you, O Lord, in the midst of your people; offer spiritual sacrifices acceptable to you; boldly proclaim the gospel of salvation; and rightly administer the sacraments of the New Covenant. Make *him* a faithful pastor, a patient teacher, and a wise councilor. Grant that in all things *he* may serve you without reproach, so that your people may be strengthened and your

Name be glorified in all the world. All this we ask through Jesus Christ our Lord, who with you and the Holy Spirit lives and reigns, one God, for ever and ever. *Amen.*[70]

Deacons: O God, most merciful Father, we praise you for sending your Son Jesus Christ, who took on himself the form of a servant and humbled himself, becoming obedient even to death on a cross. We praise you that you have highly exalted him, and made him Lord of all; and that, through him, we know that whoever would be great must be servant of all. We praise you for the many ministries in your Church, and for calling this your servant to the order of deacons.

Therefore, Father, through Jesus Christ your Son, give your Holy Spirit to N.; fill *him* with grace and power, and make *him* a deacon in your Church.

Make *him*, O Lord, modest and humble, strong and constant, to observe the discipline of Christ. Let *his* life and teaching reflect your commandments, that through *him* many may come to know you and love you. As your Son came not to be served but to serve, may this deacon share in Christ's service, and come to the unending glory of him who, with you and the Holy Spirit, lives and reigns, one God, for ever and ever. *Amen.*[71]

The prayers for the respective orders (as well as the proper lessons and addresses before the examination) highlight the ancient understanding of each order. As in the South Indian rites, there is a short address proper to each order before the examination. The bishop is high priest and pastor of the church in the diocese and successor to the apostles in the church's mission, with responsibility for guarding its faith and unity (a duty given expression in directing a new bishop to lead the Nicene Creed at his or her ordination — a variant of the Byzantine custom noted above). The diaconal nature of the episcopate is emphasized at the end of the address before the examination of a bishop elect. Priests are associates and councilors of the bishop in this ministry, with a share in the pastoral, priestly, and teaching responsibilities of the bishop. Deacons are called to a servant ministry, whose exemplar is Christ himself, and they are meant to exercise that ministry in the world as well as to serve as assistants to bishop and presbyters at worship. The present rites give special emphasis to the importance of this ministry and do not treat it as simply preparation for assuming the responsibilities of the priesthood at a later time. The movement in the church toward a vocational diaconate which has gained strength in the years since the new rite has partially realized this vision — which appears to be part of what Cranmer, influenced by the diaconate in the Reformed tradition, intended at the Reformation.

After ordination, the new minister is clothed with vestments appropriate to the order. A stole is specified; other vestments (dalmatic for deacons; chasuble for priests; chasuble, cope, or chimere for bishops) may also be put on. Presentation of stoles had become customary in the Anglican tradition, though no provision for them was made in prior rites. Vesting is particularly appropriate in the new rites, since new ministers are expected to assume the function of the office in the eucharistic celebration which follows. No formulas are intended for use at this time; if vestments are blessed, this is done before the service. The presentation of instruments has been retained, but carefully reworked. The 1979 rite follows the Church of South India in making the Bible the principal instrument for each order; there seems no good reason why the deacon should receive only the New Testament.[72] The impression that the instrument conveys authority is avoided by the new wording, which makes the Bible a symbol of the authority given by ordination. Other appropriate symbols (such as chalice and paten for priests and the pastoral staff, mitre, and ring for bishops) may also be given. A special symbol of the bishop's ministry is his chair or *cathedra*, and the rubrics of the rite provided for seating the bishop in that chair immediately after ordination.

This 1979 revision of ordination rites, like other liturgical revisions during the same era, makes constructive use of historical scholarship in an attempt to be faithful to the tradition of the church in the way the Church orders its life through its ministry. Paul Bradshaw's evaluation of this rite in his study of the Anglican ordinal is generally quite positive.[73] The chief new feature of the rites is the restoration of the prayer of consecration to a cen-

restoration of prayer to central position

tral position in the rites and its association with the imposition of hands. Bradshaw criticizes what he regards as the double prayer of the people for the ordinand in the initial litany and the silent prayer before the imposition of hands; he also questions the use of the *Veni creator* as a part of the people's prayer for the ordinand. Since the litany serves as the prayers of the people for the ordination eucharist and includes general intercession as well as petitions for the ordinands, it seems in many ways preferable *not* to use it to serve as the specific public prayer for the ordinand, and to place it either at the beginning — as in the American rites — or after the ordination in the ordinary place for the prayers of the people, as in the South Indian rite. The people's prayer for the ordinand should be sharply focussed; the inclusion of general petitions in the litany make it awkward to use for this purpose. The *Veni Creator* is a late addition to Western rites of ordination, originally associated with the anointing. Textually it is a general invocation of the Spirit upon the church rather than a specific invocation of the Spirit on those being ordained; it would seem therefore that its use in ordination as prayer for those being ordained is less apt than first appears, and it has become an optional text in the English version of the Roman Catholic rites. The prayer of the people before the ordination prayer is surely best treated as specific prayer for those being ordained, and silent prayer is perhaps the preferable option here.

Conclusion

The Ordering of the Church's Life through Ordination

Sacramental means of church ordered by god

The rites of ordination are properly understood as sacramental means by which the life of the church as the people of God, the body of Christ invested with his royal priesthood, and the temple of the Holy Spirit is ordered by God. The catechism describes ordination as "the rite in which God gives the grace of the Holy Spirit to those being made bishops, priests, and deacons, through prayer and the laying on of hands."[74] Lest we mistake the purpose for which this grace is given, we would do well to heed the words of William Wake, Archbishop of Canterbury at the end of the seventeenth century:

We do not at all doubt but that the *grace* of God accompanies this ordinance and the discharges of those ministers which are performed in consequences of it. But then this *grace* is only the *blessing* of God upon a particular employ; and is given to such persons rather for the *benefit* of *others* than for the furtherance of their own *salvation*.[75]

When we understand ordination as a sacramental rite, as the Book of Common Prayer 1979 does, it is important that it be placed in this context. It is not a pastoral office, concerned with the sanctification of the personal life of the Christian.

We have noted above that the shape of the historic threefold ministry had emerged in the life of the church by the beginning of the second century. The bishop was the linchpin in this ministry, serving as the head of the collegial ministry of the presbyterate of the local church and having collegial responsibilities with his fellow bishops for the life of the universal church. Deacons were assigned to assist the bishop in the administration of the church's charity and finances and in its worship. By the time of Ignatius the way in which these ministries ordered the church's life was revealed by the way in which they functioned at the eucharist as the heart of the church's life.

The continuity of these orders of ministry since that time easily masks, however, how deeply the understanding of these ministries was shaped, for good or ill, by the environing society.[76] First-century Christians in a Jewish milieu no doubt organized the life of their communities under the presbyterate (board of elders), much as first-century Jews did. By the second century presbyters were beginning to be understood as the associates of the bishop, in whom the leadership of the community was vested, and also acted by delegation from the bishop to preside at the eucharist. In subsidiary gatherings in large cities and in rural gatherings, presbyters began to be the primary pastors. As bishops became increasingly remote figures in the middle ages and as the diaconate became a vestigial office, the presbyters (whose ministry was understood primarily in cultic terms as celebrating the eucharist) absorbed most ministerial functions and ministry was understood primarily as priesthood. In the West, monasticism became the model of the priestly life, and the married community patriarch of the pastoral epistles had become a celibate cleric set apart from the community. Most churches of the Reformation would redefine the parish priest as the minister of word and sacrament, with strong emphasis on the minister as teacher and preacher. Celibacy was no longer required for ordination in these churches. The Catholic priest and the Protestant minister had displaced the richly differentiated ministries of the early centuries.

In the first century, bishops are not clearly differentiated from presbyters. In the second century the chief presbyter of cities assumed the title of bishop, and his ministry was understood as that of shepherd and high priest. In the urban church of the early empire, bishops assumed the status and rank of urban magistrates, while in other areas such as Gaul bishops took the lead as missionaries in still pagan regions. In the middle ages bishops took on the role of feudal lords and episcopate and presbyterate were often understood as a single priestly order, with distinction only in terms of power of jurisdiction, not in terms of power of order. As the church spread beyond the European world, bishops began to shed their status as feudal lords. In modern times they have often functioned as administrators of the diocesan bureaucracy or as corporate executives. Churches which did not retain the episcopate at the Reformation subsequently often subsequently discovered a need to create a ministry of oversight or superintendence (*episcope*) in the church, whether or not such ministers received the title of bishop.

Through their responsibilities for the church's charity and finances, deacons gained considerable power, especially when their numbers were restricted (to seven in Rome, no doubt in deference to the seven in Acts).[77] The rise of presbyters as parish priests led to the decline of the diaconate, and eventually the diaconate in the West became an apprenticeship for the presbyterate rather than a permanent ministry. Only recently have churches begun the restoration of the diaconate as a permanent order.

Recent documents show the emergence of an ecumenical consensus on the threefold ministry as appropriate to the ordering of the church's life. The description of the tasks of ministry found in the 1979 catechism is in fact very similar to that set out in the document on ministry in the 1982 report on *Baptism, Eucharist, and Ministry* by the World Council of Churches:[78]

Catechism

The ministry of a bishop is to represent Christ and his Church, particularly as an apostle, chief priest, and pastor of a diocese; to guard the faith, unity, and discipline of the whole Church; to proclaim the Word of God; to act in Christ's name for the reconciliation of the world and the building up of the Church; and to ordain others to continue Christ's ministry.

The ministry of a priest [or presbyter] is to represent Christ and his Church, particularly as pastor to the people; to share with the bishop in the overseeing of the Church; to proclaim the Gospel; to administer the sacraments; and to bless and declare pardon in the name of God.

The ministry of a deacon is to represent Christ and his Church, particularly as a servant of those in need; and to assist bishops and priests in the proclamation of the Gospel and the administration of the sacraments.

World Council of Churches

Bishops preach the Word, preside at the sacraments, and administer discipline in such a way as to be representative pastoral ministers of oversight, continuity and unity in the Church. They have pastoral oversight of the area to which they are called. They serve the apostolicity and unity of the Church's teaching, worship and sacramental life. They relate the Christian community in their area to the wider Church, and the universal Church to their community. They, in communion with the presbyters and deacons and the whole community, are responsible for the orderly transfer of ministerial authority to the Church.

Presbyters serve as pastoral ministers of Word and sacraments in a local eucharistic community. They are preachers and teachers of the faith, exercise pastoral care, and bear responsibility for the discipline of the congregation to the end that the world may believe and that the entire membership of the Church may be renewed, strengthened, and equipped in ministry. Presbyters have particular responsibility for the preparation of members for Christian life and ministry.

Deacons represent to the Church its calling as servant in the world. By struggling in Christ's name with the myriad needs of societies and persons, deacons exemplify the interdependence of worship and service in the Church's life. They exercise responsibility in the worship of the congregation: for example, by reading the scriptures, preaching and leading the people in prayer. They exercise a ministry of love within the community. They fulfill certain administrative tasks and may be elected to responsibility for governance.

The vision of the threefold ministry in the catechism and what is said about the respective orders in the addresses and prayers of the ordination rites of the Book of Common Prayer 1979 coheres very well with the ecumenical vision set out in the World Council of Churches document. The challenge, for the Episcopal Church as well as for other denominations, is to implement in the context of its contemporary life the vision set out there in ways that fulfill that vision and do not distort it. As the document says,

> All churches need to examine the forms of ordained ministry and the degree to which they are faithful to its original intentions. Churches must be prepared to renew their understanding and their practice of the ordained ministry.[79]

The restoration of the vocational diaconate is a part of that process; recovery of presbyteral collegiality is important; the way in which bishops in the contemporary church exercise the ministry of *episcope* also needs examination.

Ministry in the Community of the New Covenant

The ministry of the church as the people of God is not restricted to its ordained ministers, but brought to a focus in them. All are called to ministry in the church by virtue of their baptism. The 1979 catechism explicitly includes lay persons as ministers of the church (though it is perhaps unfortunate that it speaks of them as an "order" of ministry):

> The ministry of lay persons is to represent Christ and his Church, to bear witness to him wherever they may be; and, according to the gifts given them, to carry out Christ's work of reconciliation in the world; and to take their place in the life, worship, and governance of the Church.[80]

Similarly, the World Council of Churches declares,

> The word *ministry* in its broadest sense denotes the service to which the whole people of God is called, whether as individuals, as a local community, or as the universal Church.[81]

The challenge to the church is to enable the ministry of all Christians through the ordering of its life by ordained ministers, rather than to restrict ministry to those who are ordained. The Spirit's gifts for ministry are not limited to those who are ordained. A restored differentiation in the ordained ministry of the church should lead to a recognition of other ministries for which ordination is not required.

The Royal Priesthood of the People of God

The royal priesthood of the people of God is the priesthood of Christ in his church. It finds a focus in the eucharistic worship of the church where Christians are united to Christ in his self-offering for the life of the world, but it encompasses the whole of life and aims at the reconciliation of the world to God. At baptism Christians are sealed that they may "share the royal priesthood of Christ."[82] Because the ordained ministers of the church oversee its sacrificial life and worship, first bishops and then presbyters came to be called "priests." Theirs indeed is a priestly ministry, but that priestly ministry must be understood as a particular exercise of the priestly ministry of the whole church. The World Council of Churches declares,

> Ordained ministers are related, as are all Christians, both to the priesthood of Christ and to the priesthood of the Church. But they may appropriately be called priests because they fulfill a particular priestly service by strengthening and building up the royal and prophetic priesthood of the faithful through word and sacraments, through their prayers of intercession, and through their pastoral guidance of the community.[83]

What the church needs to avoid is the creation of a cultic ministry of priests distinct from the priestly life of the whole church — the kind of priestly caste which dominated the church in the middle ages.

The Apostolic Character of the Church and Its Ministry

The 1979 catechism describes the church as apostolic "because it continues in the teaching and fellowship of the apostles and is sent to carry out Christ's mission to all peoples."[84] The historic episcopate has been understood in Anglicanism as one of the ways in which continuity with the apostolic church has been maintained. The World Council of Churches document on ministry recognizes this function of the episcopate and episcopal succession:

> The primary manifestation of apostolic succession is to be found in the apostolic tradition of the church as a whole. . . . Within the Church the ordained ministry has a particular task of preserving and actualizing the apostolic faith. The orderly transmission of the ordained ministry is therefore a powerful expression of the continuity of the Church throughout history. . . . Under the particular historical circumstances of the growing Church in the early centuries, the succession of bishops became one of the ways, together with the transmission of the Gospel and the life of the community, in which the apostolic tradition of the Church was expressed. This succession was understood as serving, symbolizing and guiding the continuity of the apostolic faith and communion.[85]

The document also insists that continuity in apostolic faith, worship and mission be understood as genuine apostolic tradition, even in churches which have not maintained episcopal succession. The classic tradition of Anglicanism, while insisting that Anglicans retain the historic episcopate, has generally been unwilling to "unchurch" those denominations which did not maintain episcopal succession. In both American and international Anglican-Lutheran dialogues, Anglicans have come to place succession in pastoral office in a larger context, and to agree that "both the Lutheran Church and the Episcopal Church stand in Apostolic Succession."[86]

The Ministry of Women

Women played significant roles in the ministry of Jesus and in the early decades of the church's life, as the evidence of the New Testament bears witness.[87] In the Pauline literature, the apostle Paul recognizes women as his colleagues in his missionary work and women who exercised leadership in local communities. Christian literature of the first several centuries gives evidence to the ministry of women in the diaconate. We have no evidence as to whether women shared in the oversight exercised in local communities by the presbyterate and the episcopate, although by the era of the pastoral epistles these offices were restricted to male heads of households. Eucharistic presidency may have been exercised by women who provided space for early house churches, but there is no explicit evidence of any kind about eucharistic presidency in the New Testament.

It appears that the baptismal equality of all believers to which Galatians bears witness gave way to older patriarchal conventions as the church made efforts to give no scandal to the environing society in the later literature of the New Testament. As radical movements in the early centuries recognized the equal status of women, the "great church" reacted by excluding women from leadership. It was left to later generations to give expression to the equality of men and women in the body of Christ. The only ministerial roles for women to which the literature of the later New Testament and the following centuries bear witness are those of enrolled widows, consecrated virgins, and women deacons. In later centuries women deacons and ascetics had recognized but strictly limited roles in the church's ministry and worship.

The Reformation in the West brought little change, except in some of the more radical traditions. In fact, the suppression of women's religious orders brought to an end one field in which women might exercise ministry. It was not until the late nineteenth century that women began to be recognized as qualified to exercise the ministerial office in the church in any major denomination, and it was only in the twentieth century that major denominations began to admit women to ordinary ministerial offices. The first beginning for most denominations was the restoration of the office of deaconess, although the liturgical role of deaconess was a limited (and non-sacramental) one. From the last decades of the nineteenth century, churches began to issue rites for the setting apart of deaconesses through the laying on of hands (a rite for which the Episcopal Church made official provision in the *Book of Offices*, a predecessor of the *Book of Occasional Services*). This service became redundant in the 1960s, when deaconesses in the American church were recognized as within the diaconate and were ordained by the same rite as male deacons.

After earlier "irregular" ordinations of women to the presbyterate, canonical changes were made and the language of the rubrics and texts of the Book of Common Prayer 1979 were adjusted to provide for the ordination of women to the three orders of ministry. Theological arguments against the ordination of women are most frequently made in terms of a theology of ordained priesthood which argues that women cannot be an appropriate sign of the priesthood of Christ because of their gender. This is an argument not adequately rooted in tradition, which originally spoke of baptism as the act which invests men and women alike with the royal priesthood of Jesus, which speaks not of priests but of bishops, presbyters, and deacons as the orders of ministry, and which makes the diaconate (the one order of ministry to which women in Christian antiquity were indisputably admitted) the icon of the ministry of Jesus. It is important, however, to note that arguments for the ordination of women soundly rooted in Christian tradition cannot speak of the right of women to ordination, for tradition knows no individual right to ordination; they must speak, rather, of the right of the church to call women to its ministry.

The Episcopal Church and other churches of the Anglican Communion have not been unique in reconceptualizing the ministry in terms of the radical equality of men and women within the body of Christ. The document on ministry of the World Council of Churches addresses the issue as part of the present agenda of ecumenical dialogue, since consensus has not yet been achieved on an ecumenical level:

> Where Christ is present, human barriers are being broken. The Church is called to convey to the world the image of a new humanity. There is in Christ no male or female (Gal. 3:28). Both women and men must discover together their contributions to the service of Christ in the Church. The Church must discover the ministry which can be provided by women as well as that which can be provided by men. A deeper understanding of the comprehensiveness of ministry which reflects the interdependence of men and women needs to be more widely manifested in the life of the Church.

Though they agree on this need, the churches draw different conclusions as to the admission of women to the ordained ministry. An increasing number of churches have decided that there is no biblical or theological reason against ordaining women, and many of them have subsequently proceeded to do so. Yet many churches hold that the tradition of the Church in this regard must not be changed.[88]

Scandinavian Lutheran churches and the churches of the Anglican Communion are the only denominations which have maintained the episcopal succession of their ministries to move to the ordination of women. The Orthodox churches, the other Oriental Churches, and the Roman Catholic Church have all resisted this change in practice. The debate in the Roman Catholic Church[89] produced a decision by the Pontifical Biblical Commission in 1975 and 1976 that "the opinion that a clear apostolic tradition excludes women from the priesthood is not supported by the N[ew] T[estment]."[90] The Congregation on the Doctrine of the Faith, however, denied the possibility of the admission of women to the priesthood in the declaration *Inter Insigniores*, issued in 1976. The arguments presented are open to serious challenge:

1. Continuity of present practice as apostolic tradition: this argument does not do justice to the New Testament evidence of ministry by women.
2. Restriction of the twelve to men: this argument works from the assumption that Jesus instituted the eucharistic priesthood at the last supper, addressing to the twelve the command to do this in remembrance of him — an exegesis of the text which does not find contemporary support.
3. Lack of a "natural likeness" in a woman as *signum* to the *res* of the sacrament, Christ incarnate as a male human being: this argument is undercut by the baptismal likeness of both men and women to Christ to which Galatians bears witness and is a theology of the priesthood not grounded in the understanding of the presbyterate in the early centuries.

4. Vocation to the priesthood is God's call mediated through the church, not an inner call to the individual: an argument about the nature of call to ministry which is supported by the classical rites of ordination, but which does not preclude the church calling women to its ministries.[91]

The third objection is purely theological, and is based on several dubious assumptions. The order of presbyter may indeed be understood as a priestly order, but the early tradition does not base the sacramental character of presbyters on iconic likeness to Christ, nor does it define the office primarily in terms of eucharistic presidency. To do so is to think in terms of the cultic priesthood in the Old Testament, not of the royal priesthood of Christ and the Church in the New Testament. Moreover, the iconic likeness to Christ required is, according to early tradition, given in baptism when the Christian puts on Christ. In any case, theological likeness to Christ depends on his human nature, not his gender. What underlies the argument that women cannot adequately represent Christ is the subordination of women to men and the anthropology of scholastic theology — a flawed anthropology which can no longer be sustained. The inclusion of women in the orders of bishop, presbyter, and deacon to which the Episcopal Church is now committed brings to realization the vision of the new humanity in Christ which makes the church the people of God.

The rites of ordination, properly understood, articulate a vision of the church as the New Israel as it orders its life through ordination to ministerial office in the apostolic mission and priestly ministry of the reconciliation of the world to God.

ENDNOTES

[1]Exodus 19:5, 6.

[2]Alexander Schmemann, *For the Life of the World: Sacraments and Orthodoxy* (Crestwood, NY: St. Vladimir's Seminary Press, 1973), page 93.

[3]At the suggestion of Robert Prichard, I have avoided designating the church as the New Israel. This term is not found in the literature of the New Testament, though it is found in some later writers. At present, however, it

can give offense to Jews, because it suggests that they have been superseded as the Israel of God and that the new covenant abrogates the old. The early centuries saw a fierce struggle between Judaism and the Church to take a claim as the legitimate heirs of Israel. While the church cannot abandon its claim to this heritage and retain its identity, it does not need to uphold the claim in such a way that it disinherits Judaism. For the enduring heritage of "Israel after the flesh" (Judaism) see Romans 10.

[4]1 Peter 2:9.

[5]1 Peter 2:5.

[6]For analyses of the New Testament evidence, see James A. Mohler, *The Origin and Evolution of the Priesthood* (Staten Island, NY: Alba House, 1970), chapters I and II; and Nathan Mitchell, *Mission and Ministry: History and Theology in the Sacrament of Order* (Wilmington, DE: Michael Glazier, 1982), chapters 1-3.

[7]For Acts in the stricter sense the apostles were the twelve chosen by Jesus during his lifetime and granted a vision of the risen Lord. The number is made up, after the apostasy of Judas, by another who had followed Christ during his lifetime and seen him after his resurrection. Paul claims apostolic authority because he has seen the risen Lord and has received a commission from him — a claim to the title which he obviously finds it necessary to defend.

[8]On the second century, see James A. Mohler, *The Origin and Evolution of the Priesthood*, chapter III.

[9]A convenient and accessible edition of the *Apostolic Tradition* is *The Apostolic Tradition of St. Hippolytus of Rome, Bishop and Martyr*, edited by Gregory Dix and Henry Chadwick (Ridgefield, CT: Morehouse Publishing, 1992). For brief assessments of the material on the ministry, see Frank Hawkins, "The Tradition of Ordination in the Second Century to the Time of Hippolytus," and Paul Bradshaw, "Theology and Rite, AD 200-400," in Cheslyn Jones, Geoffrey Wainwright, Edward Yarnold, and Paul Bradshaw, *The Study of Liturgy*, revised edition (New York: Oxford University Press, 1992), pages 347-355 and 355-362; also, H. Boone Porter, *The Ordination Prayers of the Ancient Western Churches*(London: SPCK, 1967), pages 1-11; James A. Mohler, *The Origin and Evolution of the*

Priesthood, chapter IV; Nathan Mitchell, *Mission and Ministry*, chapter 4; Pierre Jounel, "Ordinations," in A. G. Martimort, *The Church at Prayer*, vol. 3, trans. Matthew O'Connell (Collegeville, MN: Liturgical Press, 1988), pages 139-179, here pages 141-144. For other texts of the early patristic era, see Paul Bradshaw, *Ordination Rites of the Ancient Churches of East and West* (New York: Pueblo, 1990), Part II (Patristic Texts).

[10]For an extensive discussion of the development of the key elements of the rite, see Paul Bradshaw, *Ordination Rites of the Ancient Churches of East and West*, Part I: Introduction. Bradshaw prints the texts of all ordination prayers of the early centuries.

[11]Translation adapted slightly from H. Boone Porter, *The Ordination Prayers of the Ancient Western Churches*, pages 6-11.

[12]H. Boone Porter, *The Ordination Prayers of the Ancient Western Churches*, pages xiv-xv.

[13]The sole exception is a prayer for the ordination of a bishop first found in the Leofric Missal. See the text and commentary in H. Boone Porter, *The Ordination Prayers of the Ancient Western Churches*, pages 72-77.

[14]For a discussion of *ordo* and *ordinatio*, *cheirotonia* and *cheirothesis*, see Pierre Jounel, "Ordinations," in A. G. Martimort, *The Church at Prayer*, vol. 3, pages 139-179, here pages 139-141.

[15]Translation adapted from H. Boone Porter, *The Ordination Prayers of the Ancient Western Churches*, pages 7, 9, 11.

[16]See James A. Mohler, *The Origin and Evolution of the Priesthood*, pages 66-68

[17]See Paul Bradshaw, *Ordination Rites of the Ancient Churches of East and West*, page 45.

[18]The early sacramentaries are concerned with the prayers more than ritual actions, and give no directions in regard to the laying on of hands, so that it is difficult to establish the early Roman usage in regard to the laying on of hands.

[19]See Paul Bradshaw, *Ordination Rites of the Ancient Churches of East and West*, pages 14-15 and note 61.

[20]Second prayer for the ordination of a deacon in the Byzantine rite, adapted from Paul Bradshaw, *Ordination Rites of the Ancient Church of*

East and West, page 137.

[21] The earliest (proto-)sacramentary is the Verona Sacramentary (sometimes called the Leonine). For ordination, it and the Gregorian Sacramentary have the texts of the Roman tradition without the addition of Gallican texts, which already appear in the Gelasian Sacramentary. These are the primary texts used in Boone Porter's critical edition of the Roman prayers, *The Ordination Prayers of the Ancient Western Church*. Porter treats the Roman rites in chapter II. They may be supplemented by the directions found in *Ordo Romanus XXXIV*, which gives directions for Roman usage (e.g., the use of the litany after the bidding). A translation of the greater part of this document is found in Paul Bradshaw, *Ordination Rites of the Ancient Churches of East and West*, pages 218-221. For the Roman rite, see also Frank Hawkins, "The Early History of the Roman Rites of Ordination," in Cheslyn Jones et al., *The Study of Liturgy*, pages 362-365. For the evidence of the *ordines Romani* as well as the sacramentaries, see Pierre Jounel, "Ordinations," in A. G. Martimort, *The Church at Prayer*, vol. 3, pages 139-179, here pages 151-162.

[22] Translation adapted from Pierre Jounel, "Ordinations," in A. G. Martimort, *The Church at Prayer*, vol. 3, pages 139-179, here page 158. Jounel cites the Latin text from *Ordo Romanus XXXVI:9* — a Gallicanized version of Roman usage.

[23] Translation adapted from H. Boone Porter, *The Ordination Prayers of the Ancient Western Churches*, pages 18-35.

[24] Translation from H. Boone Porter, *The Ordination Prayers of the Ancient Western Churches*, page 13.

[25] On the early Gallican rites of ordination, see H. Boone Porter, *The Ordination Prayers of the Ancient Western Churches*, chapter III (which provides texts), and Paul Bradshaw, "Medieval Ordinations," in Cheslyn Jones et al., *The Study of Liturgy*, pages 370-379, here page 370-372.

[26] For the texts of these addresses and the Gallican biddings, see H. Boone Porter, *The Ordination Prayers of the Ancient Western Churches*, pages 40-57.

[27] Translation adapted from H. Boone Porter, *The Ordination Prayers of the Ancient Western Churches*, pages 40-57.

[28]For these rites, see H. Boone Porter, *The Ordination Prayers of the Ancient Western Churches*, chapter VI; Paul Bradshaw, "Medieval Ordinations," in Cheslyn Jones et al., *The Study of Liturgy*, pages 370-379, here 372-379; Pierre Jounel, "Ordinations," in A. G. Martimort, *The Church at Prayer*, vol. 3, pages 139-179, here pages 162-172. For the development of these rites with particular attention to English usage, see Alan Detscher, *The Evolution of the Rite for the Ordination of Priests in the Protestant Episcopal Church in the United States of America from its Pre-Reformation English Origins to the Book of Common Prayer, 1979: An Historical Study*, Dissertatio ad Doctoratum in Liturgia assequendum in Pontificio Instituto Liturgico (Rome: Pontificium Institutum Liturgicum, 1921), especially pages 1-66.

[29]Tables adapted from Paul Bradshaw, "Medieval Ordinations," in Cheslyn Jones et al., *The Study of Liturgy*, pages 370-379, here pages 374-375.

[30]Translated from the formula in Alan Detscher, *The Evolution of the Rite for the Ordination of Priests*, page 98. The Sarum text continues: "In the name of our Lord Jesus Christ." Response: "Thanks be to God." There are slight variants in this formula from rite to rite.

[31]Translated from the formula in Alan Detscher, *The Evolution of the Rite for the Ordination of Priests*, page 33.

[32]For translations of the key texts from these traditions, see Paul Bradshaw, *Ordination Rites of the Ancient Churches of East and West*, Part III. For a discussion of these rites, see Paul Bradshaw, "Eastern Rites of Ordination," in Cheslyn Jones, *The Study of Liturgy*, pages 366-369, and Pierre Jounel, "Ordination," in A. G. Martimort, *The Church at Prayer*, vol. 3, pages 139-179, here pages 144-151.

[33]Translation adapted from Paul Bradshaw, *Ordination Rites of the Ancient Churches*, page 133.

[34]Translation adapted from Paul Bradshaw, *Ordination Rites of the Ancient Churches*, pages 134-137.

[35]BCP 1549, page 293.

[36]On the Anglican rites of ordination, see particularly Paul F. Bradshaw, *The Anglican Ordinal: Its History and Development from the Reformation*

to the *Present Day* (London: SPCK, 1971), and "Reformation Churches 3: Anglican," and "Recent Developments 1: Anglican" in the section on ordination in Cheslyn Jones et al., *The Study of Liturgy*, pages 385-388 and 391-394. A careful treatment of the rite of ordination to the priesthood is found in Alan F. Detscher, *The Evolution of the Rite for the Ordination of Priests*. American developments from the 1662 rite on may be followed in Paul V. Marshall, *Prayer Book Parallels: The public services of the Church arranged for comparative study* (New York: Church Hymnal, 1989), pages 574-647. For a commentary on American rites through 1928, see Massey Shepherd, *The Oxford American Prayer Book Commentary* (New York: Oxford, 1950) commentary on pages 527-562.

[37]For brief discussions, see the treatment in Paul Bradshaw, "Reformation Churches," in Cheslyn Jones et al., *The Study of Liturgy*, pages 379-381, and the articles s.v. "Ordination" in J. G. Davies, *The New Westminster Dictionary of Liturgy and Worship* (Philadelphia: Westminster, 1986), pages 400-417, esp. 404-417.

[38]For a translation of the appropriate parts of this work, see E. C. Whitaker, *Martin Bucer and the Book of Common Prayer* (Great Wakering, UK: Mayhew-McCrimmon, 1974), pages 176-183.

[39]In *De Ordinatione Legitima* he writes, "when anyone is ordained Superintendent, that is, bishop, everything is done and carried out more solemnly and at greater length than when a presbyter of the second or third order is ordained, and there is also some distinction between the ordination of presbyters of the second and third order." The translation is taken from E. C. Whitaker, *Martin Bucer and the Book of Common Prayer*, page 183.

[40]Paul Bradshaw, *The Anglican Ordinal: Its History and Development from the Reformation to the Present Day*, pages 22-23.

[41]Text from the translation in E. C. Whitaker, *Martin Bucer and the Book of Common Prayer*, pages 181-183.

[42]Paul Bradshaw, "Reformation Church," in Cheslyn Jones et al., *The Study of Liturgy*, pages 379-391, here page 385.

[43]Text from the translation in E. C. Whitaker, *Martin Bucer and the Book of Common Prayer*, page 183.

[44]BCP 1549, page 301.

[45]BCP 1549, page 311.

[46]BCP 1549, pages 316-317.

[47]BCP 1662, pages 631-632.

[48]BCP 1662, page 647.

[49]BCP 1662, pages 659-660

[50]BCP 1549, page 301.

[51]BCP 1549, page 312.

[52]BCP 1549, page 317.

[53]BCP 1662, page 632.

[54]BCP 1662, page 647.

[55]BCP 1662, page 660.

[56]See Alan Detscher, *The Evolution of the Rite for the Ordination of Priests*, pages 52-55. Originally, presbyters concelebrated with the bishop by standing with him at the altar. When the presentation of chalice and paten was added, in some rites they recited the eucharistic prayer over the elements in the patens and chalices which they had received. This practice is not attested in English pontificals, however, where deacons and priests received communion from the bishop "if they wish" (page 54).

[57]BCP 1662, page 649.

[58]The Church of England rejected the sacrificial understanding of the eucharist common in the late middle ages, but its classical authors carefully spell out the sense in which the eucharist might properly be understood as a sacrifice.

[59]Paul Bradshaw, *The Anglican Ordinal*, page 208.

[60]The Church of South India, *The Book of Common Worship* (London: Oxford University Press, 1963), pages 160-161.

[61]For the official English version of the texts of these rites, see International Commission on English in the Liturgy, *The Rites of the Catholic Church*, vol. 2 (New York: Pueblo, 1980), pages 3-108. For a commentary, see Pierre Jounel, "Ordinations," in A. G. Martimort, *The Church at Prayer*, vol. 3, pages 139-179, here pages 172-179, and Paul Bradshaw, "Recent Developments 5: Roman Catholic," in Cheslyn Jones et al., *The Study of Liturgy*, pages 396-398.

[62]See the original draft of the rite, with an introduction by the drafting

committee, Standing Liturgical Commission, *The Ordination of Bishops, Priests, and Deacons: Prayer Book Studies 20* (New York: Church Hymnal, 1970). For commentaries, see Marion J. Hatchett, *Commentary on the American Prayer Book* (New York: Seabury, 1980), pages 501-532, and Leonel Mitchell, *Praying Shapes Believing: A Theological Commentary on the Book of Common Prayer* (Minneapolis, MN: Winston Press, 1985), chapter 8. For the ordination of priests see Alan Detscher, *The Evolution of the Rite for the Ordination of Priests.*

[63]BCP 1979, page 510.

[64]Compare the statement in § 19 of the document on ministry in the report of the World Council of Churches, *Baptism, Eucharist, and Ministry*: "The New Testament does not describe a single pattern of ministry . . . . In the New Testament there appears rather a variety of forms which existed at different places and times. As the Holy Spirit continued to lead the Church in life, worship and mission, certain elements from this early variety were further developed and became settled into a more universal pattern of ministry. During the second and third centuries, a threefold pattern of bishop, presbyter, and deacon became established as the pattern of ordained ministry throughout the church." For the text of this document, see John Leith, ed., *Creeds of the Churches: A Reader in Christian Doctrine from Reformation to the Present*, 3rd edition (Louisville, KY: John Knox, 1982), pages 604-658, here pages 641-642.

[65]For a contemporary ecumenical statement, see §§ 39-44 of the document on ministry, in *Baptism, Eucharist, Ministry*, in John Leith, *Creeds of the Churches*, pages 652-655. It suggests that the key elements are invocation of the Spirit and the imposition of hands and that the ordinary context is the eucharist.

[66]See the discussion in Standing Liturgical Commission, *The Ordination of Bishops, Priests, and Deacons*, pages 30-31.

[67]Standing Liturgical Commission, *The Ordination of Bishops, Priests, and Deacons*, page 23.

[68]Standing Liturgical Commission, *The Ordination of Bishops, Priests, and Deacons*, page 23.

[69]BCP, pages 520-521.

[70]BCP, pages 533-534.

[71]BCP, page 545.

[72]In medieval rites, the deacon received the *gospels* (not the New Testament) because reading the gospel at the eucharist was a function of the order.

[73]See Paul Bradshaw, *The Anglican Ordinal*, pages 189-190, and "Recent Developments 1. Anglican," in Cheslyn Jones et al., *The Study of Liturgy*, pages 392-394. The original version of the American rite was the first of the recent revisions in the Anglican ordinal, and it is from this perspective that Bradshaw writes about it in *The Anglican Ordinal*.

[74]BCP 1979, pages 860-861.

[75]William Wake, *The Principles of the Christian Religion explained in a Brief Commentary upon the Church Catechism* (London, 1849), page 148.

[76]For the early centuries, see the James Mohler, *The Origin and Evolution of the Priesthood*, and Nathan Mitchell, *Mission and Ministry*. For more complete surveys (focussed largely on the presbyterate) see Edward Schillebeeckx, *Ministry: Leadership in the Community of Jesus Christ* (New York: Crossroads, 1981) and *The Church with a Human Face: A New and Expanded Theology of Ministry* (New York: Crossroads, 1985), and Bernard Cooke, *Ministry to Word and Sacrament: History and Theology* (Philadelphia: Fortress, 1976).

[77]Although Acts does not name the seven as deacons, they were so understood in later centuries and Stephen was recognized as the first deacon.

[78]Texts from the catechism are from the BCP 1979, pages 855-856; texts from the document on ministry (§§ 28-30) are found in *Baptism, Eucharist, and Ministry*, in John Leith, ed., *Creeds of the Churches,* pages 646-647.

[79]Document on Ministry, § 51, *Baptism, Eucharist, and Ministry*, in John Leith, ed., *Creeds of the Churches*, page 656.

[80]BCP 1979, page 853.

[81]Document on Ministry, § 7, *Baptism, Eucharist, and Ministry*, in John Leith, ed., *Creeds of the Churches*, page 656.

[82]BCP 1979, page 307.

[83]Document on Ministry, § 17, *Baptism, Eucharist, and Ministry*, in John Leith, ed., *Creeds of the Churches*, page 639.

[84]BCP 1979, pages 854-855.

[85]Document on Ministry, §§ 35-36, *Baptism, Eucharist, and Ministry*, in John Leith, ed., *Creeds of the Churches*, pages 650-651. For a recent discussion of the issue of bishops and apostolic succession in Anglicanism, see Richard Norris, "Episcopacy," in Stephen Sykes and John Booty, *The Study of Anglicanism* (Philadelphia: Fortress, 1988), pages 296-309. The Anglican theologian Paul Avis argues for the priority of a "baptismal paradigm" of the church over an "apostolic paradigm" in the last chapter of his book, *Anglicanism and the Christian Church* (Minneapolis, MN: Fortress Press, 1989). This does not mean that Anglicanism should abandon episcopacy in its own life, he argues, but it should not block relations of communion between Anglican churches and those churches which have not maintained the historic episcopal succession.

[86]"Lutheran-Episcopal Dialogue II," in William A. Norgren, compiler, *What Can We Share? A Lutheran-Episcopal Resource and Study Guide* (Cincinnati, OH: Forward Movement, 1985), page 57.

[87]For an evaluation of the evidence of the New Testament, see Elizabeth Schüssler-Fiorenza, *In Memory of Her: A Feminist Theological Reconstruction of Christian Origins* (New York: Crossroads, 1983). See also the article of Letty M. Russell, s.v. "Ordination of Women," in J. G. Davies, *The New Westminster Dictionary of Liturgy and Worship*, pages 417-419.

[88]Document on ministry, § 18, *Baptism, Eucharist, and Ministry*, in John Leith, ed., *Creeds of the Churches*, page 640.

[89]For a discussion of the state of the question in the Roman Catholic Church, see the article by Georges Tavard, s.v. "Ordination of Women," in Peter Fink, ed., *The New Dictionary of Sacramental Worship* (Collegeville, MN: Michael Glazier/Liturgical Press, 1990), pages 910-915.

[90]Georges Tavard, s.v. "Ordination of Women," in Peter Fink, ed., *The New Dictionary of Sacramental Worship*, pages 910-915, here page 913.

[91]Summary of objections as stated by Georges Tavard, s.v. "Ordination of Women," in Peter Fink, ed., *The New Dictionary of Sacramental Worship*, pages 910-915, here page 913. The analysis of the problems with the arguments is my own.

CHAPTER 7

OTHER EPISCOPAL SERVICES

CELEBRATION OF A NEW MINISTRY AND DEDICATION OF A CHURCH

The last two episcopal services were not included by Thomas Cranmer in the Reformation Book of Common Prayer; indeed, they have never been included in English editions of the prayer book. The first, which in older language was known as institution and induction, was a transaction in ecclesiastical law in the middle ages which had no liturgical expression. The second was a rite not needed in the first decades of the Reformation, though it had a long and complicated history in the history of the church. In subsequent centuries, the rites used for the dedication and consecration of churches in England were established by diocesan custom rather than by official liturgical formularies. Both services entered the American Book of Common Prayer early in its history: the rite for the consecration of churches was added in 1799; the institution of a minister was adopted in 1804.

1. The Celebration of a New Ministry

The Origins of the Rite

In the early centuries of the church's life, candidates were ordained to "titles" — that is, they were ordained for the exercise of ministry in a particular diocese or church, and ordinarily exercised their ministry in that church for the remainder of their lives. Early councils forbade the "translation" of bishops from one diocese to another. Presbyters did move from time to time, but in most cases in the early church it was presbyters who were associated with the ascetic movement, not those who had been ordained for ministry in particular parishes. For this reason there was no need for a liturgical rite for clergy beginning a new ministry in a new church.

When ordained ministry became a "career" in the middle ages, appointment to a new position came to be understood largely in terms of feudal law[1] and involved nomination by the person or institution that held the right of patronage, institution by the bishop, and induction into the parish. Institution gave the nominee the right to a particular cure (benefice); induction gave the person who had been instituted possession of the cure. Someone who was possessed of the bishop's mandate then officiated at the induction, when the person to whom the letter of institution had been issued took physical possession of the cure. After the Reformation in England, the practice of bishop Lancelot Andrewes illustrates the manner of induction:

The Manner of Induction
prescribed by the Rt. Rev. Lancelot Andrewes

The neighbour minister, that inducts you, let him read in the Church Porch (the Church being empty and the door locked) the mandate ad Inductionem [for Induction], verbatim.

That done, let him give you hold of the ring or key, and say,

By virtue hereof, I, C. D., give you, I. N., real, actual, and corporal possession of this Parish, together with all and singular tithes, rights, and commodities of and belonging to the same.

Then unlock the door, and go into the Church, alone, and lock or bolt the door, and execute these particulars, which you shall write on the back of your mandate, viz.:— Accepi clavem, intravi solus, oravi, tetegi sacra, pulsavi campanas, In nomine Patris, et Filii, et Spiritus Sancti. Amen. Per me, I. N. [I received the keys, entered alone, prayed, touched the altar, rang the bells, in the name of the Father, and of the Son, and of the Holy Spirit. By me, I. N.] (Then endorsed by C. D.).[2]

Other customary actions at induction included subscription to the 39 Articles and the reading of the articles and of the service appointed for the day. The ringing of the church bell gave the induction public status.

Other Reformation churches have devised their own rites for the induction of ministers — generally not in terms of the feudal law which lies behind the Anglican forms. In some Reformation churches with a congregational ("independent") polity, the distinction between induction and ordination was not always made. Ministers were ordained by the congregation which they served for ministry to that congregation. Should they remove to another congregation, they were not inducted but ordained for ministry in the new congregation. Such "reordination" for induction in a new ministry has now become obsolete in most such churches at present.[3]

American Adaptations of the Rite and Later Anglican Practice

American Episcopal parishes, which unlike English parishes elected their rectors, adopted a form for institution and induction in 1804.[4] For a short time, this rite had status in canon law and gave clergy tenure, but for most of the history of the American church, the rite had liturgical status but no legal force. Election of a rector and approval by the bishop are the legal requirements for assumption of a cure. The original American rite included the reading of the letter of institution and the act of induction by reception of the key of the church, incorporated into the regular services of the church, Morning Prayer and Holy Communion. It was drafted by the Rev. William Smith, rector of St. Paul's Church, Norwalk, Connecticut, and adopted in Connecticut in 1799 and in New York in 1802.

The liturgical materials for this rite seem to be made up largely of materials drawn from elsewhere in the prayer book. The rite may be outlined as follows:

Morning Prayer

Entrance of the inductor, the Person being inducted, other Clergy, and Wardens

Morning Prayer by the Inductor with Special Propers (optional in 1928)

Institution and Induction

Presentation of the Person being Inducted and Reading of the Letter of Institution

Presentation of Keys by the Senior Warden and Acceptance by Minister

Devotional Office for Induction

Prayers and Reception of Minister within the Altar Rails by the Inductor

Presentation of Bible, Prayer Book, and Canons to Minister by Inductor

Psalm(s) (Ps. 135 in 1799/1804/1808/1892; Ps. 67 in 1892; Ps. 36 or 67 in 1928)

Preces and 3 Collects by Inductor

Prayer of Self-Dedication by Inducted Minister

Intercession for Church by Inducted Minister

Eucharist

Holy Eucharist celebrated by Minister with Special Propers (optional in 1928)

Blessing by Minister, Godspeed from Congregation

___

Commentators have noted the Scottish high-church tradition of the office, indicated by such language as "presbyter," "altar," "ministers of the apostolic succession."[5] After 1928, the rite could be combined with either Morning or Evening Prayer or the Eucharist or celebrated separately; the incorporation into the "regular services" of a Sunday or holy day was no longer required. This was a loss, for the service itself — although it actually has no legal force and includes devotional material — is in form a legal transaction with appropriate prayers, and the omission of the services of Morning Prayer and the Eucharist gives an unduly legalistic emphasis to the relation of parish and rector articulated in the rite.

The most notable feature is the minister's prayer of self-dedication, which was retained in revised form in 1979 as an option:

> O Lord my God, I am not worthy that thou shouldest come under my roof; yet thou hast honoured thy servant with appointing him to stand in thy House, and to serve at thy holy Altar. To

thee and to thy service I devote myself, body, soul, and spirit, with all their powers and faculties. Fill my memory with the words of thy Law; enlighten my understanding with the illumination of the Holy Ghost; and may all the wishes and desires of my will centre in what thou hast commanded. And, to make me instrumental in promoting the salvation of the people now committed to my charge, grant that I may faithfully administer thy holy Sacraments, and by my life and doctrine set forth thy true and lively Word. Be ever with me in the performance of all the duties of my ministry; in prayer, to quicken my devotion; in praises, to heighten my love and gratitude; and in preaching, to give a readiness of thought and expression suitable to the clearness and excellency of thy holy Word. Grant this for the sake of Jesus Christ thy Son our Saviour.[6]

Subsequently, other Anglican churches have devised liturgical rites for induction. Many of these have involved the perambulation of the church to its various liturgical centers in a way characteristic of the classical Anglican rites for the consecration of a church.[7]

The Celebration of a New Ministry in the Book of Common Prayer 1979

The drafting committee charged with revising the service known as "An Office of Institution of Ministers into Parishes or Churches" in the 1928 Prayer Book carefully articulated the way in which they understood the service in the introduction to the rite:

> Its force is moral and spiritual, rather than legal. . . . The service for beginning a pastoral ministry . . . is intended to be localized in character. Indeed, it has no other function. It provides an opportunity for the members of a particular congregation to celebrate a significant event in the life of their own church in the way that means most for them. . . . The most distinctive portion of this service is the delivery of symbolic objects to the new minister with charges to fulfill various aspects of his [or her] ministry. . . .

The giving of these objects should not appear to be a supplement to ordination, nor a ceremony of investiture. Rather, these articles and substances should be visible and recognizable signs of the pastoral, fraternal, and ecclesial relationship that should exist between ministers and people.[8]

What the service does, in fact, is to make visible how the authority received by the minister in ordination will be exercised in the context of a particular congregation. It is intended for a variety of ministries — not just that of rector. It may be adapted for use for deacons or lay persons as well when the situation requires. The service, like most of the other pastoral offices and episcopal services, is set in the context of the celebration of the eucharist, for which a special introductory rite and propers are provided, and the key actions occur after the liturgy of the word:

Institution as the Introductory Rite at the Eucharist

Presentation of the New Minister to the Bishop or Bishop's Deputy
Letter of Institution or Similar Statement of Purpose
Commitment of the Congregation
Litany for Ordinations (or other litany) and Proper Collect

Proper Liturgy of the Word

Proper Lessons and Sermon

The Induction

Presentation of Symbols of Ministry by Lay Persons and Clergy with Charges
Sentence of Induction by Presiding Minister
New Minister's Prayer of Self-Dedication
Greeting of New Minister and Exchange of Peace

Celebration of the Holy Communion

Proper Preface and Postcommunion Prayer
Blessing by the New Minister at the Bishop's Invitation

The redrafted letter of institution in this rite is pastoral in character and is the bishop's official delegation of authority to minister in this place, rather than a certificate of the legal entitlement of the new minister to what the earlier letter spoke of as "accustomed temporalities" of the cure. The introduction to the rite speaks of the presentations as inspired by the perambulation to liturgical centers characteristic of other recent Anglican rites. Here, however, the tokens of ministry are presented in one place (ordinarily the chancel), and in form the presentations and sentences are analogous to the presentations of instruments of ministry in medieval ordination rites — except that here they articulate the ministry to be exercised and are not understood as investing the minister with authority to minister. The key — originally symbol of the new minister's taking possession of his cure — is included here and reinterpreted as a symbol of the use of the building for ministry. Canons, Bible, and book of prayers are presented, as in the earlier American rite, and are used to express various dimensions of the ministry to be exercised. Water, stole, oil for unction, and bread and wine are the other symbols suggested. Rubrics give permission, however, to adapt the symbols to the character of the ministry to be exercised. The new rite expresses the assumption of ministerial duties in a church, rather than taking possession of a new cure as legal property. It has proved a very effective service for this purpose.

2. The Dedication and Consecration of a Church

In the beginning, the whole world was a temple. In the new Jerusalem at the consummation of the ages there will be no temple, "for its temple is the Lord God the Almighty and the Lamb."[9] In between the beginning and the end, the fallen human race has felt a need to focus and concentrate God's presence in a sacred space where it can encounter God in worship.[10] Such places gained their sacred status at least three ways. Some places were sacred by their natural location — mountains (which reached toward the heavens into the clouds), caves (which reached down into earth's darkness), groves (where trees reached out of earth's darkness toward the heavens), springs (where life-giving waters gushed forth from the earth), and places considered the center of a territory and so the center of the earth ("earth's navel"). Second, a place might acquire sacred status because God had been revealed there in an encounter with someone or a sacred object associated with God's presence was kept there. Finally, a place might acquire sacred status because people had made it sacred by rites of consecration — kindling fire, enclosing the boundaries of the space, or erecting a building according to a sacred pattern. Consecration was sometimes resisted in the name of God, for it might be understood not only to reveal but to restrict God's presence — making a defined space sacred and reserving it for God, but also making the rest of a territory profane and reserving it for purely secular activities carried on without reference to God.

Judaism: The Temple and the Synagogue

Israel's God was not a God who knew spatial constraints,[11] but a God of sovereign freedom. Indeed, the rabbis later said that the Jew who recited all the prescribed *berakoth* prepared a place for God's *Shekinah* or presence in all things.[12] God's shrine in ancient Israel was not a house made by human hands, but a portable tent — an expression of God's sovereign freedom. But Israel frequently conceived of God in theological terms borrowed from its neighbors, and so it too had sacred places or sanctuaries. Their sacred status may first have been due to their natural location — mountains (Sinai or Horeb; Mt. Moriah where Abraham had gone to sacrifice Isaac; the temple mount; the high places throughout the land), groves (the oaks at Mamre), springs (Gihon), or earth's center (Jerusalem). Their sacredness was usually ascribed, however, to God's appearance there to the patriarchs (Mamre, Moriah, Bethel, Jerusalem), to Moses (Sinai or Horeb), or to David (the threshing floor of Araunah where the temple was to stand). Places where the ark of the covenant was kept were considered sacred — Shiloh being the most significant of these before Jerusalem.

The temple in Jerusalem had numerous sacred associations. As a mountain, it had been a Jebusite holy place even before it became part of Israel. As Israel's capital, it was considered the center of the earth. It was identified with Mt. Moriah, where Abraham had gone to sacrifice Isaac. It was here, at the threshing floor of Araunah the Jebusite, that David saw God's angel and was bidden by Gad the prophet to erect an altar; and God accepted David's sacrifice at the altar and stayed the plague. Solomon erected the temple according to a heavenly archetype and brought there the ark of the covenant, associating the temple with Israel's covenant with God. He recognized, however, in the view of the Deuteronomist, that not even heaven can contain God, much less a house built by human hands. To avoid the blasphemous idea that God's presence was limited by the temple, Jews referred to it as the place where God's name was, or as the place of God's *Shekinah* or tabernacling — a reverential way of speaking about God's presence. The ark was sometimes thought of as God's footstool or God's throne. God cannot be put at the disposal of humans, however, and even Ezekiel, the most cultic of the prophets, had a vision of God's *Shekinah* leaving the temple during the exile.

Later Judaism made the synagogue the center of the religious life of local Jewish communities and spoke of its holiness in a different way. The Jewish temple, like its pagan prototype (and heavenly archetype) was built as a place of sacrifice. The people had no place in the temple: they gathered outside in the temple precincts. The synagogue,[13] however, provided space for the people, because God's presence was to be sought in the midst of God's people, not in a cultic object. The temple was the house of God in some sense; the synagogue was the house where God's people assembled — of his synagogue in its root sense. The rabbis said that whenever ten Jews assembled to hear the torah read, God's *Shekinah* was in their midst.[14]

For its house, then, the synagogue used not a cultic building (a temple), but a basically secular assembly hall (like the Roman basilica). Furnishings of such a building included a raised platform (the *bema*), with seats for the elders of the synagogue, a chair ("the seat of Moses") for the one who expounded the torah, and a reading desk from which the scriptures might be read. The scrolls of the scriptures were kept in a curtained chest (soon called the ark), with a menorah before it. This stood before a niche in the wall (which might be oriented toward Jerusalem, thus linking the synagogue to the temple). Later, the ark might be placed in the niche itself. The congregation stood around the bema, segregated by sex. They faced Jerusalem for prayer.

The House of the Church as a Setting for Early Christian Worship

In the New Testament, true worship is not worship in a particular place, but worship "in Spirit and in truth," as Jesus tells the Samaritan woman (John 4:23). Jesus by breaking down the barrier of sin which separates God from humanity and so dissolving the spatial limitations on our encounter with God restored the sacrality of the world: when Jesus died on the cross, as Chrysostom wrote, the whole world became a temple.[15] From another perspective, Jesus reveals that it is not in a place but in a person that we encounter God: he himself is the true temple (John 2:21). In him the Word was made flesh and "tabernacled" (made his *Shekinah*) among us (John 1:14). And when two or three are gathered in his name, he is in their midst (Matthew 18:20), for he is the true torah. Holiness attaches to "the house of the church," therefore, because — like the synagogue — it provides the place for God's people to assemble for worship. It is the people that sanctify the building, not the building that sanctifies the people.

For the eucharistic liturgy of word and meal which was the characteristic rite for its assembly on the Lord's Day, the church required a place of assembly which had a platform and seating for bishop and presbyters, a reading desk for lessons from scripture, a table for the meal, adequate room for the congregation, and a nearby chamber or stream for baptism. At first it appears that the larger rooms of ordinary houses were employed for such purposes. The rooms might be loaned for such purposes, or the church might use the whole house as a kind of Christian community center. We have some idea of one way in which a house might be put to such purposes from the remains of the house church of Dura Europos, the earliest such building so far discovered (ca. 230).[16] One room, with a canopied baptismal "tub" and murals, was set apart for baptism. A larger room, with a dais at one end, was probably used for the eucharistic celebration. Legal records from Cirta in North Africa bear witness to a similar building used for the worship of the church which was seized during persecution in 303.[17] In cities such as Rome, the church may have used rooms in tenement blocks (*insulae*). Some of the early parish churches in Rome (*tituli*) probably had such origins.[18] In periods of relative tolerance in the first three centuries, the church possessed substantial property for its purposes in some areas. Rites to dedicate such buildings, if they were used, were not of sufficient importance to be included in early church orders.

Architecture and Rites of Consecration after the Peace of the Church

The Basilica: With imperial toleration, recognition, and eventual establishment of the church in the fourth century, the church had both the need and the resources for larger houses of worship. Two types of buildings were common. Buildings for congregational worship adapted the plan of the basilica — the public meeting hall. In eastern parts of Syria, it would appear that Christians simply adapted the regional synagogal plan of the basilica to their purposes.[19] In the sanctuary (*questroma*) in the apse, oriented to the East, was the space for the table for the eucharistic banquet. It was walled off from the nave, with access to it by a curtained central doorway. In the center of the nave, connecting with the apse by a raised and railed walkway, was the bema — the raised platform for the liturgy of the word, with seats for clergy and a desk for readings from the scriptures. Men and women occupied separate sections of the nave. Access to the nave was by separate doors for men and women (not by doors opposite the apse, as elsewhere).

Elsewhere, Christians conformed their use of the basilica more closely to the way in which the building was adapted as an audience chamber for civil magistrates or the emperor himself.[20] On the apse platform on the chord of the apse where the magistrate's seat or the imperial throne sat in secular basilicas was the bishop's chair (*cathedra*), surrounded by benches for presbyters. The platform (which might extend out into the nave) was railed, and columns carrying an architrave above the railing created an open screen separating the apse platform from the nave. The table was placed toward the front of the platform opposite the bishop's chair, under the triumphal arch or even beyond it in the nave. To set it off, the table often was surmounted by a canopy supported by four columns. On the half-dome of the apse, the imperial insignia were replaced by Christ represented in many different ways in mosaic — as sovereign ruler of the universe (Pantokrator), enthroned in glory; in his transfiguration; as Good Shepherd; at the last supper; or with the Virgin at his birth.

A processional pathway (solea) led to the clergy seating in the apse from the central doorways at the opposite end. Often a portion of it was raised. In the Byzantine East, a raised platform for readings (the ambo) was near the center of the church along the solea.[21] In the West, the front of this pathway was often widened to give space for the choir (*schola*) and lessons were read from the front of the *schola* or from raised lecterns attached to its side railings.[22] The congregation occupied the areas to the side of this central passageway and — at times — galleries which rose above side aisles. Above the aisles beneath the windows of the clerestory various cycles might be represented in mosaic or fresco — patriarchs, prophets, apostles, and martyrs in procession to Christ on the dome of the apse; the mysteries of Christ or his miracles (often balanced by Old Testament types).[23] Near the narthex or entrance opposite the apse the Roman tradition located the sacristy, which in Constantinople was housed in a separate building. In some areas catechumens and others excluded from communion had special areas — often the narthex — reserved for them. A colonnaded courtyard (atrium) with a fountain in the center often was placed before the narthex.

There were regional variations to these arrangements of the basilica. We have already seen the major regional variant in the East — the Syrian disposition of the church, with clergy seating in the center of the church rather than in the apse. Sacristies and vesting chambers often flanked the apse. This was a two-room arrangement, with the apse walled off from the nave. North African churches often reversed the Syrian arrangement of the apse and the bema — with clergy seating in an (open) apse, and the altar in the center of the nave.[24] Different regions developed different ways of locating clergy seating, altar table, and reading platform to meet the liturgical needs of the church assembled for the liturgy of the word and the sacramental meal.

The Martyrium: The other principal architectural form employed by the church after the fourth century was the martyrium. The basic feature of such buildings is the domed central space. The building itself may take the form of a circle, a circle inscribed in a square, an octagon, or even a domed central space superimposed on a cruciform building. In the fourth century it was employed primarily for shrines (preeminently the shrine of the resurrection in Jerusalem), tombs (such as the mausoleum of Galla Placidia), and baptistries. Unlike the basilica, a secular meeting hall in origin, the proto-types of the martyrium had sacral overtones. Perhaps the most important use initially was for baptistries, which were restricted to major churches in the fourth century and later in many regions and were frequently detached structures, particularly in the West.

In the sixth century under the emperor Justinian, a new architectural plan came into use in Constantinople and areas under Byzantine influence. This was in effect a fusion of the martyrium and the basilica — a space which retained an axial orientation but was surmounted by a central dome rather than a gabled roof. The most important example of this is the new Hagia Sophia of Constantinople.[25] This became the standard plan for Byzantine churches in coming centuries — though in smaller churches the central ambo inherited from the earlier basilicas disappeared, and side chambers off the apse replaced the exterior sacristy of Hagia Sophia.

Rites of Consecration: Fourth-century documents describe elaborate dedica-tions of the new buildings financed by imperial largesse, but behind the descriptions of the magnificent buildings and oratorical splendor it is appar-ent that what dedicates the building is its use for eucharistic celebration. There might be specially composed prayers and specially selected readings, special sermons, and an impressive gathering of dignitaries, but the rite was simply the eucharist itself. This continued for many centuries to be the basic rite for the dedication of a church. The earliest Western sacramentary, the collection of mass formularies known as the Verona (or Leonine) Sacramentary, contains for the consecration of a church no other prayers besides those customarily provided for every celebration.[26] The growing cult of the martyrs, however, provided a supplementary rite for some churches: the deposition of a martyr's relics, which might be compared to a triumphal burial culminating in the eucharist. When pagan temples were converted to use as churches, another preliminary rite was one of lustration — to purify the building from its pagan associations. But it was the eucharist, rather than either of these supplementary rites, which served to consecrate the church for public worship.

The Middle Ages: Reversion to Cultic Sacrality

The Churches: The conversion of the masses after the fourth century eventually resulted in a concomitant adaptation to popular religiosity — the distinction of sacred and profane that early Christianity had decisively rejected. In this context, there was a return to a sense of sacred spaces, and church buildings were "set apart" from the world in popular imagination. Christian worship was also understood in such terms. As a result, Christian worship was increasingly understood in older cultic terms of sacrifice; Christian ministry was increasingly understood in terms of the cultic priesthood of the Old Testament; and the church building was correspondingly understood more in terms of the temple and less in terms of the place of assembly. A need was also felt for distinctive rites to set it apart.

In the East, the architecture of the dome to which Justinian gave expression in the Hagia Sophia was interpreted in neo-Platonic terms deriving from Dionysius the Areopagite as the place where heaven and earth were joined:[27] the church was the iconic representation of heaven on earth, and programs of iconography were executed accordingly. In the hierarchical reading of reality by Dionysius, clergy and laity were also sharply distinguished. Over the centuries, the open screening which distinguished their places in church was gradually filled in, until in many regions it became in the late middle ages a solid screen which veiled the sacral actions of the clergy in the liturgy from the eyes of the congregation. Architecturally, however, the disposition of the church remained fairly constant through the centuries.[28]

In the West, the relatively open one-room basilica of Christian antiquity developed over the course of the centuries into a compartmentalized series of rooms.[29] Altars were moved back against the wall of the apse against elaborate altarpieces. In the many monastic, collegiate, and cathedral churches a separate area of stalls for the clergy (the choir) was partitioned off between the altar in the apse and the nave. In parish churches, too, the area for clergy and altar was partitioned off — creating in effect two rooms. With the rise of the daily votive mass (especially for the departed) most churches also acquired numerous subsidiary altars in chapels or chantries.

Consecration of Churches: While early Roman churches were dedicated for use by the celebration of the eucharist, with the lustration where pagan buildings had been put to Christian use and with the deposition of relics where these were available, Gallican and Byzantine rites for the consecration of a church seem originally to have been developed on the basis of Old Testament descriptions of the consecration of the tabernacle and the temple. There the rites of consecration included marking the corners of the altar with sacrificial blood, then pouring the remainder at its foot (Exodus 29:10-12), and finally anointing the altar and the rest of the tabernacle with oil (Leviticus 8:10-12).[30] The Christian adaptation of these rites included the lustration of the church with water and the anointing of the altar and the walls of the church. We note that in some rites for the consecration of a church the lustral water is mixed with wine — probably to assimilate it to the sacrificial blood in the Old Testament rites. With this shift, the church building was no longer understood as the "house of the church" with the synagogue as its prototype; it was understood as a temple and followed Old Testament prototypes. Eventually, however, the rites of consecration were reinterpreted and in some sense assimilated to the rites of Christian initiation — the altar and the building were "baptized" and "chrismated."

The eventual fusion of the Roman and Gallican traditions created very elaborate rites of consecration.[31] A further addition to the rites seems likely to have been used originally for laying the foundation of the church rather than its dedication. This was the abecedarium (alphabet ceremony) in which the bishop claimed the church for Christ by writing the Latin and Greek alphabet in ashes on the pavement of the church (perhaps originally in the earth on the spot where the church was to be erected) along two diagonal lines which formed a St. Andrew's cross between the four corners of the building. The final version of the fusion of these rites of consecration might take the better part of a day to accomplish.

The major components of the composite rites as they come down to us in documents from the twelfth century on are these:[32]

Preliminary Service
Vigil from the previous day at another church, with relics to be used in dedication

Initial Station at Church Where Vigil Was Kept
Litany and collect
Exorcism and blessing of water and salt for external lustration of church
Procession to church to be consecrated with psalmody

Exterior Lustration of Church
Triple circumambulation of exterior of church and lustration with psalmody

Preliminary Rites in Church (Alphabet Ceremony and Lustration)
Entrance of Bishop into Church
Double Inscription of alphabet on floor of church along crossed diagonal
　　lines
Blessing of water mixed with salt, ashes, and wine
Signing of center and corners of altar with lustral water
Sevenfold circumambulation of altar and aspersion with lustral water
Triple circumambulation of church and lustration

Solemn Prayer of Consecration of the Church (text below)

Preparation of Altar for Deposition of Relics (Anointing)
Double anointing of altar with oil of catechumens and censing
Anointing of altar with chrism and censing
Twelve anointings along the walls of the church with chrism

Solemn consecration of the altar with censing (text below)
Blessing of altar hangings and vessels

Deposition of Relics
Reentry of Bishop into the Church with People and Relics
Chrismation of place of deposition, deposition of relics, sealing of place
Chrismation of four corners of the altar
Vesting of the altar and censing
Illumination of the church

Consecration Eucharist with Special Propers

As we examine these complicated rites, it becomes apparent that in the
fusion of Roman and Gallican elements, components have been duplicated
in the process. The consecration involves all three features of the Roman
rites of consecration — the inaugural eucharist, the preliminary lustration

(now no longer restricted to pagan temples being converted to Christian use), and the deposition of relics. To this the characteristic preliminary Gallican rites have been added — the lustration and anointing with the oil of catechumens and chrism of altar and church that assimilated the rites of consecration to those of Christian initiation. Both Roman and Gallican rites had lustrations (purificatory in the Roman rite, initiatory in the Gallican) and anointings (related to the deposition of relics in the Roman rite, related to initiation in the Gallican). The two purposes of lustration and anointing overlap awkwardly when the rites are fused.

The key prayers of the rite are those for the consecration of church and altar. Their provenance is uncertain; the prayers for the consecration of the altar (with bidding introducing the blessing) are certainly Gallican in provenance, but those for the consecration of the church (with preliminary prayer and blessing in preface form) may be Roman. The texts are as follows:

For the Consecration of the Church

O God, who dost sanctify places set apart to thy name, pour forth thy grace upon this house of prayer, that the assistance of thy mercy may be sensed by all who here call upon thy name.

Eucharistic Dialogue

It is very meet, right, and our bounden duty that we should at all times and in all places give thanks unto thee, O Lord, holy Father, almighty, everlasting God, almighty lord of all blessings, whose faithfulness is sensed without end; O God, who dost encompass things heavenly and things earthly in thine embrace, saving thy mercy for thy people who walk in the sight of thy glory: Hear the prayers of thy servants, that thine eyes may be open upon this house day and night; and most graciously dedicate this church founded in honor of *this* saint through the holy mysteries, mercifully illuminate it, and brighten it with fitting splendor; and welcome all who come to worship in this place, graciously disposed to look upon them with mercy; and for the sake of thy great name and thy strong hand and thine out-stretched arm afford thy protection to those who pray to thee in this dwelling, hear them as is fitting, and preserve them with thine eternal defence; that they may continually persevere in the catholic faith in the holy trinity, ever happy and rejoicing in thy religion.

For the Consecration of the Altar

Let us pray for the mercy of God the Father almighty, dearly beloved brothers and sisters, that, as we fittingly implore him with our present pleas, he may sanctify with his blessing this altar and consecrate it for spiritual sacrifices; that he may be pleased to bless and sanctify at all times the offerings of his servants placed upon it with fervent devotion to him; and that, pleased and made mindful by the spiritual offering of incense, he may hear and assist his family as they pray:

Almighty God, in whose honor we consecrate this altar by calling upon thee, mercifully and graciously hear our humble petitions, and grant that what is offered on this table may be acceptable to thee, be pleasing to thee, may be anointed and bathed with the dew of thy Holy Spirit, so that thou wilt ever relieve the burdens of thy family when it prays to thee in this place, wilt cure its weaknesses, hear its prayers, receive its vows, strengthen its desires, and grant its requests.[33]

None of the funerary or initiatory imagery of the elaborate ceremonial of these rites is reflected in these two sets of prayers. The prayer for the consecration of the church asks God to dedicate it through the "holy mysteries" (the solemn celebration of the eucharist); what is asked is that God hear the prayers made in the church and receive the offerings made at the altar.

The Reformation and the Church of England

Few new churches were erected in the early decades of the Reformation in

England. While churches on the continent often radically altered the church buildings which they inherited, Anglicans did not.[34] The ornamentation of churches was simplified and shrines to the saints in the churches were removed. Different schools of thought in the church favored a Puritan iconoclasm with respect to ornamentation or a moderate restraint. But Anglicans generally retained the two-room architectural disposition of the medieval church but used it in different ways. In most churches, the nave was used for the daily office and the liturgy of the word at the eucharist, while chancel and altar were reserved for the administration of communion. After 1552, a reading pew was frequently erected in the nave for the use of minister and clerk during the services held there, while the altar table was moved into the chancel and placed lengthwise between the choir pews so that communicants could gather around the table for communion. In the seventeenth century when new churches were erected, a one-room plan came into favor, placing the altar table (now railed) against the wall once again and giving prominence to reading pew and pulpit. The nineteenth century saw a reversion to medieval styles. often with little understanding of their use in either the medieval church or after the Reformation. Twentieth century Anglicans have used a wide variety of styles, with a current preference for design that works well as a functional setting for a participatory liturgy with the congregation gathered around lectern, table, and font.

Because few churches were erected in the early decades after the Reformation, there was little need at first for a rite of consecration for churches, and none was ever incorporated into English editions of the Book of Common Prayer.[35] As the need arose, bishops drafted their own diocesan forms. Little use was made of the earlier rites, for the focus of those rites on relics, lustration, and anointing were not consonant with Reformation theology. The most influential rite was that of Lancelot Andrewes, Bishop of Winchester, first used in 1620. That rite showed little dependence on medieval services. Most subsequent English rites depended on his work, though they did not necessarily use his long prayer of consecration, and they generally did not exclude the congregation from the church during the prayers related to the various stations in his perambulation. Some forms, in fact, eliminated the perambulation during these prayers. They worked with the same principle as early Christians, that a building was consecrated by being put to use, and often celebrated as many of the church's services as possible at the consecration. The general outline of these rites is a follows:[36]

Petition for consecration and entry into church by bishop
Prayer of Consecration (various forms)
Prayers during perambulation of the church
    to font, pulpit, lectern, altar, place of marriage, place of burial
Entrance of congregation
Morning Prayer, Litany with special prayers and propers
Pastoral offices (baptism, churching, marriage, burial) as appropriate
Eucharist with special prayers and propers
    King Solomon's Prayer of Consecration (1 Kings 8:27 ff) after Nicene
      Creed
    Reading of the Act of Consecration
Later Blessing of Churchyard and Evensong

The English convocation prepared a rite for general use in 1712, but it was never officially adopted, though it was widely used. That rite worked from Bishop Andrewes' rite, but omitted the perambulation while keeping the prayers.

The Rite for Consecrating a Church in the American Book of Common Prayer

It was an adaptation of the 1712 English rite by Bishop Provoost of New York that was adopted by the American Church and incorporated into its Book of Common Prayer in 1799.[37] The situation of the American church created certain anomalies in the use of this rite. The English rite involved a surrender of title by the donor. American churches, more often acquired from building funds secured by mortgage notes than by gift of a single donor, might be in use for many years before their title was clear — something the canons required before consecration of the building. Since they could not be "consecrated" when they were first used by the congregation, they were often "dedicated" when construction was complete. But there is no fundamental theological difference between the dedication of a church for public worship and its consecration. In addition, the focus on the surrender of title lends to this rite, like the institution of a minister, a spirit that is more legal than is perhaps appropriate. The American rite did not differ significantly from its English prototype, except in one regard. It made provision for concluding the service with antecommunion rather than a full celebration of the eucharist — thus breaking with both ancient tradition and earlier Anglican usage.

The drafting committee for the 1979 rite had several purposes: it wanted to make a rite available for dedication and consecration as soon as a church went into use for public worship, working from the principle that the building is consecrated by being put to the use for which it was intended and eliminating the fictitious distinction between dedication and consecration. It also seemed appropriate to restore the expressive perambulation of the church with appropriate prayers at the various liturgical centers. The new feature of this rite is that the perambulation is integrated into the course of the service, so that the furnishings are put to use as they are dedicated. The consecration of the entire church, however, is the first action after the procession enters the building. The rite reaches its climax in the dedication of the altar and the celebration of the holy communion. This is the outline of the rite:[38]

Initial Station outside the church, bidding, and prayer
Procession (around the church) to the church door
Station at the door and signing of the threshold by the bishop with the cross
Entrance to the church
Prayer of Consecration by bishop, warden, and rector or minister-in-charge
Stations to dedicate furnishings of the church and Liturgy of the Word
    Station at the font, dedication of font, baptism or blessing of water
    Station at the lectern and/or pulpit and their dedication
    Proper Old Testament Reading, Psalm, Epistle
    Station at musical instrument and dedication; use of instrument before gospel
    Proper Gospel
    Sermon or Address

Pastoral Offices as appropriate
Prayers of the people with appropriate petitions and collect
Station at the altar and solemn dedication of altar and its vesting
Celebration of the Holy Communion with Proper Preface

There is a real logic to the sequence of components in the rite. However, at times the flow of the service is somewhat awkward. It would appear to make sense to make the font the first of the furnishings to be dedicated, since it is by baptism that we enter the church. However, the 1979 baptismal rite is integrated into the eucharist after the liturgy of the word. The service would flow considerably more smoothly — particularly when there are baptisms — if the dedication of the font came after the the gospel and sermon or address. This would also allow for the renewal of the baptismal covenant in its proper place — an appropriate component for this rite — even when there are no baptisms.

In addition, it might make more sense to make the consecration of the church itself the climax of the dedication of its furnishings, rather than a preliminary to those dedications. This could be done by incorporating the consecration of church and altar into the eucharistic prayer itself, as part of the proper preface and a supplement to the supplications after the invocation of the Holy Spirit[39] — the original plan for the new Roman Catholic rite for the dedication of a church (see below).[40] The three-part dedication prayer of the present rite could be used as a special conclusion for the prayers of the people in this case — with the warden taking the first, the minister in charge the second, and the bishop the third, adding a standard doxology rather than the final sentence of consecration.

Unlike most of the rites in the Book of Common Prayer 1979, this service was drafted before the comparable revised Roman Catholic service had been issued. The Roman Catholic rite has a very rich euchology. This is concentrated in the solemn prayer for the dedication of the church, which incorporates the consecration of the altar as well, and in the proper preface and special intercession for the eucharistic prayer.

Dedication of the Church

Father in heaven, source of holiness and true purpose, it is right that we praise and glorify your name.

For today we come before you to dedicate to your lasting service this house of prayer, this temple of worship, this home in which we are nourished by your word and your sacraments.

Here is reflected the mystery of the Church.

The Church is fruitful, made holy by the blood of Christ: a bride made radiant with his glory, a virgin splendid in the wholeness of her faith, a mother blessed through the power of the Spirit.

The Church is holy, your chosen vineyard: its branches envelop the world, its tendrils carried on the tree of the cross, reach up to the kingdom of heaven.

The Church is favored, the dwelling place of God on earth: a temple built of living stones, founded on the apostles, with Jesus Christ as its cornerstone.

The Church is exalted, a city set on a mountain: a beacon to the whole world, bright with the glory of the Lamb, and echoing the prayers of her saints.

Lord, send your Spirit from heaven to make this church an ever-holy place, and this altar a ready table for the sacrifice of Christ.

Here may the waters of baptism overwhelm the shame of sin; here may your people die to sin and live again through grace as your children.

Here may your children, gathered around your altar, celebrate the memorial of the Paschal Lamb and be fed at the table of Christ's word and Christ's body.

Here may prayer, the Church's banquet, resound through heaven and earth as a plea for the world's salvation.

Here may the poor find justice, the victims of oppression, true freedom.

From here may the whole world, clothed in the dignity of the children of God, enter with gladness your city of peace.

We ask this through our Lord Jesus Christ, your Son, who lives and reigns with you and the Holy Spirit, one God, for ever and ever. *Amen.*[41]

Eucharistic Prayer: Proper Preface:

The whole world is your temple, shaped to resound with your name. Yet you also allow us to dedicate to your service places designed for your worship.

With hearts full of joy we consecrate to your glory the work of our hands, this house of prayer.

Here is foreshadowed the mystery of your true temple; this church is the image on earth of your heavenly city:

For you made the body of your Son, born of a Virgin, a temple consecrated to your glory, the dwelling place of your godhead in all its fullness.

You have established the Church as your holy city, founded upon the apostles, with Jesus Christ as its cornerstone.

You continue to build your Church with chosen stones, enlivened by the Spirit, and cemented together by love.

In that holy city you will be all in all for endless ages, and Christ will be its light for ever.[42]

Eucharistic Prayer: Proper Intercession of Eucharistic Prayer III:

Father, accept the prayers of those who dedicate this church to you.

May it be a place of salvation and sacrament
where your Gospel of peace is proclaimed
and your holy mysteries separated.

Guided by your word and secure in your peace
may your chosen people now journeying through life
arrive safely at their eternal home.

There may all your children
now scattered abroad
be settled at last in your city of peace.[43]

The Roman Catholic rite incorporates in the prayer of dedication the dedication of all liturgical furnishings as well as the dedication of the church itself. The revisers originally intended to use the proper preface of the eucharistic prayer for this dedication. The present preface (which draws on a preface in the Ambrosian rite of Milan) in fact still echoes its original purpose. The prayer of dedication itself is in preface form and might also have been used in the same way. The original shape of the rite would have given expression in a unique way to the fact that it is the celebration of the eucharist itself which consecrates a church for the public worship of God. Further revisions of the Episcopal rite might incorporate the consecration of both altar and church into the preface and the supplication after the epiclesis of the eucharistic prayer. Indeed, this is close to the model used for the related service of Thanksgiving on the Anniversary of a Parish of the Book of Alternative Services of the Anglican Church of Canada.[44]

Conclusion

The church building, the house of the church, is, as the new Roman Catholic rites emphasize, the outward expression of the church as the people of God, the body of Christ, and the temple of the Holy Spirit in a particular place. The 1979 Episcopal rite for the dedication of a church gives fitting expression to the early Christian conviction that a building is consecrated by being put to the use for which it is intended — the public worship of God. Only in this sense is it a "sacred space," and the focus in late Christian antiquity and the middle ages on the deposition of relics and lustration and anointing were a deviation from this original insight. However, once the building is used for the public worship of God, it does acquire a kind of sacramental status: it is an icon of the world as God's temple where the human race is called to God's priestly service, of the church as the body of Christ visibly showing forth the world's redemption, and of the new Jerusalem where God is all in all — the goal toward which the Spirit moves creation. The Roman Catholic rite gives far richer expression to this truth than the Episcopal rite, and we can hope that future revisions of the Episcopal rite will find ways to incorporate this truth more fully.

ENDNOTES

[1]For English practice, see W. K. Lowther Clarke, "The Consecration of Churches and Other Occasional Offices," in idem, ed., *Liturgy and Worship: A Companion to the Prayer Books of the Anglican Communion* (London: SPCK, 1954), pages 703-728, here 714-721.

[2]Lancelot Andrewes, *Minor Works* (Library of Anglo-Catholic Theology), page 196, as cited in W. K. Lowther Clarke, "The Consecration of Churches and Other Occasional Offices," in W. K. Lowther Clarke, ed., *Liturgy and Worship*, pages 703-728, here page 717.

[3]See Paul Bradshaw, "Reformation Churches 5: Baptist and Congregational" in the section on ordination in Cheslyn Jones, Geoffrey Wainwright, Edward Yarnold, and Paul Bradshaw, *The Study of Liturgy*, revised edition (New York: Oxford University Press, 1992), pages 390-391.

[4]For commentaries on the history of the rite in the American Church, see Massey Shepherd, *The Oxford American Prayer Book Commentary* (New York: Oxford University Press, 1950) commentary on pages 569-574; Marion J. Hatchett, *Commentary on the American Prayer Book* (New York: Seabury, 1980), pages 533-539; Standing Liturgical Commission,

Dedication and Consecration of a Church; Celebration of a New Ministry, Prayer Book Studies 28 (New York: Church Hymnal, 1973). For the versions of the American rite, from the form adopted by the Connecticut Convention in 1799 to the present rite, see Paul V. Marshall, *Prayer Book Parallels: The public services of the Church arranged for comparative study* (New York: Church Hymnal, 1989), pages 648-679.

[5]See Massey Shepherd, *Oxford-American Prayer Book Commentary*, commentary on pages 569-574.

[6]BCP 1928, page 573.

[7]See the description in W. K. Lowther Clarke, "The Consecration of Churches and Other Occasional Offices," in W. K. Lowther Clarke, ed., *Liturgy and Worship*, pages 703-728, here pages 720-721.

[8]Standing Liturgical Commission, *Dedication and Consecration of a Church; Celebration of a New Ministry*, page 46. For other commentaries on this rite, see Marion J. Hatchett, *Commentary on the American Prayer Book*, pages 533-539, and Leonel Mitchell, *Praying Shapes Believing: A Theological Commentary on the Book of Common Prayer* (Minneapolis, MN: Winston Press, 1985), pages 269-270.

[9]Revelation 21:22.

[10]See Louis Bouyer, *Rite and Man: Natural Sacredness and Christian Liturgy*, trans. Joseph Costelloe (Notre Dame, IN: University of Notre Dame Press, 1963), pages 151-158. For the study of sacred space in comparative religion, see Mircea Eliade, *The Sacred and the Profane: The Nature of Religion* (New York: Harper and Row, 1961), pages 20-65, and Gerhard van de Leeuw, *Religion in Manifestation and Essence*, 2 volumes (New York: Harper and Row, 1963), pages 393-402.

[11]On Jewish shrines and the temple, see Louis Bouyer, *Rite and Man*, pages 158-165. See also biblical references to the events and places discussed in the following two paragraphs.

[12]Louis Bouyer, *Rite and Man*, page 166.

[13]For a summary of the architectural evidence, see E. M. Myers, article s.v. "Synagogue, Architecture," in Keith Crim, general editor, *The Interpreter's Dictionary of the Bible: An Illustrated Encyclopedia*, Supplementary Volume (Nashville, TN: Abington, 1976) pages 842-844.

Louis Bouyer gives an interpretation of archeological evidence in *Rite and Man,* pages 166-167. Architectural evidence and rabbinic literature are both hard to date, and Bouyer's interpretation must be treated with caution, but seems to be accurate in broad terms.

[14]Louis Bouyer, *Rite and Man,* page 165, citing *Pirke Aboth* 3:8.

[15]Second Sermon on the Cross and the Thief (*Patrologia Graeca* 49:409).

[16]For a plan, see Cheslyn Jones et al., *The Study of Liturgy,* figure 1, page 531. At the present time some remnants of the baptistry can be found in the Yale University Art Gallery, which once possessed sufficient remains to reconstruct the baptistry.

[17]See the text cited in Gregory Dix, *The Shape of the Liturgy,* revised edition (New York: Seabury Press, 1983), pages 24-25.

[18]*Early Christian and Byzantine Architecture* (Baltimore, MD: Penguin, 1975), pages 28-29.

[19]For the best treatment of this see Robert Taft, "On the Use of the Bema in the East-Syrian Liturgy," *Eastern Churches Review* 3 (1970), pages 30-39, and "Some Notes on the Bema in the East and West Syrian Tradition," *Orientalia Christiana Periodica* 34 (1968), pages 327-359; also Richard Krautheimer, *Early Christian and Byzantine Architecture* (Baltimore MD: Penguin Books, 1975), pages 150-151 (where the bema is called an exedra). For a isometric rendering of such a church, see Cheslyn Jones et al., *The Study of Liturgy,* figure 4, page 532.

[20]On Christian use of the basilica in general, see Richard Krautheimer, *Early Christian and Byzantine Architecture,* chapter 2, esp. pages 40-43. For Byzantine disposition of the basilican form, see Thomas F. Mathews, *The Early Churches of Constantinople: Architecture and Liturgy* (University Park, PA: Pennsylvania State University Press, 1971); for a study of the most important Byzantine church, Hagia Sophia, in both its fourth-century form and its later rebuilding, see Rowland Mainstone, *Hagia Sophia: Architecture, Structure, Liturgy of Justinian's Great Church* (New York: Thames and Hudson, 1988). For a typical Roman disposition of the basilica, see Thomas F. Mathews, "An Early Roman Chancel Arrangement and Its Liturgical Functions, *Rivista di archeologia cristiana* 38 (1962), pages 71-95.

[21]For an isometric rendering of such a church, see Cheslyn Jones et al., *The Study of Liturgy,* figure 3, page 532.

[22]For plates of Roman churches retaining this arrangement, see Cheslyn Jones et al., *The Study of Liturgy*, plates 22 and 23 (between pages 448 and 449).

[23]See the clerestory mosaics in S. Apollinare Nuovo, Ravenna, in Richard Krautheimer, *Early Christian and Byzantine Architecture*, figure 149, page 197 (the apse mosaics have not survived).

[24]For a isometric rendering, see Cheslyn Jones et al., *The Study of Liturgy*, figure 2, page 531.

[25]See Rowland Mainstone, *Hagia Sophia* — the best treatment at the present time of this church and its use in the liturgy.

[26]On these rites, see Pierre Jounel, "The Dedication of Churches," in A. G. Martimort, ed., *The Church at Prayer*, vol. 1, *Principles of the Liturgy* (Collegeville, MN: Liturgical Press, 1987), pages 215-225, here pages 216-218; Louis Duchesne, *Christian Worship: Its Origin and Evolution. A Study of the Latin Liturgy up to the Time of Charlemagne*, trans. M. L. McClure, 5th edition (London, SPCK, 1949), chapter 12; and G. G. Willis, "The Consecration of Churches Down to the Ninth Century," in idem, *Further Essays in Early Roman Liturgy* (London: SPCK, 1968), pages 135-173, here 135-156.

[27]See for example, the opening chapters (1-7) of the *Mystagogy* of Maximus the Confessor, in Julian Stead, *The Church, the Liturgy, and the Soul of Man: The Mystagogia of St. Maximus the Confessor* (Still River, MA: St. Bede's Publications, 1982), pages 65-86.

[28]Developments can be followed in the later chapters of Richard Krautheimer, *Early Christian and Byzantine Architecture*.

[29]These developments are treated in rapid survey in Peter G. Cobb, "The Architectural Setting of the Liturgy," in Cheslyn Jones et al., *The Study of Liturgy*, pages 528-542. For this period, see pages 535-537 and figure 8 on page 534.

[30]See John Wilkinson, "New Beginnings and Church Dedications," in Ralph McMichaels, ed., *Creation and Liturgy: Studies in Honor of H. Boone Porter* (Washington, DC: Pastoral Press, 1993), pages 251-264. See especially pages 255-258 and note the comparative table on page 256. What is at work here is a typological interpretation of the church building: the heavenly temple (as in Revelation) is the reality; the tabernacle and temple

in the Old Testament are shadows of this reality, and the Christian church is a type which participates in this reality. Hence the concern to conform the building to the heavenly pattern and the reading of the rites in the Old Testament as pointing to the Christian rites which are assimilated to baptism and chrismation.

[31]On these developments, see Pierre Jounel, "The Dedication of Churches," in A. G. Martimort, *The Church at Prayer*, vol. 3, *Principles of the Liturgy*, pages 515-525, here 218-222; Louis Duchesne, *Christian Worship*, chapter 12; W. K. Lowther Clarke, "The Consecration of Churches and Other Occasional Services," in idem, ed., *Liturgy and Worship*, pages 703-728, here 706-709; G. G. Willis, "The Consecration of Churches Down to the Ninth Century," in idem, *Further Essays in Early Roman Liturgy*, pages 135-173, here 157-170.

[32]Outline based on the rite described by Pierre Jounel, "The Dedication of Churches," in A. G. Martimort, *The Church at Prayer*, vol. 3, *Principles of the Liturgy*, pages 515-525, here 218-222.

[33]Translated from the Latin texts in Louis Duchesne, *Christian Worship: Its Origin and Evolution. A Study of the Latin Liturgy up to the Time of Charlemagne*, trans. M. L. McClure, 5th edition, pages 411-412.

[34]See the perceptive study of Anglican architecture and its use in the liturgy in G. W. O. Addleshaw and Frederick Etchells, *The Architectural Setting of Anglican Worship* (London: Faber and Faber, 1948).

[35]On the rites for the consecration of churches in England after the Reformation, see W. K. Lowther Clarke, "The Consecration of Churches and Other Occasional Services," in idem, ed., *Liturgy and Worship*, pages 703-728, here 709-713. For the text of the 1712 consecration rite, see Paul V. Marshall, *Prayer Book Parallels*, pages 680-701.

[36]Outline based on the text of the 1712 rite in Paul V. Marshall, *Prayer Book Parallels*, and on the information in W. K. Lowther Clarke, "The Consecration of Churches and Other Occasional Services," in idem, ed., *Liturgy and Worship*, pages 703-728.

[37]All editions of the American rite and the English rite of 1712 on which it was based may be studied in Paul V. Marshall, *Prayer Book Parallels*, pages 680-701. For a commentary on the 1928 rite, see Massey Shepherd,

The Oxford American Prayer Book Commentary, commentary on 563-568. For commentary on the 1979 rite and its relation to earlier rites, see the introduction in Standing Liturgical Commission, *Dedication and Consecration of a Church; Celebration of a New Ministry*, pages 7-22; Marion J. Hatchett, *Commentary on the American Prayer Book*, pages 540-550; Leonel Mitchell, *Praying Shapes Believing*, pages 270-273.

[38]BCP 1979, pages 566-579.

[39]This would preclude the use of Eucharistic Prayer C, which is structured differently, and Eucharistic Prayer D, which has a fixed preface.

[40]For the English text of these rites, see International Commission on English in the Liturgy, *The Rites of the Roman Catholic Church as Revised by the Second Vatican Ecumenical Council and Published by Authority of Pope Paul VI*, vol. 2 (New York: Pueblo, 1980), pages 185-293. For a brief commentary, see Pierre Jounel, "The Dedication of Churches," in A. G. Martimort, *The Church at Prayer*, vol. 3, *Principles of the Liturgy*, pages 515-525, here 223-225,

[41]International Commission on English in the Liturgy, *The Rites of the Roman Catholic Church*, vol. 2, pages 223-224.

[42]International Commission on English in the Liturgy, *The Rites of the Roman Catholic Church*, vol. 2, pages 229-230.

[43]International Commission on English in the Liturgy, *The Rites of the Roman Catholic Church*, vol. 2, pages 230-231.

[44]Anglican Church of Canada, *Book of Alternative Services*, 668-674.

LITURGICAL THEOLOGY AS SACRAMENTAL THEOLOGY

PASTORAL OFFICES AND EPISCOPAL SERVICES

1. Liturgy and the Mystery of Christ

The Origins of Liturgical Theology

The theology of the liturgy first developed as a theology of two of the "regular services of the church" (baptism and the eucharist) and the feasts when these rites were celebrated (Easter or the pascha in the annual cycle of feasts and the Lord's Day in the weekly cycle). This theology was, in fact, rooted in the New Testament itself, and its development continued in the era of the apostolic fathers in literature such as the letters of Ignatius of Antioch and the *Letter of Barnabas*, in apologists such as Justin Martyr, and in such second and third century authors as Origen and Tertullian. It found classic expression in the homilies given by such preachers as Cyril of Jerusalem, Theodore of Mopsuestia, John Chrysostom, and Ambrose of Milan at the end of the fourth century to candidates for Christian initiation. In these baptismal instructions or mystagogic catecheses, the preachers explored the meaning of the rites through which such candidates were incorporated into the church. Preachers had earlier explored with their congregations the meaning of Easter in such works as the *Paschal Homily* of Melito of Sardis, and in the fifth century the bishops of the church also delivered their sermons on the other great feasts of the church year to explore the meaning of those feasts. This theology found its primary focus in the relationship between Christ's death and resurrection, the church's participation in Christ's death and resurrection in its baptismal rites and the eucharist, and the feasts which celebrate Christ's death and resurrection.[1]

In the fifth century in the Latin West, we find a carefully articulated theology of the feasts of the liturgical year (including the weekly feast of the Lord's Day) and the rites proper to those feasts in the homilies and letters of Pope Leo the Great.[2] Christ himself is mystery of our salvation (the *mysterium* or *sacramentum salutis*): his humanity is the visible expression (*mysterium, sacramentum*) of God's saving presence in the world. His redemptive acts are likewise *mysteria* or *sacramenta* — the tangible form which God's salvation takes in human history. After his ascension, the saving presence of Christ became visible in the church as *mysterium* or *sacramentum*, and the liturgical rites of the church are the tangible acts (*mysteria, sacramenta*) through which Christ reaches out to save us. Christ's death and resurrection are the heart of his saving work and as such are the principal theme of Leo's theology. He relates that death and resurrection as the paschal mystery to the weekly feast of Sunday, to the annual feasts of Easter and Pentecost, and to the liturgical rites proper to those feasts — the proclamation of Christ's death and resurrection in the liturgy of the word and the liturgical actions of baptismal initiation and the eucharist by which the church participates in Christ's death and resurrection. What Leo has sketched out is the foundation of a theology of the church's liturgy of time and its distinctive rites — what the Book of Common Prayer calls the regular services of the church. The whole of the church's liturgy was sacramental to Leo and he touched at times on the pastoral offices and the episcopal services in his works, but it was the rites which we know as the regular services to which Leo devotes his attention.

The only occasional offices to develop stable forms in this period were the rites of ordination and rites of public penance and reconciliation. These rites were grounded in the New Testament itself. They did, however, show the influence of local cultures. The interpretation of ministerial authority in the church often owed as much to local social structures as it did to Jesus' interpretation of ministerial authority in terms of costly service. Even in the later literature of the New Testament (such as the pastoral epistles) patriarchal structures of authority began to displace those rooted in the ministry of Jesus, and we see considerable variation in early centuries in the way that authority was exercised in the church — a variation articulated in the process of selection of ministers and directions as to who laid hands on those ordained to various orders of ministry. In the case of public penance and reconciliation, the concept of satisfaction (borrowed from the Roman legal tradition) considerably modified the theology of penitence and forgiveness found in the literature of the New Testament.

The theological interpretation of the other occasional offices (such as marriage and religious profession, ministry to the sick, ministry to the dying, and burial rites) could not develop before those occasions found liturgical expression. For these occasions Christians by and large borrowed their ritual forms from local cultures — ritual forms which showed considerable variation from place to place and age to age. This process of what is now commonly called inculturation had mixed results. In sickness Christians often sought out popular cures from Christian, semi-Christian, or pagan healers. The ministry of prayer and anointing, attested in the New Testament itself, did not begin to take standard liturgical form until well after the peace of the church in the fourth century, and even then it continued to compete with other remedies in popular superstition. In most cases it proved possible to recast rites for the dying and burial rites of local cultures in terms of Christ's death and resurrection, so that there was a real transformation of both the rites and the way in which they were interpreted (although pagan associations sometimes lingered). It was much longer before marriage took on liturgical expression. It appears that for centuries Christians were content to make use of local rites for marriage, purged if necessary of pagan associations. The results were mixed. It appears that Christians upheld a far higher standard of marital fidelity than social conventions of the day were able to sustain. But by taking over local marriage rites, Christians on the whole accepted the understanding of the relation of husband and wife that those rites articulated. The subordination of women to men in Roman society, articulated in Roman marriage rites in the "giving" of the bride from the "hand" (authority) of her father to that of her husband and in the exclusive focus of the rites on the *bride's* change of status (the *bride* was veiled and the *bride* was blessed) was a substantial departure from Christ's own teaching.

The Theology of the Sacraments in the Late Middle Ages in the Latin West

The liturgical theology of the early centuries had a sharply corporate focus on the "building up" of the church as the body of Christ and on the church's participation in his passover. It dealt primarily with the rites which we have designated as the "regular services of the church." By the early middle ages the focus had shifted dramatically from the corporate dimension of Christian worship to the personal dimension. This shift was articulated in the emerging theology of the sacraments. It was in disputes of the third and fourth centuries in the North African Church that the terminology of this new sacramental theology began to be formulated. In the course of these disputes the focus was on certain rites as means of grace. The concern here was the objective reality of the grace offered to the Christian in the church's rites — particularly baptism, the eucharist, and ordination. A conceptual framework was developed to determine both the validity and the fruitfulness of these rites. In the process a theology of the sacraments was formulated with increasingly less reference to actual liturgical texts and actions and to the corporate life of the church. By the end of the middle ages the Western church had ceased to think in terms of the sacramental character of Christian worship as a whole and had focussed its attention on seven "sacramental" rites which were understood primarily as means of grace for the individual Christian. A theological framework had been superimposed on these rites which did not correspond to their liturgical texts and actions. As a consequence, Western sacramental theology came to be divorced almost entirely from the liturgical rites which it was meant to interpret. All the rites now defined as sacraments were understood primarily as means of

grace correlated to the course of a Christian's life.[3] The disputes of the
Reformation era were carried on largely in terms of the problematic that
was set out by late scholasticism: the focus continued to be on sacramental
rites as means of grace for the individual Christian rather than as integral
components of the church's liturgy which built up the church as the body
of Christ.

The Return from Sacramental Theology to Liturgical Theology

By the beginning of the twentieth century, the scholarship of the liturgical
movement had begun to recover a patristic perspective on the church's liturgy. Odo Casel developed a theology of the paschal mystery which set the
agenda for liturgical theology for much of the twentieth century.[4]
Subsequent scholars such as Louis Bouyer gave such a theology a more adequate biblical foundation, and Edward Schillebeeckx and Karl Rahner as
systematic theologians began to recover the frame of reference which had
been established by Leo the Great. For Schillebeeckx, Christ is the sacrament of the human encounter with God, and the church is the sacrament of
our encounter with Christ.[5] Only after he had laid out this groundwork did
he go on to speak of the sacramental rites of the church. Rahner formulated
language which spoke of Christ as the primordial sacrament (*Ursakrament*)
and the church as the basic sacrament (*Grundsakrament*) of God's self-com-
munication to us.[6]

Although they reconceptualized the framework of sacramental discourse,
Schillebeeckx and Rahner still worked primarily with sacraments as means
of grace for the individual Christian. Subsequent theologians have begun to
recover the sense of sacraments as liturgical actions of the church. The
Constitution on the Liturgy which was promulgated by the Second Vatican
Council speaks of liturgical rites from this perspective when it declares, "In
the liturgy, by means of signs perceptible to the senses, human sanctification
is brought about in ways proper to each of these signs."[7] Once we have
begun to work within this framework, however, the distinction between
sacramental and non-sacramental rites becomes arbitrary. It also becomes
apparent from this perspective that to focus primarily on the sanctification
of the individual is to take inadequate account of the corporate nature of

liturgical worship. The task of formulating an adequate liturgical theology requires us to re-examine the basic structures of the church's liturgical tradition and to articulate a theology which corresponds to those structures.

2. The Structure of the Church's Liturgy

If we turn to the actual way in which the church's liturgy is structured, what we discover is not a distinction between sacramental and non-sacramental rites, but a set of services which are organized according to the rhythms of time (the day, the week, and the year) and another set which are related to the rhythm of human life and the rhythm of the life of the local Christian community. The regular services are the first set: these services (the daily office, the eucharist, and the rites of initiation) can be regularly scheduled according to the calendar. Occasional services follow no such regular pattern, but are celebrated as the occasion arises in the life of the individual or the community.

Alexander Schmemann and Marion Hatchett have both attempted to lay out an appropriate framework for interpreting these services, utilizing the work of scholars of comparative religion on the phenomenology of religious rites.[8] Because a phenomenological approach pays attention to the structure of a rite and its place in the overall structure of the church's liturgy, this approach is generally quite faithful to the liturgical witness. Schmemann adopted the following scheme:

> The Sacraments of Baptism and Chrismation
> The Eucharist (and all that is directly related to it)
> The Liturgy of Time
> The Liturgy of the Sanctification of Life[9]

The principal problem with Schmemann's scheme is that it privileges the sacraments of initiation and the eucharist and makes them independent of the temporal cycles of the liturgy. Such a distinction, however, does not grow out of the structural shape of the church's liturgical life, but is superimposed upon it. Hatchett revised Schmemann's scheme and works with the following categories:

The Sanctification of Life,
The Sanctification of Time,
The Sanctification of Space.[10]

Hatchett's revision corrected the anomaly of Schmemann's scheme and located the rites of initiation and the eucharist within the context of Schmemann's other categories — the sanctification of life and the sanctification of time. He placed the eucharist within the context of the sanctification of time as the rite proper to the Lord's Day as the feast of the weekly cycle. He treated the rites of initiation (baptism and chrismation in Schmemann's scheme) within the context of the sanctification of life, although he recognizes them as a component of the seasonal observances of the sanctification of time as well. The sanctification of space is a useful category, but it relates to only a very small portion of the liturgical tradition.

The treatment of baptism in the classic rites of the fourth century and in the present Book of Common Prayer makes it preferable, I would argue, to classify it as part of the liturgy for the sanctification of time rather than as part of the liturgy for the sanctification of life. But the principal problem with Hatchett's scheme is the inclusion of the rites of ordination under the category of the sanctification of life. The rites in this category find their focus in personal sanctification. Rites of ordination properly understood, however, relate to the ordering of the church's life rather than to the sanctification of the individual's life.

In this work and in *Redeeming the Time* I have used a modified form of Hatchett's scheme: Its basis is the way the rites fit into the structure of the church's liturgical life.

1. **Regular Services:** the Daily Office, the Holy Eucharist, and Holy Baptism as the distinctive rites of the church's corporate worship in the daily, weekly, and annual cycles of the calendar;
2. **Pastoral Offices:** the rites found under this heading in the *Book of Common Prayer* 1979, which are concerned with turning points in the personal lives of Christians;
3. **Episcopal Services:** rites at which the bishop presides and

which structure the corporate life of the church in the diocese and in the local Christian community.

The regular services are concerned with the sanctification of time. The pastoral offices are occasional rites concerned with the sanctification of the life of the Christian. Episcopal services are occasional rites concerned with the sanctification of the life of the Christian community.

3. A Theological Perspective on the Liturgy of the Church

Liturgy as Epiphany

The Reformed theologian Jean-Jacques von Allmen, drawing on the Lutheran Peter Brunner, describes the assembly of Christians for the worship of God as "the epiphany of the Church."[11] For the Orthodox theologian Alexander Schmemann, it is more than that: liturgy is the epiphany of the true meaning of all reality in its cosmic, ecclesiological, and eschatological dimensions.[12] We might say that there the extraordinary meaning of ordinary things and actions is made manifest. For the world itself is sacramental: it makes present and accessible to us in tangible ways the God who is the world's creator, redeemer, and ultimate fulfilment; it is a link of life and love between God and the human race, whose vocation is to be a royal priesthood which offers the world to God in thanksgiving. When we make that offering, the true character of the world is revealed to us and God's purposes for it are realized.

The function of the liturgy as sacramental is thus to reveal and make accessible to us the real presence of God in the world. Liturgy is a symbolic activity. But, Schmemann insists, we must understand this symbolism correctly. It is an intrinsic, not an extrinsic symbolism. The things of the world as symbols do not *make present* an absent reality but rather *reveal the presence* of the reality which they represent and make real and accessible to us. It is in the church's worship that this epiphany occurs and it is therefore in worship that the deeper dimensions of reality become accessible to us.[13] The liturgical language of the Byzantine tradition sees this as the work of the Holy Spirit and asks that the Holy Spirit may manifest or show the true reality of things. Thus in the eucharistic liturgy the epiclesis of the Great

Thanksgiving of St. Basil asks that God *show* (*anadeixai*) the bread and wine as the body and blood of Christ, and in the baptismal liturgy the thanksgiving over the font asks that God *show* (*anadeixon*) the water as "a water of rest, water of redemption, water of sanctification, a cleansing of the pollution of body and soul, a loosening of chains, forgiveness of sins, enlightenment of souls, washing of rebirth, grace of adoption, raiment of immortality, renewal of spirit, fount of life."[14]

This Christian understanding of the sacramental function of prayer is deeply rooted in the Jewish theology of blessing, which lies behind the characteristic form of Jewish prayer, the *berakah*.[15] Before using the things of the world or undertaking an action, the Jew gives thanks to God and in so doing acknowledges the purposes for which God has given those things or intended the action, usually by citing a text of scripture which reveals that purpose. We see this understanding in the literature of the New Testament:

> [E]verything created by God is good, and nothing is to be reject-
> ed, provided it is received with thanksgiving; for it is sanctified
> by God's word and by prayer.[16]

Through this priestly act of giving thanks to God for the world and acknowledging the purposes for which God has created the world, the church in its liturgy manifests the world in its God-given dimensions and is enabled to know and participate in the world as a sacramental link of life and love between God and the human race.

Liturgical theologians have explored the theme of the liturgy as the epiphany of the world as God intended it in their study of the eucharist and the baptismal liturgy — the distinctive rites of the week and the year in the church's architecture of time. But less attention has been paid to the more personal dimensions of our world — the turning points which are occasions of grace in the life of individual Christian and of the local Christian community of which they are a part. The church gives expression to the Christian vision in its rites for these pastoral offices and episcopal services as well. They too are moments of epiphany — when God reveals the divine purposes in these aspects of our lives.

Referring All Things to Christ and His Passover

The world as we encounter it in worship is our world, not some other world. But we encounter dimensions of that world which were opaque before — closed off to us.[17] Those dimensions were closed off to us because we are estranged from God. We have turned from God as the giver of life and sought life from the world. We have made the world an end in itself, rather than receiving the world from God in thanksgiving and recognizing the world as the means by which God seeks in love to share the divine life with us. But apart from God, the world cannot give the life that we seek. Instead, it deals death. In our sin, we have shortcircuited the world as our link to God and have broken the connection.

Only in Christ is that connection restored. Only in him do we find someone who receives the world from God and offers it to God in thanksgiving. He alone fulfils the royal priesthood to which the whole human race is called.[18] Only when worship becomes the remembrance of Christ and refers all things to Christ does the world regain the purposes for which God created it. Only in Christ does the world serve as the place of our journey toward the fulfilment of all things in God's kingdom, where God is all in all. The old creation grew dark and opaque through human sin. In Christ it becomes a new creation, restored to its purposes in the providence of God. In worship the church passes over with Christ from the world to the kingdom — the ultimate end of all things.

That is why all Christian prayer is offered through Christ and all Christian worship is the remembrance of Christ. Christ recapitulates the world's return to the Father; and the church, reconciled to God in him, begins its passover with him from a world estranged from God to a world which has found its fulfilment in the kingdom of God. In him the church reaches the goal for which God created all things. But we still live in a world estranged from God, and our journey is not yet complete. In the words of Schmemann, the world revealed in worship

> is not an "other" world, different from the one God has created and given to us. It is our same world, *already* perfected in Christ, but *not yet* in us. It is our same world, redeemed and restored, in which Christ "fills all things with himself."[19]

And so the remembrance of Christ is what enables our thanksgiving to the Father to consecrate the things and actions of our world to the purpose for which God intended them. The Christian *berakah* moves from thanksgiving to the Father to remembrance of Christ in reconsecrating the world to God. Only by so doing can it pass over with him to the kingdom where the world is restored to God's creative purposes, ceases to be opaque to God, and becomes once again transparent to God.

The Trinitarian Dimensions of the Vision: World, Church, Kingdom

Christian prayer is not only Christological in nature, offered in remembrance of Christ and referring all things to Christ. It is also trinitarian, reflecting the threefold economy of the triune God in creation, redemption, and the sanctification in which God's work reaches its fulfilment. A sacramental vision of reality, Schmemann argues, holds together the three dimensions of reality — the world (creation), the church (redemption), and the Kingdom (sanctification or eschatological fulfilment). In the church's liturgy, we encounter reality as created good by God, as redeemed from its estrangement to God in Christ and in the Church as the body of Christ, and as moving toward fulfilment in God's Kingdom. We have already taken note of the first two dimensions. It is the final, eschatological dimension which we need to explore here. In this dimension the Spirit reveals the destiny of the world and moves the world toward that destiny — the Kingdom of God. It is God's Spirit which enables us to journey, if only by anticipation, where Christ has gone before us, and so makes Christ and the world as it is transfigured by Christ accessible to us. And so the church in its worship not only gives thanks to the Father and remembers Christ, it prays for the Spirit. Christian prayer in its classic form moves from thanksgiving to remembrance to epiclesis, the invocation of the Spirit, as we have seen already in looking at the solemn prayers of the eucharist and of baptism.

When this final, eschatological dimension of reality is forgotten, we fall into the danger of mistaking either the world or the church *as they are* for the kingdom of God.[20] In this case our vision is tragically stunted and God's purposes in creation and reconciliation are frustrated. On the other hand, the kingdom is a dimension of the world in which we now live; it is not some other world. It is this present world when it has been reconciled through Christ and attained fulfilment through the Spirit. All worship is the world on pilgrimage as the church to its final destination in God's kingdom. And it is in worship that the goal of this pilgrimage which gives meaning to the church's life is revealed.

4. The Liturgical Shape of the Pastoral Offices and Episcopal Services

We turn now to examine the particular shape and structure of the services which give liturgical expression to important occasions in the lives of individual Christians and local Christian communities. As the regular services of the church reveal the deeper meaning of basic realities such as sunrise and sunset, a story, and meal, a bath, anointing, and the touch of a human hand by referring them to Christ and to his passover, so occasional offices focus on significant acts at turning points in the lives of individual Christians and local Christian communities, and by referring them to Christ and to his passover reveal their deeper meanings and purposes in God's economy.

The Relationship of the Pastoral Offices and Episcopal Services to Baptism and the Eucharist

The life of both individual Christians and local Christian communities is rooted in their participation in the paschal mystery of Christ through baptism and the eucharist.[21] The occasional offices of the church's liturgy build on the foundation established by baptism and the eucharist. The commitments of the baptismal covenant are particularized to address the occasions which find expression in the pastoral offices and episcopal services. Because the eucharist is the heart of the church's ongoing participation in Christ's passover, these occasional services are structurally related to the eucharist. Rites in preparation for baptism reach their goal in the communion of the newly baptized at the eucharist of the baptismal feasts. Rites which draw their distinctive meaning from baptism (confirmation, the form of commitment to Christian service, and the reconciliation of a penitent) are sealed in eucharistic communion. Confirmation and the Form of Commitment to

Christian Service are set in the context of the eucharist, where communion seals the commitment. The reconciliation of a penitent (unlike the early rites of public penance) no longer is set in this context, but its function is to restore penitents to their communicant status when this has been disrupted by sin. It is in the context of the eucharist that the solemn commitments of marriage, *adelphopoiesis* (in the Byzantine tradition), and celibacy are sealed by the church's solemn blessing. The rites for the ministry to the sick in their full form are set in a eucharistic context — either in a celebration of the eucharist or in a service which concludes with the administration of communion from the reserved sacrament. The rites for the ministration at the time of death include communion, which has classically been understood as "food for the journey" from death to eternal life. The various rites associated with the death of a Christian conclude with the eucharist of the burial office. It is in the context of the eucharist that the church orders its life by ordaining ministers, who then exercise the ministry to which they are ordained in the context of that eucharist. The eucharist is the context for induction into a new ministry for similar reasons. Finally, the liturgy for the dedication and consecration of a church is set in the context of a eucharist in which the building is put to the use for which it is consecrated.

As we have seen, the Book of Common Prayer 1979 has established a particular pattern for the inclusion of these occasional rites in the celebration of the eucharist. It is in the eucharistic liturgy that reality is revealed in all its cosmological, ecclesiological, and eschatological dimensions, and so it is in this context that the distinctly Christian character of the occasions which find ritual expression in the pastoral offices and episcopal services is revealed.

Gathering Rite	Special forms to introduce rite (baptism, confirmation, marriage, burial, ordinations, celebration of a new ministry, consecration of a church)
Ministry of the Word	Special propers for many rites except on Sundays and feasts

Proper Rite	**Special forms of commitment** (baptism. confirmation, form of commitment, marriage, profession to celibacy, burial, ordinations, celebration of a new ministry)
	Special forms of prayers of the people (baptism, confirmation, form of commitment, marriage, burial, ordinations, celebration of a new ministry, consecration of a church)
	Ritual action and blessing proper to the rite (except burial)
	(Subsidiary formulas and actions)
	Proper postcommunion if appointed
	Special rites at burial (commendation, committal)

The special introductory rites and the liturgy of the word serve to set the context of the celebration and to root it in the story of God's saving acts to which Scripture bears witness. The distinctive ritual action and prayer of each rite follows the liturgy of the word. The celebration of the holy communion seals the rite with the reception of communion. The eucharist is the primary act of the church's corporate worship, the heart of the church's corporate life. Since the eucharist is the primary manifestation of the corporate life of the church, placing the pastoral offices in this context gives tangible expression to the church's concern for its members at the turning points in their personal lives and relates these turning points to the paschal mystery of Christ. For the same reason, it is appropriate that it is in this context that the church orders its life in ordaining and inducting its ministers and dedicates buildings for its worship.

The rite proper to each of the pastoral offices and episcopal services ordinarily has as its core a distinctive action which takes on a new significance by being placed in the context of redemption and eschatological fulfilment in the prayer which establishes its place in the context of Christian existence. A note of caution is important in regard to the ritual shape of these occasional offices. Unlike the ritual shape of baptism and the eucharist, that of the pastoral offices and episcopal services is not firmly rooted in the gospel and Christian tradition. It is dependent in large measure on the particularities of local culture and varies from age to age and place to place. Particular care needs to be taken that the liturgical form for these rites articulate an understanding of these occasions that is consistent with the gospel and not distorted by the perspectives of the culture in which they originate. The history of the rites of marriage and ordination reveal at times a patriarchal understanding of marriage and cultic and feudal understandings of the church's ordained ministry which are inconsistent with the Christian gospel.

Forms of Commitment

The commitments related to the baptismal covenant usually follow the liturgy of the word. The forms in the following rites are worthy of note.

Baptism	Baptismal covenant
Confirmation & Form of Commitment	Affirmation of the baptismal covenant (intensification of baptismal commitment)
Marriage & Religious Profession	Vows establishing the social context in which baptismal commitment is lived out
Reconciliation	Amendment of life (Some rites: Reaffirmation of baptismal covenant)
Ministry to the Sick	(Some rites: Reaffirmation of baptismal covenant)
Burial of the Dead	Reference to baptismal commitment in prayers Congregational affirmation of baptismal covenant

Ordination	Vows establishing the way in which the ordinand will lead the community in its baptismal covenant
New Ministry	Particularization of minister's commitment in context of local community

Ritual Action

These forms of commitment are frequently followed by the significant ritual acts proper to each rite:

Baptism	Threefold baptismal immersion Laying on of hands by celebrant Consignation (with chrism if desired)
Confirmation	Laying on of hands by bishop
Marriage	Joining of hands Exchange of rings or other tokens (Veiling or Crowning in early traditions)
Adelphopoiesis	Placement of hands on gospel book (Byzantine tradition)
Religious Profession	Clothing or veiling
Reconciliation	Laying on of hands or sign of the cross by officiant
Ministry to Sick	Laying on of hands and anointing by officiant
Burial	Procession (before and after service) Commendation and Burial (end of service)

Ordination	Laying on of hands (Seating, Vesting, Presentation of Instruments)
New Ministry	Presentation of Instruments
Dedication of Church	Entry of congregation into church Use of font, lectern, altar table

Prayer

The prayers serve to interpret the ritual action in order to reveal its meaning. Sometimes these include a special set of the prayers of the people and a climactic prayer of blessing or consecration. The solemn prayer of consecration often resembles the eucharistic prayer in structure and may be sung to the preface tone. In the West such prayers are found at the blessing of the font at baptism, at the nuptial veiling and the veiling of virgins (as well as later forms of monastic profession), at the solemn reconciliation of penitents on Maundy Thursday, at the blessing of the oil of unction (which was actually incorporated in the eucharistic prayer), at ordinations, and at the consecration of a church. At other times the prayers are simple in form and do not incorporate the full eucharistic structure. In the Book of Common Prayer 1979 it is only the thanksgiving over the water at baptism, the set of prayers at confirmation, and the prayers of ordination that take a solemn form rather than the traditional structure of the Western collect. The key prayers of the pastoral offices and episcopal services are these.

Baptism	Litany for Candidates Thanksgiving over the water (and chrism) Prayer for the gifts of the Spirit
Confirmation	Baptismal litany or other form of prayer Solemn prayer before and after laying on of hands
Marriage	Special form of prayers of the people

	Prayer of blessing and declarative blessing (Solemn Prayer in earlier Roman tradition)
Adelphopoiesis	Litany and Prayer with bowed heads (Byzantine tradition)
Religious Profession	Prayer (solemn in some earlier rites)
Reconciliation	(Solemn prayer after public penance in past)
Ministry to the Sick	Blessing of oil of unction (included in the eucharistic prayer in the Roman tradition)
Burial of the Dead	Special form of prayers of the people
Ordination	Litany and Hymn to the Spirit Solemn Prayer of Ordination
Consecration of Church	Threefold prayer of consecration Prayers at font, lectern, pulpit Setting apart of altar

In general, the prayers serve to reveal the particular aspect of human life related to the rite under the dimensions of God's creative purpose, Christ's reconciling work, and the final goal in God's kingdom. They are an epiphany of the fullness of this reality in God's eyes, and by revealing this reality allow the Christian to participate in it.

Other Formulas for Administering the Rites

Besides the prayer and ritual action which constitute the core of these rites, we often find subsidiary formulas for the "administration" of the rites (just as there are formulas for the distribution of communion in addition to the Great Thanksgiving at the eucharist). The earliest of these is no doubt the baptismal formula, which came into use once the interrogatory baptismal creed was no longer used during the administration of the baptismal immersions. In the East the standard formula of this sort is passive (as a way of indicating divine agency); in the West, it is active in form and in the first person, spoken by the officiant as the instrumental agent. Formulas of this sort usually conclude with the name of the Trinity.

Baptism (Eastern)	The servant of God is anointed with the oil of gladness in the Name . . . .
	The servant of God is baptized in the Name . . . .
Baptism (Western)	I baptize thee in the Name . . . .
Marriage (Eastern)	This man is crowned unto this woman in the Name . . . .
Marriage (Western)	I pronounce that they are husband and wife, in the Name . . . .
Reconciliation (Western)	I absolve you from all your sins, in the Name . . . .
Ministration to the Sick (BCP)	I lay my hands upon you, in the Name . . .
	I anoint you with oil in the Name . . . .
Dedication of a Church (BCP)	We dedicate this Font (Lectern, Pulpit) in the Name . . . .

At times such a formula may be supplemented by a clause which continues with prayer for the person (as in the formulas used in the imposition of hands and anointing of the sick).

Other formulas are addressed directly to the person to whom the rite is being administered, usually in the imperative form.

Baptismal chrismation	You are sealed by the Holy Spirit in baptism . . . . (variant formulas in different traditions)

Ordination (Imposition of hands in medieval rites and BCP before 1979)	Receive the Holy Spirit . . . .
Ordination (Presentations)	
BCP before 1979	Take authority . . .
BCP 1979	Receive the Holy Scriptures (this Bible) . . .
Celebration of a New Ministry (Presentations)	Accept this Bible . . . .
	Take this water . . . .
	. . . .
	Let all these be signs of the ministry which is mine and yours in this place.

There are other forms as well. The most common is precative — cast in the third person subjunctive as a prayer.

Reconciliation (variants)	The almighty and merciful Lord grant you absolution . . . .
	Our Lord Jesus Christ . . . of his great mercy forgive you . . . .
	Our Lord Jesus Christ . . . absolve you through my ministry . . . .
Unction (Roman tradition)	Through this holy anointing may the Lord in his love and mercy help you with the grace of the Holy Spirit.

The key to the meaning of the principal ritual action is in every case the solemn prayer proper to the rite, but the subsidiary formulas serve to elaborate the meaning and to apply it to the recipient. This was once true even in reconciliation, which in its private form has now lost the solemn prayer of its original form on Maundy Thursday. The celebration of a new ministry has no solemn prayer, but draws its meaning from the solemn prayers of ordination.

5. Lessons from the History of These Rites

The focus of the regular services of the church is the crucified and risen Christ, refracted in different ways in the offices of praise and prayer each day, in the eucharistic liturgy on the Lord's Day as the church's weekly feast and on the feasts of the annual cycle, and in the baptismal liturgies which are the distinctive rites for annual feasts of Easter, Pentecost, and Epiphany. But the focus of the pastoral offices is on the turning points in the personal lives of Christians and in the life of local Christian communities. The distinctively Christian character of these rites is found in the way they relate such occasions to Christ's cross and resurrection. Because of the shift of focus, however, it is very easy to forget what it is that makes these rites (which often borrow local cultural forms) distinctively Christian. The events to which the pastoral offices give expression are not peculiar to Christians, and Christians in fact often adapted the ritual forms that these events took in the local culture. In this process of inculturation, the distinctive witness of and transforming power of the gospel was sometimes lost or obscured.

The structural analysis of liturgical rites over the course of their development yields relatively secure results for the regular services of the church — the daily office, the eucharist, and the rites of initiation. This is also true for the rites of ordination. Later developments can be tested against the classic rites developed in the first three centuries. But the results of such an analysis of the pastoral offices and the episcopal services are much more ambiguous. The church's accommodation to the cultural environment is often revealed by the minimal adaptation it made in giving ritual expression to the turning points in human life.

Even as early as the later books of the New Testament, the church had begun to compromise its vision of the transformation of all things in Christ to avoid giving offense to the dominant culture. By the time that the church itself gained dominant status in the fourth century, it stood in real danger of losing its identity as the *ekklesia* — the people "called out" of the world to bear witness to the reconciliation of the world to God in Christ and the transformation of the world through the Holy Spirit. The fourth century, however, is the very period when the rites for the pastoral offices began to take definite shape. For this reason, even early rites for these offices must be carefully tested against the witness of the gospel.

6. Living Out the Vision

The sacramental vision of reality which is articulated in the church's worship secures the objectivity of God's presence for us at the turning points of our lives in the worship of the Church. But while this presence offers the possibility of a transforming encounter with God's grace, it is our response in faith that makes that encounter fruitful. There is a dialectic between God's gift and the response which that gift demands. That is why most of the pastoral offices give explicit expression to the commitment required of Christians at the turning points which they celebrate. In worship we pass over with Christ and are given a foretaste of the world's future in the kingdom of God. But we are then sent forth from worship to bear witness to the reality there revealed to us and to live out the life made possible by our foretaste of the life of the world to come. God's costly gift of love is freely offered to us in Jesus Christ, but this gift of love is, as Dietrich Bonhoeffer reminded us, "costly grace." To accept the gift is to walk with Christ the way of the cross, for that is the path we must take if we would pass over with him to the kingdom of God.

The regular services of the church root its life as a community in the death and resurrection of Christ. The pastoral offices particularize that saving mystery so that it transforms the turning points of our lives. Episcopal services shape the lives of particular Christian communities according to the same mystery. The cross and resurrection of Jesus Christ are the mystery of our salvation and the tangible manifestation to the world of the heart of all reality — the God whose costly love became incarnate in Jesus Christ and transforms our lives through the power of the Holy Spirit.

ENDNOTES

[1]The texts of the principal series of baptismal homilies are conveniently collected in Edward Yarnold, *The Awe-Inspiring Rites of Initiation: Baptismal Homilies of the Fourth Century* (Middlegreen, Slough, UK: St. Paul Publications, 1971). Perhaps the easiest place to begin a study of the liturgical theology of these texts is Jean Daniélou, *The Bible and the Liturgy* (Notre Dame, IN: University of Notre Dame Press, 1956). The two characteristic Eastern approaches were the anagogical or Alexandrian school of interpretation (best represented by Dionysius the Areopagite), in which liturgical rites become the material means for the Christian's ascent (*anagoge*) to the immaterial God, and the typological or Antiochene school of interpretation (best represented by Theodore of Mopsuestia and also by Cyril of Jerusalem), in which liturgical rites are interpreted in relation to their Old Testament foretypes and to the eschatological reality to which they in turn point. The fullest exposition of the later developments of this Byzantine tradition of interpretation is René Bornert, *Les commentaires byzantines de la divine liturgie du VIIe au XVe siècle* (Paris: Institut Français d'Études Byzantines, 1966). For a briefer treatment in English, see Paul Meyendorff, *St. Germanos of Constantinople on the Divine Liturgy* (Crestwood, NY: St. Vladimir's Seminary Press, 1984), pages 23-26, and Robert Taft, "The Liturgy of the Great Church on the Eve of Iconoclasm," *Dumbarton Oaks Papers* 34-35 (1980-1981), pages 45-75. Byzantine liturgical commentaries of later centuries went on to develop these two schools of interpretation. After Dionysius, however, the commentaries were restricted to interpretation of the eucharistic liturgy. For festal homilies, see the excerpts collected in Thomas K. Carroll and Thomas Halton, *Liturgical Practice of the Fathers* (Wilmington, DE: Michael Glazier, 1988). For the interpretation of Easter as the *pascha* in patristic literature, see the excerpts in Raniero Cantalamessa, *Easter in the Early Church* (Collegeville, MN: Liturgical Press, 1993).

[2]See the concluding chapter of Byron David Stuhlman, *Redeeming the Time: an historical and theological study of the Church's rule of prayer and the regular services of the Church* (New York: Church Hymnal, 1992), for a

brief study of the theology set out by Leo. There is no adequate treatment of Leo's theology in English; the best study is Maria Bernhard de Soos, *Le mystère liturgique d'après Saint Léon le grand* (Münster, Westfallen: Aschendorffsche Verlagsbuchhandlung, 1958). Leo's theology of the paschal mystery, however, has lost much of the eschatological thrust of the earlier tradition. Alexander Schmemann's liturgical theology, which speaks of the Church's *pascha* or passover with Christ rather than of the paschal mystery, captures the eschatological thrust better than much of the twentieth-century theology of the paschal mystery in the West.

[3]So understood, individual sacraments were associated with moments in life with which liturgically there was no connection — baptism with birth, "confirmation" with the age of discretion (or with puberty), and unction of the sick with the moment of death.

[4]See Odo Casel, *The Mystery of Christian Worship* (Westminster, MD: Newman, 1962), and the critique of Louis Bouyer in *Liturgical Piety* (Notre Dame, IN: University of Notre Dame Press, 1955).

[5]See Edward Schillebeeckx, *Christ the Sacrament of the Encounter with God* (New York: Sheed and Ward, 1963).

[6]See Karl Rahner, *The Church and the Sacraments* (New York: Herder and Herder, 1963).

[7]*Constitution on the Sacred Liturgy (Sacrosanctum Concilium)*, § 7. This constitution can be found in any of the collections of the documents of the Second Vatican Council.

[8]See especially Gerhard van der Leeuw, *Religion in Essence and Manifestation*, 2 volumes (New York: Harper and Row, 1963), and Mircea Eliade, *The Sacred and the Profane: The Nature of Religion* (New York: Harper and Row, 1961).

[9]Alexander Schmemann, *Introduction to Liturgical Theology*, 3rd edition (Crestwood, New York: St. Vladimir's Seminary Press, 1986), page 26.

[10]Marion J. Hatchett, *Sanctifying Life, Time, and Space: An Introduction to Liturgical Study* (New York: Seabury, 1976). See the way the categories are developed in chapter 1. They are then used to organize the succeeding chapters.

[11]Jean-Jacques von Allmen, *Worship: Its Theology and Practice*, trans.

W. Fletcher Fleet (New York: Oxford University Press, 1965), chapter 2. See also Peter Brunner, *Worship in the Name of Jesus Christ* (St. Louis, MO: Concordia, 1968).

[12]The most concise treatment of this is found in the essay, "Sacrament and Symbol," appendix 2 in *For the Life of the World: Sacraments and Orthodoxy* (Crestwood, NY: St. Vladimir's Seminary Press, 1973), pages 135-151. See also his essay, "Theology and Eucharist," in Thomas Fisch, editor, *Liturgy and Tradition: Theological Reflections of Alexander Schmemann* (Crestwood, NY: St. Vladimir's Seminary Press, 1990), where he works with the eucharistic ecclesiology of several Russian theologians. My treatment draws on those essays and various other works of Schmemann.

[13]Luther's doctrine of the real presence of Christ in the eucharistic elements was developed from a similar perspective.

[14]Translation from E. C. Whitaker, ed., *Documents of the Baptismal Liturgy* (London, SPCK, 1960), page 71.

[15]On this, see Louis Bouyer, *Liturgical Piety*, chapter 9, pages 115-128, esp. page 119.

[16]1 Timothy 4:4-5.

[17]I am here following the account which Alexander Schmemann gives of our estrangement from God and its effect on how we approach the world in *For the Life of the World*, pages 16-17 (where he is dealing primarily with the eucharist).

[18]See Alexander Schmemann, *For the Life of the World*, pages 18-20.

[19]Alexander Schmemann, *For the Life of the World*, page 42.

[20]The Western theology of the paschal mystery tends to be so exclusively Christological that its trinitarian dimensions are obscured. This is in part due to an inadequate doctrine of the Holy Spirit which distorts trinitarian theology in the West and a concomitant weakness in the development of eschatology. On recent attempts to correct this, see chapters 11 and 13 of Edward J. Kilmartin, *Christian Liturgy*.

[21]Louis Bouyer gives some attention to this relationship in chapters 11-13 of *Liturgical Piety*. Here he pays more attention to the liturgical structure of these rites than we find in most other theologians of the liturgy.

FOR FURTHER READING

The books listed below provide a general introduction to the more accessible literature on the pastoral offices and episcopal services available in English, as well as important Latin and Greek sources. They are meant as an introduction to the subject for the general reader. For other works, the student should consult the bibliographies in the works cited below.

General Studies, Handbooks, and Dictionaries

There are a several handbooks and dictionaries which provide up-to-date summaries of liturgical scholarship from a variety of perspectives. A. G. Martimort, ed., *The Church at Prayer: An Introduction to the Liturgy* (Collegeville, MN: Liturgical Press, 1985-1987) is a four-volume set of articles by leading French liturgical scholars (recently reissued in a single-volume edition) that provides concise summaries of current scholarship on the historical development of the rites of the Roman Catholic Church. It includes reference to Eastern traditions as well, but gives no consideration to the liturgies of the Reformation traditions. Volume III, which contains essays on the services in the ritual and the pontifical in the Roman tradition, covers the rites which I consider in this book. A useful dictionary with brief articles is J. D. Davies, *The New Westminster Dictionary of Liturgy and Worship* (Philadelphia: Westminster, 1986). A similar work with much more substantial articles is Peter Fink, ed., *The New Dictionary of Sacramental Worship* (Collegeville, MN: Michael Glazier/Liturgical Press, 1990). The majority of scholars who contributed to *The New Dictionary* are Roman Catholic, but there is also a good representation of scholars from other traditions. Despite the title, this work covers both sacramental and non-sacramental rites. Marion J. Hatchett provides a good overview of the historical development of services in *Sanctifying Life, Time, and Space: An Introduction to Liturgical Study* (New York: Seabury, 1976). The rites which I consider in this work are treated by Hatchett in the section of each chapter headed, "The Sanctification of Life." A similar handbook with a generous selection of texts is Herman Wegman, *Christian Worship in East and West: A Study Guide to Liturgical History* (New York: Pueblo, 1985). The revised edition of *The Study of Liturgy* (New York: Oxford University Press, 1992), edited by Cheslyn Jones and others, has a good series of articles on the rites of initiation and ordination, but omits any treatment of the pastoral offices. For these, the reader should consult the older work for which *The Study of Liturgy* was intended as a replacement — *Liturgy and Worship: A Companion to the Prayer Books of the Anglican Communion* (London, SPCK, 1954), edited by W. K. Lowther Clarke.

Texts of Historic Liturgies

The most easily accessible text of Hippolytus is Gregory Dix, *The Treatise on the Apostolic Tradition of St. Hippolytus of Rome, Bishop and Martyr, Reissued with corrections, preface, and bibliography by Henry Chadwick* (London: Alban Press, and Ridgefield, CT: Morehouse Publishing, 1992). Another convenient English translation is Geoffrey J. Cuming, *Hippolytus: A Text for Students*, Grove Liturgical Study No. 6 (2nd edition, Bramcote, Nottingham, UK: Grove Books, 1987). For texts in the early Roman tradition, the principal sources in the sacramentaries are available in these critical editions: for the Verona (Leonine) Sacramentary in L. C. Mohlberg, *Sacramentarium Veronense*, Rerum Ecclesiasticarum Documenta, series maior: Fontes 1 (Rome, 1956); for the Old Gelasian Sacramentary, L. C. Mohlberg, *Liber Sacramentorum Romanae aeclesiae ordinis anni circuli (Sacramentarium Gelasianum)*, Rerum Ecclesiasticarum Documenta, series maior: Fontes 4 (Rome, 1960); for the Gregorian Sacramentary, J. Deshusses, *Le Sacramentaire grégorien: ses principales formes d'après les plus anciens manuscrits*, 3 volumes, Specilegium Friburgense 16, 24, 28 (Fribourg, 1971, 1979, 1982). The *Ordines Romani* have been published in a critical edition by M. Andrieu, *Les Ordines romani du haut moyen âge*, 5 volumes, Specilegium Friburgense 11, 23, 24, 28, 29 (Fribourg, 1931-1961). For a critical edition of the Romano-German Pontifical, see Cyrille Vogel, *Le Pontifical romano-germanique du X siècle*, 3 volumes, Studi e Testi 226,

227, 269 (Vatican City, 1963, 1972). For guidance in the use of these sources, an invaluable tool is Cyrille Vogel, *Medieval Liturgy: An Introduction to the Sources*, translated and revised by William Storey and Niels Rasmussen (Washington, DC: Pastoral Press, 1986). Many medieval English rites are available in F. E. Warren, trans., *The Sarum Missal in English, Part II* (London: De La More Press, 1911).

The texts of the Byzantine rite are less easily accessible. The best source for the most ancient manuscript, Barberini 336, is Jacobus Goar, ed., *Euchologion sive Rituale Graecorum* (Venice: Ex Typographia Bartolomaei Javarina, 1730; reprint, Graz: Akademische Druck-und Verlagsanstalt, 1960). A critical edition of the euchology of this tradition is being published with French translation and commentary by Miguel Arranz in *Orientalia Christiana Periodica*; so far, the texts are primarily those related to the daily office and the rites of initiation. The most accessible translation of the Byzantine rites is Isabel Florence Hapgood, trans., *Service Book of the Holy Orthodox-Catholic Apostolic Church*, 5th edition (Englewood, NJ: Antiochean Orthodox Christian Archdiocese of New York and All North America, 1975). For the present Roman rite, the texts for the rites in English translation by the International Commission on English in the Liturgy are most easily accessible in *The Rites of the Catholic Church as Revised by the Second Vatican Ecumenical Council*, 2 vols. (New York: Pueblo, 1983, 1980).

Collections of texts for particular rites are listed with the bibliography on those rites.

Editions of the Book of Common Prayer

For a study of the evolution of the rites in the prayer book tradition, the most useful works for the student are the text of the 1549 and 1552 editions of the book, E. C. S. Gibson, ed., *The First and Second Prayer Books of Edward VI* (New York: E. P. Dutton, 1910), and the comparative presentation of the texts of the 1662 English book and all of the American books in Paul V. Marshall, *Prayer Book Parallels: The public services of the Church arranged for comparative study* (New York: Church Hymnal, 1989). All of these should be consulted for each of the rites studied in this book. The 1662 English edition and the 1928 and 1979 American edition are still in print and available from a variety of publishers (pagination is standard in these editions).

Commentaries on the Book of Common Prayer

The two standard commentaries on the Book of Common Prayer 1979 are Marion J. Hatchett, *Commentary on the American Prayer Book* (New York: Seabury, 1980) and Leonel Mitchell, *Praying Shapes Believing: A Theological Commentary on the Book of Common Prayer* (Minneapolis, MN: Seabury/Winston, 1985). Hatchett's work provides a detailed commentary on all the texts; Mitchell's commentary is less detailed and more theological in character. Also valuable for the study of these rites in the Book of Common Prayer 1979 are the relevant books in the series of Prayer Book Studies (New York: Church Hymnal) — *The Ordination of Bishops, Priests, and Deacons* (PBS 10, 1970), *Pastoral Offices* (PBS 24, 1970), *Holy Baptism, together with A Form for the Affirmation of Baptismal Vows with the Laying on of Hands by the Bishop* (Supplement to PBS 26, 1973), *Dedication and Consecration of a Church; Celebration of a New Ministry* (PBS 28, 1973), and *Introducing the Proposed Book* (PBS 29 Revised, 1976). *The Oxford American Prayer Book Commentary* (New York: Oxford, 1950), Massey Shepherd's commentary on the Book of Common Prayer 1928, also contains much information that is still useful.

Studies of Particular Rites

Baptism and the Rites Related to Baptism

Perhaps the best place to begin in understanding the present approach of the Episcopal Church to the very complicated issues associated with baptism and confirmation is Daniel Stevick's commentary in the Supplement to Prayer Books Studies 26 listed above. His later reflections on the issues are found in *Baptismal Moments, Baptismal Meanings* (New York: Church Hymnal, 1987). The standard collection of texts from the historic liturgies is E. C. Whitaker, *Documents of the Baptismal Liturgy* (London: SPCK, 1960). For the history of the rite in the middle ages in the West, see his *Christian Initiation: Baptism in the Medieval West* (London: SPCK, 1965);

for the Reformation period, see his *Christian Initiation: The Reformation Period* (London, SPCK, 1970). Perhaps the most influential treatment of the history of the rite and the reforms of Vatican II is Aidan Kavanagh, *The Shape of Baptism* (New York: Pueblo, 1978). The treatment by Robert Cabié in vol. III of *The Church at Prayer* also gives concise coverage of the pre-Reformation materials and the Roman tradition through the reforms of Vatican II. A good general survey of the history of initiation in the various traditions is presented in the articles on these rites found in *The Study of Liturgy*. The fullest study in English on initiation in the Byzantine tradition in Alexander Schmemann, *Of Water and the Spirit: A Liturgical Study of Baptism*, revised edition (Crestwood, NY: St. Vladimir's Seminary Press, 1974). A brief treatment of initiation in this tradition is Kenneth Stevenson, "The Byzantine Liturgy of Baptism," *Studia Liturgica* 17 (1987), pages 176-190.

Other Pastoral Offices

The pastoral offices are treated in the entries of the standard handbooks — *The Church at Prayer*, *The New Westminster Dictionary of Liturgy and Worship*, *The New Dictionary of Sacramental Worship*, and *Sanctifying Life, Time, and Space*. Since *The Study of Liturgy* does not include articles on these offices, the reader needs to rely on the older articles in *Liturgy and Worship* (which only take the historical development of these rites up to the revisions of the 1920s). A very useful set of English studies on these rites in the Roman tradition through the reforms of Vatican II is the Pueblo series (now published by Liturgical Press), *Studies in the Reformed Rites of the Catholic Church*. These studies often include reference to present rites in non-Roman traditions as well. For the rites of the Book of Common Prayer 1979 the reader should also consult the relevant works in the *Prayer Book Studies* and the commentaries by Hatchett and Mitchell. Useful information is also found in Massey Shepherd's commentary on the Book of Common Prayer 1928.

Marriage and Religious Profession: Two works by Kenneth Stevenson present a careful study of the rites of marriage in the Christian tradition — *Nuptial Blessing: A Study of Christian Marriage Rites* (New York: Oxford, 1983) and *To Join Together: The Rite of Marriage* (New York: Pueblo,

1987). Jean Evenou presents a brief but good historical survey in vol. III of *The Church at Prayer*. The rites of religious profession are studied in Adrien Nocent, "The Consecration of Virgins" and "Monastic Rites and Religious Profession" in *The Church at Prayer*, vol. III. The Benedictine rites of profession are presented in an article by Claude Pfeiffer, "Monastic Formation and Profession," in Timothy Fry, ed., *RB 1980: The Rule of Benedict in Latin and English with Notes* (Collegeville, MN: Liturgical Press, 1980).

The Reconciliation of a Penitent: James Dallen, *The Reconciling Community* (New York: Pueblo, 1986; Collegeville, MN: Liturgical Press, 1992), provides an accessible treatment of the history of penitential rites in the Catholic tradition, which he summarizes s. v. "Reconciliation, Sacrament of," in *The New Dictionary of Sacramental Worship*. See also Pierre Gy, "Penance and Reconciliation," in *The Church at Prayer,* vol. III. For a careful study of the texts relating to reconciliation in the early centuries, see Joseph A. Favazza, *The Order of Penitents: Historical Roots and Pastoral Future* (Collegeville, MN: Liturgical Press, 1988). A brief but comprehensive study by an Anglican is John Gunstone, *The Liturgy of Penance* (London: Faith Press, 1966).

Ministry to the Sick: The best current English study of the church's ministry to the sick is that of the Roman Catholic scholar Charles W. Gusmer, *And You Visited Me: Sacramental Ministry to the Sick and Dying* (New York: Pueblo, 1984). Ministry to the sick is treated in many of the papers included in the collection edited by Achille M. Triacca, *Temple of the Holy Spirit: sickness and death of the Christian in the liturgy: the twenty-first Liturgical Conference Saint-Serge*, trans. Matthew J. O'Connell (New York: Pueblo, 1983). A. G. Martimort traces the history of this ministry in his article in volume III of *The Church at Prayer*. The article by Charles Harris on the visitation of the sick in *Liturgy and Worship* is a good presentation of the ministry in the Anglican tradition.

Ministry at the Time of Death and Burial Rites: The classic study of these rites in the early Western tradition is Damien Sicard, *La liturgie de la mort dans les Églises latines, des origines à la réforme carolingienne* (Münster, Westfallen: Aschendorffsche Verlagsbuchhandlung, 1978). This author gives a brief summary of his research in the article on Christian death in volume

III of *The Church at Prayer*. For ministry at the time of death, a good summary is found in chapters 1 and 3 of Charles Gusmer, *And You Visited Me: Sacramental Ministry to the Sick and Dying* (New York: Pueblo, 1984). See also his article s.v. "Viaticum" in *The New Dictionary of Sacramental Worship*. Burial in the Christian tradition is treated in many of the papers included in the collection edited by Achille M. Triacca, *Temple of the Holy Spirit: sickness and death of the Christian in the liturgy: the twenty-first Liturgical Conference Saint-Serge*, trans. Matthew J. O'Connell (New York: Pueblo, 1983). A good study of the history of the Western tradition is Richard Rutherford, *The Death of a Christian: The Rite of Funerals* (New York: Pueblo, 1980).

Episcopal Services

Ordination: The preeminent authority on the rites of ordination writing in English is the Anglican scholar Paul Bradshaw. His key works are *Ordination Rites of the Ancient Churches of East and West* (New York: Pueblo, 1990) and *The Anglican Ordinal: Its History and Development from the Reformation to the Present Day* (London: SPCK, 1971). He has also contributed several of the articles to the section on the rites of ordination in *The Study of Liturgy*. This work provides excellent coverage of the history of these rites. The texts of early Western rites of ordination are presented in a critical edition with English translation and brief commentary by H. Boone Porter in *The Ordination Prayers of the Ancient Western Churches* (London: SPCK, 1967). Pierre Jounel's article in volume III of *The Church at Prayer* gives a useful summary of the tradition to the time of the Reformation and an analysis of Roman Catholic rites after Vatican II. For historical studies of the development of the Church's ministry, the reader will find James A. Mohler, *The Origin and Evolution of the Priesthood* (Staten Island, NY: Alba House, 1970), Nathan Mitchell, *Mission and Ministry: History and Theology in the Sacrament of Order* (Wilmington, DE: Michael Glazier, 1982), and Bernard Cooke, *Ministry to Word and Sacrament: History and Theology* (Philadelphia: Fortress, 1976) useful. The two studies by Edward Schillebeeckx, *Ministry: Leadership in the Community of Jesus Christ* (New York: Crossroads, 1981) and *The Church* with a Human Face: A New and Expanded Theology of Ministry (New York: Crossroads, 1985), provide considerable insight into the way that the church's ministry was shaped by social structures in successive periods of the church's history.

Other Episcopal Services: The rite now known as the Celebration of a New Ministry is largely a post-Reformation development. Relevant information is best found in the article by W. K. Lowther Clarke, "The Consecration of Churches and Other Occasional Offices," in *Liturgy and Worship*. Further information may be found in Massy Shepherd's commentary on the Book of Common Prayer 1928 and Marion Hatchett's commentary on the 1979 Book of Common Prayer and in Prayer Book Studies 26, *Dedication and Consecration of a Church/Celebration of a New Ministry*. For information on the dedication of a church (a rite not found in the English Book of Common Prayer) the same sources are useful. For the historical development of this rite in Christian tradition, the reader should consult the treatment by Pierre Jounel on pages 215-225 of volume I of *The Church at Prayer*; the essay by George Willis which is chapter III of his *Further Essays in Early Roman Liturgy* (London: SPCK, 1968); and the chapter on this rite in Louis Duchesne, *Christian Worship: Its Origin and Evolution. A Study of the Latin Liturgy up to the Time of Charlemagne*, trans. M. L. McClure, 5th edition (London, SPCK, 1949). The history of church architecture is presented in summary form in Peter G. Cobb, "The Architectural Setting of the Liturgy," in *The Study of Liturgy*. More detailed information on the origins and early development of this architecture can be found in Richard Krautheimer, *Early Christian and Byzantine Architecture* (Baltimore, MD: Penguin Books, 1975). For the use of the church in the Anglican tradition, the standard work is G. W. O. Addleshaw and Frederick Etchells, *The Architectural Setting of Anglican Worship* (London: Faber and Faber, 1948).

The Theology of the Pastoral Offices and Episcopal Services

Perhaps the best introduction to the early stages of liturgical theology, which grows out of the interpretation of the paschal rites of Christian initiation, is Jean Daniélou, *The Bible and the Liturgy* (Notre Dame, IN: University of Notre Dame Press, 1956). The theological basis of this theology in the typological exegesis of Christ's death and resurrection receives careful treatment in the introduction to Raniero Cantalamessa, *Easter in the Early Church* (Collegeville, MN: Liturgical Press, 1993). Leo the Great's theology of the paschal mystery as a basis for his sacramental theology of the liturgy is treated in the last chapter of my own *Redeeming the Time: an historical and theological study of the Church's rule of prayer and the regular services of the Church* (New York: Church Hymnal, 1992). The development of the theology of the sacraments and the more recent return to liturgical theology receives succinct treatment by Peter Fink in his article s.v. "Sacramental Theology after Vatican II" in *The New Dictionary of Sacramental Worship*. For a more extended treatment of the scholastic theology of the sacraments, see Edward J. Kilmartin, *Christian Liturgy: Theology and Practice. I. Systematic Theology of Liturgy* (New York: Sheed and Ward, 1988).

In the first half of this century, liturgical theology developed as the theology of the paschal mystery. Key works in this development include Odo Casel, *The Mystery of Christian Worship* (Westminster, MD: Newman, 1962), and Louis Bouyer, *Liturgical Piety* (Notre Dame, IN: University of Notre Dame Press, 1955). Succinct summaries of this theology can be found in J. D. Crichton, "A Theology of Worship" in *The Study of Liturgy*; and I. H. Dalmais, "The Liturgy as Celebration of the Mystery of Salvation" in volume I of *The Church at Prayer*. Systematic appropriation of this work is found particularly in Edward Schillebeeckx, *Christ the Sacrament of the Encounter with God* (New York: Sheed and Ward, 1963), and Karl Rahner, *The Church and the Sacraments* (New York: Herder and Herder, 1963).

The analysis of the structure of the church's liturgy in this chapter is based on the work of Alexander Schmemann in *Introduction to Liturgical Theology* (Crestwood, NY: St. Vladimir's Seminary Press, 1986) and Marion Hatchett in *Sanctifying Life, Time, and Space: An Introduction to Liturgical Study* (New York: Seabury, 1976). Ultimately the categories used are phenomenological and were borrowed by both scholars from Mircea Eliade, *The Sacred and the Profane: The Nature of Religion* (New York: Harper and Row, 1961). I develop a theological interpretation of this structure on the basis of Alexander Schmemann's presentation of the trinitarian dimensions of World, Church, and Kingdom, which he sets out most succinctly in his essay on "Sacrament and Symbol," appendix 2 in *For the Life of the World: Sacraments and Orthodoxy* (Crestwood, NY: St. Vladimir's Seminary Press, 1973), pages 135-151. The basic difference between Schmemann's liturgical theology and the earlier Western theology of the paschal mystery is his correction of the inadequate development of the theology of the Holy Spirit in Latin theology, which caused the eschatological dimensions of the liturgy to be obscured in the West. The ultimate reason for this is the difference between the Eastern and Western understanding of the Trinity. In recent decades Western theologians have sought to develop a more adequate theology of the Trinity and to work out the implications for liturgical theology. On this, see Edward Kilmartin, *Christian Liturgy: Theology and Practice*, especially chapters 11 and 13.

Schmemann's treatment of the church's liturgy as epiphany is derived from the eucharistic ecclesiology which developed in the Institut Saint Serge in France among Russian emigres and from the work of Jean-Jacques von Allmen. On the former, see Schmemann's essay, "Theology and Eucharist," in Thomas Fisch, editor, *Liturgy and Tradition: Theological Reflections of Alexander Schmemann* (Crestwood, NY: St. Vladimir's Seminary Press, 1990). Von Allmen's treatment of liturgy as epiphany is found in *Worship: Its Theology and Practice,* trans. W. Fletcher Fleet (New York: Oxford University Press, 1965).

Although the phenomenological classification of rites as pastoral offices (related to the sanctification of life) has won general acceptance, the category itself has received little serious attention in liturgical theology. In the middle ages theologians treated all the sacraments as pastoral offices — a treatment which does considerable violence to the structure of the church's liturgy, which pays little attention to the actual liturgies for these rites, and which introduces an artificial distinction between sacramental and nonsacramental rites. Recent theologians have focussed their attention on the rites most closely associated with the paschal mystery — the rites of initiation and the eucharist and their setting in the paschal liturgy — and have given less attention to the pastoral offices. Louis Bouyer develops the seeds of such a theology in chapters 11-13 of *Liturgical Piety*. The strength of Bouyer's treatment is the fact that he pays attention to the actual structure of the rites and their relation to baptism and the eucharist — something which most theologies of the sacraments as pastoral offices fail to do. Alexander Schmemann gives a popular presentation of many of the rites in *For the Life of the World*, but his treatment there relates awkwardly to the structural analysis of the church's liturgy in his *Introduction to Liturgical Theology* (where rites for the sanctification of life receive little attention). The individual services under the category of pastoral offices receive excellent treatment in Leonel Mitchell's *Praying Shapes Believing*, but the category as such receives no extended treatment.

The rites grouped under the category of episcopal services are concerned primarily with the ordering of the church for ministry. The studies of ministry listed earlier in this bibliography develop the theology of ministry in these rites with considerable care. The liturgical structure of the rites of ordination is carefully treated in Paul Bradshaw, *Ordination Rites of the Ancient Churches of East and West* (New York: Pueblo, 1990). To place the theology of ordination in an ecumenical context, the reader should consult the document *Baptism, Eucharist, and Ministry*, issued by the World Council of Churches. A convenient source for this is John H. Leith, *Creeds of the Churches: A Reader in Christian Doctrine from the Bible to the Present Day*, 3rd edition (Louisville, KY: John Knox, 1982).

APPENDIX 1

THE RELATION OF THE PASTORAL OFFICES AND EPISCOPAL SERVICES TO THE TEMPORAL CYCLE

Note: Pastoral Offices and Episcopal Services in the Prayer Book are in boldfaced type. Services from the Book of Occasional Services are in ordinary type.

Pastoral Office	Occasion in Life	Context in Regular Services
RITES RELATED TO BAPTISM (ADULTS AND OLDER CHILDREN)		
Admission of Catechumens	conversion at any time	Sunday eucharist
Prayers during catechesis	until enrollment	—
Enrollment of Candidates	maturing faith	First Sunday of Lent /Advent
Prayers for candidates	until baptism	Eucharists in Lent/Advent
Baptism [*regular* service]	mature faith	Easter Vigil/Baptism of Christ
RITES RELATED TO BAPTISM (INFANTS)		
The Blessing of Parents	mother's pregnancy	Sunday Eucharist
Thanksgiving for the Birth or Adoption of a Child		
[= enrollment for baptism]	after birth of child	Sunday Eucharist
Prayers for child	until baptism	Sunday Eucharist
Baptism [*regular* service]	—	Eucharist of Baptismal Feast
CONFIRMATION AND RELATED RITES (AFFIRMATION OF THE BAPTISMAL COVENANT)		
Welcoming of baptized Christians into a community	reawakened/deepened faith	Sunday Eucharist

Calling of the baptized to continuing conversion	continuing conversion	Ash Wednesday Eucharist
Prayers for candidates	until reaffirmation	Sunday Eucharist
Preparation for Paschal Holy Days		Maundy Thursday
Reaffirmation of Covenant	mature faith	Easter Vigil
Confirmation	mature faith	At Vigil or in Easter Season

A Form of Commitment to Christian Service	deepened faith	Eucharist

RITES RELATED TO MARRIAGE AND CELIBACY

Celebration and Blessing of a Marriage	lifetime commitment	[Special] Eucharist
The Blessing of a Civil Marriage	lifetime commitment	[Special] Eucharist
An Order for Marriage	lifetime commitment	[Special] Eucharist
Setting Apart for a Special Vocation —		
as a Novice	testing of commitment	Daily Office
in temporary vows	preliminary commitment	Eucharist
in life vows	lifetime commitment	Eucharist

RITES RELATED TO SIN AND SICKNESS

Reconciliation of a Penitent	repentance	—
Communion under Special Circumstances	inability to attend church	Sunday Eucharist
Ministration to the Sick	sickness	—
I. Ministry of the Word [Reconciliation]		
II. Laying on of Hands and Anointing		
III. Holy Communion		

RITES RELATED TO DYING AND DEATH

Ministration at the Time of Death		
Litany at the Time of Death	death	—
[Reception of the Body]	[entrance to church]	—
Prayer for a vigil	vigil before burial	—
Reception of the Body	entrance to church	
Burial of the Dead	burial	[Special] Eucharist

Ordination

of a bishop	Succession or assistance in leadership of diocese	Eucharist on Sunday or feast
of presbyters and deacons	Need for associate and assistant ministers	*Eucharist [Roman ordines, English Canons: Sunday at close of Ember weeks]
Celebration of a New Ministry	Beginning of a ministry in a cure	*Eucharist
Dedication of a Church	Opening of church for public worship	*Eucharist

Note: Because of the collegial character of the ordained ministry, Episcopal Services are now ordinarily scheduled at a time when clergy are not obligated to worship in their own parishes.

Appendix 2

BUCER'S ORDINATION PRAYER AND CRANMER'S PRAYERS AT THE ORDINATION OF PRIESTS AND BISHOPS IN 1550

Bucer

Almighty God, Father of our Lord Jesus Christ, we give thanks for thy divine majesty, and for thine infinite love and goodness towards us, through him thine only Son, our redeemer and teacher unto blessed and everlasting life.

And it has been thy will that after he had perfected our redemption by his death and sat down at thy right hand in heaven, he should renew all things in heaven and earth and give to us lost and unhappy mortals Apostles, Prophets, Evangelists, Doctors, and Pastors, sending them to us as thou didst send him to us, that by their ministry he might gather unto thee thy children scattered throughout the world, and that manifesting thee to them in his own self he might restore and renew them unto thee to the perpetual praise of thy holy name.

BCP (Priests)

Almighty God, and heavenly Father, which, of thy infinite love and goodness towards, us hast given to us thy only and most dearly beloved Son Jesus Christ, to be our Redeemer, and the Author of everlasting life;

who, after he had made perfect our redemption by his death, and was ascended into heaven, sent abroad into the world his Apostles, Prophets, Evangelists, Doctors, and Pastors, by whose labours and ministry he hath gathered together a great flock in all parts of the world, to set forth the eternal praise of thy holy Name:

BCP (Bishops)

Almighty God, and most merciful Father, which of thy infinite goodness hast given to us thy only and most dearly beloved Son Jesus Christ, to be our Redeemer, and the Author of everlasting life;

who, after he had made perfect our redemption by his death, and was ascended into heaven, poured down gifts abundantly upon men, making some Apostles, some Prophets, some Evangelists, some Pastors and Doctors, to the edifying and making perfect of his congregation:

And through the same thy Son we humbly pray and beseech thee in the name of thy Son that thou pour out thy Holy Spirit richly upon these thy ministers:

For these so great benefits of thy eternal goodness, and for that thou hast vouchsafed to call these thy servants here present to the same Office and Ministry of the salvation of mankind, we render thee most hearty thanks, we worship and praise thee;

more widely spread, and hold more powerful sway where ever it may come. Grant, we beseech thee, to this thy servant such grace,

and that by him thou teach and govern them, that they discharge their ministry faithfully and usefully to thy people, the flock of thy Son and our good shepherd.

that he may be evermore ready to spread abroad thy gospel, and glad tidings of reconcilement to God; and to use the authority given unto him, not to destroy, but to save, not to hurt, but to help: so that he, as a wise and a faithful servant, giving to thy family meat in due season, may at the last day be received into joy;

To all those for whose salvation thou dost desire them to minister, give minds that can receive thy word.

And to us all who here and in all places call upon thy name, grant that we may ever show ourselves grateful to thee for these and all his other benefits, and that through thy Holy Spirit we may so advance daily in the knowledge and faith of thee and of thy Son, that through these thy ministers, through those to whom thou hast desired us to give ministers, and through all of us, thy holy name may be for ever more fully glorified, that thy blessed kingdom may be

and we humbly beseech thee, by the same thy Son, to grant unto all us, which either here, or elsewhere call upon thy name, that we may show ourselves thankful to thee for these and all other thy benefits, and that we may daily increase and go forwards, in the knowledge and faith of thee, and of thy Son, by the Holy Spirit. So that as well by these thy Ministers, as by them to whom they shall be appointed Ministers, thy holy Name may be always glorified, and thy blessed kingdom enlarged:

more widely spread, and hold more powerful sway where ever it may come.

Through the same thy Son Jesus Christ our Lord, who liveth and reigneth with thee in the unity of the same Holy Spirit, world without end. Amen.[1]

through the same thy Son Jesus Christ our Lord, which liveth and reigneth with thee, in the unity of the same Holy Spirit, world without end. Amen.[2]

through Jesus Christ our Lord, who, with thee and the Holy Ghost liveth and reigneth, one God, world without end. Amen.[3]

[1]Translation from E. C. Whitaker, *Martin Bucer and the Book of Common Prayer* (Great Wakering, UK: Mayhew-McCrimmon, 1974), pages 181-182.

[2]BCP 1549, page 311. For ease of comparison, I have conformed the spelling and punctuation to that of the BCP 1662.

[3]BCP 1549, page 316. For ease of comparison, I have conformed the spelling and punctuation to that of the BCP 1662.

Appendix 3

COLLECTS IN THE 1550 ORDINATION RITES

Collect after the Litany

Deacons: Almyghtie God, whiche by thy deuyne prouidence, haste appoynted dyuerse Orders of ministers in the Churche: and dyd-deste enspyre thyne holy Apostles to chose unto this Ordre of Deacons, the fyrste Martyr sainct Stephyn, wyth other: mercyfully beholde these thy seruauntes now called to the lyke office and administracion; replenishe them so wyth the trueth of thy doctryne, and innocencie of lyfe, that, both by worde and good example, they may faithfully serue thee in this office, to the glory of thy name, and profyte of the congregacion, through the merites of our saviour Jesu Christ, who lyveth and reygneth wyth thee, and the holy Ghost, nowe and euer. Amen.[1]

Collect after the Postcommunion

Deacons: Almyghtie God, geuer of al good thinges, which of thy great goodnes hast vouchsafed to accepte and take these thy seru-aunts unto the office of Deacons in thy church: make them we beseche thee, O Lorde, to bee modest, humble, and constant in their ministracions, to haue a ready wyl to obserue al spiritual discipline, that they hau-ing always the testimonie of a good con-science, and continuing euer stable and strong in thy sonne Christ, may so wel use them-selues in thys inferior offyce, that they may be found worthi to be called unto the higher ministeries in thy Church; through the same thy sonne our Sauiour Christ, to whom be glorye and honoure, worlde wythout ende. Amen.[2]

Priests: Almyghtie God, geuer of all good things, which by thy holy spirit has appoynted dyuerse orders of Ministers in thy church, mercifully behold these thy seruantes, now called to the Office of Priesthoode, and replenish them so wyth the trueth of thy doctryne, and innocencie of lyfe, that both by worde and good example, they may faythfully serue thee in thys office, to the glorye of thy name, and profyte of the congregacion, through the merites of oure sauiour Jesu Christ, who lyueth and reygneth, wyth thee and the holy Ghoste, worlde wythout end. Amen.[3]

Bishops: Almightie God, geuer of all good thynges, which by thy holy spirite has appointed diuerse orders of ministers in thy church, mercifully beholde this thy seruaunt, now called to the worke and ministerie of a Bisshoppe, and replenishe him so with the trueth of thy doctryne, and innocencie of lyfe, that both by worde and dede, he may faythfully serue thee in thys office, to the glorye of thy name, and profite of the congregacyon. Through the merites of oure sauioure Jesu Christe, who lyueth and reigneth with thee and the holy gost, worlde without end. Amen.[5]

Priests: Most mercifull father, we beseche thee so to sende upon these thy seruauntes thy heauenly blessyng, that they maye be cladde about with all iustice, and that thy worde spoken by theyr mouthes may haue such successe, that it may neuer be spoken in vain. Graunt also that we may haue grace to heare, and receiue the same as thy moste holy worde and the meane of our saluacion, that in all our wordes and dedes we may seke thy glory, and the encrease of thy kingdom, thorow Jesus Christ our lord. Amen.[4]

Bishops: Most merciful father, we beseche thee to send down upon this thy seruaunt, thy heauenly blessynge, and so endue hym with thy holy spirite, that he preaching thy worde, may not only be earneste to reproue, beseche, and rebuke with all pacience and doctryne, but also may be to such as beleue, an wholesome example in words, in conuersacion, in loue, in faith, in chastitie, and puritie, that faythfully fulfilling his course, at the latter day he may receiue the croune of righteousnesse, laied up by the Lord, the righteous judge, who liueth and reigneth, one god with the father and holy gost, worlde withoute ende. Amen.[6]

Note that the prayers after the litany for deacons and priests were used after 1662 as the proper collect at the eucharist.

[1]BCP 1549, page 298. Used as the collect of the day in 1662.
[2]BCP 1549, page 302. Used as the collect of the day in 1662.
[3]BCP 1549, page 307.
[4]BCP 1549, page 312.
[5]BCP 1549, page 314.
[6]BCP 1549, page 317.